THE CHURCH IN AMERICA

THE MACMILLAN COMPANY
NEW YORK · BOSTON · CHICAGO · DALLAS
ATLANTA · SAN FRANCISCO

MACMILLAN & CO., Limited
LONDON · BOMBAY · CALCUTTA
MELBOURNE

THE MACMILLAN CO. OF CANADA, Ltd.
TORONTO

THE CHURCH IN AMERICA

A Study of
The Present Condition and Future Prospects
of American Protestantism

BY

WILLIAM ADAMS BROWN, Ph.D., D.D.

Chairman of the Committee on the War and the Religious
Outlook, Secretary of the General War-Time Commission
of the Churches, Author of *Christian Theology in Outline*

New York
THE MACMILLAN COMPANY
1922

Press of
J. J. Little & Ives Company
New York, U. S. A.

TO ALL WHO HAVE WON
FROM YESTERDAY'S EXPERIENCE
THE HOPE OF A BETTER TO-MORROW

PREFACE

THIS book expresses certain convictions concerning the opportunity and duty of the American Protestant churches which sum up the experience and reflection of many years.

The immediate occasion for the book was furnished by my experience as Secretary of the General War-Time Commission of the Churches and Chairman of the Committee on the War and the Religious Outlook. The former was the organization through which the different Protestant denominations co-operated during the war. In this commission no less than thirty-nine different bodies were represented, including communions as different as the Episcopalians and the Southern Baptists. As secretary of this Commission I was not only brought into intimate association with many leaders of the larger Protestant communions as well as with representative Roman Catholics and Jews, but was obliged for the first time to make a comprehensive survey of the tasks and problems which confront the Church as a whole.

The need which the war disclosed of a thoroughgoing co-operative study of these tasks and problems led to the organization, in 1918, of the Committee on the War and the Religious Outlook. This is a group of men and women, some thirty in number, who have spent the last four years in a co-operative study of such fundamental subjects as the relation of the Church to industry, the missionary outlook in the light of the war, the teaching work of the Church, and the problems and possibilities of Christian unity. One of the motives which has led me to undertake this book has been the desire to bring the work of this committee to the attention of a wider public, and to enlist thoughtful Christians of all the churches in the kind of inquiry it seeks to promote.

But my interest in the subject to be discussed is of older date. As a member of the Board of Home Missions of the Presbyterian Church in the U. S. A., and for many years Chairman of the Home Missions Committee of the Presbytery of New York, I have had the opportunity to study at first hand the ways in which the new influences and demands of the modern world are affecting the missionary policy of the churches. In particular, my work as Chairman of the Home Missions Committee has brought me into touch with the race problem as it meets us among our immigrants of foreign speech, with the industrial problem as it confronts us in labor and radical circles, and, above all, with the problem of Christion co-operation as illustrated in the missionary work of an important denomination in our largest and most difficult home mission field.

This study of home mission problems has been supplemented by repeated visits to the foreign field, most recently in 1916 by a trip to China and Japan as Union Seminary lecturer in the Far East, where in conferences with representative missionary groups I had the privilege of comparing the problems which face the Church at home with those which confront the Church abroad.

These contacts at home and abroad have helped me to appreciate how impossible it is for any one denomination to solve its problems alone, and have interested me keenly in the various attempts that are being made to realize Christian unity. Some of these attempts I have had the opportunity to study in practical ways: in the local field as Chairman of the New York City Missions Council; in the national field as a member of the Administrative Committee of the Federal Council and Chairman of its Commission on Christian Education.

As a result, I have come to hold with growing conviction the thesis to which this book is devoted; namely, that it is vital to the future success of American Protestantism that we re-think our theory of the Church.

When I say that we ought to re-think our theory of the Church I do not mean that we should continue our discussion of church unity in the abstract. I mean something far more important and more difficult; namely, that we should make a serious attempt to determine what should be the function of the Church in our democratic society and to come to a definite understanding as to the ways in which the existing churches can best co-operate in seeing that this function is adequately discharged. I mean that we should interpret to those who are actually participating in the everyday work of the churches the real meaning and ultimate purpose of what they are doing, so that they shall see their familiar tasks and occupations in their larger setting as necessary parts of the work of the Church as a whole.

Such an interpretation of present-day Christianity is needed because of the changes which have taken place in the environment in which the Church must work. The modern Church must follow the individual through his varying experiences in the world of to-day. It must face the social issues of our time as they meet us in the struggles of capital and labor, in the strife of race with race, in the rivalry of nation with nation, and be able to show that the Gospel of Christ has a remedy and a programme adequate for all forms of human need. We are trying an experiment which will have a far-reaching effect upon the future of democracy, an experiment which will show whether it is possible to supply the unifying spiritual influence needed in a democracy by means of a strong, coherent, free Church, and so make possible under the conditions of our modern life the coming of the new social order called by our Maker the Kingdom of God.

It remains to express my acknowledgments to the friends who have helped me in the preparation of this book. To name them all would be impossible, but a word must be said of what I owe to my fellow-workers in the Federal Council, the General War-Time Commission of the Churches, and the Committee on the War and the Religious Outlook. If in spite of many superficial reasons for discouragement I still retain an abiding faith in the promise and possibilities of American Protestantism, it is no small part because of what I have learned of these possibilities through my association with them.

In particular I wish to express my indebtedness to my friend, the Rev. Samuel McCrea Cavert, my assistant in the General War-Time Commission, and now General Secretary of the Federal Council, who has read the whole manuscript in proof and given me many helpful suggestions. To Dr. Alfred Williams Anthony, Secretary of the Home Missions Council, Dr. Robert L. Kelly, Secretary of the Council of Church Boards of Education, and my colleagues, Professors Daniel J. Fleming and Hugh Hartshorne, of the Union Theological Seminary, who have read parts of the manuscript, I desire also to express my thanks.

It had been my hope to add to the text a classified bibliography; but the range of interests covered is so wide that I have reluctantly been obliged to abandon this plan. References to some of the most convenient sources of information have been given in the notes. For help in assembling the material available in print I am indebted to Miss Hudson, Reference Librarian of the Union Theological Seminary. But much of the information on which I have relied has been secured through correspondence of which no detailed acknowledgment is possible.

As I reflect how imperfect is my knowledge of many of the subjects on which I have written I am tempted still further to postpone the publication of my book. But since any study of contemporary life must needs be provisional, I am content to send it out as it is, asking only that it be taken for no more than it professes to be, a report of progress and a confession of faith.

WILLIAM ADAMS BROWN.

UNION THEOLOGICAL SEMINARY,
    June, 1922.

CONTENTS

INTRODUCTION

PART I

FACING THE FACTS

PART III

DEFINING THE IDEAL

PART IV

ORGANIZING FOR WORK

PART V

TRAINING FOR TO-MORROW

CONCLUSION

INTRODUCTION

DEMOCRACY AND THE CHURCH

THE CHURCH IN AMERICA

CHAPTER I

DEMOCRACY AND THE CHURCH

1. *The New Interest in Organized Religion and the Reasons for It*

IN the chapters that follow I propose to inquire what American Protestantism is likely to contribute to the most significant experiment being tried in the world to-day, the experiment which is to determine whether democracy will be able to furnish on a world-wide scale the integrating influence which will make it possible to realize unity under free institutions.

One of the most significant signs of the time is the new interest in organized Christianity.[1] By this it is not meant that we are experiencing what is technically called a revival of religion, or even that there has been any considerable accession to the membership of the Christian Church. We refer to the renewed interest in the Church as a structural element in human society. Men are coming to realize that in the Church we possess a social asset with as yet undeveloped, not to say unappreciated, possibilities—an asset which has value not simply for the men and women who belong to its own membership and are responsible for the direction of its policy, but for all of whatever calling who love their kind and take thought for the welfare of society.

The war, which in so many ways has shaken us out of our easy satisfaction with things as they are, is responsible for this revived interest in the Church. We have been cataloguing our assets, spiritual as well as material, and asking ourselves how far they are

[1] It is worth noting that during the last year, since this book was begun, no less than four different books have appeared, dealing with various phases of our subject: Leighton Parks, "The Crisis of the Churches," New York, 1922; John Haynes Holmes, "Old Churches for New," New York, 1922; Charles A. Ellwood, "The Reconstruction of Religion," New York, 1922; Charles R. Brown, "The Honor of the Church," Boston, 1922.

adequate to meet the needs of the day. Most of all is this true of our institutions—the family, the school, the state, our economic and industrial systems. If the war has taught us anything it is this, that face to face with the strain of modern life the individual alone counts for little. Modern war, as we have been reminded again and again, is not an affair of armies, but of peoples and of civilizations. And the same is true of the less dramatic, but no less momentous, competitions of peace. The great word of our day is organization, and the test of the civilization of the future will be the fitness of its institutions to respond to the demands which will be made upon them.

It is not surprising, then, that we should find men turning with fresh interest to the Christian Church. Here is an institution which has lasted nearly two thousand years, whose constituency embraces nearly a third of the human race, which professes to be the teacher of Europe and America in morals and religion, and which is carrying on an active missionary propaganda among the more distant peoples who were drawn against their will into the maelstrom of the Great War. It is an institution which commands vast financial resources, disposes of an annual revenue mounting into the hundreds of millions, numbers its paid ministers by the hundreds of thousands and its voluntary workers by the million, receives state support in a country like England where the tradition of the state church still obtains, yet is no less generously sustained in a democratic country like America where the voluntary gifts of the faithful replace the taxes of the citizens. It is an institution which touches life at each of its great crises—birth, marriage, sickness, and death—which is entrusted with the moral education of childhood during its formative period, which maintains in its pulpit a forum for the weekly discussion of questions of morals and religion, which has been, and still is, the spring of private charity on an unprecedented scale. In spite of all its faults, the Church is the one social institution touching men of all races and nations and callings which exists to spread faith in a good God and to unite men in a world-wide brotherhood. Here surely is a factor with which any one must reckon who, faced by the unexampled tragedy of our own time, asks with soberness where men are to turn for help in the stupendous task of world reconstruction.

It is the more natural that men's thoughts should turn to the

Church in such a crisis because present issues bring them face to face with the unseen realities with which religion has always been concerned. These issues, ostensibly political and economic, are in essence spiritual. They have to do with the conflict of ideals. Though the weapons may be tariffs and armaments, the real contestants are philosophies and loyalties. New faiths challenge the old; old standards are called in question.

This change, everywhere in evidence, is most striking in democratic countries. Here the greater power given to the people, and the higher standard of living which they demand, puts added strain upon the government. Nowhere is there more need of some unifying and steadying influence in the realm of the spirit. And such a unifying influence, as we are coming to see more clearly every day, can proceed only from religion. It is pertinent, therefore, to inquire whether the Church can supply the element of self-control and consecration which will make a free people willing to undergo the sacrifices which are necessary to a just and stable peace.

It is a world-wide question. It is being asked in Europe and in the Orient as well as in this country. It affects all branches of the Church—Greek and Roman Catholic as well as Protestant. Bishop Nicholai [1] has recently brought before us in impressive manner the bankruptcy of Europe's statesmanship and the need of some new organizing principle to unite men of good will in every land in a constructive and inspiring programme. Archbishop Söderblom [2] has been appealing for a world-wide conference of the churches to heal the spiritual ravages of war and to create an organization which will make future wars impossible. But it is in this country especially that the responsibility of the Church appears. For in no other is the Church itself to so large an extent the creation of the democratic spirit and the expression of democratic ideals. If, therefore, the Church has a service to render to democracy anywhere, the nature of that service ought to appear most clearly here.

2. *The Differing Estimates of the Function of the American Church.*

For every reason, therefore, the place which the Church occupies in America in the popular estimation and the views which are generally held of its function should be peculiarly significant.

[1] Bishop of Ochrida, in Serbia.
[2] Archbishop of Upsala, in Sweden.

That the Church has still a strong hold upon public sentiment and respect there is no reason to doubt. Although complaints are made of the slight influence exercised by the ministry as a profession, of the failure of the ministry to appeal to the best of our young men as a life work, of the lowering of professional standards in the ministry, and of the divisions and competition among the denominations, we still continue to find men in every walk of life who, having found nowhere else the moral leadership which the hour demands, turn with hope to religion and to the Church as the institution of religion. This appeal to the Church comes from the most varied groups—from editors, from men holding public office, from military commanders, from leaders of political parties, most recently from men of business.

But for the most part the appeal is made blindly, and few have more than a vague conception of what the Church really is and what it can reasonably be expected to do. To judge whether the Church has so far succeeded or failed in performing its function in our democracy, and to gain a clear conception of what that function should be, requires more thought than is usually devoted to such questions by those outside the Church.

Nor is this uncertainty as to the duty of the Church confined to outsiders. Among church members also we find a wide difference of view as to what function the Church should fulfil in the life of our time. There are still Christians who fix all their hope upon the visible coming of Christ and believe that the chief duty of believers is to warn men of His speedy return to judge the world; while others are chiefly concerned that the Church should be an active agent in the reformation and even the reconstruction of society.

And as Christians differ in their view of the function of the Church, so they differ in their view of the way in which that function should be discharged. Some believe that the Church's primary responsibility is to preach the Christian ideal and to inspire the men and women who, in their several walks of life and through different institutions of society, will make this ideal prevail. Others believe that the Church as an institution is directly responsible for social betterment and should itself undertake as an organized body the works of charity, of education, of healing, of economic and industrial reform, which are now largely in the hands of secular agencies.

It would seem, then, that the time had come for an impartial and objective study of the function of the Church in human society and of the nature of the contribution which it may fairly be expected to make to the progress of mankind. When times were easy and issues relatively simple, one could be content with the traditional formula, equally acceptable to evangelical Protestant and to radical socialist, that religion is an affair of the individual conscience, and that the Church concerns those only who choose to belong to it. But we are coming to see that the matter is not so simple. The boundaries that separate one man's personality from his neighbor's have been embarrassingly obscured, and of institutions most of all it proves impossible to say where the limit of their influence is to be fixed.

3. Purpose and Scope of the Present Study.

Let us, then, take up these two questions: (1) What has modern democracy a right to expect of the Church? (2) What reason is there for believing that the Church will do the work which may reasonably be expected of it by the forward-looking men and women of our generation?

We must begin by knowing what we have a right to expect. Many demands are made upon the churches which in the nature of the case they cannot meet. They are asked to do things which are the proper responsibility of other institutions and agencies, and sometimes in their desire to be all things to all men, they try to do these things. Such easy compliance can have only unfortunate results. It diverts attention from the Church's true and unescapable responsibility. It wastes energies that ought to be expended on more important matters. It leads people to expect from the Church service which they have a right to ask of state or school, and thus they overlook the greater thing which the Church alone can do. Before we measure the Church's performance we must first determine the standard which should be employed. Primary among the needs of the day is a sound theory of the nature and function of the Church.

Such a complete theory this book does not profess to give. That must be the work of many minds working through many generations. What is offered here is such a contribution as one man can make who believes profoundly in the unique service which the Church can render and whose duties during recent years have brought him into close touch with leaders in all branches of the Church during a period in the history of the co-operative movement when new experiments were being tried and old theories brought again to the final test of practice.

This desire to keep theory in close touch with fact must be our excuse for confining the present study to American Protestantism.[1] We shall not forget the wider relations of our subject so far as they affect other churches and other countries. Indeed, our study will bring fresh evidence of the impossibility of doing this even if we were disposed to do so. But for the time being we shall concentrate so far as possible upon the narrower field. We shall inquire what opportunity now opens before the Protestant churches of America, and what reason there is for believing that the churches will rise to this opportunity and do the thing to which the need of man and the Spirit of God alike seem to point.

This restriction to the narrower field is the less to be regretted, because even within the limits thus set we shall find problems too difficult and many-sided for immediate solution. Almost every question of principle which meets the student of religion in any country or in any age confronts the student of American Protestantism. If we are to make progress at all it will be necessary to ignore many attractive side issues and hold ourselves rigidly to the main track. We must try to see the big things big and the small things small.

[1] A word should be said in explanation of the use of the term "Protestantism." The author knows American Christians who dislike this term because it seems to them divisive and narrowing and he would gladly use another if one could be found. The fact remains that the term has come into general use to describe the group of churches which broke away from Rome in the sixteenth century and which have this in common, that they lay greater stress on the Bible as the supreme revelation of God and on the right of the free spirit to interpret the Bible for itself, than was the case with the older church from which they separated. Within this group there are many who are reverent of the Catholic tradition and conscious of ties which bind them to the churches of the past which they are not willing to sever. For Christians of this type the author has great respect, and recognizes that no comprehensive plan for unity can hope to succeed which leaves them out. He trusts that they will not be deterred by the title from reading this book.

Above all we must endeavor to distinguish that which is alive and growing from that which has had its day. "History," once said a great scholar, "is full of ghosts"—movements and ideas which profess to be alive when they have really died long ago. For the historian of the past most of these ghosts have been laid. For one who wishes to interpret the history which is being lived they are a haunting presence and may easily divert him from his proper path.

It will help us to find our way through the intricacies of our subject if, at the outset, we remind ourselves of the main topics of our inquiry. We shall begin with the environment in which the Church must do its work. This will require us to consider briefly the present spiritual condition of America and to point out the chief needs and problems to which the churches must address themselves. We shall study the religion of the average American and ask ourselves how it came to be what it is. We shall point out the deeper problems which emerge when we begin to look below the surface and consider the exceptional groups who are out of touch with the Church. We shall remind ourselves of the larger setting in which this life is placed and of the ways in which the spiritual problems of America are affected by this larger setting, which includes Asia and Africa as well as Europe.

Having studied the people to whom the Church is to minister, we shall next examine the Church itself. Here our thought must follow the changes produced by the war. We shall begin by asking what the American Church was like when the war broke out. What were its outstanding characteristics and what were their historical antecedents? Wherein did the churches show themselves weak and wherein strong when in common with all other American institutions they faced the test of war? How, in the next place, did the churches fare in the war? How did they meet the new opportunities which the war brought and what services did they render to the country and to mankind? What lessons did the churches learn which will be fruitful for the future? Where, finally, did the war leave the churches? In what spirit are they facing the new problems which confront them now that the war is over?

Having thus cleared the ground we shall be ready to enter upon the main course of our inquiry. This requires us to define the standard by which the Church must be judged. What have we a right to expect of the American Church if it is to realize our ideal of what a Church should be? The Church professes to be the institution of a world religion. What is the Christianity of which it is the expression and on what grounds does Christianity appeal for the allegiance of men? There are forces in the modern world which challenge the Christian claim—forces in the realm of the intellect, forces in the realm of affairs. There is that silent and pervasive influence we call the scientific spirit. There is that loud and disturbing group of forces which make up the industrial movement. These have their own tests for contemporary institutions. The Church cannot evade their scrutiny. We must look their criticism in the face. We must ask ourselves what effect the scientific movement will have upon the Church's ancient faith in a self-revealing God and His promise of a present spiritual salvation. We must know how the Church is to meet the demands of the modern man for a religion which conforms to the facts of the real world; what it has to offer to the individual, not simply in his private and personal relations, but as a member of society, meeting new questions—economic, racial, political, international. Above all, we must learn what changes the Church must make in organization in order to cope with the present situation; how far and in what sense we ought to expect the churches to become *the Church.*

In the light of this preliminary discussion of principle we must next study the Church as it is. We must learn what the churches are doing and planning in the local community, in specialized forms of service, in the country at large. This survey will introduce us to the problem of unity in its practical form as it meets us in the efforts which are being made to bring various sections of the Church together in organic union or to devise ways of expressing the spiritual sympathy which unites those who are not yet ready to surrender their corporate independence. It will show us how large a part theory plays in the decisions of practical men and will prove to us that the key to the Church's future progress lies with the teacher.

This brings us naturally to the fifth and final division of our study; namely, the educational agencies of American Protestantism. Having learned to know the Church as it is to-day, our next step must be to find out what it is doing to prepare for to-morrow. Admitting, as all must admit, the gulf between ideal and reality, what steps are being taken to bridge that gap? What are the Protestant churches of America teaching their young people? What are they doing to fit themselves to become more effective teachers in the future? How far does American Protestantism contain within itself the principle of improvement which warrants our hope that it will prove the unifying and inspiring influence which American democracy needs?

Such in briefest terms is the ground to be covered in the discussion that follows. We shall speak first of the environment in which the Church must work; secondly, of its equipment for its task; thirdly, of the standard of judgment to be applied; fourthly, of the organization through which the Church functions; and finally, of the creative forces at work within the organization.

Since we are proposing a study of institutional Christianity, much time must be spent in talking about organization and methods, but we should never allow ourselves to forget that these are only part, and by no means the most important part, of the Church's life. Like all institutions the Church is conservative in the literal sense of that much abused term. It hands down with reverent care to each new generation habits and customs which have grown out of the creative activity of the past. But creation in religion, as in the wider universe, is not over. It is going on to-day, and those who shape the life of institutions must take this into account. We may plan as we will, but when all is done, there is always something incalculable about religion. Chief of all the factors in the life of the soul is the free Spirit of God who touches the spirits of men and arouses them to new and undreamed-of activities. The Spirit of God is the refreshing and quickening shower. The Church is but the channel through which the water is conveyed. But water may be wasted for lack of a proper conduit, and those who build the reservoirs and lay the pipes have an essential part in the preparation of the Kingdom of God.

PART I

FACING THE FACTS

CHAPTER II

1. *Opportunity Afforded by the Army for the Study of the Religion of American Young Men*

WE begin our study, then, with the environment in which the Church must do its work. The first fact to note is that it is an environment of persons. In order to understand the Church we must make the acquaintance of the men and women to whom the Church ministers. To estimate correctly the opportunities and prospects of the American churches we must appreciate the spiritual needs and problems of the people who live in America.

This is by no means easy. It is hard enough to weigh the spiritual values of an age which is past, when the records are all in and the deeds done have worked out their inevitable consequences. But what standards shall we employ in our own age and among our own people? In the mass of material which comes to hand how shall we distinguish the significant from the adventitious? It has been truly said: "He who would decipher the meaning of his own time must lead an anxious life."

Certain distinctions we may make with confidence. We may distinguish between the attitude of religious people in general and the exceptional groups who are critical of the Church or hostile to it. We may differentiate the demands which the individual makes upon the Church for solace and guidance from the social needs and tasks which affect masses of men and involve political and economic as well as more narrowly religious interests. We may separate those interests which are primarily American from those larger issues which affect man as man and require us to consider religion in its inter-racial and international relationships.

Our first attention must be given to the average American, the person who lives on Main Street. We must try to learn what is thought about religion by the rank and file of Americans, and what they expect from it; who are found within the Church and what these persons are doing and receiving while they are there; why

15

those are outside who are outside; whose fault it is, theirs or the Church's, that they do not take a more active part in organized religion; whether it is because they are not interested in religion or capable of religious experience, or because the kind of religion which the Church has to offer does not appeal to them. The answers to these questions may not carry us far, but they will supply a point of departure.

When the Great War broke out it lifted us for the moment above our local prejudices and limitations, and forced us to consider the condition of the country as a whole. What is more important, it furnished us with information which enabled us to do so intelligently. Our early adoption of the military draft made the war in the strictest sense a national affair. For the first time in our history a group of men was gathered from the whole country, without distinction of occupation, wealth, race, or geographical location. This afforded a rare opportunity for the study of American conditions. We secured data that we could not otherwise have obtained about the health of our people, their physique, their education, their morale, and, about that which particularly interests us here, their religion.

These facts have been preserved for our information in a volume issued by the Committee on the War and the Religious Outlook, entitled "Religion Among American Men." [1] It is a study of the religion of the average American as revealed by observation of conditions in the army. Compiled by a representative committee of Christians of different denominations, based upon the experiences of a large number of chaplains, Young Men's Christian Association secretaries, and other religious workers, it gives us the most comprehensive and reliable information we have on the subject under discussion.

It is true that any conclusions derived from such a study must be supplemented by evidence dealing with other groups and other ages. Extensive as was the material utilized, it was yet too restricted to be fully representative. The subjects of this study were all young men, and men selected for exceptional health and vigor. They were living under strong emotion, faced suddenly with the possibility of the loss of all that they loved most. The conditions

[1] "Religion Among American Men: As Revealed by a Study of Conditions in the Army." Association Press, New York, 1920.

of their life were unnatural and artificial. They were removed from home and familiar work. They were cut off from association with those of other ages and of the opposite sex. They were relieved of all responsibility to think for themselves. They were subjected to a rigorous discipline. Even within this restricted sphere their actual experiences differed widely. Some were on the fighting line, face to face with all the tragedy and horror of war; while others never crossed the sea, or rendered their service in the reserve area behind the lines. Obviously in studying the experiences of men under such conditions there is need of great discrimination and reserve.

This was recognized by the Committee, and determined their method of procedure. They distinguished between the religion which men brought with them to the war, and their religious experience under the new conditions. They distinguished, further, between what they experienced under normal conditions, and what they lived through in times of exceptional crisis and shock. Finally, they distinguished between what they said about religion, and the faith their actions revealed. With these qualifications their reports furnish us the material for certain generalizations which we may take as the basis for further discussion.

2. What Young America Thinks about God and Religion

In the first place it may safely be said that the rank and file of the young men in America are religious. They believe in God and in a life after death, and they have some connection, at least nominal, with the Christian church. Just what proportion of the men were church members it is not easy to say. Doubtless the number did not differ appreciably from that in the nation at large. The interesting thing is that so many men should have confessed to some connection with the Christian church. Estimates vary from the great majority to ninety per cent. and even higher.[1]

---

[1] Cf. "Religion Among American Men," p. 10. A striking example is that of Camp Devens, Massachusetts, where through the co-operation of the Young Men's Christian Association, the camp pastors, and the military authorities, a religious census was taken in July and August, 1918, which covered 25,607 men. Of this number only 586 failed to express some church preference, approximately two per cent. of the whole number. In a religious census of 1,487 men in a base hospital in a Southern camp, only sixteen expressed no preference. *Op. cit.,* p. 9.

This contact, indirect if not direct with the Christian Church, helps to explain an attitude in many of the young men of the American army which was frequently remarked by foreign observers. Drawn in large numbers from homes where religion was respected and the Church taken for granted, they brought with them to their new life a background of association and habit which made prayer and the singing of hymns a natural vehicle for the expression of their deeper emotions. This was true even when, as was often the case, their lives contradicted their ideals or yielded all too readily to the solicitations of the new environment.

In an unpublished letter written by a chaplain of the American Expeditionary Force [1] we find the following description: He is speaking of a service which he had been holding near the front during one of the intervals when his regiment was relieved from active service.

The service this morning was one of the most satisfactory that I have had. After a great deal of palaver I finally secured the use of the church in this village. The French chaplain had mass at eight-forty-five, and my service came at ten-thirty. The whole thing would make a good story. First of all, the argument with the French chaplain through an interpreter, then the securing of a detail of men to clean the building. A big shell had gone through the roof leaving a great hollow place in the centre aisle. Another shell had come in through the side wall. Of course, all the glass in the windows was broken. Outside, the little graveyard had suffered in the same way. One grave-stone had been made in the form of a big stone coffin and the shell had torn one end of it off, leaving the stone standing near by like a partly opened door. It reminds me somewhat of the pictures you sometimes see of the Day of Resurrection.

The band had been practising on some hymns for me. At twenty minutes past ten the bugler blew the church call and then the band started and marched up through the street playing a march composed of "Onward, Christian Soldiers," and "Stand up for Jesus," and "Oh, Come, All Ye Faithful." They stopped outside the door and marched quietly in and up the aisle to the front on the right-hand side where I had a place for them. Then the fellows began to come in. I suppose there were about two hundred of them. You cannot imagine how it helped to have a real church building with seats and music. And when after a few opening sentences the band started "Praise God from Whom All Blessings Flow," I just thought I was standing up once more in the pulpit of the dear old University Place Church. Shell holes, dangling plaster, the band, and the men in uniforms disappeared and I was right back home. And that is the way the whole lot of us felt. A picture of all the memories that were before our eyes would have been a very beautiful and precious one.

[1] Rev. Guthrie Speers, Chaplain of the 102d Infantry Regiment, 26th Division, A. E. F.

My forty-five little hymn books did not go around, but there were a whole lot who did not seem to need them, who just put their hands behind their backs, looked up toward the ceiling a little, and seemed to get the words by special messenger from the old church back home. We sang "Come, Thou Almighty King," "What a Friend We Have in Jesus," "Onward, Christian Soldiers," and "The Son of God Goes Forth to War." But the best of them all to me was the Doxology. It was a fine service, not because of anything I did, but because of the things that came to all of us, the precious memories and thoughts.

It may be said that this was an exceptional instance. Let me cite a witness whose testimony covers a wider field of observation. Dr. Talbot, senior chaplain of the First Division of the American Expeditionary Force, writes:

> Pick up a magazine from home. You read of the religious work of the cantonments, and how soldiers flock to the services. I hope it is so. I have never seen it. We are not so fixed here that we can flock. But let me tell you what I have seen. During the first two weeks' fighting in the Argonne, my chaplains buried between fourteen hundred and fifteen hundred dead. The personal effects came through my hands. I did not count them. But I venture to say that in ninety per cent. of the personal effects of the dead soldiers there was a Bible, or a Prayer-book, or a crucifix or scapula, or some indication that religion was an element in that man's life. More than that. The force of which that treasured object was an outward sign was vital and necessary. By September, 1918, we had hiked through enough mud and rain to scrap anything not essential.[1]

But if all observers agree that the young men in the American army were religious, there is equal agreement that the religion which they had was exceedingly vague and undeveloped. Not only did the difference between the different churches play a small rôle, but even the differences between Christianity and other religions. God was a power controlling destiny, to whom one prayed, but His character was ill-defined, and He could almost as easily be identified with the fatalistic God of Mohammed as with the God and Father of our Lord and Saviour, Jesus Christ. Prayer was instinctive and chiefly for personal and private matters. Christ was a vague, ideal figure, not the personal Saviour of traditional religion. The sense of personal sin was conspicuous by its absence. God was Companion and Protector, not Judge or Saviour. The Bible, as we have seen, was carried even when it was not read, but there is little evidence of intelligent and sympathetic acquaintance with its contents. There was indeed but a meagre understand-

---

[1] Quoted in part in "Religion Among American Men," p. 89.

ing of the Church's teaching, and Christian doctrine was either ignored, or was referred to in connections which did not show any adequate comprehension of its meaning.[1]

There were, of course, many exceptions to this rule. There were individuals whose grasp of religious subjects was refreshing. In the case of some denominations, notably the Roman Catholic and the Lutheran, there was evidence on the part of some men of systematic religious instruction in the tenets of their religion.[2] But of the great majority of Protestant church members of all denominations, our generalization holds good. No single conclusion is reinforced by a larger mass of testimony than that of the failure of the churches to furnish the young men who had been under their instruction with an intelligent understanding of Christian beliefs, Christian ideals, and Christian history.[3]

Especially noticeable was the lack of contact between the Church as an institution and the wider social ideals and purposes which called forth what was best in these young men. No prominence was given to the Kingdom of God, as a better social order for which to work. Indeed, there was almost no evidence of any connection in the minds of most of them between religion and social betterment. Where social ideals and aspirations were present, they were not associated with Christianity or the Church.[4] This is the more significant in view of the fact that, as we shall see later, there has been a growing tendency in certain sections of the Christian Church to emphasize the social aspects of Christianity. It would seem, therefore, that this emphasis has not yet affected the educational work of the churches to any considerable extent.

The absence of the social note in religion was the more noteworthy because of the ready response of many of the men to the

[1] Cf. "Religion Among American Men," Chapter III, "The Faith of the Majority."

[2] "Religion Among American Men," p. 16. Cf. the following testimony from a Lutheran minister of wide experience: "Among the Lutherans of the Eastern states I should say that probably less than ten per cent. have ever had any parochial school training; in the Western states the percentage would be higher but would hardly reach one-half. The real secret of the thing is the catechetical training which precedes confirmation and which is universal in the Lutheran churches." P. 16, note 13.

[3] Religion Among American Men," pp. 14, 15. Note that the same situation is reported as true of the English army. Cf. Cairns, "The Army and Religion," London, 1919, pp. 99 sq.

[4] "Religion Among American Men," p. 137.

ideals of social service. Among the ethical qualities most admired by them, unselfishness, courage, and loyalty were conspicuous.[1] The response to the first call for troops was the best proof of this. No one whose privilege it was to go into the camps and meet the men under the impulse of that first enthusiasm could feel that Ambassador Harvey's description of the motives which led to America's entrance into the war was anything but a libel. There may have been older men whose attitude Mr. Harvey has correctly reported. Applied to the young men of our country his words were far from the truth.

It is all the more striking that these generous and unselfish qualities should not in the minds of most men have been associated with Christianity. On the whole Christianity was regarded as a self-centred and a negative religion, having to do primarily with one's own personal welfare here and hereafter.[2] Yet when the Christian appeal was made by men who could talk simple language, the response was instant and generous. It would seem, then, that the fault at this point was not with the men, but was due to the fact that they had not been properly taught the true nature of the Christian Gospel.

All students of the religious life of the army agree in reporting a great impatience with denominationalism and a widespread lack of interest in the differences between the churches.[3] Yet there is almost equal agreement as to the responsiveness of the men to worship under the stress of emotion. I have already referred to the men's enjoyment of the hymns. The same was true of the sacrament.[4] It was widely observed and apparently much appreciated. Both in the home camps (as in the great communion services at Camp Dix and Camp Meade, which were attended by thousands), and under the more trying and dangerous conditions at the front, it seemed to appeal to something in the men which the spoken word could not as effectively reach. In view of the infrequent use of the sacrament in the non-liturgical churches this responsiveness is worthy of serious consideration. Was this only a passing phase, to disappear with the crisis which had called it forth? Or have we

[1] "Religion Among American Men," p. 45.
[2] Cf. the chapter on "The Men and the Church," p. 21 sq., especially pp. 22 and 23.
[3] *Op. cit.*, p. 29.
[4] *Op cit.*, p. 103.

here the revelation of a need in human nature, to which some of us have as yet given too little heed?

Much has been made of the soldiers' criticism of the Church. That there was serious criticism cannot be denied. It is, however, easy to exaggerate its extent. The fact seems to be that many men were indifferent to the Church because it did not seem to stand for the great ideals in which they were most interested. If we try to sum up the criticisms in definite form, we find that they have to do partly with the inadequacy of the Church's moral ideal and the failure of church members to live up to their profession; partly with the unreality or triviality of the religion of the Church, the fact that the churches have been so much concerned with matters of routine and externals that they have not succeeded in relating their message to the living needs of the day.[1]

One further point requiring notice is the lack of evidence of any widespread intellectual difficulty in connection with religious belief.[2] The theoretical obstacles to faith were conspicuous by their absence. What difficulties remained were moral rather than intellectual—the selfishness of Christians, the rivalries of the churches, the concern of religion with another life to the neglect of this, and the like. The one conspicuous exception was the problem of evil, which the war kept ever before men's minds.[3] Here, too, there is food for thought for those who are responsible for the religious teaching of the next generation. We need to consider whether we have not been giving too much time to theoretical and imaginary difficulties, and ignoring the real obstacles that keep men from faith in Christ. In the army we had a chance to learn what these obstacles are. We saw that to deal with them effectively we must show men a working religion grappling with the fact of evil, as it meets us in this present life. Yet there is a good deal of testimony to show that while for many men the experiences of the war made faith in God and immortality easier, there were others for whom the reverse was true. Many who had never seriously faced the ultimate problems in their own lives were suddenly confronted with these world-old mysteries and found the strain upon

[1] Cf. "Religion Among American Men," pp. 22–29; Fosdick, "The Trenches and the Church at Home," *Atlantic Monthly,* January, 1919.
[2] This was particularly noticeable in connection with belief in immortality. Cf. "Religion Among American Men," pp. 84 sq.
[3] *Op. cit.,* p. 82.

faith greater than they could bear. So much was this the case that a well-known clergyman of wide experience, whose position in London gave him the opportunity to speak with numbers of the soldiers who were coming and going, summed up his own impression of such conversations in the paradoxical sentence that the war had made those who were irreligious before, believers in God, while it had shattered the faith of those who had supposed they were believers.

Such, then, in barest outline is the picture of the average American young man as it was revealed by a study of conditions in the army. Sincerely and simply religious, a believer in God and in prayer, even when he forgets one and omits to practise the other, he is an admirer of unselfishness and loyalty to great ends, which he has not yet succeeded in associating in any definite way with the religion which has been preached to him as a matter of individual salvation. He respects the Church and feels a vague attachment to it; and while he does not see how it bears very directly on his personal life, or has any very definite message to him on the matters in which he is most interested, he is ready to turn to it for inspiration and comfort in the greatest crises of his life.

3. *The Attitude of the Older Generation*

Helpful and reliable so far as it goes, this evidence needs supplementing in several important respects. Three groups in particular should be taken into account before our survey of American religious life can be even approximately complete: the older men, the women, the children.

Apart from war conditions, any account of the state of religion drawn from the experience of young men alone would be misleading; for youth has its prejudices and limitations which later experience tends to correct. With the responsibilities of later life come new estimates of value. One grows less impatient of half measures, readier to compromise, more willing to learn from the past.

In two respects especially the religion of older people differs from that of the younger generation. It differs in its greater appreciation of the objective and the institutional. It differs in its greater distrust of novelty.

Older people appreciate more fully than those who are younger the values that are embodied in institutions. They have come to the time of life when permanence means more to them than it once did. They have seen so many changes which are not for the better that they are disposed to put up with the evils of existing institutions for the sake of the good which they contain. It is not that they do not sympathize with the ends which the radicals seek. Indeed, there is much to be said for the thesis that the older one grows the more radical he becomes in his ideals. But they distrust the plans by which it is proposed to make us better. Like Bernard Shaw's revolutionist, their dissatisfaction with things as they are goes so far as to include the proposals to reform them.[1] This affects their estimate of the Church. They see its faults as clearly as those who are younger. Indeed, they often see them more clearly, but they see its virtues, too, and they are less ready to risk a certain good for a doubtful gain. To them the Church is a social asset of proved value, and they are not ready to give it up for any substitute which has not stood the test of time.

It is only natural, then, that we should find many older men looking with suspicion at proposals to extend the range of the Church's activity in the social field. They doubt whether it is wise for ministers to interest themselves actively in politics or to try to commit the Church to remedies for our social evils of whose economic soundness they are not sure. Sometimes this disapproval expresses itself in active opposition as in a widely read letter of the Pittsburgh Employers' Association,[2] in which the Young Women's Christian Association is criticized for its endorsement of the Social Ideals of the Churches.[3] More frequently it shows itself in the demand that the churches confine their activities to their proper sphere, which is religion. "Let the minister stick to the simple Gospel," we are told. By the simple Gospel is meant the message of personal forgiveness and salvation which was characteristic of the older evangelistic preaching. Like their sons, the fathers think

[1] Cf. "Man and Superman," 1903, p. 183: "All who achieve real distinction in life begin as revolutionists. The most distinguished persons become more revolutionary as they grow older, though they are commonly supposed to become more conservative, owing to their loss of faith in conventional methods of reform."

[2] Quoted in the *Christian Advocate*, February 10, 1921. Cf. the interesting defence of the employers' position by Mr. Long, Vice-President and General Manager of the Employers' Association, in a letter to the *Christian Work*, March 19, 1921. Cf. also *Industry*, February 1, 1921.

[3] Cf. p. 89.

of religion as something separate from the rest of life—a spring of inner contentment and satisfaction, reconciling men to the limitations and failures of this life through the promise of compensation in another rather than as an active social force in the life that now is. But while to the young man this is a reason for dissatisfaction with the Church, or at least for the absence of any active interest in its work, to his senior it is the best proof of the Church's value both to the individual and to society.

Not all older men, however, hold this negative view of the Church's function. Many value it for the opposite reason, because it inculcates in the individual the habits of self-reliance and industry which are the mainspring of social progress. They have come to see that a religion which can do no more for a man than reconcile him to his failures will not meet the needs of this restless and aspiring age. They are wise enough to perceive in the social unrest of our time not simply a danger to be guarded against, but a source of new power to be utilized. They look to the Church for leadership which will direct this new power into fruitful and beneficent channels.[1]

The most convincing evidence of the strong hold of religion upon the rank and file of the American people is the widespread habit of church attendance. Much has been said and written in recent years about the decline of church attendance in the United States, but there is no reliable evidence to prove that it is growing less. Indeed, taking the country at large, it is doubtful if there has ever been a time in our history when more people were in the habit of attending church every Sunday.[2] When we consider the number of rival attractions in the shape of golf, baseball, and the movies, and reflect how far the old sanctions which made church attendance a badge of social respectability have broken down, the wonder is not that so many men remain away from church, but that so many go. In its ability to bring large numbers to its weekly service the

[1] Mr. Roger Babson's widely read book, "Religion and Business," New York, 1920, is typical of this point of view. Cf. also "Enduring Investments," 1921, and "The Future of the Churches," 1921, by the same author.

[2] A recent canvass of student church attendance at Urbana showed that on a particular Sunday, more than thirty-five hundred undergraduates attended church—probably fifty per cent. of those who were in town that day—not a bad showing for a state university, where attendance is entirely voluntary. Cf. *Christian Century*, March 30, 1922, p. 402.

Church gives a signal proof of the strength of its hold upon the conscience and conviction of its members. They believe in the Church in spite of its faults as answering to some deep need of the soul. In times of routine the bond which exists between the members and the Church may be loosened and may even seem to part altogether, but in times of crisis it tightens and gives evidence of holding power.

The very general disposition on the part of American parents to send their children to Sunday school is another witness to the influence of the Church. They may not themselves have any active part in church life. They may not be church members or even regular church attendants. But they feel that the Church stands for certain great values and interests in human society which they would like their children to share. The Church inculcates certain virtues in which they believe. It holds up certain ideals of which they approve. It fosters habits of reverence, loyalty, and respect for authority which they regard as essential to the stability of society, and they wish their children to grow up in an atmosphere where a respect for these qualities is cultivated.

Of such facts as these Dr. Gilkey has reminded us in his recent pamphlet on the effects of the war on the local church.[1] He tells us that if we really wish to understand the religious experience of America during the war, we must study it not only in camps but in the hearts of the fathers and mothers who stayed at home. We have no formal record of the experience of these older people, but if the pastors of our churches could write the story of the last six years it would reinforce our faith in the central place of religion in human life, in the unique opportunity of the Church to minister to the deeper needs of men, and in the power of old associations to assert themselves in time of strain. Among the people who filled the home churches we find little desire for novelty, small trace of intellectual difficulty; a readiness to take the Church at its face value as a ministrant to the simple needs of every day. If it be said that those who desire novelty are not in the Church, this is doubtless true. The significant thing is that there are so many who seem satisfied with the churches as they are.

---

[1] Charles W. Gilkey, "The Local Church After the War," published by the Committee on the War and the Religious Outlook, Association Press, New York, 1920.

4. What American Womanhood is Likely to Contribute to the Religion of the Future

Thus far we have been considering the religion of the average American as it is revealed to us by a study of American young men and the kind of men they are likely to grow into when they become older. But there is another important factor which needs to be considered, and that is the new attitude of women toward their rights and responsibilities—social, economic, political, and religious. Here we have a set of influences which are bound to affect religion in novel and unexpected ways. Can we venture any prediction as to what their effect will be?

In the first place, as women become more highly educated, we may expect them to become more critical of the Church. Such criticism, as we have already seen, has been confined to limited groups and has not as yet largely affected any considerable number of church members. But with the increasing intellectual activity of women we must expect their attitude to change. In other walks of life we find women bringing to the conventional methods which have hitherto had the right of way a questioning and inquisitive mind. Why should not the same be true of religion? With the accession of women to the ranks of those who are thinking independently about religion we should expect a reinforcement for those who are trying to better conditions in the Church.[1]

This interest of women in the problems of the Church will be particularly valuable because it is the reflex of a parallel process which is going on in their attitude to personal religion. Their attitude to religion is a natural result of the new conditions in which many of them are working side by side with men, and the responsibilities which are being put upon them. Out of these conditions special questions arise and a fresh type of religious experience is being developed. This modern religious experience must also be taken into account in any effort to estimate the possible contribution of women to the future of religion.

When we speak of a new type of religious experience we do not mean that we are to expect any abrupt break between women's at-

[1] As an example of this new critical attitude of women toward the Church we may refer to the stimulating pamphlet of Miss Rhoda McCulloch, "The War and the Woman Point of View," published by the Committee on the War and the Religious Outlook, Association Press, New York, 1920.

titude to religion in the past and their present outlook. We mean simply that the conditions into which women are entering put upon their religious life a strain which is bound to have some corresponding effect on the type of their religious experience. They are facing in many interesting ways that change from the older religion of authority in which everything was taken for granted and one did simply what one was told, to the modern religion of freedom and responsibility which puts questions which each must answer for himself and lays loads which cannot be shifted to other shoulders. This fact will make a study of the religious experience of women in the next generation peculiarly instructive.

In a most interesting and significant way women are concentrating in a few brief years a development which has been going on in the race during many centuries. It is the change from the narrow and sheltered life of the home to the wider contacts and more exacting problems of life in society. Women are experiencing the sense of comradeship and responsibility that comes through the larger life of business or politics. To the old ties of family or friendship they are adding new ties of class or race or nationality. This transition is going on to-day in the lives of millions of men and women, and it will have momentous consequences for religion. Apart from the simple needs and experiences which have hitherto concerned us and which together make up the religion of the average American, we find that interests and problems are emerging which affect special groups and combinations of people. These interests and problems come to American women with peculiar freshness and power just because their life has been more sheltered than the life of men.

An inevitable consequence of the greater independence of women will be to give them a larger share in the administration and government of the Church. As the number of highly trained and self-supporting women has increased there has been a corresponding increase in the number of those available for active service in the Church. But as yet this energy has found no adequate outlet. Until recently, with a few minor exceptions, all official positions in the Protestant churches have been reserved for men. But this was true also until a few years ago of the other learned professions. When women were admitted to the law and medical schools, the natural consequence was bound to follow, and we see women taking their place beside men at the bar and in the operating room, as they had already made their presence felt in business, in industry, and in commerce. Is there any reason to doubt that what has been true of the other professions will prove true also of the Church? Is it conceivable that woman with her deeply religious nature and her profound conviction of the importance of spiritual issues will be content to remain a mere spectator, a runner of errands in the Church? Here is a fund of trained energy available for the highest form of service, ready to be utilized in a hundred ways, if those who are responsible for the conduct of the Church's affairs appreciate the opportunity and provide proper channels for the use of the powers already demanding expression.

In the foreign field this change is taking place. The practical exigencies of the situation have made it necessary to grant women a greater share in the administration of the Church's work than is common in the home Church. In many of the missions women have an equal vote with men in the determination of the affairs of the mission and they are represented on the Continuation Committees in which the larger questions of missionary policy are decided. But the same causes which have produced this result in the foreign field are beginning to operate at home, and there is no reason to doubt that they will make their influence felt in increasing measure in the near future.

Already we see signs that the home Church is waking up to this fact and is preparing to make use of this unutilized power. For a long time the women have had their own agencies of missionary service. But their admission to a share in the management of the affairs of the Church as a whole is comparatively recent. The Episcopal Church, to be sure, has an order of deaconesses, and the same is true of the Methodists, but the proposal to create this office in the Presbyterian Church has thus far been voted down. The Methodist Church South has provided for women's representation on its Board of Missions, and the same is true of the Disciples and the Friends. The Presbyterian Church is considering similar provision both in the case of Home and of Foreign Missions. The Congregationalists, the Baptists, and the Disciples, admit women to their highest representative body, and the same is true of the Methodists.[1] In the Diocese of Massachusetts a woman this year for the first time took part in the election of a Bishop. Most striking of all was the recent action of the Northern Baptist Convention in electing a woman, Mrs. Montgomery, its president.

It may well be that as a method of self-education and discipline it may be desirable for women still further to develop their independent agencies for missionary and philanthropic work. But as we shall see later, any such device must necessarily be temporary and provisional. The real unit with which the Church deals is not man alone, or woman alone, but the family, and to deal adequately with the spiritual needs of the family men and women must co-operate on equal terms. This fact must ultimately express itself in the constitution of the Church. We are not attempting here to forecast what form that co-operation is to take, but simply pointing out that in the capacity of women for executive work and their interest in the larger questions which determine the Church's policy, we have a factor which must be given serious consideration in any attempt to appraise the present condition of American Christianity.

This reference to the family as the moral and spiritual unit suggests one further point to which reference must be made, and that is the strategic position which, as the home maker, the American woman holds for the future of religion. With the entrance of women into industry and the extension of their interest to other spheres of service, there has been for the time being a shifting of interest from that industry which has always been woman's peculiar specialty; namely, making the home. No intelligent student of contemporary affairs believes that it will be possible, even if it were desirable, to turn the wheels back and make women content with the narrow and limited life which they once lived. But it must be possible, and for the future welfare of the Church it is essential, to use the wider training and insight which women are gaining through their entrance into the world of affairs to make their work as home makers more efficient and successful, and so fit them to become in the new age what they have been so conspicu-

---

[1] In 1904, the Methodist Church admitted women to its General Conference. In addition women may serve as stewards, may act as trustees for church property, and as presidents of the Epworth and Junior Leagues. They are recognized as members of the Quarterly Conference, and of the District Conference, but not as yet of the Annual Conference, a purely ministerial body. Since 1920 they have been licensed as local preachers.

ously in the past, the dominant influence in forming the character and determining the destiny of the children who are to be the makers of the American Church of the future.

5. *Changing Conditions Affecting the Religion of American Children*

With the mention of the children we have touched the last of the factors to be considered in our estimate of present-day Christianity. A generation is growing up under influences the effects of which it is too early for us to forecast. What is to be the attitude of these young Americans when they come to the place where they must make up their own minds, and choose for themselves? Will they repeat the experience of their elders whose attitude toward religion we have tried to analyze; or will the new factors at work produce changes in their experience, and, if so, of what kind?

Some of these factors we can already distinguish, and they are such as to cause us grave concern. For one thing, there is the breaking up of family life, with a consequent decay of religion within the home. It is increasingly true that if the children of the next generation are to be saved for religion it is the Church which must save them. Their fathers and mothers no longer teach them the Bible at home or gather them in the morning for family prayers. For a home some degree of permanence is requisite, but in America permanence seems a vanishing art. The rapid changes of residence due to economic and industrial conditions; the shifting of population from country to city; the increase of women's work, particularly in factories, and other occupations taking them from home many hours in the day; the growing love of excitement; the increasing pace at which life is lived—all these create for the children of the next generation a problem the like of which the world has never yet seen.

Into the causes of this state of things we cannot enter here. They are many and complex. Some of them will appear in the next chapter. In part we may hope they will prove temporary, the natural aftermath of the Great War which has detached so many people from their old moorings and set them adrift in the world. In part they have deeper causes and are a result of the intellectual and moral revolution which we associate with modern science both in its theoretical and in its applied forms. The breaking down of the old sanctions of religion with the resulting loss of standards by which to judge right and wrong, the easy disregard of law when individual interest or taste is at stake, the enormous increase in the facilities for cheap amusement and the prevailing tendency to subordinate duty to pleasure in the world's estimate of values—these are some of the factors which have helped to produce the world in which the children are growing up with whom the future Church is so vitally concerned.

On the other hand, there are encouraging factors to be noted. We have gained a truer appreciation of the importance of the child, and pay more attention to his needs and welfare. Our attitude toward the child in industry is different. We are limiting the hours of child labor; we are lengthening the years of schooling and improving the instruction given. Increased attention is being devoted to the study of child psychology, and this in turn is making possible better methods of education. In a word, we are becoming conscious that the child is a social asset whose welfare concerns the community as a whole.

This new attitude reappears in religious circles. The conception of the child as a depraved creature who must run his course of evil before he can be won back to the Church by conversion no longer prevails. Bushnell taught us long ago that the child born in a Christian home should grow up a Christian as naturally as the acorn develops into the oak.[1] But we are only now beginning to draw the full consequences of this insight for religious education. A good Sunday-school has long been regarded as essential to the life of the Church, and the number of children who are not reached by any formal religious instruction has been recognized as a national menace. We realize to-day that it is not enough to have Sunday schools. We must have good schools, and teachers who know what children need, and are competent to supply it.

But this deeper insight into the spiritual possibilities of the American child will amount to little unless we have homes in which to produce Christians. The Church can do much to assist parents in training their children for religion, but it cannot take the place which God has assigned to them. In Christian education no single

[1] Cf. his "Christian Nurture," written in 1846.

factor can operate effectively. Only through the intelligent co-operation of home and school and church can we hope for success. The way to make Christian children is to have Christian fathers and mothers, and the time to begin making them is when they are children. We must keep this fact constantly in mind as we pass from this general survey of the religion of the average American to a more detailed study of particular problems. Though we may re-define the Church's task, we cannot alter its nature. Now as in every past age the function of the Christian Church is to win men and women to allegiance to Jesus Christ and to make His principles regnant in their lives wherever these lives may be lived.

CHAPTER III

1. *New Elements Affecting the Religious Situation—The Shifting of Population—Immigration and the Negro*

THUS far we have been considering the religion of the average American—the impression of the religious condition of the country which we gain from a cross-section of the population—men, women, and children—without distinction of occupation, geographical location, or personal taste or idiosyncrasy. But already our study has brought to our attention disturbing features which render a more careful analysis necessary. There are large groups whose attitude toward religion would not be correctly represented by the preceding description, and there are widespread influences operating on the country at large which are producing changes in the existing situation and are likely to do so to an increasing degree. These new influences we have now to consider.

Some of them we have already briefly referred to: the changing conditions under which people are living; the rapid shifting of population from country to city, with its consequence in the growth of great cities, and the denuding of the country districts and the smaller communities. With the economic effects of this change we are already familiar, but the spiritual consequences are even more serious. It produces a sense of instability which prevents the formation of permanent attachments. Like the ancient Arab, the modern American is a dweller in tents, or, what comes to the same thing, in trunks. New York City is only the most conspicuous example of a tendency which is nation-wide. Its buildings are being continually torn down to be replaced by new ones, and while in use are occupied by a ceaseless stream of tenants. At whichever extreme we take our point of observation the result is the same. Twenty-seven years ago the author was a member of a committee to choose a site for the proposed Union Settlement on the upper East Side. Wandering through One Hundred and Fourth Street he questioned a man standing at the door of a tenement: "What can you tell me of this neighborhood?" "You have come to the right man," was the answer. "I have lived here longer than any one else." "And how long may that be?" "Three years." When the corner-stone of the new buildings of Union Theological Seminary was laid on Lenox Hill in 1884, Dr. Hitchcock, then president, congratulated the institution on having at last acquired a permanent home. To-day not one stone of the old buildings remains upon another. The eternity to which the eloquent speaker looked forward was in fact less than thirty years.

The difficulty which results from this incessant change is magnified by the character of the units which are changing. From the first, different strands have entered into the making of the American people, and in recent years the complexity of our population has enormously increased. Immigration has been pouring into the country year by year streams of people, ignorant of our language, our traditions, and our ideals, attracted to us by the promise of higher wages, greater comfort; but, above all, larger freedom. At first drawn largely from the British Isles and central Europe, they now come from Russia and the Balkans, as well as from the Near and the Far East. Calling upon the Protestant pastor at Baalbek in Syria twenty years ago I was accosted in good English by the wife of the local Greek priest. She had spent five years in New York as a peddler on the lower East Side, and she was expecting to return. It was a hope that seemed in every one's mind. The man who drove my camel in Egypt begged me to take him back to America, "the land of unlimited possibilities."

With the consequences of this migration of the peoples we are only too familiar. Foreign cities have been growing up in the heart of America, preserving in language, customs, and ideals the habits of the country from which they came. New York has its Ghetto, its Little Italy, its Chinatown, its Bohemia, its Hungary. It has its Greek coffee-houses, and its Syrian restaurants where the newcomer may fraternize with men from his own country. In Harlem, which was yesterday a white man's city, one hundred thousand Negroes now make their homes. It is the same on a lesser scale the country over. A single ward of San Francisco contains thirty thousand Italians. In New Britain, Connecticut, a city of forty thousand people, twenty-six different languages are spoken.

At the Student's Cosmopolitan Club [1] in New York City one can meet students of sixty-five nationalities.

The war awakened us to the extent to which we had become a nation of nations. We discovered the foreign-language press.[2] We learned how many of our foreign-born fellow Americans remained loyal to the country of their birth. But we learned also how effectively the great majority had been won to a new allegiance. The comrades in arms of our soldiers of foreign birth know how completely many of them identified themselves with the objects for which they were fighting; how truly America represented to them the cause of human liberty and progress.

In 1915, there was organized in the Labor Temple of New York City the American International Church. Five different nationalities were represented in the services, and five different languages were used in the worship. Besides English-speaking Americans there were Italians, Russians, Hungarians, and Galicians. Their fellow-countrymen were fighting on opposite sides in the Great War —Italian and Russian against Hungarian and Galician—yet here they met on equal terms, as members of the Christian Church.

Of special interest to the student of church affairs are two races whose presence within our borders presents peculiar problems, the Japanese of California, and the Mexicans who during these years of revolution have been pouring across our southern border in large numbers. Most Americans know something of the crisis caused by the presence of the Japanese on the west coast; but few Americans realize the gravity of the situation caused by the huge Mexican immigration of recent years. While no definite figures are obtainable, the most reliable estimates available put the number of Mexicans now in this country at about a million and a half,[3] and already the question as to what can be done to assimilate them and fit them to become worthy citizens of the country in which they have found a home has become a pressing one.

Most serious of all in its magnitude and complexity is the prob-

---

[1] A club on Morningside Heights, which brings together the foreign students of Columbia University and the affiliated institutions.

[2] At a single news-stand on East Forty-second Street you may buy any morning a daily in any one of the following languages: Spanish, French, German, Russian, Ukrainian, Greek, Slovak, Italian, Hungarian, and in many cases you may choose between two or three.

[3] Cf. Stowell, "The Near Side of the Mexican Question," New York, 1921.

lem of the American Negro. A dozen years ago we thought of this as a Southern problem, but to-day we realize that it has become a national one; for the Negro, as little as the Italian, or the Slav, is content to remain in the situation in which his father left him. He, too, aspires to better himself in respect to property, education, and social standing. So great Negro communities are growing up in our Northern cities, and the problems with which we have become familiar in the South are repeating themselves on a smaller but still unmistakable scale in the North. Here, too, the problem is not simply economic and social, but in its deepest sense personal and religious. What do we propose to do with these black fellow-citizens of ours, brought here generations ago without their consent, but now linked to us by an indissoluble bond? One thing is certain, that the old attitude of subjection and docility inherited from the days of slavery has gone, never to return. The war taught the Negro that he was good enough to fight for his country by the side of the white man. Now he asks his country what sort of life he is to live with his white brothers since the war has been won.

2. The Effect of Modern Industry—The Growth of Class Consciousness

These more obvious difficulties of residence and race are accentuated by serious problems growing out of the economic and industrial situation. The rise of big business with its attendant factory system is itself one of the causes of the complications which we have been considering, but it brings with it other and more far-reaching consequences.

We have spoken of changes in habits of life—of the breaking up of the family, due to the lack of permanent homes; of the uncertainty of employment, due to the fluctuation of supply and demand; of the entrance of women and children into industry. But all these are but symptoms of something deeper, a change in the attitude of mind on the part of large numbers of people toward those earlier democratic ideals of liberty and equality which are celebrated in the school books as peculiarly American, and which gave their tone to the America of an earlier day. For many people in this country those ideals have vanished, or are vanishing. In their place we find the growth of a class consciousness which puts the group before the individual and is jealous of any advance that carries the favored few beyond their less able or gifted comrades. Any position in the commonwealth was open to the traditional schoolboy. But many thoughtful people in the ranks of labor no longer believe this to be the case. They have accepted the philosophy of class with all that this implies. They do not believe that it is possible for them to be anything else than what they are, nor do they desire it.

We often meet Americans who deprecate the existence of class consciousness and try to ignore it. They would like to think that America is still the land which they believe that it ought to be; the land which they have found it to be in their personal experience. It is natural that they should cherish this wish, but it is dangerous to let our eyes be blinded to the fact that for multitudes this America no longer exists. If there are no classes in America, it is true that there are many people who *think* that classes exist, and who shape their lives accordingly.

A conspicuous example of class consciousness is the labor union. Both in its craft form as represented in the American Federation of Labor, and in its industrial form, as represented by the Amalgamated Garment Workers and similar unions, its leaders accept the conventional division of mankind into capitalists and laborers, and devote their energy to increasing the rewards and improving the condition of the latter.[1] This is quite consistent with the recognition of the fact that the contrast is not an exclusive one; that the laborer may be a capitalist to a certain extent, and the capitalist may contribute his share of useful work. But this recognition can not obscure the fact that the livelihood of great numbers of men and women depends and, so far as we or they can see, will always depend upon the wages they earn; just as there are many who need never work at all unless they desire to, but may live at ease upon the in-

---

[1] While many of the older unions, particularly those connected with the American Federation of Labor, are conservative in their view of the relations between capital and labor, emphasizing their common interest in the industry which both alike serve, not a few of the more recent unions, particularly of the industrial form, have embodied the doctrine of the class war in the preamble of their constitutions. The most radical statement of this doctrine is that of the Industrial Workers of the World.

"The working class and the employing class have nothing in common. . . . Between these two classes a struggle must go on until the workers of the world organize as a class, take possession of the earth and the machinery of production, and abolish the wage system."

come of their capital, and pass on the possibility of a similar life to their children.

The labor movement in all its forms takes this fact for granted, and builds upon it not only a certain method of procedure, but, what is more important, a definite philosophy of life. It is a philosophy in which loyalty to class is the major virtue, and the scab (or the man who seeks private advancement at the cost of his class) is the incarnation of all the vices.

It must be added that such class consciousness is not confined to the workingman. There are employers of labor who share it to the full. To them it seems natural that the few should command, and the many obey; and labor, instead of being the sum total of aspiring, hoping, suffering human beings, is a group which cherishes ambitions to which it has no right, and must be taught its place.

This rivalry, implicit in the present relation of capital and labor, is deliberately and cleverly reinforced by the propaganda of the radicals. This propaganda takes many forms according to the school which it represents. Its more conservative form is represented by the orthodox Socialists; its more extreme form by the communism of Lenine and Trotzky. The Industrial Workers of the World, with their repudiation of state socialism, and their theory of the One Big Union, are especially significant because of the field in which they operate. A less radical variant is Guild Socialism, which advocates the control of each industry as a whole by the workers, while vesting the ownership of the industry in the state.

It is difficult to estimate the extent or the influence of this radical propaganda. According to the Lusk Committee,[1] it is sufficiently extensive and influential to make legislative inquiry necessary.[2] Other informants who have every motive to emphasize the strength of the radical forces wherever they can discover them, are convinced that the radicals have thus far made little progress,

[1] The Lusk Committee is a committee appointed by the legislature of the State of New York "to investigate the scope, tendencies, and ramifications of . . . seditious activities and to report the result of its investigation to the Legislature." Its report of 4450 pages in four volumes was issued in 1920.

[2] Cf. "Resolution Authorizing the Investigation of Seditious Activities." "It is a matter of public knowledge that there is a large number of persons within the State of New York engaged in circulating propaganda calculated to set in motion forces to overthrow the Government of this State and of the United States," p. 1.

and that the great body of the American labor movement, like the nation of which it is a part, is conservative. Certainly if deeds are to be the judge rather than words, there is little reason for alarm, provided our national industrial policies are sane, just, and progressive. But discontent thrives on repression, and if our reactionaries have their way, they may yet succeed in bringing about the consequences they profess to fear.

One fact concerning the radical movement deserves serious consideration. It knows what it believes and why. It has a gospel to preach, and it preaches it in the only way in which any gospel can be preached, by the personal communication of man to man. It has its press and its schools, and whether we like it or not, it is teaching men to think who never thought before. Worthy of serious consideration is the following remark made in my hearing by a well-known agitator of the I. W. W., who had spent many months in jail. "You may say what you like about the I. W. W. But you cannot rob us of this, that we were the first people to put a social conscience into the casual laborer."

In the radical labor movement, as in the race movement to which we have already referred, we have a point of contact with the wider world of international affairs. For America, as for all the other countries of the world, the great experiment which is being tried in Russia has been of crucial importance. As long as it was possible to represent this as a glowing success, our radicals were in possession of ammunition of which they knew how to make good use. Now that the weakness and probable ultimate failure of the Russian revolutionary programme has become apparent, the conservative element in the labor movement has been correspondingly strengthened.

3. Resulting Changes in the Church's Missionary Task

Our intention is not to describe the present condition of the labor movement, but to sketch briefly the conditions which the Church must face under the conditions of the new day. It is evident that these conditions are extraordinarily complex, necessitating many changes from the organization and methods of a simpler age.[1]

[1] Cf. W. P. Shriver, "The New Home Mission of the Church," Committee on the War and the Religious Outlook, Association Press, New York, 1919.

One of the cherished traditions of the author's family is of John Adams, once headmaster of Phillips Academy, Andover, who in his old age accepted service under the American Sunday-School Union and went out in his buggy through the newly settled districts of Illinois, bringing the people into the schoolhouse and organizing Sunday schools which later grew into churches. During the twelve years of his service he organized no less than three hundred and twenty-two schools with more than twenty-five hundred teachers and brought under the influence of the Christian religion more than sixteen thousand scholars.[1]

It is a typical picture of the life of the old-time home missionary, at once strenuous and simple. Our haunting problems of the why and the how were unknown to him. His duty was to take the Gospel, which all Christian people accepted, from the eastern and central parts of the country which were already adequately churched, to the frontier, ever pressing westward, in order that these new churches in turn, when they were strong enough to support themselves, might take up the work of home missions for the regions farther west.

How different is the situation to-day! How different it is in extent! No single part of our country is home-missionary territory to the exclusion of the rest. Everywhere we face the same problem of an unchurched population; in the East as well as in the West; in the city as well as in the country. Indeed, there is a sense in which New York City itself is the greatest home-mission field in the world. Our task is not to plant a few home-mission churches in frontier states where they will presently grow to self-support. It is to mobilize all the resources of the Church for the Christianization of the country as a whole.

Nor is the change simply in the range, but also in the nature of the task. It is not a matter of converting individuals simply, but of changing their environment. The social consciousness, which we have already had occasion to note in connection with the woman movement and the labor movement, has pervaded home missions as well. We see that we have to deal not simply with individuals as individuals but with members of definite and sharply contrasted groups, each with its own background of race, religion,

[1] M. E. and H. G. Brown, "The Story of a New England Schoolmaster," New York, 1900.

economic and political ideals. We must study these ideals if we are to understand the people who cherish them, and this requires a much more elaborate preparation than the buggy and the Bible which were once the sufficient stock in trade of the successful missionary.

These new demands require far-reaching changes in organization. We shall later on study these changes more in detail.[1] We notice•now that they involve a growing specialization. Departments are created for the study of special phases of the work. Surveys are made to serve as the basis of intelligent planning. The relation to the home church is being re-studied. It is clear that the time has come when we must re-define the responsibility of the national boards to those smaller and self-supporting units like the diocese, the classis, and the presbytery, which we have hitherto been in the habit of regarding as independent and self-sufficient.

Above all, we are coming to see the importance of sound methods of education. As in all teaching, the point of contact is the key to mastery. In the case of the people we have been trying to describe, this requires constant study and experiment.

4. *Emerging Problems—The Problems of Race, of Class, and of Nationality*

In the course of this study of the new home missions three major problems have emerged, the understanding of which is essential for the definition of the future task of the Church: the problem of race, the problem of class, the problem of nationality.

In the first place, the problem of race. What ought to be the attitude of the Christian to these deep-seated differences which we have passed in review? In what sense ought the Church to recognize race as a fundamental fact, to be taken account of and provided for in our planning? What ought to be the Church's attitude to these new Americans coming to us as prospective citizens, yet still cherishing affection and loyalty for the land that gave them birth? Shall we discourage this loyalty and affection, or shall we see 'in it an asset to be used in the making of a better America? What shall we do with the languages they speak, with their literature, their art, their religion? Can we use these as helps to the building of a finer character than could otherwise have been attained? And

[1] Cf. Chapter XII.

if so, how? How, in a word, in this most difficult and baffling field, shall we realize the Christian ideal of unity in variety—the body with the many members?

The problem presses most heavily in connection with that race which forms so substantial a part of our population—the American Negro. How shall we treat these ten millions whose lives are so inextricably intertwined with ours, and who are increasing in numbers every day? To our Christian faith they are sons and daughters of God our Father, disciples of Jesus Christ our Saviour, potential citizens in the Kingdom of God. How shall we express this faith in the practice of our American church? How far is the current practice of race segregation consistent with Christian principles? If not, in what respects should it be changed, and what steps should be taken to bring this change about?

These are not simply theoretical questions. They meet us in practical forms which cannot be evaded. The doctrine of inherent race rivalry preached by such books as the recent "Rising Tide of Color"[1] is given practical effect in the conduct of multitudes of men; and here again, since we meet not simply the clash of practical interests but the strife of ideals, the Church has a stake in the matter. It is the Church's responsibility, if not to settle all the questions at issue, at least to lay down the principles by which they can be rightly settled, and what is even more important, to create the atmosphere in which the desire to settle them rightly can be born.

Secondly, the problem of class. What shall be our attitude to the questions at issue between capital and labor? How far does the class consciousness which we have above briefly described represent a fact of human nature, of which honesty compels us to take account? How is it to be reconciled with the Christian doctrine of the brotherhood of man, and the infinite worth of each human soul? It will not do to say that these are economic and industrial questions with which the Church as such has nothing to do; for the fundamental fact about the labor movement is not economic but spiritual. It is an attitude of mind with which we are confronted, a philosophy

---

[1] Stoddard, "The Rising Tide of Color against White World Supremacy," New York, 1920. Cf. especially this sentence from Mr. Madison Grant's preface: "Democratic ideals among an homogeneous population of Nordic blood, as in England or America, is one thing, but it is quite another for the white man to share his blood with, or *entrust his ideals* to, brown, yellow, black, or red men." (Italics are author's.)

of life; an attitude and a philosophy which call forth loyalty and devotion in many who hold them which can only be described as religious. How far are the new forces which this movement has released hostile to Christianity? How far are they merely the expression in a different form of the same social forces and spiritual aspirations of which the Gospel was born? What has the Church to offer the leaders of this movement? What, on its part, can it learn from them?

Many radicals maintain that the Church has been in the past, and still remains, an organ of privilege. They look upon it as the rich man's club or, if not that, at least the almoner of his bounty. They insist that it is committed to the maintenance of the present capitalistic system. At its best it is concerned with individual and personal matters, preaching a religion of contentment here in hope of a better world to come by and by.[1] We cannot allow this picture of the Church to go unchallenged. But a mere denial will not be enough. We must show men the alternatives which we have to offer, and we must show them these alternatives so clearly that they will be understood.

Finally, there is the problem of nationality, in many respects the most urgent and the most baffling of all. What shall be the attitude of the Church to the wave of patriotism which is sweeping over America, as it is sweeping over all the other nations of the world? How far is patriotism a Christian virtue? How shall we reconcile the internationalism of the Gospel with the emotions which every true American feels when he looks up at the Stars and Stripes?

The question meets us in a hundred forms. It is implicit in almost every decision that we make. No vote we cast, no business transaction in which we engage but forces us to consider—if indeed it does not determine for us without consideration—how far we have a right to treat our country as ours alone, how far it is our duty to consider the needs and aspirations of other lands.

The Christian view of nationality lies at the heart of the tariff question, the immigration question, the question of our mercantile marine. Our fathers came to this country as exiles and refugees to seek freedom of conscience, and a place in which to worship God

---

[1] A sympathetic interpretation of the radical point of view is given by J. J. Coale, in his article, "Protestantism and the Masses," *Yale Review*, October, 1921.

in their own way. But there are still countries where people are oppressed and where men are denied the right to worship God as their conscience dictates. Has the time indeed come when the refuge America offered to our fathers can rightly be denied to these other oppressed and needy children of God, for whom He cares as truly as for us?

The same issue meets us in our foreign relations. Senator and ambassador may repeat Cain's ancient question: "Am I my brother's keeper?" But we are learning that blood brotherhood is a tie which cannot so easily be severed. We may try to ignore Europe, but Europe will not ignore us. Evade the issue as we may, we shall find that our very denial of international responsibilities brings us face to face with international dangers. What is there in this fact of nationality that seems to lead so inevitably to conflict with men who ask only the right to feel toward their own country as we feel toward ours? The Church has something to say about this conflict of patriotisms. It has a loyalty to offer which makes place for all the lesser loyalties of race and class and nation. It opens a horizon which carries us beyond the confines of our country and requires us to envisage the world as a whole.

CHAPTER IV

1. *Chief Points of Contact between American Christianity and International Problems*

THUS far we have been analyzing the task of the American Church from the point of view of the homeland, for whose Christianization we are primarily responsible. We have studied the religion of the average American, as it is revealed to us in the life of the young men gathered in the camps by the military draft and in the experience of the fathers and mothers from whose homes they came. We have taken into account the exceptional groups whose changing occupation forces them into new conditions; children facing the disintegration of the home; women entering industry in ever larger numbers, and sharing for the first time the responsibilities and problems of men; immigrants introducing into the relatively homogeneous life of the older America new factors of language and of tradition; the labor movement with its growing class consciousness, and its challenge to the older theory of American democracy. Out of this situation we have seen three problems emerging with which the Church of the future must deal: the problem of race, the problem of class, and the problem of nationality. But these are not problems confined to any one country or to any one branch of the Church. To approach them understandingly we must see them in their larger setting, as they affect other nations than our own.

During the early days of the war the author's work as Secretary of the General War-Time Commission of the Churches took him to the Brooklyn Navy Yard which had been transformed into a naval training station. In company with the resident chaplain he visited the men's barracks and made the acquaintance of the new recruits, clean, manly-looking fellows of whom any country might be proud. But what impressed him most was the fact that they had come so largely from the fresh-water states. Many of them had never seen the sea. To most of them, enlistment brought the first oppor-

46

tunity to leave their own country and touch the wider world of which America is a part.

What was true of the navy was true on a far larger scale of the army. The war carried to the remotest hamlet of the nation the news that America was no longer an isolated country, but a member of the family of nations, linked to the fortunes of her sisters across the sea by indissoluble ties and prepared, if need be, to spend all that she had in a contest which was fought three thousand miles from her own shores.

To millions of Americans this was a revolutionary experience. The war brought a rude shock to their former preconceptions and habits. Even when they were convinced that it was inevitable and had resigned themselves to do what was necessary to bring it to a successful conclusion, they could not shake off the conviction that it was, after all, but an episode. When peace came, or at all events very soon after, they were confident that the nation could resume its interrupted occupations where they had been broken off, keep its sons at home, and leave Europe to deal with its own difficulties. It was this widely spread feeling which made it possible for a little group in the Senate to block President Wilson's attempt to secure the whole-hearted co-operation of the American people in the task of international reconstruction. Only slowly and by a process of education which will take wisdom and patience can the country as a whole be brought to realize that what has happened is not an episode, but only the last and most dramatic chapter of a history which reaches back to the beginnings of the nation's life.

Long before the first troops of the American Expeditionary Force took ship for France, others of their fellow-countrymen had preceded them in international enterprises. Some of them had gone in quest of trade, like the early merchants whose admission to Japan was made possible by the peaceful embassage of Commodore Perry. Others had been moved by missionary zeal, like the Williams College students who went from their meeting by the haystack to win the world for Christ. Still others went in search of learning or art, or in the simple human desire to relieve suffering. All through our national history in varying degrees these motives have been operating, and the experiences gained and the contacts formed in these ways have helped to prepare America to meet understandingly the new problems and responsibilities which she faces

to-day. Of the many points of contact between our own country
and other nations two have special importance for our present purpose: that furnished by foreign missions in the widest sense of that
term, and the more recent appeal made to the sympathies of the
American public by the suffering which was the aftermath of the
war.

2. Foreign Missions, a Factor in Educating America for Internationalism

The most direct point of contact between American Christianity
and the outside world before the war was the foreign-missionary
enterprise. Through this enterprise generations of Americans had
been educated to realize their kinship with other peoples and to feel
responsibility for their welfare. But this contact was confined to
a relatively small section of the American people, and its far-reaching significance for our international relations is only now for the
first time coming to be realized. The war has put a knowledge of
the habits and aspirations of other peoples at a premium, and
besides knitting closer the ties which already bind this country to
Europe has made the nation realize the possible significance, for
weal or woe, of those great masses of men who inhabit the Near and
the Far East.

It will give us the true perspective for judging the closer and
more intimate relations into which the war has brought us with
Europe if we begin by considering the world situation as a whole,
as it appears to those observers whose judgment as to the significance of what they see has been ripened by long acquaintance with
the foreign-missionary enterprise. We can do this the more readily
as the information has been gathered for us in convenient form in
a recent publication of the Committee on the War and the Religious
Outlook, entitled, "The Missionary Outlook in the Light of the
War."[1]

The book is the joint contribution of more than fifty persons
from different countries and societies, and is an interesting illustration of the educative effect of foreign missions upon those who
participate in them. Mr. Israel Zangwill recently expressed in the
New Republic[2] his surprise at finding a missionary review which

[1] Association Press, New York, 1920.
[2] June 25, 1919.

chanced to fall into his hands so alert and well informed on international questions. Had he read this volume his surprise might have been greater still. Its authors agree in reporting a new self-consciousness on the part of the peoples of the East, which takes the form of a demand for national independence and self-government.[1] In Asia and Africa, as in Europe and America, nations as well as individuals aspire to be their own masters, to lead their own lives, and to direct their own destinies. What Irishmen are demanding of England, Hindus and Egyptians are also asking. What Poland and the Balkans desire for themselves is the aspiration of Armenians, Syrians, and Arabs. The legitimate desire of the Japanese for territory in which to expand so that they may feed their rapidly increasing population, is met by the stout resistance of Chinese and of Koreans who claim sovereignty over their own territories and refuse to recognize the rights of the invader.

This tide of national self-consciousness carries with it other changes of a far-reaching character. We find a strong interest in education, a changing economic and industrial system, and, above all, the beginnings of a new position for women. It is true that these changes are only in their infancy. But no one can predict how rapid their growth will be or how far they will lead us.

A striking illustration of what these new forces mean in the educational life of the East is furnished by Professor Dewey's recent experience in China. For centuries China has been conspicuous for the conservatism of its educational system. Yet the Chinese invited the foremost educational authority of the Western world to lecture to them on the philosophy of education. All recent visitors to China report an extraordinary educational revival, and those who have had the opportunity of meeting the students who are finding their way to this country in increasing numbers realize that in native ability, power of concentration, and maturity of judgment, the Chinese student can, to say the least, hold his own with the students of other countries.

It is too soon to forecast the outcome of the new movement. We have seen in Russia what may take place when a premature attempt is made to graft a different system upon a stock which is not prepared for it. In China popular education is a thing of yesterday, and though the invention of the modern script removes one

[1] Cf. "The Missionary Outlook in the Light of the War," p. 28.

of the most serious difficulties in the way of teaching the masses to read and write, it will be long before the experiment has gone far enough to make confident prediction as to its outcome possible.

The economic and industrial life of the Eastern peoples is also changing. Japan offers the most instructive example. In Japan as in our own country the rapid rise of great manufacturing centres, drawing their labor from all parts of the country, has affected the habits of the masses. All the vexed problems of human relationships and ideals at which we have already glanced in previous chapters are involved in such a process.

What is going on in Japan on a large scale is beginning in China and in India. In Shanghai there are cotton mills owned, operated, and managed by Chinese who have received their training in the University of Texas. The same will be true in other cities as soon as the proper facilities for transportation have been created.

The movement for the enfranchisement of women,[1] though still in embryo in countries like India and China, is very much alive and no one can foresee what its ultimate outcome will be. One of the recent unofficial delegations to this country in connection with the Disarmament Conference included Madame Yajima, a lady who represents what is best in the spirit of the new Japan. Such a visit would have been unthinkable a few years ago. The leaven is working even in Mohammedan countries, and there are indications that the women of the Near East as well as of the Far East will soon no longer be content with the intellectual seclusion to which the marriage customs of their country have hitherto condemned them.

Race kinship as well as national self-consciousness is asserting itself in various ways, as in the Zionist movement among the Jews and the recent Pan-African movement among the Negroes. This fact is being used in certain quarters to check the growing international spirit. We are warned that the rising tide of color is a menace to the world's peace and to meet it the white peoples should arm to the teeth.[2] There seems little reason for such fear. Race is indeed a powerful tie, but by itself it has not proved as strong as some alarmists would have us believe. There are rivalries between peoples of the same race which are as bitter and have been as pro-

[1] "The Missionary Outlook in the Light of the War," pp. 67 sq.
[2] Cf. p. 43.

longed as those between peoples of different race. The World War amply demonstrated this point. Even if this were not true such a race menace would be an argument for more international friendliness rather than for less.

Yet while the growing race consciousness may not lead to war it is none the less true that it may hamper the Christian spirit in many ways. We have seen this already in our own country in connection with the Negro question. In the international sphere it reappears on a larger scale and creates difficulties of a formidable kind.

Noticeable among the effects of the war has been the loss of confidence in Western leadership. The war which has shattered so many ideals has given an irreparable blow to European prestige. The early respect for the superior knowledge of the foreigner, the willingness to take his counsel and follow his advice, which was apparent in the earlier relations of the East with Europe, has been sadly shaken. Asiatics and Africans fought in Europe against white men during the war and have carried back to their homes a very different report of the state of European civilization from that which has been given to them by the missionaries. They have seen its weakness as well as its strength and are not likely to forget what they have seen. Henceforth the peoples who have been content to accept Western models mean to judge for themselves and to shape their lives in their own way.

The reflex influence of these tendencies upon Christianity has on the whole been less unfavorable than might have been anticipated. Far from disproving the Christian religion, the war has made it seem to many thoughtful Eastern observers more desirable and admirable. What has been disproved is the claim of Europe and America to be Christian nations. Had they been Christian (so reason thoughtful Chinese with whom the author has talked) the war would never have been possible.

Unquestionably those who go to China and Japan as representatives of Western civilization will be subjected in the future to a more rigorous scrutiny than in the past. They will be obliged to prove their disinterestedness by helping the Asiatic peoples to develop their own methods of progress and cannot hope to impose upon them unmodified Western ideals.

True in all departments of social life, this will be particularly true in religion. In Japan a native Christian church is already

in existence.   In China and India its beginnings are apparent.[1]
Chinese and Hindus are no longer content to reproduce in their own
country the divisions of our Western Christianity. If they must
divide they will divide on their own.lines and on issues which have
present meaning for them.

These issues, if present indications are any guide as to the
future, will be, far more largely than with us, moral and social issues. The theological disputes which gave us the ancient creeds
have lost meaning to Eastern Christians; but questions of social
justice, national independence, and individual morals are living
questions, and on them they expect the Church to take a stand.
What, they ask, has Christianity to say about the sale of opium
in China? What about Shantung? What about the treatment of
the Japanese in California? What about the situation which has
been created by the Japanese conquest of Korea?

Under these influences the foreign-missionary enterprise develops
and expands before our eyes.   From the first the missionaries were
many-sided men, keenly interested in the social conditions of the
countries to which they came, and eager to provide for them the
broadest possible ministry.[2] But the consciousness of a responsibility for changing the environment as well as the spirit of men
has been greatly reinforced by recent events.   Modern missionaries
take it for granted that their calling may lead them to study economic and industrial as well as theological questions and to establish
colleges and hospitals in addition to churches.

Especially noticeable has been the effect of the new problems
upon the attitude of the missionaries to one another. The differences which divide Christians have shrunk into relative insignif-
icance in the face of the needs of a non-Christian civilization.
Nowhere has co-operation between the churches been carried so
far. Union schools and hospitals exist in many mission fields.
Even in theological education the obstacles have not proved in-
surmountable. There is not a single theological seminary in the
United States supported jointly by the authorities of different
denominations. There are six such institutions in China.[3]

[1] Cf. "The Missionary Outlook in the Light of the War," pp. 87, 96 sq.
[2] Cf. Speer, "The Social Spirit of the Missionary Founders," *Constructive
Quarterly*, March, 1921.
[3] It is quite true that the elementary character of the instruction given in
these schools has made co-operation easier than would be the case with insti-

This consciousness of a united responsibility has found signal expression in such gatherings as the Edinburgh and Panama Conferences. It has created organs for its activities in the various Continuation Committees at home and on the field;[1] most notably in the Foreign Missions Conference of North America which brings together annually for mutual counsel and deliberation all the more important foreign-missionary agencies of the United States and Canada. In the *International Review of Missions* it has an organ which serves not only as a reliable source of information as to what is being done in the various mission fields, but also, what is far more important, as a forum for the discussion of principles and policies as between the missionaries in the field and those who are supporting them at home.[2] In a later chapter we shall study the co-operative movement in the home church, and we shall find that at almost every point it is following a course which has been anticipated in the foreign field.

The foreign-missionary movement is peculiarly instructive because of the light which it sheds upon the course which is likely to be taken by our home Christianity. It shows us not only that our problems in America are *like* the problems which other nations are facing; they are *the same* problems, and because they belong to all of us alike, they can only be solved together.[3] It was not

tutions of higher grade. The real test will come when Young China claims the right to shape its own theological instruction after the models of the free institutions of the West. The campaign now being carried on by the Bible Union in China in favor of a literal interpretation of the Bible and the resulting theological tension among missionaries is an indication of the fact that the same differences of belief which have made unity difficult in the home field are certain to reproduce themselves in the foreign field. Much will depend for the future of Christianity, not only abroad but at home, upon the spirit in which these difficulties are met.

[1] *E.g.* the International Missionary Council, which is the successor of the Continuation Committee of the Edinburgh Conference; the Committee on Co-operation in Latin America, the organ of the Panama Conference; the China Continuation Committee; the National Missionary Council of India, organized as a result of Dr. Mott's tour in 1912 and 1913. Action taken at the last meeting of the National Missionary Council proposes a reorganization of the Council on a more representative basis, in which churches as well as missions shall become the units of representation. Cf. "Resolutions of the National Missionary Council," Poona, 1922, pp. 20 sq.

[2] Cf. W. Adams Brown, "Ten Years . . . of the Review," *International Review of Missions,* January, 1922.

[3] Cf. the author's pamphlet, "Modern Missions in the Far East," New York, 1917, pp. 20 sq.

an accident that the writers of the missionary review which so impressed Mr. Zangwill were keenly interested in international politics. It is not an accident that writer after writer in the volume on "The Missionary Outlook in the Light of the War" discusses the League of Nations.[1] These topics are forced upon the missionaries by the nature of the situation in which they find themselves. They preach Christianity to the Chinese, but influences emanate from Europe and America which make the Christianization of the Chinese difficult if not impossible. They hold up an ideal of brotherhood and peace, but forces are in operation which constrain their converts to separation and war. How can we expect Japan to treat China on Christian principles if France, England, and the United States decide their relations to weaker peoples on grounds of self-interest or expediency? Unless we can show that Christianity is practicable everywhere it is difficult to see how it can be practicable anywhere. The old principle of each for himself has broken down in politics no less than in religion. All nations must learn to live together in peace if there is to be hope of peace for any nation.

So a study of the foreign-missionary enterprise brings us into the heart of present international questions. These, too, form part of the problem with which the Church must deal, for they bear directly upon the lives of the men and women to whom the Church ministers.

3. Suffering as a Teacher of International Brotherhood and Responsibility

A second point of contact between American Christianity and the international situation is the appeal that comes to us for relief from the suffering peoples of the war-stricken lands. Touching human sympathy in the most elementary way, it reaches many who have not yet felt the importance of the missionary enterprise.

There was a time when suffering was accepted as the natural lot of man, to be endured with as much fortitude as one could command. There are countries where this opinion still prevails. Famine, pestilence, war with its devastation are accepted as natural phenomena like storm or drought. The Chinese pilgrims have for centuries thrown coins to the beggars that line the road leading from Hangchow to the monastery of Lin Yin. But it is to acquire

[1] Cf. pp. 17 sq., pp. 294 sq., p. 301.

merit for themselves, not out of compassion for the sufferers. It has never occurred to anyone that this suffering could be prevented or these diseases healed. "Remove the beggars!" exclaimed a Buddhist abbot to one who asked why the Church did not care for these sufferers; "That would never do. Kwannon (the goddess of mercy) would be angry. How could we worship her acceptably if there were no beggars to whom to give alms?"

Once in a while we discover this attitude of mind at home. There is an island in Maine where a plague of tuberculosis recently threatened to destroy the little population. A nurse was sent by the Sea Coast Missionary Society to try to check the plague and to save the lives of the children by teaching them sanitary habits. Soon after her arrival she was asked by one of the older inhabitants to cease her nursing work on the ground that she was interfering with the will of God. "You stick to religion," he said to the nurse, "and don't go interfering with our health. The Almighty sent this sickness to plague us. When He gets through punishing us He will stop."

This primitive conception of suffering is, however, rare among us. Suffering wherever found, in whatever nation, or race, or class, is considered among Western nations a challenge to help. Charity has become an international virtue. The Red Cross knows no frontier. So when a calamity like the late war falls upon the world, it annuls the boundaries of nationality and reveals our kinship as human beings. The thirty million dollars raised by Hoover for the starving peoples of Europe, the vast sums secured by the Near East Relief Commission, and the yet other millions contributed for the China Famine Relief Fund are but conspicuous examples of an outreaching charity which has made America loved in great areas of human suffering.

But the question continually recurs: "Why should we spend our substance in repairing war's damage when the causes which produce war are suffered to operate unchecked?" Charity is no doubt a Christian duty, but at best it is a makeshift, a device to tide over a crisis till some more permanent help can be supplied. The true ideal for the Christian is not to give alms to the man who is down, but to help him to stand upon his feet. We do well to feed suffering Austrian children, but we shall not have done our full duty until we have helped Austria to feed her own children.

The same is true of all the peoples to whom we are asked to extend help.

Armenia is a case in point. During the past three years the American people through the Near East Relief Fund have expended more than sixty million dollars to care for the unhappy peoples of the Near East. The larger part of this has gone to the Armenians. Yet after all these years of labor and effort the situation seems as precarious as ever. Many sufferers have been relieved and many orphans fed and sheltered, but the causes which have produced this condition still continue. Still Turkish vengeance threatens the remnant of this afflicted people and the rivalries of the great powers and our own policy of non-interference have made it impossible to take effective steps to protect them. How futile to go on treating symptoms while we allow the disease to rage unchecked! How impossible to pretend indifference to the political situation in Europe when it affects directly not only the pocket-books but the Christian sympathies of more than ten million Americans!

We have spoken of Armenia because it is a case which to an extraordinary degree has awakened the sympathies of Americans; but it is only one of many points of danger on the international horizon. Some we have already touched on, but only a few. In the Far East there are Korea and Manchuria; in the Near East, Syria, Asia Minor, and Egypt; in Europe, the Balkans, Poland, and Silesia, not to speak of the ever-threatening menace of Russia. England must deal with India, and we must consider our relations with Mexico and Japan. While these conditions continue, statesmen cannot but be anxious and efforts to bring about disarmament meet with resolute opposition.

But our dissatisfaction with the present international situation goes even deeper than this. It involves our entire philosophy of life. As Christians we are committed to the ideal of world-wide co-operation and brotherhood. The present system proceeds on a diametrically opposite assumption. It takes for granted an inherent antagonism of interest between nations and races. Christians believe that all men are children of a common Father, meant by Him to live together in mutual helpfulness and peace. So believing, we cannot rest until we have found a way to live out this faith, not simply as individuals but as citizens and as patriots.

4. *The Church and the League of Nations*

That is why the proposal for a League of Nations met with so enthusiastic a response on the part of Christians everywhere. It was a definite attempt to deal with this ever-present danger at its source. It was the suggestion of a new method of approach to international relations—the method of conference and co-operation instead of secrecy and isolation. It invited a different attitude on the part of statesmen, an attitude of trust and confidence, instead of one of suspicion and fear. The acclamation with which the proposal of the League was received in the most widely separated circles, no less than the deep despondency and even despair with which its momentary failure has been followed, is the best witness to the fact that it touched some deeper chord than is reached by our conventional politics; that it expressed those underlying yearnings which belong not to any one nation or group of nations, but to man as man; that, in short, its appeal passed beyond politics into religion.

It was inevitable, then, that religious people should actively interest themselves in the League of Nations. No political issue for a generation received such instant and whole-hearted support from the churches.[1] While it is true that the recent campaign against the League has led many of its former advocates to recognize weaknesses and dangers in its present form which will need to be corrected, those who are responsible for the present conduct of the nation's affairs will make a grave mistake if they interpret the present disposition of their constituency to allow them large latitude in finding the way in which that correction can be made, as indicating any loss of faith in the central purpose for which the League was created or any weakening of the will to realize it. When all has been said against the League that can be said, the fact remains that it is the first serious attempt to write into the law of nations the principle that there is a sovereignty higher than that of the individual nation; the first real effort to devise machinery through

---

[1] Between February and July, 1919, the League was endorsed, among others, by the General Assembly of the Presbyterian Church in the U. S. A., by the Northern Baptist Convention, by the Protestant Episcopal Synod of New England, by the Congregational Conference of Southern California, by the Methodists, at their Centenary Celebration, as well as by the Federal Council of the Churches of Christ in America.

which common human interests can find orderly recognition and protection. The particular plan which President Wilson brought back from Paris may need to be modified or replaced by a better, but the ideal which it enshrines will never die. For it is the old ideal of Isaiah and of Jesus—the ideal of a family of nations, worshipping one God, conscious of one destiny, co-operating in one brotherhood. If the churches are silent in the face of such an issue; if in this crisis of the world's history their influence is not felt on behalf of some ideal which transcends that of the individual nation, they will be recreant to their calling and will see the moral leadership of the nation pass to other hands.

The appeal of General Bliss to the churches [1] about disarmament has been often quoted. It will bear quoting again. Speaking to the preachers of the United States he said, "If the clergymen of the United States want to secure a limitation of armaments they can do it now without any further waste of time. If, on an agreed-upon date, they simultaneously preach one sermon on this subject, in every church of every creed throughout the United States, and conclude their services by having their congregation adopt a resolution addressed to their particular congressman urging upon him the necessity of having a business conference of five nations upon this subject, the thing will be done. If the churches cannot agree upon that it will not be done, nor will it be done until the good God puts into them the proper spirit of their religion. The responsibility is entirely upon the professing Christians of the United States. If another war like the last one should come, they will be responsible for every drop of blood that will be shed and for every dollar wastefully expended."

Limitation of armaments is but the first step in the campaign against war. Armaments are effects which are produced by states of mind. General O'Ryan was quite right when, in a recent address to the students of more than forty Eastern colleges, assembled at Princeton to discuss disarmament, he said, "If you wish to abolish war you must go back further than a limitation of armaments or even beyond absolute disarmament. Men will fight with scythes, stones, and any other weapons they may have . . . unless something is done to stop this by looking after men's emotions and creeds." [2]

[1] In a letter to the Church Peace Union, in May, 1921.
[2] *New York Times,* October 27, 1921.

These emotions and creeds—the raw material out of which wars are made—are built up slowly step by step by what you and I do in our daily lives as citizens, as we pass judgment on the various questions which involve the relation of our own nation to others in the practical conduct of its everyday affairs. It is because we have formed the habit of thinking of our own nation as an independent moral unit, claiming the allegiance of its own citizens, but in its relation to other nations bound by no law but its own self-interest, that we allow ourselves to become involved in situations which, when they arise, force us into war against our will. When that time comes it is too late to draw back. The mischief is already done. If ever a nation tried not to go to war, we tried from 1914 to 1917, but we found it impossible. What has happened once may happen again. It will happen again unless while there is time we take steps to see that it shall not.

Thus this matter of armament becomes a symbol of something far deeper and more momentous, something which cuts to the very heart of the life of mankind. Bishop Nicholai expressed it in these moving words to the students of the Cosmopolitan Club:[1]

"I find myself to-night speaking to the whole world. Who can speak to the world but He who loves the world? God alone can do it, for He alone really loves the world. Christ tried his best to teach men we are the sons of God. Europe throughout the nineteenth century tried her hardest to teach men they were animals and the sons of animals. The first teaching leads to humanity and peace; the second teaching leads to disdain of humanity and war. Friends, we must train ourselves systematically for love of humanity. First we must learn to have compassion with suffering humanity; then we must learn to respect its efforts and struggles; and finally, out of compassion and respect, love will be born in our hearts."[2]

It seems so simple. We have time for everything else. We are training men for this and that—to be doctors, lawyers, diplomats, soldiers, sailors. Has not the time come to train men for love? No one of all the multiplying contacts of our modern world but carries with it the opportunity for an enlarged fellowship, if rightly understood. This interpretation is the Church's business. We must

[1] Cf. p. 36, note 1.
[2] Reprinted in "Pan-Humanity," New York, 1921.

train men for love by showing them the bearing of the common things they do upon the great ideals they profess. Only by patient, intelligent, long-continued training can we create the habits of feeling and thinking, or as General O'Ryan would put it, "the emotions and creeds," which will make co-operation with men of other nations seem natural and desirable.

A renewed confidence in the efficacy of love is the world's paramount need to-day.[1] Trace any one of our troubles to its source and we come to a difficulty of the spirit. When we lose faith in our neighbor's capacity for good we open the door to fear. Until this fear is exorcised we can make no real progress. When trust is restored, all else will be possible. To replace fear with trust is the Church's supreme mission. By its success or failure here it must finally be judged.

[1] In a recent number of the *New York Evening Post* appeared two letters under date of December 30, 1921, which, written for different purposes, are alike in bearing testimony to the efficacy of love as a solution of the world's practical difficulties. The first, commenting on Lord Shaw of Dunfermline's recently published "Letters to Isabel," quotes the following from a letter by Sir Henry Campbell-Bannerman, written at the close of the Boer War: "It is not by force of arms that South Africa will be lost, but by misgovernment, and instead of blustering about reinforcements and army reform, or—shall we say—platitudinizing about commercial education, it would be well if our eminent ones applied themselves to this problem, How to make those love us who now hate us. A fine New Year's sentiment, if ever there was one." The author adds: "Many a time in the years since then I have thought of that sentence, 'How to make those love us who now hate us.' It is the pure gold of statesmanship."

The other repeats the last message of Lord Grey, the late Governor-General of Canada, who said when dying, "I want to say to people that there is a real way out of all this mess materialism has got them into. It is Christ's way. We've got to give up quarrelling. We've got to realize we are all members of the same family. There's nothing that can help humanity—I'm perfectly sure there is not—except love. Love is the way out, and the way up. That is my farewell to the world."

PART II

WHERE TO BEGIN

CHAPTER V

1. *The American Church, an Experiment in Democracy*

LIKE the nation which it serves, the American Church is a complex phenomenon. No historian has yet been found to attempt such a comprehensive interpretation of its genius as Viscount Bryce has given us of the genius of the nation in his "American Commonwealth." A generation ago Dr. Philip Schaff called attention to this need, but the American Church history which he edited is little more than a series of denominational histories, and the last of these appeared more than twenty years ago.[1] A summary of the main facts concerning the denominations is given by Dr. Carroll in his "Religious Forces of the United States," [2] and more fully in the United States Census of Religious Bodies for 1916.[3] But these give us only the body, not the spirit, of American Christianity. The needed interpretation of American Christianity as a whole has not yet been attempted.

Yet the attempt would be singularly rewarding. For in the American Church, we have a contribution to the history and possibilities of religion worthy of far more attention than it has yet received. In the United States we see religion coming to terms with democracy; rejecting state control, and with this rejection all claim to state support; declaring itself competent to meet its own problems and discharge its own responsibilities without outside aid, even the supreme responsibility of training the rising generation for religion. We have had occasion already to note some of the points in which it has failed. It would be a mistake not to be equally appreciative of its successes.

[1] "American Church History," New York, 1893–97, thirteen volumes.

[2] H. K. Carroll, "Religious Forces of the United States," Revised edition, New York, 1912.

[3] "Religious Bodies, 1916," Vol. I, "Summary and General Tables"; Vol. II, "Separate Denominations." Published by the Federal Census Bureau, Washington, D. C. Cf. Peter G. Mode, "Source Book and Bibliographical Guide for American Church History, Menasha, Wisconsin, 1921.

Perhaps the greatest of these is the extent to which it has succeeded in impressing the average Christian with his responsibility for supporting the institutions of religion. We see the weakness of the American Church; its irregular and in many respects unlovely development; the curious types of religion to which it has given rise; the multiplicity of rival sects; the lack of the sense of beauty and of dignity; the loss of the consciousness of the historic past of which it is heir. We do not always realize as we should that these are only the counterpart in religion of the democratic experiment in the nation—the price of an experience which, with much that is uncouth and regrettable, has yielded also much that is of inestimable value to mankind.

The history of the American Church, could it but be studied with the sympathy and understanding which it deserves, would give us a key to the understanding of the American people. In both we see the same irregular and unplanned development. In both we find the spirit of the pioneer reaching out into the uncharted wilderness, careless of the conventions of the home-land from which he came, yet a child of that home-land none the less, carrying with him into his new environment ideals and aspirations that he did not create. We see him played upon by a thousand influences both old and new. Each ship that brings him his supplies of food and tools brings him also ideas embodied in men and women. Puritan and Cavalier build side by side and worship as they build, each in his own way. Yet the Episcopacy of Virginia differs from the Anglicanism that gave it birth as truly as the Congregationalism of New England differs from the older Puritanism from which it sprang. Immigrant follows immigrant: Scotch, Irish, Welsh, Dutch, French, German, and each group brings its own type of religion. To understand the story you must consult the United States Census of Religious Bodies, as well as the records of the commissioner on Ellis Island. Each separate religious type, being free to develop as it will, tries its own experiment and comes to terms as it may with the new influences that surround it. Under these many forms religion shares in the struggle against nature in forest and prairie; in the rapid immigration from state to state; in the new problems of government, civil and religious; in the world-old problem of reconciling liberty and order. Each type responds in its own way to the influences that are welding the nation into a unity. The growth of the democratic spirit, the jealous purpose to guard a newly won freedom against European encroachment, the strengthening of the national consciousness in the Civil War, the sense of unbounded possibilities that came with the great development which followed the war—all these interacting influences have helped to make out of the American churches, in a far deeper and truer sense than we ourselves realize, the American Church.

Let us sketch, if we can, some of the salient features of the Church to which the country looked for inspiration and spiritual guidance when in 1917 it found itself at war.

2. *Strength of the American Church in Numbers and Resources.*
Distribution of This Strength Among the Denominations

And first a word as to the externals of the Church—its strength in numbers and in resources, personal and financial. The last Census of the United States, that of 1916, puts the number of church organizations in this country at 227,487, and of church members at 41,926,854.[1] 194,759 Sunday schools were reported with a total membership of 19,935,890. These organizations were divided between 206 denominations, owned 203,432 church buildings valued at $1,676,600,582, on which there was a debt of $164,864,899, and parsonages valued at $218,846,096. Their annual expenditures totalled $328,809,999, and their gifts to missions and philanthropy, $62,050,571. They employed 191,796 ministers who conducted services in 43 different languages, and of whom the 63,543 who reported full salaries received on an average $1,078. These were divided by denominations as follows, reckoning those only which had more than 50,000 members:

Roman Catholics	15,721,815
Members of the Eastern Orthodox churches	249,840
Methodists	7,166,451
Baptists	7,153,313
Lutherans	2,467,416
Presbyterians	2,255,626
Disciples	1,226,028
Episcopalians	1,092,821
Congregationalists	791,274
Reformed	537,822
United Brethren	367,934
German Evangelical Synod	339,853

[1] Cf. "Religious Bodies," 1916, Part I, pp. 25–99, from which the figures here given are taken.

Churches of Christ	317,937
Dunkers	133,626
Adventists	114,915
Christians	118,737
Evangelical Association	120,756
United Evangelical Church	89,774
Unitarians	82,515
Mennonites	79,363
Universalists	58,566

In addition there were 462,329 Latter Day Saints and 357,135 Jews. The number of Christian Scientists is not reported in the Census.[1]

[1] Figures in the Year Book of the Federal Council for 1921 show the following changes since the Census of 1916: church organizations, 233,999, with a membership of 46,242,130 (an increase of 6,512 and 4,315,276 respectively); 199,154 Sunday schools with a membership of 23,944,438 (an increase of 4,395 and 4,008,548 respectively); 199,154 ministers (an increase of 7,358). During the same period the population of the country increased from 102,017,312 to 105,710,620, or 3,693,308.

The figures for the denominations with over 50,000 communicants are given as follows:

Roman Catholics	17,885,646
Eastern Orthodox churches	411,054
Methodists	7,918,557
Baptists	7,835,250
Lutherans	2,466,645
Presbyterians	2,384,683
Disciples	1,210,023
Episcopalians	1,117,051
Congregationalists	819,225
Reformed	510,905
United Brethren	383,329
German Evangelical Synod	274,860
Churches of Christ	317,937
Dunkers	134,110
Adventists	136,233
Christians	97,084
Evangelical Association	160,000
United Evangelical Church	90,096
Unitarians	103,936
Mennonites	91,282
Universalists	58,566
Latter Day Saints	587,918
Jews (estimated)	400,000

It must be remembered, however, that these figures are only provisional and cannot claim the accuracy of those of the United States Census. Thus the source of the figures for the Roman Catholic Church is the Catholic Directory which in 1917 reported over 17,000,000 Roman Catholics for the year 1916, in place of the 15,721,815 given by the United States Census.

In determining the significance of these figures we must not overlook the fact that the basis of estimation varies in different bodies. Thus the Roman Catholic Church reckons as full church members all baptized children, the Baptists those only who can speak for themselves and have received believers' baptism. An ordinary Roman Catholic congregation is a section of the Roman Catholic population as well as of the Roman Catholic Church membership. An ordinary Baptist congregation, on the other hand, is made up both of persons whose number is included in its reported membership and of other persons not reported in the Census of Religious Bodies, to whom appeal is being made to make the public profession which will lead to their inclusion in the organized church. The number of persons under direct Baptist influence must be computed. In the case of the Roman Catholic Church those numbers are reported.

A similar contrast exists in the case of other churches, like the Presbyterian, the Methodist, the Lutheran, and the Episcopal, which, like the Roman Catholic Church, practise infant baptism, but unlike it do not include baptized children in their list of reported church members. It is clear, therefore, that in order to get a correct impression of the relative strength of the Roman Catholic and Protestant element in the American Church, it is necessary to take account of that proportion of the reported church membership which consists of children under thirteen. This proportion in the case of the Roman Catholics is 24.96 per cent. In the average Protestant Church it is slightly over 5 per cent. Even this does not fully represent the situation, for while in the case of the Roman Catholics a large number of baptized persons are included in the rolls who have only a nominal connection with the church, in the case of the larger Protestant communions many regularly attend church services and contribute to the support of the church who never become church members at all. Taking these facts into account, Dr. Laidlaw estimates the Roman Catholic element in the United States in December, 1916, at 15.5 per cent, while the Protestant element ranged between 69.2 and 76.1 per cent, according to the basis of calculation.[1]

As our plan does not permit any detailed consideration of

[1] Cf. his suggestive pamphlet, "Roman Catholicism and Protestantism," from which the figures here cited are taken. Cf. esp. p. 5.

the Roman Catholic Church in the United States, it is sufficient to say that the same influences which have moulded the work of American Protestantism have been active in the history of the American Catholic Church. New problems meet the church in America and new emphases appear in its teaching and organization. The old orders reappear in this country—Dominicans, Franciscans, Jesuits, etc., and in addition new orders like the Paulist Fathers, which have for their purpose the interpretation of Catholic Christianity to Protestant America. Much important information about the church and its operations may be gained from the Catholic Encyclopedia.[1] But it is as true of American Catholicism as it is of Protestantism that it still lacks its sympathetic interpreter.

Two further facts need brief mention in order to complete the picture of the composition of the American Church: the number and strength of the Negro congregations and of the foreign-speaking churches.

The Census of 1916 reports 39,655 Negro organizations with a total membership of 4,602,805. Of these 51,688 are in Roman Catholic and 4,551,117 in Protestant congregations. They own church property worth $86,809,970, with a debt of $7,938,095, and parsonages worth $6,231,459. They expended for the support of religion $18,529,827, and had 37,426 Sunday schools with 2,153,843 pupils.[2]

Churches maintaining services either in whole or in part in foreign languages reported a membership of 11,329,487, distributed roughly as follows: [3]

Germans	3,923,000
Italians	1,773,000
Poles	1,613,000
French	1,190,000
Spanish, including Mexicans	606,000
Norwegians	344,000
Slavic	307,000
Lithuanian	214,000
Bohemians	210,000
Slovaks	181,000
Hungarians	146,000
Greeks	132,000

[1] 16 vols., New York, 1907, sq.

[2] "Religious Bodies," 1916. Part I, Summary and General Tables, pp. 132–138.

[3] "Religious Bodies," 1916, Part I, p. 85.

Slovenian	122,000
Yiddish	116,000
Portuguese	112,000

It is interesting to note that of these approximately 7,677,171 were in Roman Catholic and 249,840 in Eastern Catholic congregations, showing to how large an extent the Catholic Church remains a church of people of foreign antecedents and speech.

One striking feature which comes out in the religious statistics is the small proportion of Jews who are reported in the synagogues as compared with the total population. In this country only 357,-135 Jews [1] were reported in 1916 as having religious connection out of a total Jewish population estimated at 2,349,754. In New York City, out of 975,000 Jews, only 93,819 were reported as in the synagogues.[2] In estimating the significance of these figures it should, however, be remembered that they include only heads of families. To form a proper basis of comparison therefore they should be multiplied by four.

In contrast to the weakness of organized religion among the Jews is the rapid growth of the two new religions to which America has given birth in our time, Mormonism and Christian Science. As to the exact size and progress of the latter we have no official statistics, but in the former case the figures show 462,329 church members, although in this case it should be noted that 30 per cent. are under thirteen, the largest proportion of any reporting church.[3]

Such figures as these present a bewildering picture. So seen, the religious history of America would seem to be a confused medley of rival and conflicting sects. Closer inspection, however, tends to bring order out of chaos. Some of the divisions which the Census records are due to differences of language; others are the survival on this side of the water of Old World controversies which have largely lost their meaning; still others are due to individual or transient causes. Of the 25,000,000 Protestant church members, the greater number are found in seven or eight large groups;

[1] "Religious Bodies," 1916, Part I, p. 30. The number, according to the Year Book of the Federal Council, had risen in 1921 to 400,000. During the same period, according to the figures given in the World Almanac, the number of Jews in the country increased nearly a million, and those in New York City from 975,000 to 1,500,000.

[2] Laidlaw, "Roman Catholicism and Protestantism," p. 13.

[3] According to the figures given in the Federal Council Year Book for 1921, the number of Mormons had risen to 587,918. Cf. Laidlaw, *op. cit.,* p. 3.

namely, the Methodists, Baptists, Lutherans, Presbyterians, Disciples, Episcopalians, Congregationalists, and Reformed. Two millions are distributed among a dozen smaller denominations, of whom the German Evangelical Synod, the United Brethren, and the Churches of Christ together account for nearly half. The problem, therefore, of uniting American Protestantism resolves itself largely into the attitude of about a dozen large groups to one another.

In most of the larger denominations there is free interchange both of ministers and of members. The type of service which prevails is in the main similar and the consciousness of membership in the one Church of Christ common to all. Of the larger bodies the Lutherans, Episcopalians, and Southern Baptists draw the line of demarcation between their own members and those of other churches most strictly, but for the others the differences which separate them are rather differences of history and of administration than of profound religious or ecclesiastical conviction.

There are, however, two exceptions to this statement which should be noted: one, the difference caused by the race question; the other, that due to doctrinal differences. In three of the larger Protestant denominations—the Methodists, the Baptists, and, to a less extent, the Presbyterians—the most serious line of cleavage, namely that between the Northern and Southern churches,[1] is due in part to the different attitude taken to the Negro. In the Northern church the Negro minister is admitted to full parity with his white fellow-minister in presbytery, council, or conference, whereas the South has organized the Negroes into separate self-governing churches.[2] While there are other questions at issue be-

[1] The terms Northern and Southern are used for convenience, though they are not strictly accurate. The Methodist Episcopal Church (frequently though inaccurately known as the Northern Church) has in the South and on the border between 700,000 and 800,000 members. The Presbyterian Church in the U. S. A. (the Northern Church) also has many members in the South. Nor are the Baptists divided by any strict geographical line.

[2] It should in fairness be said that while the law of the Northern churches permits colored pastors to sit with white pastors in the same conference or presbytery, and individuals do so, the great bulk of the Negro membership is distributed in Negro conferences or presbyteries. In General Conference and General Assembly, however, white and Negro delegates sit side by side. This could not, under present conditions, occur in the Southern denominations.

tween the Northern and Southern churches, this difference of attitude toward the Negro to-day presents one of the most serious difficulties in the way of their reunion.

To theological difference is due the existence as separate churches of the Unitarians and the Universalists, the former owing their origin to differences of view as to the person of Christ and His relation to the Godhead; the latter to differences of view as to the extent of God's saving purpose for mankind. The conservative character of the American Church as a whole, as well as the difficulty of founding a church on doctrinal considerations alone, appears in the relatively small membership of these two churches whose influence has been rather indirect through their contribution to liberal thought and sentiment than through any large accessions from the older churches.

But though doctrinal differences alone have not been the determining factor in bringing about denominational divisions,[1] they have had, and still have, an important influence in shaping the policy of the different communions. In each of the larger bodies we find a party which advocates a liberal interpretation of the standards of the church and a party which holds to strict construction, and the fear of each of these parties of what the other might do, if it gained the upper hand, is, as we shall see later,[2] an important factor in determining its attitude to the various proposals for co-operation and union which we shall take up in the present discussion. Thus in the debate which is now going on as to reunion between Northern and Southern Presbyterians the more liberal views of the former church have frequently been cited by conservative members of the latter body as an argument against organic union; and the hospitality of many Northern Baptists to modern views of the Bible and their less rigid view of baptism are viewed with suspicion by their Southern brethren. Similar theological differences are found in other bodies, a conspicuous illustration being the difference between the Protestant and Catholic parties in the Protestant Episcopal Church.

[1] Even in the case of the division of the Presbyterian Church into Old and New Schools in 1837, when theological controversy was so acute, practical as well as doctrinal considerations were operative.
[2] Cf. p. 256.

Such in brief is the present condition of American Protestantism as seen by the statistician.[1] What are the outstanding characteristics of the group of churches whose numbers and denominational distribution we have passed in review?

3. *Outstanding Characteristics of the American Church—Its Provincialism and Individualism—Influence of the Denominational Spirit*

Taking the American Church as a whole, the first characteristic that strikes us as worthy of note is its provincialism. By this I mean the tendency of each local congregation or group of congregations to think of itself as a self-sufficient whole. That which has been true of the political life of the nation, and which has rendered any large national policies so difficult of attainment, has been equally, perhaps even more, true of its religion. Not only has there been little contact with European religious problems, but there has been little effort to grasp the problems of the country as a whole. The place in which a man has lived and voted, or at least the state to which his primary political loyalty has been due, has been the centre of his religious interest and responsibility.

This limitation has been accentuated by the differences in the character of the religious life of different sections of the country. The Episcopal church in Virginia, the Congregationalism of Puritan New England, the Presbyterianism of Pennsylvania and the Middle West, the Lutheranism of Missouri and the Northwest, the Baptist churches of the South, all have their marked characteristics, separating them from their fellow-Christians of other communions and

---

[1] In the above sketch no attempt has been made to take account of relative gain or loss. Reference to previous Census reports shows that relatively to the population of the country the churches have held their own and on the whole have gained ground. Where there were 21,699,432 members in the churches in 1890, there were in 1916 nearly 42,000,000, whereas during the same period the population of the country as a whole increased from 62,622,250 to 102,-017,312. Since 1916 the increase has been even more rapid. While the Roman Catholic Church remains first in numerical increase, in the proportion of its increase relatively to other churches it ranks 36. From 1906 to 1916, the period covered by government Census returns, the Catholics had a growth of 10.6 per cent. while the various Protestant bodies grew from 17.4 to 28.2 per cent. It is interesting to note that in ten years the English-speaking Catholic churches grew 1.5 per cent., while the foreign-speaking churches grew 22.1 per cent. Cf. Laidlaw, quoted in the *Christian Century*, January 19, 1922.

making it natural for them to conceive of Christianity as a whole after their own type.

This provincialism has been in part corrected, in part accentuated, by the denominationalism of American Christianity. From one point of view the denomination has been an enlarging and liberating influence. It has extended its work beyond the local community, and in the case of the larger communions, has taken in the country as a whole. It has extended farther than this, for, as we shall see, it has been the point of contact between the local community and the missionary enterprise of the Church in the widest sense—home and foreign. But on the other hand, it has had its limiting influence as well. It has accentuated the divisive features in American Christianity. It has applied an absolute standard to local peculiarities and made it easy for a man to identify his own particular type of Christianity with that of the Church universal.

This feature of denominational Christianity has been often criticized. But it is possible to over-emphasize it and to minimize the good effects of the denominational system. The picture of American Christianity as a strife of warring sects is a serious misrepresentation. The chief danger of denominationalism is not that it leads us to attack our fellow-Christians, but that it makes us content to ignore them. Denominationalism may identify its own enterprises with those of ecumenical Christianity and lead its adherents to regard other forms of Christian belief or worship as negligible or unimportant; but at least it reminds them of a world larger than Smithtown and Jonesville. It is the means through which the members of the local congregations realize their membership in the Church universal.

The ecumenical character of denominationalism appears most clearly in Methodism. One of the youngest of the larger denominations, the genius of John Wesley has stamped upon this new and flourishing branch of the Church a missionary zeal and organizing power which has made it within the compass of a single century the strongest of all the Protestant denominations. In no other church is denominational unity more systematically cultivated. In no other is the world-wide mission of the denomination more largely conceived or more vigorously prosecuted. It was entirely natural that the Interchurch World Movement should have been conceived and most largely promoted by Methodists.

A third characteristic of the American Church, closely associated with the preceding, is its individualism. By this is meant the extent to which religion is conceived in terms of the relation between the individual soul and God. This was a direct inheritance of American Christianity from the Puritanism to which it owed its origin. It is true that Puritanism had another side. The stricter Protestants not only believed that it was the duty of the Church to set the individual soul right with God, but that the soul so redeemed should organize society so as to conform to the divine ideal of conduct. Calvin in Geneva and Knox in Scotland were statesmen as well as preachers, and Cromwell incarnated for a few brief years the Puritan ideal of the theocratic state. But with the early separation of church and state in this country the theocratic side of Puritanism fell into the background and its individualism was accentuated. The great revival movements which from time to time swept over the country had for their primary purpose the conversion of sinners, and Methodism, the most powerful as well as the most highly organized of all the American denominations, shared and indeed accentuated the evangelistic passion.

The individualistic type of religion, common to all the larger denominations in spite of their differences, is but the reflex in religion of the democratic spirit of the American people. The sense of individual responsibility for one's own life, and a willingness to accept the consequences of one's own acts in success or failure, has been from the first a characteristic of life in America. Each man is expected to carve out his own life as he can. It is not for his neighbor to dictate what he shall do.

This individualism, while it has accentuated the sense of responsibility in religion, has reinforced the tendency to narrowness which we have already noted. Taking American Christianity as a whole we find no large and comprehensive plan for the country. Each denomination works out its own programme for itself and, in spite of certain promising movements toward unity to which we shall have occasion presently to refer, has hitherto maintained its own autonomy and independence. And what is true of the denomination is still more true of the local church. We shall study in a later chapter the ways in which the local church is beginning to minister to the needs of the community in which it is located. The tall white spire rising to heaven is not only a reminder of religion; in many an American village it is an invitation to fellowship. The church is social club as well as place of worship, and the kitchen and the library are features of its architecture for which one looks in vain in European countries. But this social consciousness is only beginning to reach beyond the local community. It has not yet made itself the dominating factor in the life of the Church as a whole.

In this respect, the experience of the Protestant bodies presents a marked contrast to that of the Roman Catholic Church in America. Always the church of a minority, the Roman Catholic Church has visualized its task as a national one and planned accordingly. In the great cities it has chosen the strategic sites for its churches years before they were needed, has laid out its programme on a parish basis, where Protestanism was content to let chance or liking decide, and financed its enterprises by an every member canvass long before Protestantism discovered the envelope system. As a result it occupies a place and wields an influence in the country out of all proportion to its numbers, as Protestants learned to their surprise when the war came.

The lack of a nation-wide constructive policy is the more surprising because of the genius of the American for organization. In no other country has the study of machinery been carried so far. In no other have large views of what can be accomplished by organized effort been more systematically cultivated. But in America this genius has been put at the service of private and individual interests—a particular business, a private philanthropy. Each group has tried to promote its own interests as if they were the only thing to be considered. There has been little sense of responsibility to the nation as a whole, still less to mankind of which the nation is a part. This characteristic phenomenon of great organized power serving interests which are partial, if not in themselves narrow, reappears in American Christianity.[1]

---

[1] Interesting illustrations of this power of organization as applied to religion appear in the two new religions which owe their origin to America—Mormonism and Christian Science. In each case reasons can be given for the growth of the religion which are independent of the intelligence and organizing skill of the promoters, but in each case it is equally true that this skill has powerfully reinforced the other motives to which the religions appeal. This is the more noteworthy in the case of Christian Science, which as a mystical religion would not seem fertile soil for the growth of a strong denomina-

In this connection we may refer to another feature of American Protestantism which has frequently subjected it to criticism; namely, the fact that in contrast to Roman Catholicism it has become to a large extent the Church of the well-to-do. So far as this is true—and taking the country at large it is far less true than the critics would have us believe—it is the natural result of the principle of freedom which we have seen to be inherent in American Protestantism. With the rejection of the state church, the support of religion has been thrown entirely upon private initiative, and under the circumstances it was natural, indeed all but inevitable, that those who had the largest means should come to have a disproportionate share of the control. One would not minimize the evil, but it would be no less a mistake to magnify it. What we see to-day is not the final stage of American Protestantism, but only a phase through which, in common with the democracy of which it is a part, it is passing. The remedy is not in the abandonment of the principle of the free support of religion, but in its extension until the basis of control is shifted. The Roman Catholic Church raises large sums from people of moderate means because it insists upon systematic giving. The same thing can be done in the Protestant churches. Indeed, as we shall see in later chapters, it is already being done on a nation-wide scale. With this change in the method of the support of religion we are witnessing a corresponding broadening of the basis of control. Where no other remedy is possible, there remains always for those who find existing organizations too narrow the way of the first Protestants. Let them form new organizations of their own to express their deepest convictions. These in time, like the older denominations, when their educative work has been done, will find their place in the larger unity of a reformed and truly democratic Protestantism.

4. *The Relation of the American Church to the State—Similarities and Differences in Organization and Spirit*

It will help us to understand the characteristics of which we have been speaking if we remind ourselves of the attitude of the

tional consciousness, but which in the course of its history has developed a central organization of a highly autocratic character, thus giving us a new illustration of the truth of which the history of Roman Catholicism is so signal an example, that mysticism and autocracy are congenial companions.

American people to the other great institution which claims their allegiance—the state. The statement has sometimes been made that our present national government was modelled after that of the Presbyterian Church, but there seems no ground for such an assertion. Nevertheless, there are similarities in the˙ attitude of the American people toward government both in state and church which make a study of their relationships illuminating.

Like the founders of the republic, those who were responsible for shaping the polity of our American churches had a lively fear of a strong central government. Theocratic government passed with the aristocratic state of which it was a part, and in its place came the representative system with its elaborate arrangement of checks and balances. As the national government came into existence through the federation of pre-existing state governments, each jealous of its independence and prerogatives, so the nation-wide ecclesiastical units we call denominations were built up gradually through the combination of various smaller groups—the presbytery, the classis, the conference, the diocese, as the case may be, as these in turn had been built up through the union of individual local congregations. The history in each case is a different one, varying with the genius of the denomination in question. Of these differences we shall have presently to speak. But common to all the churches, even such highly organized bodies as the Presbyterians and the Episcopalians, was the distrust of a strong central authority, the determination to keep for the local body, whether it were parish or presbytery, its inherent right of self-government and self-determination.

This explains a feature of American Protestantism to which we have already referred and to which we shall have occasion to recur more than once again; namely, its inability to carry through any strong and consistent national policy. This is due in no small degree to the fact that the different churches of which it is made up have no permanent executives through whom such a policy can be put into effect. The supreme judicatory in each case is a body meeting at considerable intervals, consisting of representatives elected by the subordinate judicatories whose personnel changes from year to year and which in any case exercise strictly limited powers. This is true not simply of bodies like the Congregationalists and Baptists, where final authority rests with the local congregation, but of more highly organized churches like the Presbyterians and Methodists. Even of the Episcopalians it is true that unlike their sister churches of other lands they have no archbishop in whom the unity of the Church is symbolized and to whom the permanent conduct of its affairs is committed.

A second feature of American Church polity, in which its democratic character is apparent, is the large share given to laymen in church government. Unlike many of the churches of other lands, the American churches almost without exception give laymen an equal share with clergymen in the management of their affairs. Laymen sit in their highest judicatories. They are represented on their permanent committees. They share with the clergy the responsibility not simply for the financial affairs of the church, but for the administration of its missionary policy. Indeed, it may be said with confidence that there has never been a group of churches since Christianity began in whose management laymen had so responsible a part. And while it is true, as we have already seen,[1] that women have only recently been admitted to any large share in the management of the Church, it is yet significant that long before they won political suffrage, they enjoyed the right, as members of local congregations, to vote on all parish affairs, including so important a matter as the choice of a minister. It would seem, therefore, only to be a matter of time when this privilege will be extended to include membership in the larger representative bodies, as indeed has already been done in the Methodist, Congregational, and Baptist denominations.

But if the American Church is like the state in its lack of centralized power and its broad basis of representation, it differs from it in the absence of any officially recognized party system. This does not mean, of course, that there are no parties in the American Church in the sense of groups of men who voluntarily associate themselves for the purpose of promoting the policies in which they believe. Wherever there is government there are parties. It belongs to human nature that men should differ in their views of what ought to be done and that they should organize in support of the policy in which they believe. What differentiates the party system as we have it in America from the party system elsewhere is that the existing parties are recognized by law and surrounded

[1] Cf. pp. 29, 30.

with official sanctions which make them an essential part of our system of government. There is nothing corresponding to this in the polity of the American churches. Whatever differences there may be remain unofficial and private. The conservative of yesterday may become the liberal of to-day and vice versa. When men of good will in the Church wish to unite in some constructive policy and are able to convince the majority of their fellow-Christians that their views ought to prevail, they are not hampered by the obstacles which the existing party system puts in the way of similar action in the political sphere.

The best illustration of the Church's ability to unite men of different views in common action is furnished by the missionary and educational agencies. In their Boards of Home and Foreign Missions, as well as in their College Boards and Sunday-school agencies, the churches have created powerful administrative bodies which raise and spend large sums of money for purposes which require continuity of administration. These powers are cheerfully granted because the purpose for which the boards exist commands the confidence of all parties in the Church and so makes them the most effective of all possible organs of unity.

In general the relation between church and state in this country is one of mutual co-operation and respect. The principle of separation between state and church is generally accepted and its wisdom all but universally approved. The principle has its drawbacks, to be sure, as in the matter of the teaching of religion in the schools, but these are generally regarded as a cheap price to pay for the advantages which it secures, and any attempt to divert public funds to religious purposes (as, for example, for the support of parochial schools) would meet with instant disapproval.

There is, however, one conspicuous exception to the principle of the absolute separation of church and state, and that is the provision in the laws of the various states which exempts the property of religious and charitable bodies from taxation. This is in effect a method of subsidizing religion, but it operates in so general a way as to involve no discrimination between different forms of religious belief and to maintain the central interest which underlies the separation of church and state, namely, the equality of all religions before the law.

A second point of contact between the Church and the state is found in the laws which regulate the administration of trust funds. From the point of view of the state, the Church is a corporation like other corporations, holding its funds under a charter derived from the state.[1] In the administration of these funds the state is disposed to allow the Church every latitude, particularly in matters affecting the interpretation of the religious purposes for which the funds were given. Only in case of dispute between the church members themselves is the state forced to act as arbiter in ecclesiastical matters, as, for example, in the case of a controversy between a local congregation and the denomination to which it belongs as to the use to be made of certain property, or between the majority and the minority of a denomination in the case of a proposed merger with another body as to the right to control the denominational funds. In all such cases, the initiative comes from the Church, not the state. So far as it is possible to do so, the secular authorities are disposed to grant the representatives of the churches the most complete autonomy.

But while jealously guarding the principle of the separation of state and church, the American people are equally insistent upon the fact that their country is a Christian nation. This appears in the practice of opening Congress with prayer, in the President's annual Thanksgiving proclamation, and in the provision by Congress for chaplains in the army and navy. The Presidents of the United States have been almost without exception members of some recognized Christian church and have shown their respect for religion by regular church attendance. The churches have always been free to address the chief magistrate in matters which seemed to them of spiritual significance, in the confidence that their right to do so would be recognized and their address received in a sympathetic spirit. A recent example was an open letter apropos of disarmament addressed to President Harding, through the editorial columns of a leading Protestant religious journal[2] under the caption, "To President Harding, Christian." In this letter the writer appeals to the President to approach the problems of the disarmament conference not simply in the spirit of the statesman and the politician, but as one who voices the hopes and aspiration of

[1] On the law governing religious corporations, cf. Frank White and Godfrey Goldmark, "Non-Stock Corporations," New York, 1913, pp. 301-422.

[2] *Christian Century*, October 20, 1921.

millions of his fellow-Christians. Most Americans, whatever they might think of the substance of the letter, would agree that in making such an appeal the writer was entirely within his rights.

5. *Significant Denominational Types*

Thus far we have had in view American Christianity as a whole and have tried to point out its outstanding characteristics. But within this territory there are significant differences. These differences correspond roughly to the larger denominational groups with which our survey has made us familiar. It will add vividness to our sketch and help us to approach our later study more intelligently if we remind ourselves briefly what the more important of these groups are like.

At one pole of our American Protestantism stands that large group of churches which make the local congregation the constitutive element in the Church. Of these the Congregationalists may be taken as typical. The Congregationalists inherited the Puritan tradition in its independent form and gave spiritual tone to New England during the formative period; and while in the course of time Congregationalism has softened the rigidity of its earlier Calvinism and has become hospitable to new ideas in religion, it still retains a belief in the autonomy of the local congregation, and a suspicion of all forms of prelacy. Among the large denominations, the Congregationalists have been one of the slowest to yield to the centralizing tendency of our day, and their Mission Boards still remain in theory voluntary societies maintained by the contributions of individual congregations and Christians.

In their emphasis upon the right of the individual congregation to complete independence and autonomy, the Baptists are at one with the Congregationalists, but they carry their individualism still farther. Congregationalists generally share with the older churches the belief that the family is a spiritual unit and they therefore retain the practice of infant baptism. In their reaction against sacramentarianism the Baptists reject this practice. They insist on believers' baptism and hold a theory of the Church which makes individual faith a prerequisite to baptism. It was their protest which won freedom from the restrictions of the early theocracy, and to this day they reject in theory all man-made creeds and carry out more consistently than any other body of their fellow-

Christians, with the possible exception of the Disciples, the original Protestant principle that the Bible and the Bible alone is the rule of faith and practice. Yet on the basis of free co-operation they have been able to build up powerful missionary agencies and in their recently established Board of Promotion the Northern Baptists have created a central council through which they are able to function effectively for common ends and to co-operate with other churches.[1] With over 7,800,000 communicants, North and South, the Baptists share with the Methodists the numerical leadership among American Protestants, and no one who desires to understand the genius of American religious life can afford to pass them by.

It is a natural consequence of the democratic philosophy of the Congregationalists and Baptists that they should be more hospitable than other Christian bodies to the ministry of women. In the Baptist Church there are already a number of ordained women preachers, and the same is true, though not to so large an extent, of the Congregational Church.

Most extreme of all Protestant Christians in their opposition to forms and ceremonies and in their interest in a purely spiritual religion are the Friends. Relatively few in numbers, they have remained from the first a leaven in our American Christianity whose value to the whole can scarcely be over-estimated. It is not too much to say that in proportion to their numbers they have done more to foster vital religion and make faith bear fruit in works than any other equal number of American Christians.

Of the Unitarians we have already spoken. They represent the left wing of American Protestantism, the group which has carried freedom of thought to greater length than any other body of American Christians and made it the constitutive principle of their church.

---

[1] It should be stated that this tendency to centralization is strongly resisted by the Southern Baptists. These sturdy Christians who constitute the extreme right wing of Protestantism are unwilling to do anything which would seem to limit the freedom of the local congregation. Carrying distrust of centralized authority farther than any other body of their fellow-Christians, they hold aloof even from such innocent forms of co-operation as the Federal Council. Yet with this extreme insistence on the autonomy of the local congregation goes also, curiously enough, a doctrine of close communion which makes them, in spite of their extreme individualism, the most exclusive body in Protestantism, with the possible exception of the high-church party in the Episcopal Church.

At the other pole of American Christianity stand the Episcopalians. Beginning their career in Virginia as the Congregationalists did in New England, they have spread, like them, to all parts of the country and to-day possess a nation-wide organization with eighty-seven dioceses [1] and over a million communicants.

In the Protestant Episcopal Church the sacramentarian and mystical type of religion finds expression in American Christianity. More conservative than the other branches of the Church in its attachment to antiquity, the Episcopal Church values the Catholic tradition which it has inherited and cherishes the ties which bind it to the older churches. Especially close has been the relation of the American Episcopal Church to the Church of England from which it is directly descended—a fact evidenced by the presence of American bishops in the great Councils of the Anglican Communion. Tolerant in its theology to widely divergent views, it attaches great importance to unity of organization, and more than any other single communion, except perhaps the Disciples, feels the present divided condition of the Church as a scandal. Among the distinctive features of its organization, apart from the Episcopate itself, is its consistent adoption of the parish system, its retention of the liturgy in public worship, and the central place given to the sacraments. More than any other American church the Episcopal lays stress upon beauty and dignity of worship, and side by side with its parish churches it is building stately cathedrals in the great centres of population which accommodate large numbers of worshippers and minister to the community as a whole. In spite of the limitations to which reference has already been made, the Episcopate provides this church with a leadership which makes for continuity of policy and gives it an influence in the religious life of America out of all proportion to its numbers.

Midway between the Congregationalists and the Episcopalians stand the Presbyterians—like the former in their independence and insistence upon local autonomy; like the latter in their closely articulated organization and their inheritance of a tradition of order and dignity in worship. Largely recruited from English and Scotch-Irish sources, they have organized their Presbyteries from New York to California, and through their membership in the Alliance of Presbyterian and Reformed churches retain close affilia-

[1] According to the Census of 1916.

tion with the Presbyterians of other lands. Like the Episcopalians, Presbyterians have been earnest in their advocacy of Christian union and have taken a prominent part in various plans for co-operation both in the national and in the local field. Accepting as their standard the Westminster Confession, with a highly developed system of church law and a strong sense of ecclesiastical tradition, they have not made their own orthodoxy a reason for denying the Christianity of other churches or refusing to co-operate with them in any practicable plan for the establishment of the Kingdom of God.

In the course of their history, Presbyterians have frequently divided, sometimes on doctrinal grounds, at others for reasons of policy or temperament. But to-day the several branches of Presbyterians are co-operating practically in various ways, and the movement for a reunited Presbyterianism cannot much longer be delayed.[1] The two sister churches of Presbyterian polity, the Dutch Reformed and the German Reformed, each with its own distinctive genius and honorable history, will no doubt be included in the movement for reunion, since they belong to the same general polity and inherit similar traditions.

A distinct type in American Christianity is represented by the Lutherans. One of the larger Protestant bodies (they number more than two million communicants), they have until recently been one of the most isolated and independent. As the Episcopalians represent the conservative tendency of the Reformed movement in the sphere of polity and worship, so the Lutherans represent it in the field of doctrine. Like the Episcopalians in emphasizing the value of the sacrament, to them the creed, or as they would say, the confession, is the formative principle of the church, and its acceptance is consistent with wide variations in forms of government and administration. By the creed they understand the type of doctrine represented in the Augsburg Confession and the older confessional literature which interprets it, and upon the perpetuation of this type of doctrine and the securing of its intelligent acceptance they lay great stress. The devout Lutheran believes that it is the Christian's supreme privilege and duty to bear witness to Christ as the all-sufficient Saviour; and he can allow no word or act of his to obscure this testimony, or to detract from the

[1] Yet cf. p. 256.

glory of Christ as the only Lord and Saviour. The Lutheran holds that the Church's proper function is to preach the Gospel and administer the sacraments, and that it must not trespass upon the domain of the state. It must provide for the instruction of its people, and especially the children, in the faith and duties of the Christian religion, and must commend its Gospel to the world by works of ministering love. Many of the Lutherans maintain their own parochial schools.

In carrying out this ideal the Lutherans have not always found it possible to agree among themselves on every point of faith and doctrine. They have differed also in regard to the safeguards against the possible corruption or obscuration of their testimony. Such differences account in part for the divisions among Lutherans; for to them unity in the faith is of greater importance than union in external organization. Their divisions are due also to factors of language and nationality. On the other hand, tendencies toward union among themselves have been at work for many years, and aided by the strong impulse given by the war they have resulted in several large unions and in important co-operative relationship between bodies not organically one.

No account of the genius of American Protestantism would be complete which did not include an appreciation of the Methodists. One of the latest of the larger denominations to arise, they have proved one of the most vigorous and effective. In Methodism the genius for organization, which is a characteristic feature of American life, finds a fitting vehicle of expression. Beginning modestly in Wesley's mission to the United States and the labors of the pioneers who succeeded him, the Methodists have built up a nation-wide organization which includes nearly eight million communicants.[1] Among the American churches they alone have solved the problem of the vacant pulpit and made ministerial unemployment a thing of the past. Fervent in the character of their religious life, laying great stress on personal experience and the practice of holiness, they have been one of the most powerful factors in evangelizing the needy parts of the country and in carrying missions to the other nations as well. On the whole they are conservative in their theology, yet they have proved open to modern ideas. In ideal at least they believe that a man's education does not end with

[1] Cf. p. 66.

his entry into the ministry and have made provision for this continued education in their system of annual conferences. With unfailing appreciation of the need of personal conversion and consecration, they have been hospitable to the social aspects of the Gospel, and in their genius for organization was found the inspiration
of that great enterprise of co-operative Christianity which we know
as the Interchurch World Movement. Indeed, so effective is their
own work that they are sometimes tempted to forget that there
are other churches as well and to under-estimate the contribution
which they might render to the co-operative movement if they
would throw themselves into it as whole-heartedly as in theory
they confess they ought to do.

One more group of American Protestants needs brief mention
and that is the Disciples. Special interest attaches to them because of the fact that they arose as a protest against denominationalism and even to-day many of them refuse to be called members of a denomination. They believe that there can be only one
Church and to that end would have all Christians return to the
primitive standards and ideals of the New Testament. Like the
Baptists they reject all man-made creeds. Like the Baptists they
practise baptism by immersion. Like the Baptists in turn they
have found that the rejection of a written creed does not free them
from theological differences. Within their membership we find the
same two parties, the liberals and the conservatives, which show
themselves in every human organization and which move toward
the goal of unity which both alike have at heart by the two roads
that conservatives and liberals have taken in every generation, the
former by asking others to agree with them, the latter by trying
to find some common ground on which all good men and true can
unite. To-day the Disciples have become for all practical purposes a denomination among denominations, retaining as a reminder of their original motive only this: that among their various
Mission Boards they have one whose sole function it is to promote
the unity of the Church.

Such, then, are some of the more outstanding types of American Protestantism. Each of these in turn has its own divisions
and sub-divisions, in some cases more, in others less, numerous and
important. Each has its parties emphasizing different aspects of
the common faith, and trying to shape denominational policy ac-

cording to its own conviction. And about these larger groups clus-
ter a number of smaller bodies ranging in size from many thousands
and even hundreds of thousands to a few hundreds in membership,
expressing aspects of Christian faith and life and preserving the
memory of episodes in Christian history into which, however fas-
cinating and rewarding, our space forbids us to enter.[1] Looking at
them one by one and observing in each in varying degree the limitations which we have seen to be characteristic of American Christianity as a whole, we might well question whether any large degree of unity is possible between bodies so organized and who inherit
such differing traditions.

6. *Factors Making for a Larger and More Catholic Christianity*

But this is only one side of the picture—true so far as it goes,
but unless qualified, misleading. Side by side with these divisive
influences other forces have been at work in American Christianity,
preparing for a larger future. These we must now consider to
make our picture complete.

We are not thinking here of the permanent capital of historic
Christianity, the resources laid up in the Christian religion and always available, but of certain special factors which have gone into
the making of our American Christianity, which have helped it to
adjust itself to present needs more quickly and more effectively
than it could otherwise have done. Of these the most important
for our purpose are the following: the foreign-missionary movement, the new home missions, the social-service movement, the
movement for church unity, the Christian Associations and other
voluntary societies of Protestantism.

First in importance we must put the foreign-missionary move-

---

[1] Of the denominations with more than 50,000 members, the United Brethren, with 367,000, are Methodist in polity, as is true also of the Evangelical
Association (120,000) and the United Evangelicals (89,000) who together have
more than 200,000 members. The German Evangelical Synod (339,000) is
Presbyterian in polity and carries on the traditions of the Union Church in
Germany. The Churches of Christ with 317,000 members belong to the same
family as the Disciples, and the same is true of the Christian Church with
118,000 members. The Dunkers with 133,000 are Presbyterian in polity. The
Adventists with 114,000 members and the Mennonites with 79,000 are Congregational. The same is true of the Unitarians and the Universalists.

ment. This movement, never stronger or more influential than at the time the war broke out, had, as we have seen, given to American Christianity certain great gifts which have proved of incalculable importance. It had raised up a group of men and women who had acquired the habit of world vision. It had set for multitudes of earnest Christians a standard of consecration that made the giving of one's all seem a matter of course. It had enlarged the range of the Church's ministry until it took in the whole of life. Religion, as modern missions conceive it, is a ministry to the whole man—man as an individual to be sure, but as a member of society as well, citizen not of his own nation only but of the world. The true prophets of the League of Nations, the men who have done most to prepare the way for the ideal of a new world order, are men like George Washburn and Timothy Richards and George William Knox who, in their own persons, have crossed the barrier that divides race from race and made Christianity an effective organ of international friendship. Above all, the foreign-missionary movement has carried into our American Christianity a sense of unlimited possibilities. It has broken the shell of tradition and habit and made initiative a Christian virtue.

Foreign missions enlarge the significance of denominationalism by giving it a wider outlook and a more catholic purpose. We have seen how the denomination expands the horizon of the individual Christian in the local community by making him a member of a body which is national in its reach. But the denominations are much more than this. They are themselves missionary agencies committed to a world-wide programme, and through their literature and propaganda they are continually reminding their members that no conception of the Christian church is adequate which is less inclusive than humanity.

The foreign-missionary movement not only widens the horizon of the American churches; it gives them a new conception of their responsibility at home. When one is giving for schools and hospitals in China, it cannot seem out of place that the Church in America should be occupied with questions regarding education and health, and the discovery of the missionaries that Baptists and Methodists and Presbyterians can work together without loss of efficiency in foreign lands is bound to exercise a reflex influence upon the movement for unity at home.

The effect of this enlarging conception of the task of the home Church appears in an increasing emphasis upon the social aspects of the Church's missionary activity. The leaders of the new home missions insist no less strongly than their predecessors upon the necessity of individual conversion. But they associate education and social service with evangelism as its necessary consequence. Every phase of the individual's activity, we now see, must be Christianized, and for this we must develop a nation-wide programme that includes all the varied groups in the country with their differing needs—the immigrants clustering in our great cities, the workers in factories whose hours of labor cut them off from the ordinary ministries of the Church, the multitudes of people in small villages and through the open country, who miss the inspiration and fellowship enjoyed by those who live in larger communities, and not least, the great city churches, many of which have been limiting their responsibility to their own parish instead of thinking of themselves as part of the one great field of national Christianity.

This new conception of home missions has found expression in the Social Ideals of the Churches,[1] a statement adopted at the meeting of the Federal Council in 1908,[2] which sums up in concise form the main points in a number of similar pronouncements by individual denominations. That statement attempts to formulate in a series of brief propositions the Christian attitude toward current industrial questions. It deals with such matters as wages and hours of labor, the protection of women and children in industry, the right of the workman to proper sanitary conditions of labor, and to proper representation in matters in dispute between himself and his employer. Originally put forth by a single denomination, it has gained significance from its acceptance by the Federal Council, a body including more than thirty of the leading Protestant churches; and the fact that it has recently been attacked by certain powerful business interests would seem to indicate that it expresses a movement within the Church which is sufficiently pronounced to deserve recognition.[3]

[1] Cf. Ward, "A Year Book of the Church and Social Service in the United States," New York, 1916, pp. 198-201.

[2] Revised and amplified in 1912. At the meeting of the Council at Cleveland in 1916, four additional articles were added.

[3] Cf. *Industry*, June 15, 1920. Cf. also p. 24.

It is true that this movement, so far as it affects the Church, is still young. It is an island, let us say rather an archipelago, in the sea of individualistic Christianity, and yet the archipelago exists. To trace its origin would require us to recall the history of the Social Settlement, to follow the rise of the social-service movement in the churches, to tell of the work of social prophets like Washington Gladden and Walter Rauschenbusch, and of living leaders whose accomplishment it is too early to appraise. It would bring before us the series of experiments through which church leaders have been trying to bridge the gap between the Church and organized labor, such as the institution of the fraternal delegate, or the establishment of the open forum. As a result of these and other influences the attention of the churches is being directed to their social responsibilities, and a new social conscience is being developed.

A fourth factor to be considered is the movement toward Christian unity.[1] The interest of the Church in unity appears not only in the more ambitious attempts to secure the organic union of Christendom, but in a wide variety of co-operative movements which bring Christians of different denominations together for practical purposes. While advocates of the former method have been content to focus their attention on the longer future and have discouraged efforts at early action as premature, those who have been engaged in the more immediate tasks, feeling the urgency of the situation, have preached co-operation as a present duty to constantly increasing audiences. Acting through the Federal Council, they have organized commissions on such subjects as evangelism, social service, international justice and goodwill and Christian education. They have fostered the creation of local federations in cities and states. This movement has been paralleled or preceded by similar movements on the part of the responsible administrative agencies of the larger Christian communions which have come together in such effective bodies as the Foreign Missions Conference, the Home Missions Council, the Council of Church Boards, and the International Sunday School Council. Through these agencies relationships had already been established between the different denominations which had created a common senti-

[1] Cf. Chapters X and XIII.

ment and understanding and made it possible for them to work together when the war came.

More prominent in the public eye, but needing special mention because representing a different principle, are the great voluntary societies of Protestantism, of which the most important are the Young Men's Christian Association and the Young Women's Christian Association. The story of the rise and growth and service of these powerful religious agencies is one of the most interesting and instructive of all the chapters of American church history, and some day will receive the detailed and discriminating attention which it deserves. In these bodies the Church possesses indispensable auxiliaries with the power to function quickly and effectively in crises such as war. It is not strange that the Associations should have taken the leadership when the World War came and should have filled the place in the public eye to which their great services justly entitled them.

One more asset needs to be mentioned, and that is the democratic spirit itself. We have seen the weakness of this spirit, its tendency to isolation and narrowness. We must not overlook its strength. It expresses the sense of individual responsibility which is so characteristic a feature of our American life—the willingness of the individual to assume his share and bear his part and work out in forms that seem congenial to himself the type of life he wishes to live. It has its unlovely features, for there are few individuals who have the training and the culture to order their own lives to the best advantage. But culture may be acquired if there is individual initiative and responsibility, whereas where these are lacking true democracy is impossible. The democratic spirit is a spirit of life and energy. It is active, responsible, unafraid, and this spirit, present in the republic from the first, has reflected itself in the character of the American Church.

Such was the Church upon which the war broke, to test its powers and to reveal it to itself.

CHAPTER VI

WHAT THE CHURCH LEARNED IN THE WAR

1. *Differing Estimates of the War Work of the Church*

In a frequently quoted article in the *Atlantic Monthly* an American clergyman writes thus of the temper of the Church during the months that preceded our entry into the World War: "Thoughtful men and women are asking what became of the spiritual leadership of America during those thirty-two months when Europe and parts of Asia were passing through Gehenna. What prelate or bishop or ecclesiastical dignitary essayed the work of spiritual interpretation? What convocation or conference or assembly spoke so convincingly that the national conscience must perforce listen? What book from a clerical study gave the sanctities of humanity and the sanctions of law the foremost place in current thought? What voice from altar or pulpit liberated a passion of righteous indignation and set the continent aflame with holy wrath?" [1]

The sin of which Dr. Odell calls his brother clergymen to repent is that they did not together and at once arouse the nation to the duty of immediate participation in the World War. Other critics of the Church have condemned it for exactly the opposite reason. In their view the clergy were blameworthy not because they were slow in throwing themselves into the war, but because they had not made the war impossible; or, if that could not be, did not refuse to take any part in it. [2]

These criticisms reflect the divided sentiment in the nation when the war broke out. To many Americans—no doubt the large majority—the war presented itself as a simple issue of right and wrong. The peace of the world had been suddenly interrupted

[1] Joseph H. Odell, "Peter Sat by the Fire Warming Himself," *Atlantic Monthly*, February, 1918, pp. 145 sq.

[2] Cf. the thoughtful editorial in the *Churchman*, "War is Sin," November 12, 1921.

by a marauding nation, and it was the plain duty of all law-abiding peoples to band themselves together to put down the offender. For a considerable number of thoughtful persons, however, the matter was not so simple. To them war itself seemed the evil of evils, the inevitable outcome of an unchristian social order for which we were all alike—even if not all in equal degree—to blame. Germany might have applied the torch, but others had helped to lay the fagots. In their thought, the one hope for the future of mankind was to find some nation which would have nothing to do with war in any form.

We see to-day the limitations of both points of view. We recognize that when the war came it was too late to stay the destructive forces it had set in motion, and that all that could be done was to try to mitigate the evil, so far as might be possible. But we see also that to multitudes who had been living little and selfish lives, the war was a reminder of a larger world, a call to self-forgetful service. Who can doubt that to thousands of our young men the call to service was in a true sense the call of religion?

Yet we know now how much more complicated were the moral issues than we at first supposed. One need not minimize Germany's guilt in the war or question the righteousness of the cause for which the Allies fought in order to show in how many ways on both sides evil was intermingled with good. The intolerance that cloaked itself as patriotism; the willingness—when two alternatives were possible—to believe evil rather than good; the systematic suppression and perversion of the truth when it bore against our purposes instead of for them; the loss of faith in the capacity for good in multitudes of men; the forgetfulness of the fact that in the eyes of God all alike are sinners, offenders against His law and in need of His forgiveness: [1] all this we can perceive more clearly now than five years ago when action jostled thought aside and reason often abdicated in favor of passion. It will not seem strange if in such a situation the Church was slow to express a final judgment, and required time to find its way to the truth. There was no agreement even as to the facts; how much less as to their significance. Where the wisest individuals differ it is only natural that

[1] Cf. W. Adams Brown, "The Place of Repentance in a Nation at War," *North American Student,* May, 1918.

there should be no unified policy in the institution to which they belong. Before censuring the churches for what they failed to do, it is only fair to give them credit for what they did do.

2. *Success of the Church in Caring for the Soldiers and Keeping up the Morale of the Nation*

Three plain duties lay before the Church when the war broke out. It was its duty, first, to minister to the spiritual needs of its own sons and keep alive their faith in God and the higher life; it was its duty, secondly, to reinforce the morale of the nation and to inspire men and women to sacrifice by reminding them of the ideals for which the war was fought; it was its duty, finally, in time of strain and misunderstanding, to keep alive the international spirit, the spirit of brotherhood and goodwill, and in time of war to prepare the world for the healing tasks of peace. By its success or failure in these respects, its claim to have rendered faithful service must be judged.

As to the first two there can be no question. Both in their ministry to the troops who were fighting and to the people who stayed at home, the churches performed a service of incalculable value—a service that will be rated most highly by those who knew it best.[1]

At the outset, the Church was fortunate in having as auxiliaries the two Christian Associations, undenominational agencies definitely Christian in character, of large resources, wide experience, and exceptional initiative. Both had already had training in work in other countries. Both had worked with our army on the Mexican border, and in addition the Young Men's Christian Association had had three years' experience in caring for the prisoners of war both of our Allies and of the countries against which we were presently to fight. In the Young Men's Christian Association, therefore, the Christian forces of America possessed the machinery through which they could act quickly and effectively in the service of our army, called into existence almost over-night. What was done through

---

[1] A convenient summary of the war work of the churches is given in "War-Time Agencies of the Churches," New York, 1919. A fuller account may be found in the publications of the General War-Time Commission, the Christian Associations, and the various denominational War Commissions. Cf. also Williams, "American Catholics in the War," New York, 1921.

this agency both here and across the sea is known in every home in America.[1] It is as needless as it would be impossible to add anything to the well-deserved tribute recently publicly paid to the Young Men's Christian Association by an authoritative witness, General Pershing.[2]

But the Young Men's Christian Association was only one of a number of agencies through which the Church discharged its ministry to the army. What the Young Men's Christian Association did for the men, the Young Women's Christian Association did for the women. For this was a war, we must never forget, in which women did their part side by side with men in army and navy alike. The Young Women's Christian Association looked after the women relatives of our soldiers and sailors, cared for women serving in various capacities with our troops, for trained nurses, signal-corps operators, secretaries, laundresses, etc., and for the industrial army of women in our own country and in France who served behind the lines.[3]

Less prominently before the public eye, but of increasing importance with every passing month, was the work of the army and navy chaplains.[4] The camp pastors or voluntary chaplains, furnished by the War Commissions of the different churches, rendered a useful service during the earlier months of the war, when the regular chaplains were still few.[5] The churches in the neighborhood of the camps opened their rooms for recreation and rest and offered the recruits from distant sections of the country a place

[1] Cf. Summary of the World War Work of the American Y. M. C. A., printed for private distribution, New York, 1920; Katharine Mayo, "That Damn 'Y'," 1920.

[2] "In the field of education, athletics, and recreation after the armistice, the Young Men's Christian Association took the lead, without any sort of question, and as a matter of fact about nine-tenths of the welfare work that was carried on in the A. E. F. was carried on under the direction and guidance of the Young Men's Christian Association."—"General Pershing and the Young Men's Christian Association," p. 7.

[3] Cf. Report of the National War Work Council of the Young Women's Christian Associations of America, New York, 1919.

[4] No complete account of the work of the chaplains has yet been printed. Extracts from the report of the Chief of Chaplains are given in the Report of the Secretary of War, Washington, 1921.

[5] For an account of their work cf. the reports of the various War Commissions, fuller reference to which may be found in the bibliography included in "War-Time Agencies of the Churches."

where they could feel at home.[1] In other national organizations, such as the Red Cross, the Library Association, the War Camp Community Service, etc., worked representatives of the churches, helping to create the environment that would sustain the men's morale and uphold their ideals. Probably since the world began, there has never been an army upon whose morale such solicitous care was expended.

Scarcely less notable than the contribution of the Church to the welfare of the army was its service in sustaining the morale of the nation. To all the various forms of national service which contributed so largely to the winning of the war—the work of the Red Cross, Food Control, Liberty Loans, and the like—the churches were generous contributors. When Mr. Hoover wished to reach every home in America with his appeal for co-operative action, he found an invaluable ally in the churches, for the churches have their representatives in every community and can touch, at will, every section of the people.

The service of the churches was the more creditable because of the modest and self-effacing way in which it was rendered. In all the organizations which have been named, ministers worked as volunteers. Especially significant was the work done by ministers as camp directors and Y. M. C. A. secretaries. Cheerfully accepting the limitations which the government regulations put upon their freedom,[2] they took the positions offered to them by the Association and made up in the spirit of their service what it lacked in formal and official character. Indeed, one of the chief reasons why the churches received so little credit for the work done in the war was that so much of their work was done in co-operation with others. They were content to work where work seemed needed,

---

[1] No complete record exists of the work which was done by these churches. Taken together it would make an impressive story. The Catholic War Council has undertaken to compile a complete record of what was done in this way by the different Roman Catholic parishes. Unfortunately the limitation of funds at the disposal of the General War-Time Commission made impossible any such record of the work of the Protestant churches.

[2] *E.g.*, in such matters as administering the sacraments. According to the theory of the government the work that was done by the Y. M. C. A. was primarily welfare work, and while no objection was made to the secretaries carrying on religious services, they were supposed to do so as laymen, and everything of a denominational or indeed of a formal ecclesiastical character was strictly excluded.

supplying the personnel through which other organizations worked as well as rendering the distinctive service which experience showed that they alone could give.

3. *Failure of the Church Adequately to Uphold the Ideal of International Brotherhood and the Reasons for It*

When we turn to the third of the great tasks of the Church in the war—that of keeping alive the spirit of international brotherhood—the record is less clear. There were individuals who were able in singular degree to combine loyalty to their country's cause with the larger outlook. But for many ministers the identification of the national cause with that of humanity was so complete that they found it hard to pass discriminating judgments. The steady stream of atrocity stories, the suppression of all evidences of better feeling on the part of any section of the German people, the disheartening effects of the pronunciamento of the German intellectuals, the honest and sincere revulsion of feeling against a nation the action of whose leaders had plunged mankind into these unspeakable horrors—all worked to make righteous anger seem a Christian duty. The tone adopted by some pacificists in regard to the issues at stake did not tend to make the cause of internationalism any more attractive. The fact remains that in the heat of the struggle the judgment of many a minister did not conspicuously rise above that of the average citizen. The universal note, so signally sounded by Israel's prophets in times of similar crisis, was less in evidence than we could have desired.

Yet, thank God, the note of brotherhood was never entirely absent. When the Church spoke officially, its utterances were not lacking in Christian character. Of many illustrations that might be given, the declaration of principles adopted by the Federal Council at the time war broke out may be taken as a representative example.[1]

This declaration reads as follows:

After long patience, and with a solemn sense of responsibility, the government of the United States has been forced to recognize that a state of war exists between this country and Germany, and the President has called upon

[1] Cf. "The Churches of Christ in Time of War," New York, 1917, pp. 129–133.

all the people for their loyal support and their whole-hearted allegiance. As American citizens, members of Christian churches gathered in Federal Council, we are here to pledge both support and allegiance in unstinted measure.

We are Christians as well as citizens. Upon us, therefore, rests a double responsibility. We owe it to our country to maintain intact and to transmit unimpaired to our descendants our heritage of freedom and democracy. Above and beyond this, we must be loyal to our divine Lord, who gave His life that the world might be redeemed, and whose loving purpose embraces every man and every nation.

As citizens of a peace-loving nation, we abhor war. We have long striven to secure the judicial settlement of all international disputes. But since, in spite of every effort, war has come, we are grateful that the ends to which we are committed are such as we can approve. To vindicate the principles of righteousness and the inviolability of faith as between nation and nation; to safeguard the right of all the peoples, great and small alike, to live their life in freedom and peace; to resist and overcome the forces that would prevent the union of the nations in a commonwealth of free peoples conscious of unity in the pursuit of ideal ends—these are aims for which every one of us may lay down our all, even life itself.

We enter the war without haste or passion, not for private or national gain, with no hatred or bitterness against those with whom we contend.

No man can foresee the issue of the struggle. It will call for all the strength and heroism of which the nation is capable. What now is the mission of the Church in this hour of crisis and danger? It is to bring all that is done or planned in the nation's name to the test of the mind of Christ.

That mind upon one point we do not all interpret alike. With sincere conviction some of us believe that it is forbidden the disciples of Christ to engage in war under any circumstances. Most of us believe that the love of all men which Christ enjoins demands that we defend with all the power given us the sacred rights of humanity. But we are all at one in loyalty to our country, and in steadfast and whole-hearted devotion to her service.

As members of the Church of Christ, the hour lays upon us special duties:

To purge our own hearts clean of arrogance and of selfishness;

To steady and inspire the nation;

To keep ever before the eyes of ourselves and of our allies the ends for which we fight;

To hold our own nation true to its professed aims of justice, liberty, and brotherhood;

To testify to our fellow-Christians in every land, most of all to those from whom for the time we are estranged, our consciousness of unbroken unity in Christ;

To unite in the fellowship of service multitudes who love their enemies and are ready to join with them in rebuilding the waste places as soon as peace shall come;

To be diligent in works of relief and mercy, not forgetting those ministries to the spirit to which as Christians we are especially committed;

To keep alive the spirit of prayer, that in these times of strain and sorrow men may be sustained by the consciousness of the presence and power of God;

To hearten those who go to the front, and to comfort their loved ones at home;

To care for the welfare of our young men in the army and navy, that they may be fortified in character and made strong to resist temptation;

To be vigilant against every attempt to arouse the spirit of vengeance and unjust suspicion toward those of foreign birth or sympathies;

To protect the rights of conscience against every attempt to invade them;

To maintain our Christian institutions and activities unimpaired, the observance of the Lord's Day and the study of the Holy Scriptures, that the soul of our nation may be nourished and renewed through the worship and service of Almighty God;

To guard the gains of education, and of social progress and economic freedom, won at so great a cost, and to make full use of the occasion to set them still further forward, even by and through the war;

To keep the open mind and the forward look, that the lessons learned in war may not be forgotten when comes that just and sacred peace for which we pray;

Above all, to call men everywhere to new obedience to the will of our Father God, who in Christ has given Himself in supreme self-sacrifice for the redemption of the world, and who invites us to share with Him His ministry of reconciliation.

To such service we would summon our fellow-Christians of every name. In this spirit we would dedicate ourselves and all that we have to the nation's cause. With this hope we would join hands with all men of goodwill of every land and race, to rebuild on this war-ridden and desolated earth the commonwealth of mankind, and to make of the kingdoms of the world the Kingdom of the Christ.

This utterance gains significance from the circumstances under which it was put forth. It was not the expression of a small or uninfluential group, but of the most representative body of American Christians which up to that time had ever assembled. It was prepared with great care by a large and carefully selected committee which subjected every line to repeated and rigorous criticism. It expressed to an extent which is not often true of such documents the mature conviction of the men and women best able to speak for the Church as a whole.[1]

[1] Four and a half years after the utterance which we have just quoted, a delegation of the same Council met again in Washington. The war had come and gone, and in November of 1921 representatives of the allied powers had come to the national capital at President Harding's invitation to take part in a conference on disarmament. On Friday, the eleventh, the third anniversary of Armistice Day, it was proposed to bury in the National Cemetery at Arlington, with all the honors of a grateful nation, an unknown and unidentified soldier, symbol and representative of the nameless dead who had given their lives for our country. On the Thursday preceding, the body lay in state in the rotunda of the Capitol and delegations representing different interests were permitted to enter at appointed times to bring their tributes to the honored dead. The first of these delegations represented the Federal Council of the Churches. In the early morning of a gray November day they gathered on the east steps of the Capitol, and just before eight o'clock struck, a moment or two before the doors were opened to the general public, were admitted to the rotunda where they placed their tribute, a white cross over the Stars and Stripes, in the place which had been prepared for it. After a brief prayer by Bishop McDowell, Chairman of the Washington Committee on Army and Navy Chaplains, in which he expressed the nation's gratitude to God for the valor of the men who had given their lives for its defence and invoked His blessing upon the homes from which they came, the Secretary of the General War-Time Commission, on behalf of the churches represented in the Federal Council, voiced their consciousness of the indissoluble bond which unites men of goodwill of every land and race, their hope that in work for the common weal those who were once enemies might find reconciliation and peace, and their unconquerable faith in the possibility of a warless world.

A similar note is struck in an open letter sent out a few days earlier by the heads of twenty-four of the largest Protestant communions, acting in co-operation with the Federal Council. It is addressed to all lovers of humanity, and voices the deep conviction of the churches in an impressive statement from which we take the following paragraphs:

"The Conference is to deal with difficult and complex problems of politics and economics. But underlying them all are eternal moral principles of international life. We firmly believe that nations no less than individuals are subject to God's immutable moral laws; that only through just dealing and unselfish service can people achieve true welfare, greatness, and honor; that for nations as well as individuals, goodwill and mutual helpfulness are the true way of life. No considerations of political expediency or of selfish economic advantage can supersede these basic principles without bringing ultimate disaster and ruin in their train.

"More than all else, there is need for a new spirit in our international life. Penitence there must be first of all, for our own past sin in thinking too much of our own rights and others' duties, too little of our own duties and others' rights. We must learn to think of our nation not as an end in itself, but as a member of a family of nations under a common Father. All unneighborly attitudes toward other peoples, all prejudice against other races, must be put away. Our hearts must be open to the incoming of the divine

ר ו 5 3

4. *What the War Taught the Church Concerning the Need of Effective Agencies of Unity*

So far we have been considering what the Church did for the nation. It remains to point out what was the reflex influence upon the Church. For one thing the war revealed to American Protestantism its essential unity. We have already seen how much the different denominations had in common, how far their past history and similar experiences had already welded them into a spiritual unity. But it remained for the war to bring this fact home to the consciousness of American Christians. Each denomination met the crisis in its own way. Each reacted after its own fashion. Yet the reaction was surprisingly similar, and the different agencies which the war called into existence found little difficulty in working together.[1]

But while the war disclosed to the churches their essential unity, it showed them at the same time that they lacked agencies through which that unity could express itself effectively in action. Both in the larger matters which required interdenominational co-operation and in the narrower sphere where each denomination was able to act for itself, the needed machinery had to be improvised almost overnight. The Presbyterians, the Baptists, and the Congregationalists, whose annual meetings took place soon after the war broke out, created War Commissions to act for them in the crisis. Other denominations which met less frequently relied upon their existing agencies to tide them over the emergency. In the Episcopal Church, Bishop Lawrence was authorized by the presiding bishop, acting

Spirit of life which alone can bring lasting peace to a world torn by war and staggering under the colossal burden of unnecessary armaments."

[1] Cf. the testimony of Dr. Speer, in "Christian Unity: Its Principles and Possibilities," p. 26.

"One of the most striking things about these denominational commissions was that their organization, point of view, and lines of action bore testimony to the underlying community of view and feeling in the American churches. No other institutions in America acted with more identity of mind and spirit. They set themselves to almost identical forms of service. There were many obvious differences, but they were as nothing in comparison with the significant evidence of the substantial unity of mind and temper characteristic of our churches. There were a few which believed that they were particularistic and different, but the interesting fact, almost the amusing fact, was the similarity of spirit and ideal. Actions spoke louder than words. Our American churches revealed their unity of character as a present reality."

upon his own authority, to create a War Commission, relying upon the General Convention to ratify what had been done.   The Southern Baptists made their Board of Home Missions the official agency of their war work, and the same was true at first of the Methodists.   The Lutherans, the most divided of the Protestant groups, found in the war a welcome stimulus to denominational unity.   Waiving all minor differences, they recognized their common interest in effective war service and created a National Lutheran Commission for Soldiers' and Sailors' Welfare, through which they could all function together.[1]

What was true in the field of the denomination as a whole was true also of the local community.   Individual churches were exceedingly active.   The War Camp Community Service was represented by earnest and enthusiastic agents.   In a few communities the existing federation of churches served as a unifying agency.   But the churches as a whole had no single central organization through which they could promptly unify their local service in time of war.

In spite of all obstacles, in one way or another, the needed machinery was created and the churches addressed themselves to the tasks which lay at hand.   There were chaplains to be provided for the government, and furnished with the equipment they needed; there were voluntary workers to be supplied in the camps.   Literature was needed for the soldiers.   The churches near the camps must be strengthened and supplied with workers.   In some places there were buildings to be erected or enlarged.   For these funds were required and workers, and soon in all the larger denominations a stream of activity was under way.[2]

If it had only been one stream!   But unfortunately there were more than thirty, each pouring its supplies of men, money, and literature into the camps.   It was clear that such a situation could not continue indefinitely.   The only access to the camps was through the government.   But the government recognized three great bodies of religious people, and only three—the Protestants, the Roman Catholics, and the Jews.   If, then, the Protestants were to work effectively, they must find some way of working together.

[1] Cf. "War-Time Agencies of the Churches," pp. 53 sq.
[2] For information in detail cf. the reports of the various denominations in "War-Time Agencies of the Churches."

5. *The Organization and Work of the General War-Time Commission—Principles Controlling the Work of the Commission*

This necessity led to the appointment of the General War-Time Commission of the Churches, the agency through which united Protestantism functioned during the war. The importance of this commission and its significance for the history of the co-operative movement in Protestantism justify a brief account of its origin and activities and of the principles on which it operated.[1]

The General War-Time Commission of the Churches was a body of one hundred persons chosen from the different churches and other religious agencies which were dealing in direct and responsible ways with the new problems which the war had raised.

It had its inception at a meeting of the Federal Council held at Washington on May 8 and 9, 1917. At this meeting, called two weeks after the United States entered the war, there were in attendance, besides the delegates of the Federal Council, representatives of the Home Missions Council, the Foreign Missions Conference of North America, the Federation of Woman's Boards of Foreign Missions of North America, the Council of Women for Home Missions, the International Committee of the Young Men's Christian Associations, the National Board of the Young Women's Christian Associations, the American Bible Society, and the World Alliance for International Friendship through the Churches. In all, no less than thirty-five different bodies were represented. The sessions of the meeting were devoted to the preparation of a message to the churches and the discussion of methods by which the churches might meet the duties of the hour in the spirit of the message.[2]

The discussion at the meeting developed the fact that besides the temporary committees for which provision was made, some permanent representative national body would be needed to deal with the new problems created by the war, and the Administrative

[1] Cf. General War-Time Commission of the Churches: Its Origin and Its Purpose, September, 1917; Report of the General War-Time Commission of the Churches, December, 1917; The Record of a Year: Progress of the Work of the General War-Time Commission of the Churches, 1917–1918; Report of the General War-Time Commission of the Churches, December, 1918; The Service of the General War-Time Commission of the Churches, May, 1919.

[2] Cf. pp. 97-99.

Committee was authorized to bring this about. Acting under this authority, Dr. North, the President of the Council, invited a carefully selected group of persons from the different religious bodies whose co-operation was essential to serve as members of a Commission of One Hundred. Dr. Robert E. Speer became chairman of the Commission, Bishop Lawrence of Massachusetts, vice-chairman, and the writer of the present volume, secretary.

The Commission was organized on September 20, 1917, and appointed an executive committee and other committees. After defining its relation to the various religious agencies dealing with the war work of the churches, it expressed its own purposes as follows: [1]

"1. To co-ordinate existing and proposed activities and to bring them into intelligent and sympathetic relationship so as to avoid all waste and friction and to promote efficiency.

"2. To suggest to the proper agency or agencies any further work called for and not being done.

"3. To provide for or perform such work as can best be done in a co-operative way.

"4. To furnish means of common and united expression when such is desired; and finally,

"5. To provide a body which would be prepared to deal in a spirit of co-operation with the new problems of reconstruction which may have to be faced after the war."

Beginning modestly as a means of mutual acquaintanceship and a clearing-house of information, the influence of the Commission increased rapidly. Besides the executive committee, more than twenty-five other committees functioned at one time or another, and enlisted the service of a large number of voluntary workers.[2] The expenses of the Commission, at first defrayed by voluntary contributions, were afterward underwritten by fourteen of the co-operating bodies and when the war ended it had raised and expended more than $300,000, and was operating on a budget of $200,000 a year.

From the long list of activities mentioned by the Commission in

[1] "War-Time Agencies of the Churches," p. 154.
[2] *Ibid.*, pp. 158–176.

its final report,[1] the following may be selected as worthy of special comment:

In the first place the Commission served as a clearing-house of information. When it came into existence there was no single body which possessed accurate knowledge of what was being done by the religious forces of the country for the soldiers and sailors. The government did not possess it; the Associations did not possess it; the churches did not possess it. Each covered a part of the field and could tell what was being done by its own representatives, but there was no one whose business it was to cover the field as a whole. The Commission set itself at once to remedy this lack. It undertook a careful survey of the work being done in all of the military camps of the country and made its information accessible to all who needed it.

More important than the sharing of information was the work of the Commission in bringing about personal contacts and rela-

[1] The activities which were undertaken co-operatively by the churches through the Commission were summed up in its final report as follows: "Securing and furnishing information concerning needs and opportunities for religious work by means of a series of surveys; furnishing to the religious and secular press information concerning the co-operative work of the churches; promoting a better mutual understanding of plans and purposes and establishing more effective co-operation between the churches and the welfare agencies; securing the appointment of an adequate number of well-qualified army and navy chaplains and assuring them of the united support of the churches in the endeavor to have them provided with equipment, rank, and organization adequate to the effective performance of their duties; co-ordinating the activities of the chaplains and other religious workers within the camps with the work of the several churches in the neighborhood; ascertaining the special needs and providing for the moral and religious welfare of Negro troops; providing religious ministration for interned aliens; supplying printed matter needed for the use of chaplains and churches; reinforcing the efforts of the government to maintain a high moral standard in the army, both here and overseas, and to conserve for the future the results of the present interest in social hygiene; providing for the religious and moral welfare of the workers in communities engaged in the manufacture of munitions of war and in the shipbuilding industry; securing recruits for the work of the churches at home and abroad from men in military and naval service; stimulating local churches to mobilize their resources for war-time tasks; bringing the denominations together for co-operative effort in raising funds for war work; arranging for an exchange of ministerial service by the ministers of America and those of Great Britain and other Allied countries; encouraging the churches to welcome soldiers and sailors upon their return to civilian life and co-operating with the government in helping to secure for them prompt employment; deepening the spirit of penitence and intercession among the people."

tionships. There were, in the first place, the different denominational war commissions which needed to be made known to one another. Next there were relationships to be established between the Associations and the representatives of the churches. Thirdly, there were contacts to be brought about between the Protestant religious forces and the Roman Catholics and Jews. Finally, there were problems affecting the relationship of the religious forces as a whole to governmental agencies like the Commission on Training Camp Activities, which were charged with the moral and social welfare of the soldiers. With all these agencies the Commission was in touch. For each it tried to establish a natural point of contact with the others to the end that misunderstandings might be removed and more effective co-operation made possible.

Much of the time of the Commission was given to increasing the number and promoting the efficiency of the chaplains. When the war broke out the status of the chaplain was exceedingly unsatisfactory. In theory the official representative of religion in the army and navy, in practice he held an anomalous and ill-defined position. His relation to the Church was of the loosest. On the funds so liberally contributed to equip the religious activities of the Young Men's Christian Association he could make no claim. From the government he received only his commission, and while all other branches of the army had been elevated in dignity and in rank to meet the new emergency of the war, his status remained still what it was at the time of the Spanish War.

The Commission devoted much time and energy to changing this situation. Through its Washington committee it served as the agent of the government in securing for army and navy an adequate supply of efficient men for the chaplaincy. In its New York office it maintained a bureau which furnished equipment for the chaplains and supplied them information on matters of interest to them. It took an active part in the movement for the Chaplains' School, which did much to improve the training and increase the efficiency of the service. From the first it worked with Roman Catholics and Jews to secure adequate recognition of the chaplains from the government and provide them with the kind of organization which would enable them to discharge their work effectively. Such recognition was early secured for the chaplains of the American Expeditionary Force through General Pershing's organization of a chaplains' corps under Bishop Brent, but it proved exceedingly difficult to bring about similar action at home, and it was only after the war was over that the desired end was fully attained.

Much of the time of the Commission was given to the work of the camp pastors or voluntary chaplains who were sent into the camps by the different denominational war commissions when the war broke out. The need for the services of these men was due partly to the slowness with which the regular chaplains were appointed, partly to the limitations put upon the religious activities of the Association secretaries during the early days of the war.[1] Their presence in large numbers raised many difficult questions of adjustment which taxed the skill and patience of all concerned. Conferences were held in different centres attended by representative camp pastors of different denominations, and principles of co-operation worked out which did much to remove the causes of friction and promote harmony and good feeling.

The Commission proved particularly useful in the case of the smaller denominational bodies whose limited numbers and resources made it impossible for them to create effective agencies of their own. These found in the Commission a natural outlet for their energy and responded liberally to its appeal for money and men.

Of the special pieces of work undertaken by the Commission on behalf of the churches, the following deserve a word of further mention: first, the work done by the Commission in interpreting the needs of the Negro troops to the responsible authorities;[2] secondly, its success in bringing about a united approach of the churches to the munition workers employed in the large plants operated by the government; and finally, its work in securing from the army authorities for candidates for the ministry the privilege of continuing their professional studies under army auspices during the period between the signing of the armistice and their mustering out of the service.

In the office of the Secretary of War at Washington, there gathered for conference one day early in the war a group of seventeen men. They had been brought together at the invitation

[1] Cf. p. 96.
[2] Cf. "War-Time Agencies of the Churches," pp. 167, 168.

of the War-Time Commission to talk over with the representatives of the government the needs of the Negro troops. They came both from the North and from the South. Half were white and half were colored. The spokesman of the committee was Dr. Ashby Jones, the son of Robert E. Lee's old chaplain. In that impressive historic setting, with Grant and Sherman and Sheridan looking down from their places on the wall, this son of the Confederacy, addressing a general of the United States Army, also born south of Mason and Dixon's line, spoke on behalf of colored soldiers fighting side by side with white men in a cause which was now the common cause of all Americans—the defence of liberty under law.

The service of the Commission to the munition workers was rendered through the Joint Committee on War Production Communities.[1] This was an interdenominational committee including representatives of the Home Mission Boards and of the Associations, both men and women. Through this committee one hundred and fifteen different communities were surveyed and thirty others visited, and the information gained was put at the disposal of the interested parties. A plan of common action was adopted as a result of which the different bodies represented co-operated in establishing Liberty churches in centres where denominational work was impossible and in securing the support of these churches by the co-operating denominations under a plan mutually agreed upon. In other communities where it was possible to work through denominational agencies, the committee succeeded in bringing about effective co-operation between the bodies represented. In these plans the two Associations heartily co-operated.

The work for prospective theological students was carried on through the Committee on Recruiting and Training for the Work of the Church at Home and Abroad, an interdenominational committee including well-known educators like Presidents J. Ross Stevenson and William Douglas Mackenzie, as well as representatives of the Boards of Education of the churches and of the Young Men's Christian Association. Through this committee a united front was presented to the army authorities and privileges gained for Protestant theological students which could not have been obtained in any other way. Under the arrangement made possible by this

[1] Cf. "War-Time Agencies of the Churches," pp. 193–199.

committee more than one hundred students of different denominations carried on their studies in theology in selected universities in England and Scotland for a number of months, and but for an unfortunate delay in the time of the announcement of the plan this number would have been largely increased.

Thus serving as a clearing-house of information, a co-ordinating agency, and, when desired, a means of joint administration, the General War-Time Commission enabled the churches to face their new problems and responsibilities together. In the war work of the churches it is not too much to say that unity was not only worked for but to a very considerable degree achieved.

This unity came to clearest expression in the Interchurch Emergency Campaign—a campaign carried on by fourteen of the larger denominations to secure the funds needed for their common war work. In this campaign the needs of the General War-Time Commission were presented side by side with the needs of the various denominational war commissions, and provision was made for the former in the budgets of the latter. In the course of the campaign, impressive meetings were held in the interests of Christian unity in a number of different cities, the most notable being that held in the Cathedral of St. John the Divine at the invitation of Bishop Greer.[1]

This gratifying result was possible because of the scrupulous care with which the Commission observed the limitations of its authority. Including members of widely different bodies, representing different and often conflicting ideals of religious duty, it was careful not to go further than its constituent bodies would approve. The executive committee met every two weeks during the war, and its members, all of them responsible officers of important organizations, came to know and to trust one another. Many a difficulty, which at first sight seemed insuperable, yielded to persistent attack, and unities were revealed which surprised those who discovered them.

A second reason which accounted for the success of the Commission was the fact that though unofficial in character, it was composed of men who were themselves officials. The men who

---

[1] At this meeting, which was addressed by representatives of the government and of different denominations, the building was packed to the doors and many hundreds could not gain admission.

served on its executive committee were not only persons who commanded the confidence of the religious denominations to which they belonged, but who because of their positions as secretaries of the denominational war commissions were able to carry their bodies with them in any course of action they recommended. This accounts for the generous contributions made to the funds of the Commission by the co-operating bodies, contributions which, coming as they did from the denominational treasuries, relieved the Commission after the first few months of the necessity of making any appeal to individuals and made its work in the fullest sense representative of the Church as a whole.

As a visible symbol of the spirit of the Commission we may take the chapel at Camp Upton. Midway between the administration building of the Young Men's Christian Association and the headquarters of the Knights of Columbus, a visitor to this camp might have seen an attractive building which bore the title, "Church Headquarters." It had a chapel of dignity and beauty, where under conditions that ministered to reverence the more sacred and more intimate services of religion could be conducted. It had offices for pastoral conference, where chaplains, regular or voluntary, met men for private interviews on matters of personal religion. It had residence rooms for visiting clergymen, and above all a conference room, where from week to week chaplains and other religious workers met to take counsel for the spiritual interests of the camp as a whole. The building was erected and paid for by seven different denominations [1] acting through the General War-Time Commission. It was opened with a service participated in by Protestants, Roman Catholics, and Jews, at which the commanding general delivered the address. From that time until the camp was discontinued in 1920 it was used by all the religious forces of the camp, chaplains, Y. M. C. A. secretaries, and voluntary workers, in the utmost sympathy and harmony.

Far more important than any particular thing which the Commission did was its demonstration of the fact that at a critical time it was possible for American Protestants to act together. Through the Commission not only the bodies which were constituent members of the Federal Council, but churches like the

[1] Presbyterian, Episcopal, Congregational, Lutheran, Baptist, Methodist, and Reformed.

Lutheran, the Episcopal, and the Southern Baptist which had hitherto had no direct representation in the Council,[1] found an organ of common expression. In this fact above all others lies our hope for the future. What has been done once can be done again. It must be done again unless we are to slip back into the old habits of isolation and rivalry from which for a brief few months we escaped into a larger and more unselfish life.

6. *The Committee on the War and the Religious Outlook*

In the light of these facts we must appreciate the significance of the last of the committees of the General War-Time Commission, one which, while it had its inception during the war, has continued to function in time of peace. We refer to the Committee on the War and the Religious Outlook.[2]

Long before the war was over those who were responsible for the work of the Commission began to realize that when peace came their work would be only half done. There would be problems connected with demobilization quite as serious as any which had been faced by the churches during the war; and the whole question of after-war conditions and plans would require careful study and preparation for which it was impossible to begin to get ready too soon. With this in view, on April 2, 1918, the Committee on the War and the Religious Outlook was formed. This was an interdenominational committee of some thirty members, consisting of representatives of the larger Protestant churches as well as of the two Christian Associations. It was constituted by the joint action of the General War-Time Commission of the Churches and of the Federal Council of the Churches of Christ in America. Its purpose, as defined at the time of its appointment, was "to consider the state of religion as revealed or affected by the war, with special reference to the duty and opportunity of the churches, and to prepare its findings for submission to the churches." Conceived under the shadow of war strain and of war responsibility, and beginning its work while the Armistice was still in the in-

---

[1] It is true that the Episcopal Church co-operates with the Council through its Commissions on Social Service and Christian Unity, but it is not a constituent member of the Council.

[2] Cf. the author's pamphlet, "The Church Facing the Future," published by the Federal Council, 1921.

definite future, it has continued its studies during the years of reconstruction, and found the reasons which at first sight seemed to justify its appointment reinforced by a closer acquaintance with the new conditions under which the major part of its work has been done. Indeed, if the Committee rightly interprets the significance of its work, it is to be understood less as a contribution to a passing emergency than as a new method of approach to problems which are always with us—an experiment in co-operative thinking which, if it has any measure of success, will warrant its repetition or continuance.

While created by the initiative of the Federal Council and the General War-Time Commission as a result of their conviction that the war had laid upon the churches the duty of the most thorough self-examination, the Committee was given entire freedom to act according to its own judgment as to method of procedure, subjects to be studied, and persons to be associated in the work. Originally consisting of nine members, it has added to its number until its present membership consists of twenty-eight, representing nine different denominations, as well as the two Christian Associations. In addition, a large number of other persons—one hundred and twenty-three in all—have served on its sub-committees, and to a still larger number it is indebted for active assistance and helpful suggestions. It has already to its credit five substantial volumes, with a sixth to follow,[1] as well as a number of pamphlets on important contemporaneous issues.[2]

[1] The volumes referred to above are "The War and Religion: A Bibliography," 1919; "Religion Among American Men: As Revealed by a Study of Conditions in the Army," 1920; "The Missionary Outlook in the Light of the War," 1920; "The Church and Industrial Reconstruction," 1920; "Christian Unity: Its Principles and Possibilities," 1921, Association Press, New York. A sixth volume is soon to appear entitled, "The Teaching Work of the Church." With the appearance of this volume, the work of the Committee will be completed.

[2] Robert E. Speer, "The War and the Religious Outlook," 1919; W. H. P. Faunce, "Christian Principles Essential to a New World Order," 1919; Harry Emerson Fosdick, "The Church's Message to the Nation," 1919; Francis J. McConnell, "Christian Principles and Industrial Reconstruction," 1919; William Douglas Mackenzie, "The Church and Religious Education," 1919; William P. Shriver, "The New Home Mission of the Church," 1919; Herbert N. Shenton, "Christian Aspects of Economic Reconstruction," 1920; Rhoda E. McCulloch, "The War and the Woman Point of View," 1920; Charles W. Gilkey, "The Local Church After the War," 1920. Association Press, New York.

It had been hoped that these studies would be far enough advanced before peace came to serve as a contribution toward a peace policy for the Church. Unfortunately this was not the case. When in November, 1918, the Armistice was declared, it found both church and nation no less unprepared than at the outbreak of war. In the unexpected relief at the sudden lifting of the war cloud, future difficulties and dangers were under-estimated. The war machinery of the churches was discarded as rapidly as it had been devised. The Church like the nation moved forward into the new conditions introduced by demobilization with little suspicion of the gravity of the issues confronting it.

CHAPTER VII

1. *The Situation in Which the War Left the Church*

WE have seen where the war found the Church. We have seen what the Church learned in the war. It remains to point out where the war has left the Church; to show in what spirit and with what resources the Church is facing the problems of the new day.

Three things the war did for the churches. It showed them the inadequacy of their present organization and methods; it revealed to them the existence of unsuspected resources; it inspired them with an extravagant hope. The inadequacy consisted in the churches' failure to provide the necessary organization for effective co-operation. The resources were the latent idealism in the heart of the American people and their undreamed-of capacity for self-sacrifice in a worthy cause. The hope was that by some simple concerted effort these resources might be effectively mobilized for the service of religion, and the churches, which had showed that they could work together during the war, might continue their united effort on an even larger scale in time of peace.

In the first place, the war revealed to the churches the inadequacy of the present denominational system. Individuals in the different churches had long realized this inadequacy. Their knowledge was now shared with multitudes of Christians. They realized for the first time the price they had been paying for the independence in which they had gloried. They had had the experience of working together for a great cause and they had found it satisfying and inspiring.

But the war taught them more than this. It revealed to them the latent possibilities in human nature and not least in themselves. It translated the great words about sacrifice and service which had been so often on their lips into sober and familiar realities. Old words about the cross took on a new meaning. They realized, as they had never realized before, what it meant

114

to serve a Master who, though He was rich, yet for their sakes had become poor. They, too, had given up what they most prized and had been content to make the sacrifice.

What they had experienced in themselves they had witnessed in others. Men and women outside the Christian church, who made no profession of religion, people whom they had regarded as narrow and selfish, often as downright bad, had responded, like themselves, to the country's call. They perceived that the capacity for sacrifice is not confined to any group or creed; that it is a human capacity, waiting only the occasion to call it forth, and with this insight came a great desire to utilize this capacity in the cause of religion.

Out of this double insight—of failure and of capacity—was born a great hope—the hope that the lessons the war had taught might be learned at once and for all time; that the churches, confronted by so splendid an opportunity, might meet the challenge in a spirit as splendid; might throw aside all pettiness and provinciality, pride of sect or advantage of position, and ask only what each could contribute to the welfare of the whole. This ideal of a national church, conscious of its aim and of its power, cherished now and again by some exceptional spirit, became for one brief moment the inspiring motive of multitudes of Christians.

2. *The Interchurch World Movement as the Attempt to Express the Church's Post-War Ideals in Action. The Reasons for its Failure*

The most signal expression of this hope was the Interchurch World Movement.[1] It crystallized into a definite programme the emotions and aspirations called forth by the war. It was the religious counterpart of the League of Nations, and it shared the splendor and the weakness of that daring venture.

We are too near both these great experiments to judge them

[1] On the Interchurch World Movement cf. "Handbook of the Interchurch World Movement," New York, 1919; "World Survey by the Interchurch World Movement," two volumes, New York, 1920. Cf. also Oldham, "The Interchurch World Movement: Its Possibilities and Problems," in the *International Review of Missions,* Vol. IX, pp. 182 sq. "The Truth About the Interchurch, by a member of the General Committee," *Christian Work,* December 11, December 18, 1920; "Christian Unity: Its Principles and Possibilities," pp. 140 sq.

justly. In our reaction from our extravagant hopes it is easy for us to exaggerate their weakness and their failure. No great ideal is ever realized over-night, and it may well be that the historian of the spiritual progress of mankind will look back to these two great essays in co-operative endeavor as landmarks by which to date the progress of the race. We must be content with the more modest task of learning what they can teach us of the spiritual state of America immediately after the war.

The Interchurch World Movement was the attempt to unite all the benevolent and missionary agencies of American Protestantism in a single campaign for money, men, and spiritual power. It originated in a conference of representatives of various missionary and benevolent boards held in December, 1918, and differed from previous efforts of a similar nature in that it included all forms of the Church's work both at home and abroad. Its General Committee early defined the movement as "a co-operative effort of the missionary, educational, and other benevolent agencies of the, evangelical churches of the United States and of Canada to survey unitedly their present common tasks and simultaneously and together to secure the necessary resources of men and money and power required for these tasks." [1]

The purposes which the movement set for itself were as follows: [2]

"1. To make a thorough analysis of the total world task of the church, locality by locality and item by item, to the end that neglected fields might be discovered; important existing work strengthened; unjustifiable work eliminated; and helpful relationships between all agencies and workers established.

"2. To conduct a continuous campaign of education, making use of ascertained facts, projected upon broad and varied lines and carried out upon a scale adequate to secure the attention of the nation at large, and, if possible, to convince the judgment and awake the interest of millions of people now wholly or largely untouched by Christ's call to world service.

"3. To give co-operative leadership to the Church in the fields of industrial relations, philanthropy, evangelism, and education, to

[1] Cf. "Christian Unity: Its Principles and Possibilities," p. 140.
[2] *Op. cit.,* p. 143.

the end that the Church may more wisely and amply meet her obligations in these areas of service.

"4. To conduct a campaign for recruits to the ministry and mission service.

"5. To make simultaneous and united appeal for funds, sufficient in amount to support the sort of effort at home and abroad demanded by the conditions of the hour."

Beginning as a voluntary enterprise of the participating boards, the work soon assumed such proportions that the official endorsement of the parent bodies proved necessary. The interest of the co-operating churches was recognized in the provision adopted in September, 1919, that at least two-thirds of the membership of the General Committee should consist of persons approved by the various denominations.

Those who were active in the movement disclaimed any purpose to set up a new agency with independent administrative powers or even to undertake to determine the policy of the co-operating churches. They confined their purpose to the "ascertaining and portraying of facts, to calling the attention of the churches and their agencies to the needs revealed by these facts, and to encouraging the churches, through co-operative effort, to work out the problems involved."[1] Yet in the nature of the case the large scale on which the movement was projected, the number of persons employed, and the vast sums of money expended gave those who were directing it a power out of proportion to the modesty of their professions.

If the responsibility of the movement to the co-operating churches was recognized in the statement just quoted, its relation to the existing interdenominational agencies was left undefined. No provision was made for these in the budget which was to be raised[2] and their part in shaping the Church's policy on the basis of the facts to be disclosed was left for the future to determine. The plan of the Interchurch Movement contemplated two things only: the raising of the budgets of the different co-operating denominations as these should be determined by the preliminary survey, and

[1] Statement of the General Committee at Atlantic City in January, 1920, quoted in "Christian Unity," p. 141.

[2] The only exception was in the case of the Missionary Education Movement.

an appeal to friendly citizens, both within and without the Church, for an extra sum which would not only defray the expenses of the movement, but provide a margin for worthy objects long neglected in the denominational field. This sum was placed at forty million dollars.

In its year and a half of existence the movement conducted an extensive and vigorous campaign of publicity through conferences, addresses, and the daily press; initiated surveys in the fields of home missions, foreign missions, and religious education; undertook through its Committee on Industrial Relations an investigation of the steel strike and both directly through its central office and in co-operation with the organizations of the various denominations canvassed the churches in the interest of the budgets which had been agreed upon. In the case of the denominational bodies a large measure of success was reached,[1] but the campaign among the friendly citizens was a serious disappointment. Scarcely three million dollars of the forty millions asked was raised and the denominations which had expected this fund to take care of the expenses of the movement were called upon to make contributions for this purpose from their own treasuries, which amounted in the case of the larger denominations to many hundred thousand dollars. The criticisms called forth by this result led to the appointment of a reorganization committee in 1920, which, while commending the movement for what it had already accomplished, recommended radical changes in its methods and ratio of expense. Some months later it was voted to discontinue the movement altogether and to turn over the survey material which it had gathered to other organizations.

The wide publicity given to the Interchurch World Movement and the extravagant hopes which it raised make it important to

---

[1] No exact statistics of the amount raised are available. An incomplete list furnished by the secretary of the movement puts the amounts actually received by the co-operating churches during the year from May, 1920, to May, 1921, at approximately $39,000,000. This list does not include the Methodists, who had already completed their campaign, and it takes no account of pledges which would greatly increase the total.

The total amount raised by all the co-operating bodies is put by a writer in the *Christian Work* at scarcely less than $200,000,000. This sum includes pledges covering a five-year period. Cf. "The Truth about the Interchurch," *op. cit.*, December 11, 1920, p. 713.

learn what it can teach us both as to the causes which inspired the movement and the reasons for its failure.

For one thing it teaches us the power of a great ideal to unite and inspire. No one who was present in the upper room on that momentous December day when the Interchurch World Movement was born [1] can forget the thrill of expectation which stirred those who had gathered there. They were men of long experience—secretaries of church boards, professors in theological seminaries, veteran workers in the cause of home and foreign missions, and they knew the weaknesses and limitations of the bodies they served to the full. But they had seen a vision—the vision of a united church uniting a divided world, and under the spell of what they saw all things seemed possible. Difficulties were waved aside, doubters were silenced. In the face of an opportunity so unparalleled there seemed but one thing to do, and that was to go forward.

What followed we know only too well. The causes which led to the failure of the movement have been so fully explained that it is needless to linger over them here—the failure to take account of the time element; the disposition to make expectation do duty for accomplishment; the difficulty of securing an efficient staff for a work which must be done quickly if at all; the lack of a proper sense of proportion as between income and outgo; above all, the failure to lay a sound basis for the work by the quiet conferences and careful planning which are essential to permanent success—these were some of the more obvious reasons for failure. But above and beyond all these, there were two which need more careful consideration, for they give us the key to our understanding of the situation in which the Church found itself after the war. The first was the failure to take account of the strength of the denominational spirit in the country; the second was inability to foresee the widespread moral reaction into which the sudden cessation from the strain of war would plunge the nation and the Church.

When the Interchurch World Movement was first conceived, those who were responsible for its initiation hoped to make it an

---

[1] The meeting which initiated the Interchurch World Movement was held at 25 Madison Avenue, New York City, on December 17, 1918, at the invitation of the Board of Foreign Missions of the Southern Presbyterian Church.

all embracing movement. They planned a single central committee in which all the different interests should be represented, not only the denominational church boards, and other official bodies, but the Christian Associations and similar voluntary agencies as well. It was their wish to provide a single treasury into which all monies contributed should be paid and from which the due proportion should be distributed to each of the co-operating agencies.[1]

But such an arrangement proved impossible to effect. The same influences which had led to the desire for effective interdenominational co-operation had been operating in the denominations as well. To them as well as to the Church at large the war had been a revelation at once of weakness and of strength—weakness in the ineffectiveness of their denominational organization, strength in the spiritual resources of their members. To them, too, the war came as a call to set their house in order, and the result appeared in a number of denominational forward movements, of which the Interchurch World Movement was compelled to take account.[2]

For one thing it found the denominations already committed to definite plans which had gone too far to be recalled, even had the will to change them been present. But more significant still

---

[1] Cf. "The Truth about the Interchurch," pp. 712, 714.

[2] A list of the more important movements is as follows: The New World Movement of the Northern Baptist Convention (now under the direction of the General Board of Promotion); the Forward Movement of the Christian Church; the Congregational World Movement; the Cumberland Presbyterian Educational Endowment Commission; the United Christian Missionary Society; the Centennial Movement of the Churches of God; the Department of Nation-Wide Campaign of the Presiding Bishop and Council of the Protestant Episcopal Church; the Forward Movement of the Evangelical Association; the Forward Movement of the Evangelical Synod; the Forward Movement of Friends in America; the Committee on Conservation and Advance of the Council of the Boards of Benevolence of the Methodist Episcopal Church; the Centenary Movement of the Methodist Episcopal Church, South; the Forward Movement in the Methodist Protestant Church; the Larger Life Movement of the Moravian Church; the New Era Movement of the Presbyterian Church in the U. S. A.; the Presbyterian (U. S.) Progressive Program; the Progress Campaign of the Reformed Church in America; the Forward Movement of the Reformed Church in the U. S.; the New Forward Movement of the Seventh Day Baptist General Conference; the United Enlistment Movement of the Church of the United Brethren in Christ; the Forward Movement of the United Evangelical Church; the New World Movement of the United Presbyterian Church.

it found a purpose to perfect and strengthen the denominational organization which left little energy and leisure for effective co-operation in a movement so ambitious as the Interchurch World Movement. In two important respects it proved necessary to modify the original plans. It was necessary, in the first place, in order to preserve the interchurch character of the movement, to restrict the co-operating bodies to the official agencies of the denominations; it was necessary, in the second place, to abandon the central treasury, except for the purpose of financing the movement itself, and for such further objects as the generosity of the general public might make possible.

A similar situation met the General War-Time Commission of the Churches on a smaller scale a year before, but it was dealt with in a different way. Here, too, it was at first proposed to finance the entire war work of the churches from a central treasury, and here, too, the plan was abandoned because of its conflict with the denominational programmes. All that it proved practicable to do was to provide for common publicity, as was done later by the Interchurch World Movement on a far larger scale. The cost of this publicity was assumed by the bodies which united in the campaign from the funds of their war commissions, whereas in the case of the Interchurch it was hoped to cover all the expenses of the movement from the contributions of friendly citizens. But there was this further difference between the two plans, that in the former case the expenses of the co-operative work carried on by the Commission itself were assumed by the co-operating bodies as a part of their own denominational programme, whereas, in the latter case, no provision at all was made for the interdenominational agencies like the Federal Council, the Home Missions Council, the Foreign Missions Conference, the Council of Church Boards of Education, etc., whose work corresponded in time of peace to the work done by the War-Time Commission in time of war. Thus the net result of the campaign, appealing as it did to the sources from which these agencies had been accustomed to draw their support, was to leave them for the moment weaker than before. The bond between the denominational and interdenominational programme which had been knit by the war was parted, and in the discouragement caused by the failure of the campaign, so far as its interdenominational features were concerned, many were led to lose faith in the co-operative programme of the churches.

One reason for what would otherwise appear a surprising oversight is doubtless to be found in the extravagant hopes entertained for the friendly citizens' campaign. From the funds raised in this way it was hoped to finance not only the movement itself, but also to take care of the interdenominational interests referred to above. The nearly complete failure of this campaign left these most important enterprises almost wholly unprovided for.

But even had the campaign been successful, the moral effect would have been different from that reached in the case of the General War-Time Commission. There the co-operating churches themselves became directly and wholly responsible for the interdenominational work done by the Commission. In this case the responsibility would have been assumed by the general public. But this would have left the interdenominational work interdenominational in name only and would have made of the Interchurch World Movement, in spite of the fact that it disclaimed responsibility for determining policies, the only really responsible agent directing the Church's work along interdenominational lines.

There was a deeper cause for the failure of the Interchurch World Movement, and that was the failure of its leaders to anticipate the psychological effect of the coming of peace. With the cessation of the long strain, there was a sudden let-down that manifested itself in unexpected and disheartening ways. Those who had carried responsibility bravely were now eager to throw it off. Those who had thought only for others now remembered that charity begins at home. Two years of self-denial and renunciation were followed by a feverish demand for excitement and self-indulgence. The prevailing spirit was intensified by the temper of the returning soldiers. Surfeited with the discipline of camp life and wearied with its unutterable monotony, they wanted change at any cost. The thought of new sacrifices and abnegations revolted them.

Their attitude to the prohibition amendment is a case in point. Even those who cared nothing for drinking were indignant that a question of such national importance should have been decided while they were away. They drank, not for the sake of drinking, but as an affirmation of personal liberty. Their attitude toward this question was symptomatic of a spirit which showed itself in other directions—in the extravagance in food and dress, in the mad thirst for pleasure, in the breaking down of the old standards of restraint between the sexes. All these phenomena of after-war psychology were natural—we now perceive, inevitable—results of the situation in which the country found itself.

This was not the atmosphere in which to launch such a movement as the Interchurch. It is easy to see this now; but at the time no one was wise enough to do so. Church and country were still under the spell of the past. Only gradually and by a process of disillusionment as painful as it was salutary did they wake to the realities of the present. When they did so, it was too late to correct the mistakes that had already been made.

We have an almost perfect parallel in the League of Nations. Here, too, an extraordinary situation gave birth to an extravagant hope which was disappointed because those who entertained it tried to crowd into a few short months results possible of attainment only through a slow process of education requiring years, if not decades. It is clear that such a situation presents dangers which can be guarded against only as they are understood.

3. *Dangers to be Guarded Against: (a) an Unreasonable Condemnation of the Denominational Spirit; (b) the Abandonment of the Co-operative Ideal*

To one who has lived through the exaltation of the war enthusiasm, the revival of the denominational spirit which we see to-day is hard to bear.[1] It seems a deliberate turning back upon the lessons plainly taught us—a definite refusal of the opportunity unexpectedly put in our hands. But there is another side to the matter. The denominational revival which we are witnessing does not necessarily mean loss of faith in the co-operative ideal. On the contrary, it may be a step toward its ultimate realization.

Our war experience has much to teach us here. It was not the presence of highly efficient denominational organizations which proved the greatest obstacle to our successful co-operation in

[1] For an exceptionally severe criticism of the denominational spirit as applied to missions, cf. McAfee, "Some Unchristian Aspects of Christian Missions," *Christian Century,* October 27, 1921.

the war, but their absence. For effective work more is needed than goodwill. There must be persons familiar with the situation and armed with ample power to act for the whole. But these were lacking in more than one important communion. It was not the denominations of Congregational polity that gave the most effective help to the General War-Time Commission, but highly organized churches like the Lutheran, the Episcopalian, and the Presbyterian —and if in the case of the Baptists there was a happy exception to the rule, it was because they had themselves become convinced of the weakness of their former methods and had set themselves resolutely to correct them.[1] A chain is only as strong as its weakest link, and if the churches are to co-operate effectively with one another, they must first learn to co-operate effectively within themselves.

This fact should not blind us to the dangers of the denominational spirit or the fact that added strength always carries with it a temptation to be indifferent to the needs of others. We shall have abundant occasion to be reminded of this as we proceed. But it should serve to guard us against unqualified condemnation of a tendency which may well prove—when seen in its larger perspective—to have its own contribution to make to the progress of the Kingdom of God.

For this reason the present revival of denominational loyalty is not wholly to be regretted. Through the various denominational movements which the last two years have brought into being—the Methodist Centenary, the Presbyterian New Era, the Baptist New World Movement, and the others, new powers have been released and new resources uncovered, which, if rightly guided, are full of promise for the future of the American Church. The vision of a new day has been brought to many a rural community hitherto untouched by the spirit of progress. Many a weak church has learned to its surprise that it had money enough and to spare. These facts we must take into account if we would estimate the real significance of the Interchurch World Movement. Its campaign for its own funds may have failed signally. But the great totals rolled up for the various denominational movements which co-operated in it are the best proof that

[1] Cf. p. 82.

its message found a wider hearing than the official returns would lead one to suppose.

To return to our parallel of the League of Nations. Here, too, the apparent failure may prove less serious and less complete than at first appeared. The opposition to the plan as first proposed did not spring wholly from selfish and unworthy motives. In part it was due to an unwillingness to commit to a distant and already over-burdened body the decision of questions which could only be rightly worked out with the co-operation of those immediately concerned. As with churches, so with nations, only the union of the strong with the strong produces strength, and for the realization of the great ideal which has appealed so persuasively to the men of our day—a league of free peoples for the preservation of world peace—we must first have peoples who are free and who desire peace.

For this reason the present period of hesitation and discussion is not without its compensations. Inquiry into the reason for the failure of the plan first proposed is having an important educational effect upon the different nations. In our own country especially it is showing us faults in our own organization and spirit which we must remedy if we are ever to hope to co-operate effectively with other peoples in international affairs. Conversely it is showing us how impossible it is for us to deal effectively even with our own domestic affairs unless we assume a right attitude toward the other peoples with whose destiny our own is ever more inextricably interwoven. As in the Church the choice is not between denominationalism and interdenominationalism but between the right and the wrong kind of each, so in the nation the antithesis is not between nationalism and internationalism but between the right and the wrong type of each. The more earnestly we seek our own highest interests, the more inevitably we shall be compelled to seek the interests of others and *vice versa*.

The first danger to be guarded against, then, is an unreasonable condemnation of the denominational spirit. But there is another danger even greater, and that is that in our disappointment at immediate failure we may lose faith in ultimate victory. For the Christian the one unpardonable sin is lack of faith. If the vision that we saw of a united Church seemed to our enthusiasm nearer than the facts warrant, that does not prove that it was a delusion. What we learned of man's deepest self in those days of exceptional testing was a true revelation. All that is necessary is for us to use it in the right way.

A year after the war ended an American visitor found his way to England, anxious to learn how the fiery trial of those five years had affected a country to which he owed much and which he had left in the fall of 1914, when the war had scarcely begun. It was a painful experience. Weariness and depression were everywhere evident. One looked in vain for any large movement for national, or for international, reconstruction. To the questions: "What are you doing to get ready for the new day? What is being planned to carry out the programme of the Archbishop's commissions?" [1] this answer was made: "You have come too soon. We are tired and need rest. Give us another five years and you will find a different situation. This is not the time to act, but to think and to plan." The longer the visitor stayed in England and the more he learned of what was really going on in the minds and the hearts of the men and women to whom the future belongs, the more he was convinced that this answer was correct.

It is in a similar spirit that we must judge the present situation in the American Church. This is a period for thought and for preparation. What we have learned about the spiritual resources of the country and of the Church we shall never forget. But we have not yet learned how to make effective use of the resources we have discovered. For this time is needed and patience—the open mind and the open heart. In the meantime let us do the things that lie nearest at hand, the obvious and necessary things in our parishes and in our denominations. They will put us just so much farther forward when the time comes for the larger co-operative movements which so certainly lie ahead.

[1] At the conclusion of the war the Archbishops of Canterbury and York appointed a number of commissions to study various phases of the church's post-war duty and to make recommendations. The most important of these dealt with such subjects as the following: "The Teaching Office of the Church"; "The Worship of the Church"; "The Evangelistic Work of the Church"; "Administrative Reform of the Church"; "Christianity and Industrial Problems."

4. *The Present Condition and Prospects of the Protestant Ministry*

Before we leave this preliminary stage of our discussion there is one more question which needs to be raised, and that is the effect of the present situation upon the men who have the most direct interest in the success of the Church—its ministers.

When the war ended, there was a very general hope on the part of those who were responsible for the leadership of the Church that there would be a great accession to the number of candidates for the ministry. That expectation has not as yet been realized. At first, indeed, it seemed as if the tendency were the other way. Many seminaries reported a falling off in attendance, and in more than one of the larger communions it seemed as if the question of the supply for the ministry might become a serious one. Later developments have been more reassuring.[1] Taking the country as a whole, the number of students entering the seminaries is increasing and the reports as to their quality are excellent. It is too soon, however, to draw any conclusion from the limited evidence which is available. In what follows we shall ignore the special influences which the war has set in motion and consider the prospects of the ministry in the light of the general situation which our previous study has revealed.

When we approach the matter from this point of view we must admit that there is matter for disquietude. Those who are acquainted with conditions in ministerial circles have observed a certain restlessness and anxiety on the part of many of their clerical friends. It is not that they are less loyal to the cause to which they have given their lives or less convinced of the unique opportunity before the Christian ministry. On the contrary, there has never been an age when that opportunity was greater or when a more impressive appeal could be made to young men and women

---

[1] Cf. the careful study by O. D. Foster, "Student Attendance at the Protestant Theological Seminaries," in *Christian Education,* December, 1920; also Robert L. Kelly, "The Rising Tide of Ministerial Enlistment," *Christian Work,* October 29, 1921. The report of the Life Work Committee of the Council of Church Boards of Education at their meeting in January, 1921, shows a marked increase over the preceding year in the enrollment in the theological seminaries of practically all the Protestant denominations.

to enter the service of the Church. But there is a feeling that the conditions under which the rank and file of ministers are working are not such as to provide an adequate outlet for their best powers and that the profession as a profession does not furnish that guarantee of permanent employment which the wise man naturally seeks in the choice of his life work. In the past one of the great sources of supply for the ministry has been the sons of the manse, and the manse is to-day the greatest single influence in leading men into the ministry. It is all the more significant that now and again one finds a minister shaking his head over the thought of his son's following him in his profession and raising the question in his own mind whether he could not serve God more effectively in some other way.

This is due in no small part to the increasing appeal of other forms of life work. The time when the ministry had a *prima facie* claim upon any man who desired to lead an altruistic life is long past. There are many other professions which open the way to an unselfish career—medicine, philanthropy in its various forms, teaching. Even business is losing its exclusive association with money-getting and is coming to be regarded in a new light as a form of public service. From a letter from a young man looking forward to international banking as a life work, I quote the following lines written under the impulse of the new contacts which service in a foreign country had brought about:

"I want to be a force some day in the training and inspiring of our new professional foreign banking class. I want them to be filled with the idea that their only excuse for existing is the fulfilling of a certain essential economic function, considering themselves as servants of both their own and other peoples, and receiving compensation only in proportion 'as the laborer is worthy of his hire.' Only in this frame of mind can they justify their existence in a socially-minded world. They are the real ambassadors of their country. On them rests the real development of the country's foreign policy. They work with the forces that have caused wars to be fought, and only by their help and the help of other business men can the wisest and most lofty plans of statesmen be given content and meaning."

This is typical of what more than one young man is thinking to-day whose spirit a generation or even a decade ago would have led him into the ministry. The labor movement is attracting not a few men of this type. Graduates of theological seminaries of ripe intellectual power and thoroughgoing consecration are to-day finding scope as labor leaders for the gifts which others of their fellow-students are exercising in the ministry.

But quite apart from the competition of other forms of service, there are conditions in the ministry itself which give cause for serious thought. For one thing the salary paid the average minister is such as to make one wonder how it is possible for him to support a family without outside help. As a matter of fact, the statistics which we have already quoted show that the 63,000 ministers who report full salaries received on an average less than $1,100 a year.[1] So striking are these figures that defenders of the United States Steel Corporation against the criticism of the Interchurch Report found it a convenient retort to say, in answer to the contention that the corporation did not pay a living wage, that the churches would do well to raise their own salaries to the point which made a decent living possible before they undertook to criticize what others were doing.

Yet necessary as it is to take account of this matter of salary in estimating the present appeal of the ministry as a life work, it is not the determining factor. The ministry has never promised large financial rewards, and those who are attracted to it by the opportunity of service it offers will not be deterred by the sacrifices it entails. All such men ask is a living wage and some decent guarantee for old age, and the legitimacy of this request is being generally recognized. Signs are not wanting that the same readjustment of the salary scale which we have seen in the teaching profession is taking place in the ministry, and the attempt of the larger denominations to establish pension funds to care for the minister and his family in sickness and old age is meeting with gratifying success.[2] The more influential pulpits

[1] It should be remembered that these figures, taken from the United States Census returns for 1916, do not furnish us with such relevant facts as whether the minister receives a manse as well as a salary, nor, in the case of ministers serving more than one congregation, whether the salary represents the total amount received from all sources, or only that paid by a single congregation.

On this matter of ministerial salary, cf. the statistics gathered by the Interchurch World Movement, *World Survey*, American volume, pp. 267 sq.

[2] The present capital of the combined pension and annuity funds of the Congregational, Protestant Episcopal, Methodist Episcopal, Presbyterian, and Northern Baptist churches already totals over $50,000,000.

of the large denominations care generously for their ministers, and the standard of compensation for the ministry as a whole is steadily rising.

More serious in its bearing upon the prospects of the Christian ministry is the condition which lies back of the low salary which the average minister receives. His salary is small because his congregation is small, and his congregation is small because there are so many churches. The spirit of individual initiative and independence which, from one point of view, has been the strength of the American church here reveals its characteristic weakness. Churches have been planted all over America—Baptist, Presbyterian, Methodist, as the case may be, but no one has stopped to ask whether a particular church was needed in a particular place or whether a combination of forces would not have made possible a stronger and a more effective appeal. We are to study elsewhere the effects of this disastrous policy, or rather lack of policy, upon the local church and to consider what steps are being taken to bring about a change.[1] We are now speaking of the effects of the policy upon the life of the minister himself.

It must be admitted that these have been most unfortunate. Conditions have been created which have made it difficult for a man of initiative and ability to find adequate scope for his powers in many of our Protestant churches. Christian people have been accustomed to think of their church as designed to minister to their own private interests and needs rather than as a part of the great spiritual enterprise that has for its purpose the bringing in of the Kingdom of God. For a small task only a small man is needed, and the suspicion that the ministry as at present organized offers a man a little job is one of the most serious obstacles in the way of attracting strong men to the profession.

It is not strange, then, that we should find a large part of the Christian ministry recruited from men who have not had a college or even a seminary training. This is perhaps natural in bodies like the Baptist and Methodist which have been doing work on the firing-line and make large use of an itinerant ministry. But it is true also of churches which inherit a different tradition and have long prided themselves upon their high standard

[1] Cf. Chapter XI.

of ministerial education. Recent figures show that of the present Congregational ministry, large numbers have not had a college education,[1] and the condition in the Presbyterian Church is not dissimilar. This is an inevitable result of the unsatisfactory condition to which reference has already been made, and we shall not expect any great improvement in the character of our ministerial supply until we alter the character of the demand which that supply is designed to meet.

It is true that there is abundant evidence on the other side. In every part of the Church, in city and in country, we find contented and successful ministers proving by their present experience that the ministry to-day offers scope for the best powers of the strongest men. At no time in its history has the Church been able to offer the man of independence and initiative a more varied field of service. At no time has there been a larger constituency conscious of their need of the kind of ministry that the Church alone can render. The fact remains that in wide sections of the country the old, narrow, self-satisfied spirit still lives on. Until that is banished we must expect to find young men who want to make their life tell to the uttermost looking doubtfully at the Christian ministry.

One more difficulty remains to be named, in some respects the most perplexing of all, and that is the insecurity of the minister's tenure. Let us suppose a minister fairly started in his career, happy and successful in his work. What guarantee has he that this success will continue? We have all heard of the ministerial dead-line, that mysterious line as invisible as the equator which separates the years of a man's active work from the time when he suddenly finds that his services are no longer in demand. There is such a line in other professions than the ministry. In teaching it lies somewhere between sixty-five and seventy. The time when a man becomes eligible for a Carnegie pension would be a convenient way of indicating it. But in the ministry this line is determined by public opinion, and public opinion has been pushing it farther and farther back, until to-day

[1] The Secretary of the National Council of Congregational Churches expresses the judgment based upon the information at present available that "probably not more than one-half of the Congregational ministers in the United States are college or seminary men."

we are told that it is nearer fifty than sixty.[1]   Just when a man ought to be reaching his ripest power, just when many a man has really reached his ripest power, he finds himself pushed aside for younger men.

Two causes have combined to produce this unfortunate and, let us hope, temporary state of affairs. The first is the lack of any adequate system for locating ministers; the second the same narrow and individualistic conception of the Church to which we have already more than once referred.

Most serious of all the consequences of the decentralizing tendency in American Christianity is the lack of any central authority which is responsible for the placing of the individual minister in the field where he is fitted to do his best work. Different churches have their committees on supply, some local, some national,[2] but in the great majority of cases the minister finds his job by the same hit-or-miss system which has hitherto regulated employment in other industries. The Methodist Church alone, with its system of rotation in office, has been able completely to solve the difficulty. In the Methodist Church there is a place for every man and a man for every place, and some one whose business it is to put the man in the place. The Episcopal Church through its diocesan system comes next, but the bishops are limited in what they can do by the powers of the local congregation.

But the lack of provision for any central means of placing ministers is only the outward sign of a deeper and more fundamental cause. This is the lack of a realizing sense of the essential unity of the Church's work. The local congregation is thought of as an independent unit to be managed by its officers

[1] Cf. the suggestive article in the *Continent* for March 2, 1922, "Why I Have Lost Hope," by a pastor fifty years old.

[2] The most noteworthy example of the latter method is the Presbyterian Church in the U. S. A. which has created a national Department of Vacancy and Supply with its headquarters in Columbus, Ohio. From this centre an effort is being made to create similar committees in every synod and presbytery, through which the problem of locating ministers can be dealt with in a self-respecting way. In the churches of Congregational polity little has as yet been done. A well-known Baptist minister, being asked as to the method followed in his own communion, answered, "With us it is every man for himself and the devil take the hindmost." Light on present conditions in the Congregational churches is shed by a recent pamphlet issued by the Congregational Educational Society entitled, "American Congregationalism and Our Pastorless Churches," 1921.

on business principles with the primary aim of making both ends meet, rather than as a part of a great spiritual society in which each unit co-operates with the others in work for a common cause. With such a system we cannot but expect to find waste in the human material with which the system is concerned. There are ways of dealing with the problem of the older man in the ministry just as there are ways of dealing with the older man in other walks of life, but there is no way which does not require the co-operation of all those responsible for the Church's work in a common plan which covers the field as a whole.[1]

We have a suggestion of what may be done in the case of our mission boards, both home and foreign. Here the missionary enterprise is conceived as a unit and each missionary is sent to the place in the field for which he is believed to be best fitted and transferred from place to place as experience shows that such change is needed. More is accomplished by this than a change of machinery. A new spirit is introduced into the entire enterprise, a sense of common responsibility and brotherhood which dignifies the work of each individual who takes part in it.

Such a conception of the Christian ministry is needed in the Church at large. The older individualism is breaking down and a new spirit is abroad in the churches, but it has not yet devised the proper machinery for its expression. If in what has thus far been said emphasis has been laid upon the weakness of our present system, this is not due to any lack of confidence in the future of the ministry or doubt that to-day, as in every past age, the ministry offers the man of ability and consecration the finest of all fields of service, but rather to call attention to the greatness of the issues at stake and to reinforce those influences in the Church which are working for a better day. What these influences are we shall consider in the chapters that follow.

[1] One of the finest pieces of work done in the war was done by a Presbyterian minister over sixty years of age, who entered one of the large industrial establishments in a Western city as welfare worker. Through his tact and resourcefulness he so altered the morale of the workers that the output of the plant more than doubled. Yet this same man had been seeking a church in vain for years.

PART III

DEFINING THE IDEAL

CHAPTER VIII

1. *Principles which Determine Our Ideal for the Church*

THUS far we have been giving a bird's-eye view of the situation before the Church. We have described that situation as it meets us in the life of the individual Christian, in the country as a whole, and in the world at large. We have seen a number of independent and conflicting factors operating, some old, some new, presenting baffling problems in the field of education, of politics, of social and industrial reform. But there is one problem which is more important and more perplexing than all the rest, and that is the nature of the Church itself. What exactly is the function of the Church in human society and what must it become if it is to realize the divine ideal? Interesting as it is to learn what the churches have been doing in the last dozen years, it is still more important to know what they have been *thinking;* for upon the clear conception of an ideal depends in no small measure the ability to realize it.

There is no ready-made source of such information. Unlike Roman Catholicism, Protestantism has no official spokesman to define the Church's ideal. That ideal shapes itself little by little in the minds of multitudes of men, but few formulate their conclusions in clear and concise form. We must glean our information here and there from the books of individuals and of social groups, from the action of official bodies in times of crisis or responsibility, from the press, religious and secular; above all, from the trend of events which express more accurately than words can do the unconscious faith of men. We must be on our guard against the ghosts of which we have said that history is full— ideas and movements which have had their day but still maintain the semblance of life. Especially important for our purpose are

[1] Cf. W. Adams Brown, "The Old Theology and the New," *The Harvard Theological Review,* Vol. IV, pp. 1-24.

the tendencies which appear in student circles and in groups of thinking men, old and young. These, too, we must use with caution, remembering that permanence is the one sure test of truth and correcting present impressions by the longer look.

Some truths we may take for granted as having been confirmed by the experience of the past few years: first, that the primary concern of the Church is with religion; secondly, that the mission of the Christian Church is to interpret and to illustrate the principles of the Christian religion, and to win men everywhere to allegiance to Jesus; thirdly, that it is the special responsibility of the Protestant churches to guard what has been won by the Protestant emphasis upon freedom, and to work out appropriate forms in which freedom may express itself in unity.

It seems elementary to say that the primary concern of the Church is with religion. But it is none the less necessary to do so. The Church exists to remind men of the fact of God and to help them to realize their personal relation to Him. Many other activities it shares with other institutions. Worship is its specialty.

But there are various forms of religion, and each has its own church. The mission of the Christian Church is to witness to the revelation which God has made of Himself through Jesus Christ. This carries with it a distinct philosophy of life and a corresponding view of human duty and destiny. The Christian believes that there is one God who is all men's Father, who cares for their welfare and seeks their salvation, one Master who came to save the world and who has given in His own person the supreme demonstration of self-sacrificing love, one Spirit who pleads with men to be reconciled with God, to accept His forgiveness, and to take as their standard of conduct and service the example of Jesus.

This gives the Christian religion a point of contact with the wider human problems of which we have been speaking. They are not irrelevant to the main business of the Church, which is to be a witness to God. For God as revealed by Christ is interested in men, cares for their welfare, and wishes His human children to share His redemptive purpose.

The Christian therefore knows that the mission of the Church must be as broad as humanity. He has learned from his Master that each human individual is a child of God and a potential member of his Kingdom. Difference of nationality, race, or class must therefore be included within a larger unity. Because Christ broke down the middle wall of partition between Jew and Gentile and offered salvation freely to men of every race, the Church must be a brotherhood as wide as mankind.

This sets the Christian Church its distinctive task, which is not only to satisfy our need of worship but also to put before men the character of the God who is to be worshipped, and the life He requires of His worshippers. This the Church must do as Jesus did, by making a direct appeal to the conscience of each individual. There is no wholesale way of saving men. Each must face the supreme issues for himself and decide accordingly. Through all the chords of the Social Gospel should run the deep undertone of personal religion.

One further conclusion we may presuppose, and that is the importance of conserving the gains won for mankind by the Protestant Reformation through its emphasis upon freedom. This follows from what we have already said of the importance of the individual. Without liberty you cannot realize Jesus' ideal for humanity. In His Church therefore free assent must furnish the bond of union.

It is true that the religious liberty we enjoy has been bought at a heavy price. The Reformers, to attain their chief end, temporarily sacrificed values in the older religion which must be recovered for the Church of the future. Abuses have resulted from our over-emphasis upon freedom, with a resulting depreciation of institutional religion. We have already had occasion to comment on the weaknesses of our American Christianity, its individualism, its provincialism, its denominationalism. But when all is said, the Reformation represented a great step forward in human history. It was the counterpart in religion of the movement which in politics we call democracy; at least it was the first step toward such a movement. To attempt to ignore it or to belittle it is futile, most of all in a democratic society like our own. Our way lies forward, not back, and this is true for those who are most conscious of the value of our Catholic inheritance.

But if we go forward along the path of freedom we must not forget that the goal to which it leads is unity. Our fathers gave us a principle and a method. They would have been the last to claim finality for the application of it. In the interest of liberty they sacrificed unity. It is equally true (as we shall see when we come closer to denominationalism) that in their desire for unity they were not willing to grant to others the liberty they claimed for themselves. We must achieve a Church which makes room both for liberty and for unity.

This, then, is the task of the American Church to-day: to express in forms adapted to our modern democratic society that type of Christian faith and experience which has proved its validity by the supreme test which democracy recognizes—the test of free experiment co-operatively undertaken.

But is this possible? Can the old religion still maintain itself under the strain of the new conditions? Can it sustain the theoretical test of the intellectual movement which we call modern science? Can it meet the practical test of the social and economic movement which we call industrialism, with its political counterpart in the rivalry of races and of nations for prestige and for power? To ask these questions is to raise the whole question of the relation of church and state, with the deeper question still to which it points back, the question of the relation of institutions to the spiritual life they express and foster.

2. *Effect of the Scientific Movement upon the Ideals of the Older Protestantism*

We begin with the intellectual test; the problem presented to the Christian Church by that complex of new influences and ideas which we sum up under the name of modern science. Science forces Christian people to re-examine the reasons for their beliefs and to test the process by which they have arrived at them. It substitutes for the atmosphere of unquestioning trust, the spirit of critical inquiry, and with the substitution raises a host of detailed questions which demand an answer.

While it is not easy to over-emphasize the importance of the issues raised by modern science for the Church, it is well to remember that the number of persons directly and consciously affected by them is less than we are apt to suppose. Those who move in the academic atmosphere of our colleges and schools find it difficult to realize how slowly ideas move, and what vast sections of our population still live their lives and think their thoughts as if Galileo had never lived nor Darwin written.[1] For most people, science affects religion indirectly through the changes which it produces in social organization, rather than through any immediate alteration in the form of their beliefs. Still, even in the latter sphere, the influence of science upon religion has been far-reaching, and no attempt to define the ideal of the modern Church would be complete which did not take it into account.

There are two ways in which modern science has affected the task of the Church. It has affected it as pure science by its challenge of the assumptions on which the older theology was based. It has affected it even more profoundly as applied science by the changes which it has brought about in the external environment in which the Church must work.

To begin with the former, the effect of the modern scientific spirit upon the assumptions upon which the older theology is based. From the beginning of Christian history we find Christian teachers attaching immense importance to right thinking in religion; and this emphasis is justified by the close relation between belief and conduct. Our beliefs are important, in the first place, because they define our aims. They are important, in the second place, because they reinforce our motives. This is especially true of a religion like Christianity, which professes to bring a definite Gospel and is committed to a world-wide missionary enterprise. It is clear that whatever weakens faith in the correctness of the premises on which the enterprise is based must weaken the motives which lead its adherents to engage in it.

This intellectual interest, implicit in the very nature of Christianity, was powerfully reinforced by Protestantism. The Reformers rejected external authority and substituted individual conviction as the true bond of union between believers. They recovered the Bible from the obscurity to which the mediæval church had relegated it, and urged each believer to study it for himself. They were convinced that the central verities of Christian faith were so self-evident that it needed only contact with them to bring conviction; and they laid on the conscience of the believer the duty of that first-hand study of God's word which would give him an intelligent comprehension of its message.

---

[1] Mr. Bryan's recent campaign against the teaching of evolution in our tax-supported institutions has brought unexpected confirmation of this fact.

So long as they were content to confine their emphasis to the central truths of salvation, this attitude was largely justified. The Reformation produced a group of Christians who to a remarkable degree knew what they believed and why. But as time went on and the adherents of the new way of thinking increased, differences began to appear. It became necessary to define the Church's position not simply with reference to the central verities of the Christian experience, but on matters of organization and government which were in controversy between the Reformers and the Church of Rome. So Protestantism in its turn began to produce its written creeds which multiplied until they became a formidable library. Orthodoxy in the sense of uniformity of belief was insisted on; not for its own sake indeed (the most rigid Protestants never did this) but because it was believed to be the natural expression of that saving faith to which it was the Christian's supreme duty and privilege to bear witness.

It is evident that to one trained to think of faith in this way the application of the methods of modern science to religion must present difficult problems. It is not so much the actual changes of belief which are disturbing (though these are serious enough), but the change in temper of mind and in attitude of spirit. One of the most obvious effects of the scientific spirit has been to weaken the unquestioning acceptance of the authority of the Bible which, as we have seen, was one of the characteristic features of the older orthodoxy. This has not been confined to those who have definitely accepted the modern point of view. It is equally noticeable in the case of many who in theory reject it. It is not that they have ceased to believe what they believed before, but that the grounds on which they justify their belief have insensibly shifted. Where their fathers were content to rely upon the letter of Scripture, they welcome analogies derived from present-day experience, and when they speak of miracles they explain them as instances of the operation of a higher law not yet perfectly understood.

If this is true of those who look upon the new movement with suspicion, or at least with indifference, the results upon those who accept its conclusions *con amore* have been far more revolutionary. The new point of view when applied to religion has yielded changes as great as those in other realms of human knowledge.

The Bible has been restudied as a human book, as the literature of a nation slowly ripening through centuries of experience. The history of the Christian Church has been rewritten. The creeds, the theologies, the institutions of the Church have all been subjected to critical analysis and presented in new and constantly changing perspective.

One whose youth was spent under the influence of this movement can remember the extraordinary interest and enthusiasm which it called forth. Criticism was studied as if it were a new Gospel, and the discovery that there were two Isaiahs, and that David did not write many of the psalms that bear his name, was welcomed as if it were a message of salvation to the people. Candidates came before examining committees in the mood of martyrs anticipating execution, and the trial of Dr. Briggs for heresy by the Presbyterian General Assembly occupied scarcely less space in the daily press than was recently given to the battle between Carpentier and Dempsey for the championship of the prize ring.

To-day we have discovered the limitations of criticism. After all, what does it matter whether there was one Isaiah or seven, whether the Bible occupied a thousand years in its writing or only a few hundred? What matters to us is the content of its teaching. What has it to say about God, man, and immortality? Is its witness on these subjects still credible? Whatever Jesus Christ may have said or done in detail, has He a message which is still valid for us? Is he still to us Master, Saviour? Can we still see in Him the eternal God expressing Himself in human form?

So theology passes into a new phase. Criticism is replaced by construction, science by philosophy. Beneath the differences in interpretation we detect permanent similarities of interest and our attempt now is to bring these to expression. The new theology —at first intent upon emphasizing its contrast to the old—is to-day interested in establishing its continuity with the past; in pointing out how, under new names, the old convictions survive, and the old faith is still confessed.

This change of attitude is made easier because of the central place held by religious experience in the theory of the older Protestantism. Faith to our fathers was not blind belief. It was the response of the soul to a revelation of the personal God conveyed, indeed, through external means, but manifesting itself in present experience.   Their interest in having men think alike was due to their conviction that uniformity of belief was the natural accompaniment of similarity of religious experience, but their concern was not for the belief as such, but for the experience it evidenced. So the new theology with its strong emphasis upon the primary importance of experience for belief finds a natural point of contact with the old.

3. *Negative Results—Disillusionment Resulting from the Discovery of the Limitations of Pure Science—Different Effects of This upon Different Groups*

Paralleling the new constructive interest in theology we find a clearer perception of the limitations of science. There was a time, not so long ago, when there seemed no limits to what men expected from science. It was hailed as the great deliverer, making possible by its inventions a better life for all the peoples of the world. "Only let us know enough," men said, "and all will be well." Comte and Spencer were the prophets of the new Gospel. They urged us to put away theology and metaphysics and to get back to the facts of life.   Let man reverence Mother Nature and master her laws and a new era would dawn for humanity.

But to-day we are not so confident. What science has given us, as we now see, is an opportunity, but what we do with it depends upon ourselves. Power by itself is morally neutral. It may be used either for good or for evil. Science, which is only another name for knowledge, is power. Many questions it can answer for us. Undreamed-of resources it puts at our disposal. But when we turn to it for help in the great issues which divide the modern world it fails us. Only conscience can help us here. Henry Adams, in that remarkable work in which in so masterly a way he interprets to us the deeper experience of the last generation,[1] has given expression in classical form to this mood of disillusionment.

This mood, already in evidence in many quarters, has been

---

[1] "The Education of Henry Adams," 1918, cf. esp. pp. 486 sq. "The idea that new force must be in itself a good is only an animal or vegetable instinct. As Nature developed her hidden energies they tended to become destructive. Thought itself became tortured, suffering reluctantly, impatiently, painfully, the coercion of new methods."

powerfully reinforced by the war. The war has revealed to us the gigantic power for evil which science has put into the hands of modern man. A gun that can shoot seventy miles, a boat that can navigate under the sea, an airplane that can fly a hundred miles an hour and carry poison gas enough to annihilate in a few hours a city full of men—these are some of the gifts that modern science has given us; these are some of the powers that it has put into our hands.[1] What has the Church to say to such an ally? In what spirit shall it meet the bringer of these perilous gifts?

Some Christians find that this revelation of the destructive power of modern science reinforces their conviction of its essentially irreligious character. In the practical effects of modern science, even more than in its theoretical affirmations, they see the natural result of infidelity. To them the remedy is a yet more rigid orthodoxy. Still sharper must the line be drawn between reason and revelation, humanitarianism and Christianity, the devil and God. In the spirit of the modern age they see Antichrist at work and science as his tool. The premillenarian has no hope for the world through any human instrumentality. He believes that the world must grow steadily worse until the great salvation of the last day when Christ—the number of His elect made up —shall descend in bodily presence to establish His kingdom on earth.[2]

[1] For a convenient summary of this aspect of the situation cf. Irwin, "The Next War," New York, 1921

[2] At the present time the churches in America are witnessing a revival of this militant premillenarianism. Appealing to the despondency and disillusionment caused by the Great War, its advocates challenge the entire conception of Christianity as a Gospel of social salvation and declare the present order doomed to destruction both in church and state. They regard every attempt to redeem the present institutions of society as a form of apostasy and look for the speedy advent of Jesus Christ to establish His personal reign on the earth. With this belief in the literal fulfilment of Biblical prophecy they combine a distrust of the methods of science all along the line. They maintain schools in which many hundreds of pupils are being trained in this literalistic interpretation of the Bible (*e.g.,* the Bible Institutes at Chicago and Los Angeles), and by organized propaganda in this country and on the mission field are trying to drive from the Church all who do not agree with them. This propaganda is especially active at the present time in the Northern Baptist Church (cf. the literature of the so-called Fundamentalists), but it is felt also in other churches. On the mission field, notably in China, it is a powerful and disturbing factor.

Others receive solace by means of the mystical element in religion. The destructive criticism of science has strengthened those churches which make the institution the bond of union rather than the creed. Such a church as the Protestant Episcopal Church, for example, which makes the sacrament the centre of religious worship, is less affected by the challenge of modern science than churches like the Presbyterian and the Congregational, which have always made much of doctrine. There is a symbolic element in the institution which appeals to feeling rather than reason, and which is therefore better able to stand the strain produced by the conflict of ideas.

A third way of meeting the difficulty is found by those who would substitute conduct for belief as the basis of Christian unity. An organization like the Young Men's Christian Association, for example, which makes practical ministry its primary object and leaves to the churches to which its constituent members belong the responsibility for settling the vexed questions which the modern scientific movement has raised, finds many to respond to its appeal. In such work as the Association is doing for boys and young men is found an occupation which leaves little time for speculation. In this the Association is only giving clear expression to a tendency widespread in all the churches. If science puts into our hands undreamed-of powers, let us see that we use them rightly. If some men use them for evil, that is all the more reason why we should use them for good.

One noticeable effect of the new situation for which we may be thankful is the breaking down of the arbitrary and artificial divisions which have separated Christians, and the creation of a new understanding between many who have hitherto held aloof from one another. We are learning that we can agree even while we differ, provided only that the things in which we agree are more important than the things in which we differ. A dozen years ago historians and critics could work together, but there was a deep-rooted suspicion that the only way to keep theologians at peace was to keep them apart. We have found out our mistake. Every year groups of theological teachers meet for conference in their theological clubs and societies, and every two years representatives of the leading theological seminaries spend three days together in helpful discussion of their common problems and tasks.

As a result we see the formation of new alignments corresponding more exactly to the real differences between men. Such is the difference between liberals and conservatives; the difference between those who believe in a thorough education for religious teachers and those who do not; above all, the difference between those who believe in a spiritual conception of the world and those who do not. In this new atmosphere of mutual understanding and sympathy it is possible to approach with greater hope of a successful result those more difficult and perplexing questions of definition which will later present themselves to us.

4. *Positive Results—the Contribution of the Scientific Movement to Religious Faith* [1]

But the effects of the modern scientific movement upon religion have not been simply negative. In positive ways also science has a contribution to make to religious faith.

For one thing the scientific approach to the study of religion is bringing new evidence to confirm the immemorial Christian contention that religion is a permanent human interest, not to be ignored or denied. As long as men believed that religion came to man from without, as a revelation from a world otherwise inaccessible to human reason, it might be possible to ignore it. But if man is religious by nature, one cannot be indifferent to what science may have to tell us of what religion has meant to man in the past and what it may do for him in the future.

Again, the scientific study of religion is making clear the experimental basis of our faith in God. We see that the arguments we give to justify our belief are arguments after the fact. We must find God in our experience before we can reason about Him. Our arguments are only ways in which we translate into logical form what John Caird has well called "the unconscious logic of religion." [2] They remind us of the way in which we came

[1] Cf. W. Adams Brown, "Modern Theology and the Preaching of the Gospel," New York, 1914.

[2] "An Introduction to the Philosophy of Religion," p. 133, New York, 1880. Cf. W. Adams Brown, "Why I Believe in God," *Biblical World,* September, 1920.

to believe in God. Or rather, it should be said, the different ways. For while one man rises from nature to God, another turns within and finds Him in the still small voice of conscience. To one man God speaks in solitude, and to another in the majestic appeal of some ancient institution. Personal need opens the door of religion to one, while the opportunity of service speaks to another the enfranchising word. William James showed himself a true man of science as well as a religious believer when he chose for the subject of his Gifford lecture "The Varieties of Religious Experience." [1]

This reference to the varieties of religious experience calls attention to another important contribution which modern science has been making to our knowledge of religion. It helps us to distinguish between religion as a permanent and universal human interest and the different forms in which from time to time it manifests itself. The study of comparative religion shows us how much all the greater religions have in common, how marked the contrast between the religious view of the world with its faith in meaning and goodness at the core of things and all philosophies that are atheistic and materialistic. Thus science works against denominationalism and in favor of a catholic and unifying faith.

But at the same time science shows us that there are permanent differences in the types of the religious experience and so gives denominationalism a relative justification. The difference between the Protestant and Catholic types of experience is a permanent difference, found in other religions besides the Christian, and mysticism, with its introspective and self-centred faith, is a very different thing from the practical religion of good works illustrated by the writer of the Epistle of James. By calling attention to such facts, modern science is forcing Christians to find a bond of union which at once underlies and transcends these differences and which expresses the distinctive character of Christianity in contrast to other religions, which, like it, are divided within themselves.

This unifying principle is found in Jesus Christ, the founder of the Christian religion and the one whom all Christians agree in taking as their Master, their Saviour, and their Example. In Christ we find the vitalizing principle of Christian theology, the bond of union between those who in all else are separate, the figure

[1] New York, 1902.

at once human and divine, who gives us at the same time our supreme revelation of God, our highest ideal for man, and our leader in the effort to realize this ideal in the life of individuals and of society.

This rediscovery of Jesus carries with it a new emphasis upon the Kingdom of God as the social ideal which Jesus is seeking to realize in the world. We have seen how this ideal is being forced upon us by other influences growing out of the practical needs of the time. The new theology reinforces this emphasis by its study of the nature of the Christian religion as revealed to us in the life and teaching of its founder. It shows us that Jesus, deeply as He was concerned for the individual man, highly as He rated his value for God and his capacity for service, never conceived of him as an isolated individual. He was one of many sons, potential citizens in a society in which loving service was to be the law of all men's life. So science gives us a direct point of contact with the social and economic problems which the pressure of the time is forcing upon the attention of the Church.

With this reference to the Kingdom of God we pass from the direct effect of modern science upon theological theory to its indirect result in changing the environment to which that theory must relate itself. We have seen that the social and economic changes of the day set the Church a distinctive problem. But these changes are themselves the result of the scientific movement. It is science with its discovery of the secrets of nature which has put into man's hands the powers which have made these changes possible. It is science with its invention of the steam-engine and the cotton-gin which has created the modern industrial system. It is science which has built our great cities and moved our population from continent to continent and which seems on the verge of discoveries which may make possible changes even more revolutionary.

We shall speak in the following chapter of the problems which this change presents for our definition of the Church's function. We are now thinking only of its indirect effect upon the spirits of men. How has it affected the spiritual attitudes with which the Church is primarily concerned? What effect, if any, is it likely to have upon the ideal of the Church as a teacher of religion?

5. Consequences for the Church as a Teaching Body

Two contrasted attitudes are taken by modern men toward the historic beliefs of the Christian Church. On the one hand, we find those who would discard them altogether,[1] either on the ground that belief is a negligible element in religion, or, if this be not true, that each new generation must formulate its own beliefs without reference to what has been done by the Church of the past. On the other hand, we find those who would reaffirm the ancient creeds in the literal sense and make acceptance of that sense the condition of church membership. It does not seem likely that either of these attitudes will permanently control.

So far as the first position is concerned, we have already seen that belief is inseparable from experience and that to reject all creeds is to abandon the possibility of any effective concerted action. To say, as is so much the fashion at present, that we are to unite on our purposes rather than on our beliefs is an evasion of the issue. For purposes are themselves beliefs, differing from other beliefs only in that they voice convictions which are capable of expression in action. The choice is not between beliefs and no beliefs, but between beliefs imposed from without in the form of law as is the case in the Roman Catholic Church, and beliefs which express convictions freely formed in response to some appeal which verifies itself in experience. Protestants are convinced that Christian faith should be of the latter kind and for that reason must be reformulated from age to age in the light of enlarging experience.

This does not mean that the older beliefs are to be regarded as valueless, any more than this is the case with similar beliefs in science, but only that they are to be included in a wider synthesis. The Ptolemaic astronomy was not proved false by the Copernican. It was only proved inadequate. It is true that to the man who stands on the earth the sun rises in the east and sets in the west. But Copernicus has shown us that there are other points of view from which one may contemplate the sun, and for these the Ptolemaic formula is no longer adequate. So the Christian creeds express truths in forms natural to the day in which they were

[1] Cf. Drake, "Shall We Stand by the Church?" New York, 1320, pp. 125 sq.; Holmes, "New Churches for Old," New York, 1922, p. 232.

given, but which need to be supplemented and corrected by the new experience and insight of later generations.

Those who insist that the ancient creeds must be accepted in the literal sense in which they were held by those who formulated them are not therefore likely to be successful. Much which the old creeds tried to say about God and man and salvation we modern men believe and affirm, but we interpret the old affirmations in the light of a new universe and give the old words new and larger meaning. When we say that Christ is coming again to judge the world, our vision ranges not simply over the few decades spanned by the men who first put this phrase into the creed, but over the whole course of human history since then, and the statement to us expresses a larger faith and makes demands for new forms of consecration. We think of that coming as a spiritual process in which little by little the institutions of society as well as the lives of the men and women who live under them are to be conformed to the mind of Christ. So the old word about God as Maker of heaven and earth acquires a profounder significance in the light of our present understanding of the extent and duration of the universe so described. We still read the fortieth chapter of Isaiah and the one hundred and thirty-ninth Psalm, and find our faith expressed in what we read. But how immeasurably vaster the range and sweep of the vision to which modern science has opened our eyes. Christ is still to us the centre of human history, the Saviour for whom the world has been looking, but what the words mean science has helped us to understand as, apart from its teaching, we could never have known.

If, then, we retain the old creeds it will be in a spirit of freedom not possible to the men who formulated them. As each generation writes its own commentaries on the Bible, and what is more important, lives them, so of the creeds. We shall reinterpret the old creeds and write new ones, each generation of us. The Social Ideals of the Churches [1] is an example in point. But they will not supersede but interpret the older words about the Saviour Christ, and His Kingdom. The living Spirit in whom we profess to believe will lead us into more truth as the Master promised, and we shall rejoice in this truth for ourselves, accept it gladly,

---

[1] Cf. p. 89.

and pass it on to our children, knowing well that for them, too, it will not be final, but that they will receive light from the same living Spirit and pass on the torch to their children.

In assisting us to cultivate this spiritual attitude, science can help us most. The qualities which inspire science at its best are the qualities by which religion lives—faith, co-operation, service. Faith in the significance and consistency of nature, and in man's ability, if he persevere, to find his way to the truth; co-operation with all other seekers after truth in an enterprise in which success is given to no individual alone, but becomes possible only through the union of all; unselfish service rendered with no thought of fame or reward, but only to advance the cause:—these are qualities which are characteristic of religion at its best. Substitute for nature the unseen Spirit who inhabits nature, whom religion calls God; substitute for co-operation in the world of thought the wider co-operation which takes place in human activity in all its forms; substitute for the service of truth for its own sake the service of the spiritual beings who live by the truth, and you will have a good description of the spirit of religion at its best. Without this spirit there can be no future for religion and no hope for mankind.

CHAPTER IX

1. *The Church's Stake in the New Social Order*

IN our review of the effects of the modern scientific movement we have been interested, thus far, in the bearing of the movement upon individual faith. We have tried to discover what changes modern science has made in men's attitude to the beliefs and loyalties of the past; whether and how far they can still honestly use the old creeds, practise the old rites, and keep their place in the historic institution to which the Christian religion has given birth. But Christianity has never claimed to be simply a religion for individuals. It has always upheld an ideal for society. Side by side with His preaching of personal repentance, Jesus announced the coming of the Kingdom of God. In every age the Church has interpreted His message in its own way. The social aspects of the Gospel, which our individualistic Protestantism has too long overlooked or subordinated, are being forced again into the foreground by the changes which we have studied. We have considered the effect of these changes upon the character of our contemporary religious life. It is time to examine in more detail their relation to the function of the Church. What exactly is the Church's responsibility for the welfare of society as distinct from the individuals who compose it? In what sense and by what right may the Church speak with authority upon the political and economic issues which divide men?

A year ago a car strike broke out in a Western city. It went through the usual course of such disputes. When the men went out strike-breakers were brought in. They were housed by the company in places to which the strikers were denied access and sent to their work under armed guards. Ill-feeling was engendered and a riot occurred in which shots were fired and several persons were killed. After running on for weeks the strike was finally won by the company and many of the men lost their jobs and were obliged to leave the city in search of work in other places. Many of them

153

had worked for the company for years.[1] They were sober and respectable men, fathers of families, many of them owners of their own homes.[2] A surprisingly large number, in view of the statements often made about the absence of the workingman from the Church, were members of the local churches.[3] Yet they were obliged to leave home and church and go out to begin life over again with all the loss, religious as well as economic and personal, which that change involved.

This familiar experience brings before us the most obvious point of contact between the Church and contemporary social questions, and that is, the people in the churches. The minister must concern himself with economic and political questions not because he is interested in them for their own sake, but because the forces which operate in business and politics work out their practical consequences in the lives of the men and women in his congregation. We begin to see that the issues joined in the present industrial struggle are not simply material, but spiritual. Moral values are at stake—a man's right to self-determination and self-expression, the possibility of decent conditions in which to bring up his children, the assurance of just treatment in the partition of the fruits of common toil. When under the leadership of the local Commission of Religious Forces a number of Denver ministers came together to study the causes of that strike and see if something could not be done to prevent the recurrence of similar social waste in the future, they were doing the plain duty which came to them in the course of their ministry as pastors.[4]

What is true on a smaller scale of the communities affected by industrial strife is true of the nation as a whole in connection with the great upheaval of war. We have tried to describe the effect of that upheaval upon the religious life of the young men who were called from their homes to take part in this new and unprecedented experience, but what we were able to study was but the first chapter of an unfinished story. The sequel is only beginning to unfold itself in the spirit of inertia and suspicion which has spread like a

---

[1] 237 out of 412 had worked for the company more than five years; 174 more than ten years; 71 more than twenty years.

[2] 345 were or had been married; 164 owned their own homes.

[3] 210 were church members. Others had less definite church relationship.

[4] Cf. "The Denver Tramway Strike of 1920." Report by Edward T. Devine, Ph.D., Rev. John A. Ryan, D.D., John A. Lapp, LL.D., Denver, 1921.

miasma all over the civilized world and which reaches down in a hundred ways into the lives of the individual men and women who make up our congregations. This affects the work of the Church in many ways. It creates an atmosphere of suspicion and strife which makes it difficult, if not impossible, for sincere Christians to live out their Christianity. The Christian religion teaches me that I ought to love my neighbor and wish him success; that I ought to further his welfare in every possible way and co-operate with him in helping others; but the conditions under which we are living to-day are often such as to make this practically impossible. When a strike takes place on the large scale in which strikes occur in modern industry, the first effect is to interrupt the direct relations between the parties to the dispute with all the possibilities of suspicion and misrepresentation which inevitably result. The ethics of peace give place to the ethics of war, and the first article of the ethics of war is that everything is right which helps my side to win. If human sympathy makes me feel for my enemy and want to help him rather than injure him, then steps must be taken to put a stop to that sympathy. If the knowledge that he has some right on his side weakens my will to win at any cost, then that knowledge must be suppressed. So we see side by side with the machinery for mobilizing the economic and physical resources of the contestants a propaganda which is directed to securing unity of spirit, and this propaganda—not because of any deliberate choice on the part of those who engage in it, but by the inherent logic of the situation —operates with the motives of suspicion, fear, and hate. For the purpose of winning a temporary victory, those who conduct it attribute base motives to their opponents, not realizing that by doing so they imperil the foundations on which their own future peace must rest.

It is no doubt true that individuals here and there manage to resist the contagion of their environment. Even in time of industrial strife they succeed in keeping alive that kindly human feeling which is the normal relation between man and man, just as there are soldiers who even in the most dreadful war never lose their sense of the common humanity which unites them with the enemy. The fact remains that it is immensely more difficult to do this in time of war than in time of peace, and that while war exists, industrial as well as international, the larger ministry of the Church is hampered and restricted in many ways. Were this situation permanently to continue, the Christian ideal of a world-wide brotherhood would be proved forever impracticable.

But there is a more compelling reason which calls the Church to action. It is not simply that the existing situation makes it hard for Christian men to act out their Christianity, but that it threatens to rob them of their faith in God. A creed which cannot be lived cannot command whole-hearted assent. If, as we profess to believe, God be really like Jesus Christ, we should expect to find indications of this fact in the world that He has made. A Christlike God can express Himself completely only through a Christlike society. Unless we believe, therefore, that such a society is possible—we may go further and say, unless we see evidence that such a society is actually in process of formation—our reason for believing that God is like Christ is correspondingly weakened. The greater the contradiction between our ideal and the real world, the greater the strain upon faith. Men reject faith not because they would not like to believe, but because the facts make faith difficult. They accept struggle, whether between individuals or nations, as the last word in human life because they see everyone else doing so. To hold our own against such influences we must be able to show that they do not account for all the facts; that side by side with the competitive element in human nature there is another element which seeks co-operation and fellowship, and that as between the two the second is the stronger and the more enduring. In a word, we must be able to show that Christianity is a practicable religion, not simply for individuals here and there, but for society as a whole.[1] This is possible only as we leave the shelter of a purely individualistic religion and move out into the world of business and of politics. To keep God for myself I must be able to show that He can rule the world where my fellow-men are living.

2. *Principles which Determine the Nature and Limit of the Church's Social Responsibility*

If, however, we accept the principle that the Church has a responsibility for social standards as well as for individual salvation, we must do so with our eyes open. Such acceptance opens the door to all kinds of difficulties. Some of them grow out of the inherent

[1] Cf. W. Adams Brown, "Is Christianity Practicable?", New York, 1916.

complexity of the social situation. Where so many factors enter in, it is not easy to tell just where the Church's responsibility begins and where it ends. Even when we are clear on this point, we are only at the beginning of our troubles. It is one thing to realize that the present system of society is wrong; quite another to know how to remedy it. In matters of economic and industrial reform we find men equally sincere and equally learned differing on almost every point. Most puzzling of all are the problems which result from different stages of intellectual or spiritual development. All social action involves an element of compromise. In such matters as industrial and political reconstruction, many of the men with whom we must work do not share our premises, or, if they accept them, do not understand them as we do.

In such a situation the only safety for the Christian is to confine his action strictly to the religious field. The Church's pronouncements on social and economic questions must be such and such only as grow out of the distinctive function of the Church as a religious institution, concerned primarily with motives and ideals. They must take their departure from Jesus' view of human personality and express His conception of the true relations of men in society. The unity they seek must be secured by free assent. The converts they win must be gained by the contagion of personality.

It is important to keep these principles clearly in mind because so many good people in our day are tempted to forget them. Once admit that the Church has any responsibility for bettering the conduct of society and you will find people who will hold it responsible for everything. Every fault in our present economic situation is attributed to the negligence of the Church. Every cause which deserves support for any reason claims the right to appeal for the Church's endorsement. A new calendar threatens to supersede the Christian year, as Sunday after Sunday is appropriated by Boy Scouts, Mothers' Day, and the like. What is more serious, a persistent effort is made to secure the Church's approval of plans whose economic practicability is still to be demonstrated, or which are phrased in such vague and ambiguous terms as to invite misunderstanding.

It is necessary, therefore, to remind ourselves of the dangers to which we are exposed by too hasty pronouncements. We can not distinguish too carefully between the central Christian principles on which general agreement may be anticipated, and those matters of interpretation and application as to which honest men may differ. This reminder is especially necessary in the case of social service commissions and others who claim to speak for the Church as a whole. They will do well to remember that their utterances will carry weight in proportion as they grow inevitably out of the Christian message, and convince the reason as well as the conscience of those to whom they are addressed.

Even more formidable than the difficulties which are due to the limitations of our knowledge are those which grow out of differences of character. Not all people have reached the same point of moral development. Many reject the principles of the Gospel altogether. Others interpret them differently. We look forward to a time when these differences will be overcome and all men will honestly endeavor to do what is right. But in our existing society this is not yet the case and the presence of these conflicting elements raises puzzling questions for the Christian conscience. Social progress is possible only through the co-operation of many different kinds of people. What shall we do when people refuse to co-operate or ask a price which we do not think it right to pay?

These considerations bring us face to face with the age-long question of the relation of church and state. Our democratic institutions assume that the majority must rule. But this majority consists of many who are not Christians or who, if nominally Christians, do not accept the full logic of their profession. What shall we do then? Shall we acquiesce in the decision of the majority when that decision seems to us to contravene Christian principles? If not, how can we make our own convictions prevail?

It will help us to find our way through these perplexing questions if we remind ourselves of the views which have been held by our fellow-Christians in the past.

Roman Catholics believe that both church and state are divine institutions, but with different functions and authority. The state is concerned with secular morality and enforces its decrees by physical force. Justice is its great word and law the agency through which justice finds expression. The Church, on the other hand, has to do with the higher morality of religion. It appeals to inner motives and makes love supreme. But this dualism is not final, for God has given the Church authority over the state. The state is an agent which the Church may use to promote the ends of religion, and by using this agent the Church may in effect employ force and enact law. It is the duty of every good Christian to obey the Church in all things, but the state so far and so far only as its acts accord with the teaching of the Church. In the exercise of its function as a teaching body the Church may from time to time pass judgment on the economic and political theories which affect the life of man in society and as a matter of fact does so frequently. When Rome has spoken it is the duty of all good Christians to obey her voice and to do what she commands.

The older Protestant ethics took over the contrast between church and state, but rejected the Roman claim of authority on the part of the Church. Echoes of this claim lingered on in the Geneva of Calvin and the theocratic state of the older Puritanism. But the conscience that had broken with Rome would endure no lesser substitute, and with the rejection of the Church's authority in matters of politics the older method of affecting a reconciliation was abandoned. Some Protestants were content to assign to the state the lower sphere of civil justice—the justice of the natural and unregenerate man. Others, like the English Erastians, were inclined to put the state in the supreme place once occupied by the Pope. On the whole, Protestantism has regarded obedience to the state as a religious duty, though recognizing that in times of crisis revolution may become necessary. Protestants and Catholics alike have failed to apply the full Christian standard to man's political relations, with the inevitable result in a dual standard of ethics.

The German theologian of the last generation who gave most prominence to the social aspect of Christianity was Albrecht Ritschl. The Gospel of Christ, he taught, is an ellipse with two foci, of which one is redemption through Christ and the other the Kingdom of God. In his theology, therefore, if anywhere, one would expect to see the Christian ideal for society explained and applied. Yet when one turned to the section which dealt with the state and its duties,[1] one found a strange hiatus. The state, it seems, is an exception to the operation of the principles which govern the life of the ordinary Christian. Unselfishness should be the law of the individual life. The state, on the other hand, must maintain the rights

[1] "Unterricht in der Christlichen Religion," Bonn, 1875. English translation by Swing, "The Theology of Albrecht Ritschl," New York, 1901, pp. 171 sq.

of its own citizens against the aggression of others. While the state is never justified in the use of criminal means, it is yet not bound by the same rules which govern the Christian individual.[1] In the sphere of politics, Christian principles do not apply.

Stripped of the veil of pious phrases with which it often cloaks itself, the doctrine of Ritschl is the doctrine of the modern state everywhere. The supreme attribute of the state is sovereignty, and since there is no super-state to which all others are subject, each nation is ethically justified in asserting its own rights against others whenever it honestly believes them to be imperilled. Thus preparedness, in the sense of military armament, becomes the patriotic duty of every loyal citizen, and the possession of an army and navy strong enough to assert any rights to which the nation may reasonably lay claim is the foundation-stone of foreign policy.

Such an attitude, if accepted as a finality, is fundamentally unchristian. It overlooks the fact that nations, like the individuals who compose them, are not isolated units, but members of a family of which God alone is sovereign. Isaiah pictures the ancient rivals, Egypt, Assyria, and Israel, as having the same Saviour and worshipping the same God.[2] Jesus carries the thought farther in His teaching concerning the Kingdom of God. It is our duty as Christians to formulate a standard for society which shall be true to this ideal and to define our duty as patriots accordingly.

Such a formulation is attempted by the radical Protestants who are known as pacifists. They not only believe that Jesus' principles are applicable to state as well as to church, but that they are applicable now. They insist that Jesus has laid down a definite method by which His principles are to be applied, which, if practised by all Christians, would render possible the immediate realization of the Christian social ideal. In particular this method precludes the taking of human life for any purpose whatever. It outlaws war not only for the selfish purpose of moral aggrandizement or conquest, but even for self-defence and, what is still more difficult

---

[1] "Unterricht in der Christlichen Religion," Bonn, 1875. English translation by Swing, "The Theology of Albrecht Ritschl," New York, 1901, p. 246. "So long, however, as statecraft has to defend the rights of a people or a state against hostility from other nations, while it is never justified in the use of criminal means to this end, it is yet not bound by the same rules which hold for the legal and ethical action of the individual Christian in his relation to the state and in intercourse with other men."

[2] Isaiah xix, 23–25.

to accept, in defence of others. The fact that the state has approved a war cannot alter its essentially unchristian character. On so fundamental an issue the individual conscience must assert itself. To yield to the majority would be to deny the faith.

We have referred to pacifism not to debate again the question whether it is ever right for the Christian to fight, but because it illustrates one of the possible views which Christians may hold in regard to social questions, the view, namely, that there is one particular method of social action which is applicable to all individuals at all times. Such an opinion overlooks the fact that men grow in insight as they grow in experience. What is right for a man at one stage of his development may be wrong at another. Moreover, all social action requires some degree of compromise. In the realm of motive we face right and wrong in their purity. But when it comes to action, duty is far less simple than the catechism represents. Life does not always present us with a choice between good and evil. Far more often we are required to choose between a greater and a lesser evil.

The most familiar example of such a choice of evils is war. If war always represented the self-assertive, and peace the self-sacrificing principle, one could confidentially require of the Christian that he be always a man of peace; but in experience this proves not to be the case. To fight for oneself is one thing; to fight for others quite another; to fight as an assertion of the fundamental principles of liberty and justice, which refusal to fight would imperil, another thing still. There is no doubt that to multitudes in the late war the issue presented itself in the latter form. War seemed to them so great an evil that it was hardly possible to conceive a greater. Yet a time had come when to refrain from fighting would involve them in a worse evil still, and so with a clear conscience they gave themselves to the service of their country and believed that in so acting they were serving Christ as well.

What is true of war is true of all the lesser compromises of which social life is full. In our collective action our choice, we repeat, is seldom between good and evil. Most frequently it is between a greater and a lesser good or a greater and a lesser evil. Confronted with such an alternative, one must choose the course which, on the whole, comes closest to the Christian ideal and throw all one's strength against the evil which seems most seriously to conflict with it.

There are different spheres within which such compromises must be made. There are compromises rendered necessary by degrees of knowledge. There are others made inevitable by differences of spirit. Some things we have to do because our fellows have not yet come to see what we see; others because they do not yet desire what we desire. But our reason in each case for doing what we do and refraining from doing what we leave undone should be that we believe that of the possible courses of action open to us, the one we choose will, on the whole, do most to hasten the time when all men will accept the Christian standard, and society as a whole in all its elements be perfectly conformed to the mind of Christ.

These principles determine the relation of the Christian to law. In a democratic society, law is the instrument of social progress. It registers the average opinion of society. A change in the law is the most effective proof that the ideals of society are changing and the social conscience being educated. The Christian, therefore, like all other good citizens, must see to it that so far as possible his ideals are embodied in the law; but he must be clear as to the significance of what he is doing. A law that is imposed by a majority on a minority may be a useful instrument in public education and a significant register of social progress; but from the Christian point of view it fails of success unless it becomes the free expression of the sincere conviction of those who live under it. Law, as the Apostle long ago perceived,[1] is a schoolmaster to discipline men for freedom; but the ideal is not realized until men choose freely what the law prescribes, and would do what it orders even if it were absent.

We must distinguish, then, between the function of the Christian as a citizen, helping to form the public opinion which determines prevailing social standards, and his special responsibility for bringing men to accept the inner motives which are characteristic of the Gospel. Faith and love are the distinctive marks of the Christian social order, faith in the Father God who is planning all for His beneficent end, love for the human individuals who are progressively striving to realize His principles in the world. Where these are absent society cannot be Christian. Whatever helps to promote these is a legitimate object of social effort.

[1] Gal. iii, 24.

We have already pointed out three main aspects of our modern life in which we feel pressure for the social application of the Gospel —the conflict of race, the competition of industry, the rivalry of politics. In each we need to work out a method of procedure in which sincere Christians can unite.

3. *Illustration of these Principles in the Relation of the Church to Industry*

One of the publications of the Committee on the War and the Religious Outlook is a volume entitled, "The Church and Industrial Reconstruction." [1] It is an attempt to do in this particular sphere the thing which we have all agreed needs to be done; namely, to work out a mode of procedure in industrial matters which shall express the common convictions of enlightened modern Christians. The book is a product of more than two years' study by a representative interdenominational group. It may therefore be taken as a convenient guide for our present purpose.

The book begins with an analysis of the principles which should determine the Christian attitude toward the industrial situation, the principles of personality, of brotherhood, and of service, which all Christians in theory accept. It paints the picture of what society would be like if these principles were everywhere lived up to, and men respected one another's personality, felt and acted toward one another as brothers and made the service of each by all, and of all by each, the general law. It contrasts with this picture the existing state of society and shows how this violates the law of personality, the law of brotherhood, and the law of service. Its authors then raise the question how far these violations are due to the system itself, how far to faults of character and insight on the part of the men who use the system. This leads to an analysis of what is meant by a social system, and the complicated ways in which systems rise and are modified. It appears that there is a wide field of agreement among students as to changes which are possible and desirable in the present system. There is a further field in which there is honest disagreement as to whether change would be for the better or the worse. In this latter field, the authors contend, the Church should proceed with caution, but where con-

[1] Association Press, New York, 1920.

ditions exist as to whose unchristian character all are agreed,[1] it is not only the right but the duty of the Church to deal with these evils without delay.

Having thus defined the Christian ideal, the book proceeds further to inquire how this ideal is to be realized. There are steps which can be taken now to realize the Christian social ideal, which indeed are being taken by more and more people. These the authors proceed to catalogue, illustrating the different methods which are being tried and the results which they have thus far yielded. After a further discussion of those more remote and far-reaching changes which must wait for the longer future, the book goes on to inquire what are the duties of individual Christians in their several capacities of employer, employee, investor, consumer, and citizen, and concludes with a consideration of the responsibility of the Church in its organized capacity to illustrate the Christian social ideal.

More important than any specific conclusion reached in this volume is the method which it uses. It is the co-operative method. The book expresses the conclusions of a carefully chosen body of Christians representing different churches and types of social philosophy, who have come together with the sincere desire of discovering for themselves and interpreting to their fellow-Christians the teaching of the Gospel as to man's economic duties and relationships. The authors take their departure from the principles of the Christian religion and enter the field of industry at those points only where these principles seem clearly to be at stake. They attempt to separate the obvious Christian duties which all men of goodwill must recognize, and the disputed territory of theory in which men equally honest and sincere may differ. The effort is made to keep the discussion as concrete as possible, and the principles laid down and the duties enjoined are illustrated from

---

[1] Note the difference between this point of view and that which finds expression in the well-known phrase, "the zone of agreement." This phrase, frequently used to describe the attitude of the Young Men's Christian Association to disputed questions in industry, is ordinarily understood to mean that in any question at issue between an employer of labor and his employees, the Association will refuse to take sides. The principle here formulated refers only to differences between Christians and states that as between those matters as to whose wisdom there is general agreement and those more doubtful questions as to which Christians equally sincere and honest still differ, preference should be given to the former.

cases where these principles and duties have proved their practicability by use. Finally, a clear distinction is made between the Christian ideal for society and the Christian way of realizing that ideal.

For it cannot be insisted upon too often that there is not simply a Christian ideal, but a Christian way of realizing this ideal, and it is quite as important for us to know the latter as the former. There are some results which can be secured only in one way, and the Kingdom of God is one of these. Impressive and substantial as are its outward manifestations, it develops from within as the plant from the seed, as the leaven in the lump. It spreads by the contact of spirit with spirit. Outward change may smooth the way for its advent, but it is an inward experience. The Kingdom of God is not eating and drinking, but righteousness and peace and joy in the Holy Spirit.[1]

It is one of the merits of the volume under review that the authors perceive this so clearly. Much as they are interested in finding out whither we ought to go, they are equally concerned to know how we are to get there. The answer they give is the old answer of religion from the beginning. We are to get there by trusting God, loving our brother, and overcoming the obstacles created by his ignorance or wilfulness in the only way in which such obstacles can ever be finally overcome, by the change which time brings in those who have been growing out of their old selves into better selves, under the influence of education in the truth.

It is encouraging that so many realize this and are taking time for the study which is necessary to overcome the difficulties in the way. In England this study has been carried further than here.[2] But even in this country there are many persons who appreciate the importance of the subject and are giving it their best attention.[3]

[1] Rom. xiv, 17.

[2] Cf. "Christianity and Industrial Problems," London, 1918 (Archbishops' Fifth Committee of Inquiry); "Quakerism and Industry: Being the Full Record of a Conference of Employers, Chiefly Members of the Society of Friends," Darlington, 1918; Tawney, "The Sickness of an Acquisitive Society," London, 1920. Cf. also the stimulating article by Mr. Seebohm Rowntree on the need of killing the war spirit in industry, *New York Evening Post*, November 10, 1921.

[3] From recent correspondence with a well-known employer, the vice-president of a large manufacturing company, the following is taken:

"A good many years' experience in business, employing large numbers of men, has impressed me that the chief obstacle in the way of remedying the

The cordial welcome given to the bulletin of information issued by the Social Service Commission of the Federal Council [1] is an encouraging indication of this awakening interest. The appearance of volumes like the Interchurch investigation of the steel strike,[2] and the Report of the Denver Commission of Religious Forces on the street car strike [3] in that city is another. The increasing emphasis given to social questions in the classrooms of our theological seminaries is still another.

What has been done so far, however, is only preliminary. The number of persons who are giving their attention to these questions needs to be vastly increased and the angles from which they approach the subject multiplied. Group study should be undertaken not only by employers, but by workmen, and within each industry by the men who are familiar with its particular problems. Consumers and investors should study their special form of responsibility and all these studies should be unified by some central body interested in the larger aspects of the subject and bringing to bear

evil is the almost universal failure of capital and labor to understand each other's difficulties and to get each other's point of view. They appear to be equally stupid, though it is only fair to labor to say that, as a rule, employers are much more difficult to teach than employees. In considering what can be done to make capital and labor less blind to each other's problems, I am impressed that before any real co-operation can be expected, there must be an awakening of the individual conscience, and a lessening of the spirit of intense commercialism. There is no greater power or influence for the accomplishment of both than the Church; in fact, I doubt if there is any other influence than the Church which can do it, provided it goes about it in a way which appeals to both capital and labor.

"There is no place, or ought not to be, where men should feel so free and willing to express themselves, to meet each other halfway, to agree upon definite policies for mutual good, as in the Church."

This letter is typical of many similar ones. Thus the president of a large insurance company, to whom the author had written expressing his appreciation of his attitude in a certain industrial matter, writes: "I believe and am convinced that the way out of our very serious difficulties to-day is in practicing the principles which have been taught by the Christian Church for years.

"In this instance I am merely trying to bring to bear one of those great principles, namely, the Brotherhood of Man."

[1] A bimonthly bulletin issued by the Research Department of the Commission on the Church and Social Service.

[2] Cf. Report on the Steel Strike of 1919 by the Commission of Inquiry of the Interchurch World Movement, 1920; Public Opinion and the Steel Strike of 1919: Supplementary Reports to the Commission of Inquiry, Interchurch World Movement, New York, 1921.

[3] Cf. p. 154, note 4.

upon the differences which arise the wider vision and impartial judgment which comes from the Christian view of life as a whole. To this subject we shall return again in another connection when we discuss the educational work of the Church in its larger aspects.[1]

4. Need of a Similar Application to the Questions of Race and of Nationality

What the volume on "The Church and Industrial Reconstruction" endeavors to do for the subject of industrial relations, it is equally important to do for the vexed questions of race and of nationality. A short time ago a riot occurred in a Western city of more than 100,000 inhabitants in which more than fifty persons were killed, many more wounded, millions' worth of property destroyed, and ten thousand Negroes rendered homeless by the burning of the district in which they lived, while thousands of white men looked on without raising a hand to put out the flames and even threatened to shoot the members of the fire department if they attempted to save life or property. The occasion of this lamentable occurrence was the complaint of a white woman elevator operator who had been inadvertently jostled by a Negro who stumbled as he was leaving the car. Behind this simple incident lay a long story of misunderstanding and neglect which had so strained the relations between the races that it needed only a spark to start a moral as well as a physical conflagration.[2]

What happened at Tulsa is a reminder of conditions which obtain in many parts of the country. We hear of particularly flagrant abuses, as when peonage leads to murder in Georgia, or some crime, real or suspected, leads to lynching in some hitherto peaceable community in the West or North. Of the causes that lie back of these outbreaks we know far too little. When a Southerner like Governor Dorsey risks misunderstanding and persecution by a bold statement of the facts we applaud his courage.[3] It seldom occurs to us that as members of the Christian Church we are equally responsible with him for seeing that these evils are abated and a more Christian relation between the races introduced.

Yet surely no responsibility could be plainer. How can we

[1] Cf. Chapters XIV, XVI.
[2] Cf. *Nation*, June 15, 29, 1921; *Survey*, June 11, July 2, 1921.
[3] Cf. *New York Times*, May 1, 1921.

preach brotherhood to Chinese and Japanese if we are unbrotherly to our own colored Americans? Some things we may not be able immediately to accomplish. On others we may honestly disagree. A few elementary matters we may surely take for granted. The Negro has a right to humane treatment, to a just trial before the law, to an opportunity to earn an honest living and have a decent home, to an education for his children and a sphere of self-expression for himself. An obligation rests on us as Christians to find out wherein our present treatment of the Negro involves the denial of these elementary rights and to see what we can do to remedy the evil.[1]

What is true of the relation of the races in our own country is equally true of the relation of nations to one another. In this field full of difficulties and perplexities, there must be careful thinking if Christian principles are to prevail. That they can be made to prevail is clear from the widespread response to the first proposal of the League of Nations, and the equally marked revulsion of feeling which swept over the nation when it began to appear that the public sentiment of the different peoples was not yet ripe for a Christian solution and that there was danger that the League of Nations might become simply a device for enforcing the right of the victor over the vanquished. Surely there is some other and better way than that which has led the nations to this "Pentecost of Calamity."

What we need, then, is a sober and careful study of the international situation with a view to determining the sphere in which the moral influence of the Church should operate and how it is to be effectively brought to bear. In the midst of much on which we differ, we shall find some things on which we can agree. The first step toward the better international future to which we look forward is common action within the territory of agreement. Out of the habit of working together will grow confidence in one another, and each step forward will point the way to the next.

---

[1] An encouraging beginning has been made through the creation of the Federal Council's Commission on the Church and Race Relations, a representative group of men and women of both races and different ecclesiastical and geographical connection.

In this connection reference should be made to the excellent work done by the Inter-Racial Commissions functioning in many Southern communities, as well as by the University Commission on Race Relations.

5. *Consequences for the Social Mission of the Church*

The foregoing discussion will help us to define more clearly the nature and limits of the Church's social responsibility. This responsibility is fourfold. The churches are responsible (1) for keeping the Christian ideal for society constantly before men's minds; (2) for producing men and women who in their several spheres of activity apply Christian principles to social relations, thus increasing the evidence that Christianity is socially practicable; (3) for keeping people informed of what is being done in the social application of Christianity, and so helping to create a public opinion which will make it possible to Christianize all our institutions; (4) and in the meantime, while the process is still incomplete, for conducting their affairs in such a way as to give a convincing demonstration that a Christian institution is possible.

(*a*) All four of these are important, but the first, under the conditions of our modern life, is all important. The most serious of all the obstacles to realizing the Christian ideal for society is the fact that so many, even among professing Christians, have not yet accepted it as an ideal.

What would society be like if Jesus could have His way? Let the authors of the volume on "The Church and Industrial Reconstruction" answer for us.

"It would be a co-operative social order in which the sacredness of every life was recognized and everyone found opportunity for the fullest self-expression of which he was capable; in which each individual gave himself gladly and whole-heartedly for ends that are socially valuable; in which the impulses to service and to creative action would be stronger than the acquisitive impulses, and all work be seen in terms of its spiritual significance as making possible fulness of life for all men; in which differences of talents and capacity meant proportional responsibilities and ministry to the common good; in which all lesser differences of race, of nation, and of class served to minister to the richness of an all-inclusive brotherhood; in which there hovered over all a sense of the reality of the Christ-like God, so that worship inspired service, as service expressed brotherhood." [1]

[1] Pp. 31, 32.

The acceptance of such an ideal does not require the surrender of the related ideals of patriotism, or of race or class loyalty, any more than the acceptance of these supersede the primary duty of each man to his own family and his own individuality. I do not love wife or children less because I love my country. I am not less conscious of my duty to develop my personality to its fullest capacity because I respect my friends and rejoice in their happiness and success. As each social unit is made up of lesser units, each of which in turn has its independent life and value, so society as a whole is made up of smaller social groups whose welfare and progress contribute to the success of the whole. As the welfare of each individual is essential to the well-being of the family, so the prosperity of each nation is essential to the progress of mankind. In the foreign-missionary enterprise we have recognized this in principle. It remains to draw the consequences for our political and economic life. We must take the general principles of the Gospel—principles to which all Christians would assent in the abstract—and translate them into such concrete terms as hours and wages, tariffs and immigration acts, the protection of women and children, the right of workers to organize for their own advancement, and their interest in the product of the industry of which they are a part.

(b) Words alone are not enough. Unless the witness of Christians is translated into terms of human life, the Church will find scant hearing for its social message. Men and women must be found who in their several spheres will apply Christian principles to their relations to their fellows and so make their contribution to the proof that Christianity is socially practicable.

There is nothing new in this. It is only the repetition under modern conditions of the demand for personal consecration and discipleship which has always been characteristic of Christianity. What is new is the environment in which this ministry must be rendered. In the mass production of modern industry the individual has been lost in the machine. Direct contact between employer and employee is no longer possible. More and more, human beings tend to be looked upon as the raw material of production, like pig-iron or coal. They have become hands on the lever, numbers in the balance-sheet. The Church must help to restore them to their true status as human beings with spiritual aspirations and ideals. What Jesus said to His first disciples, "Come ye after me, and I will make you to become fishers of men," [1] we must repeat to-day. But the method by which we must reach the men we are seeking has become infinitely more complex than it was in Jesus' day. Often it is no longer possible for one individual directly to touch another. If he is to be reached at all, he must be reached through others. All our relationships must be organized in such a way that the human significance of what we do shall appear at each stage of the process. For this there must be intelligent co-operation on a world-wide scale.

(c) This suggests a third responsibility of the Church; namely, its responsibility for forming a Christian public opinion. The Church must inspire in its own members a desire to apply Christian principles to the part of life they can control. It must be able to point to particular groups who are living in the Spirit of Christ and proving in their own experience that His ideal is a practicable ideal. But this alone is not enough. These isolated individuals must be related to one another, these independent experiences correlated and interpreted. The lessons learned by the few must be shared by the many, and a public opinion be formed which in time will make it possible to Christianize all human relationships.

As a force for the formation of public opinion, the American Protestant churches command resources of which they have scarcely begun to realize the magnitude. The case of prohibition reminds us of what can be done by the churches when they are alive and organized. Prohibition, however, deals with but a single evil. Once let the churches realize their responsibility for the greater causes of which we have been speaking, the cause of social justice and of international brotherhood, and there is no limit to what they may hope to accomplish.

(d) Whatever may be true of social institutions in general, there is one sphere in which it would seem as if the Christian social ideal could at once be completely realized. That is in the Church itself. The Church is an epitome of human society. Like the state, it is a government with laws and officers to enforce them, and it faces in principle all the problems of government. Like Big Business, it is an owner of property, and an employer of labor on a colossal scale. Like the nation, it includes men of every race, but

---

[1] Mark i, 17.

unlike the nation it is itself an international society. In the Church, then, we have an experiment station in which we may test the social practicability of the Gospel. Where can we find a better opportunity to put our principles to the proof? [1]

Yet, as a matter of fact, the demonstration which the Church might give has not yet been given. Institutional Christianity is itself only in part Christian. The Church, like the society of which it is a part, is the scene of compromise and limitation. Instead of being an argument for, it is often an argument against, the practicability of the Gospel. How often we hear men saying, "I could be a Christian if it were·not for the Church." Must this condition of things continue? If not, what is the remedy?

[1] Cf. W. Adams Brown, "Can We Keep the Church Christian?" *Christian Century*, June 2, 1921.

CHAPTER X

1. *Possible Attitudes Toward the Divisions of Christendom—The
Movement for Church Unity and the Questions of
Principle It Raises*

A STUDY of the responsibility of the Church for the social application of the Gospel brings us face to face with a new question;
namely, what we mean by the Church and how it is to function.

At first sight there seems to be no such thing as the Church, but
churches, partly independent, partly rivals, often working at cross-
purposes, always more or less ineffective, illustrating in their own
life and conduct all those phenomena of hesitation and compromise
which we have seen to be characteristic of the life of men in society.
Granting that we can solve our theoretical problems, that we see
clearly what the Church ought to be and to do, how can we bring
this standard to bear upon the existing churches?

To this question the Roman Catholic Church has a definite
answer. The reason for the weakness of the Church lies in its
divisions. By human wilfulness and frailty men have transformed
a divine institution into a group of human experiment stations, and
with the transformation have sacrificed the authority and majesty
which is the distinctive attribute of the true Church. For this evil
there is but one remedy—repentance and amendment. The schismatic bodies should confess their error and return to their original
allegiance. They should acknowledge the supremacy of Peter,
and accept his leadership. Then, the wounds of Christendom
healed, the Church would be once more revealed in its divine ideal,
and would reassume the spiritual leadership which is its divine
prerogative.

It is a solution as appealing as it is simple, if it were not for
one awkward and incontrovertible fact—the presence of other
churches, as conscious of their divine prerogatives as Rome, which

question her authority and compete for the right to rule over their fellow-Christians with a confidence as unshaken as hers. The Greek Orthodox Church regards Rome herself as schismatic and heretical. The rival sects of Protestantism may differ in many things; they share the conviction that they have preserved the pure and unadulterated Gospel from the corruption of Rome.

A further difficulty with the Roman solution is the inability of the churches that adopt it to show any such monopoly of the Christian virtues as would seem to justify their claim. If the reason we require an infallible Church is that it is our only means of delivery from the effects of human sin and ignorance, then we should expect to find the Church which possesses this unique revelation illustrating in an exceptional degree the Christian qualities which divine revelation was designed to produce; but no such demonstration can be given. In the court of morals no church can lay claim to a monopoly of the virtues, nor can all the churches together deny to those outside some share at least in the faith and love which are the choicest possessions of the Christian. The Church, as Roman theologians have long ago clearly perceived, is a *corpus permixtum*—including in its membership good and evil, saint and sinner. Like every human institution, it depends for its success upon the men and women who administer it, and these—in the Church as in the state—are fallible and sinful.[1] Dante, good Catholic as he was, found room for more than one Pope in hell. Harnack, from the Protestant side, has summed up his view of the situation in the pregnant sentence: "Where there is a church, there is always a little bit of the world!"

Confronted with these facts, the extreme liberals discard altogether the idea of one outward visible church. They believe that the true Church, the Church of the New Testament, is an invisible and spiritual thing. It is the fellowship of believers, the company of all the men and women who share Christ's ideal and are working for His ends. This society has no fixed limits. It is not confined to any ecclesiastical organization, nor to all of them together. It is like the spirit in the human body—an inward presence, felt

---

[1] The only exception which is admitted by the Roman Church is the Pope, and then only when he speaks *ex cathedra;* that is, "when in discharge of the office of pastor and doctor of all Christians, by virtue of his supreme Apostolic authority he defines a doctrine regarding faith or morals, to be held by the universal church."—Dogmatic Decrees of the Vatican Council, Chapter IV.

rather than seen, known by its effects but not exhausted by them. It is therefore a waste of breath to talk of outward unity. Whether there be one Church or a hundred matters little, provided that the ideals for which the churches stand find expression in consecrated human lives.

There are two reasons why this view of the Church is unsatisfactory. In the first place, it overlooks the fact that outward organization seems to be the inevitable consequence of spiritual unity. In the second place, it is blind to the equally obvious fact that ineffective organization produces unfortunate spiritual results.

We have already seen illustrations of this truth in connection with the labor movement. At heart the labor movement is a spiritual movement, embodying men's desire for self-expression and self-realization. But this desire is impotent unless it can create instrumentalities through which to function. So we see the growth of labor unions, and their association in the Federation of Labor, and the formation of Socialist clubs, and their incorporation in independent political parties, not arbitrarily or because of the selfishness and wilfulness of individual leaders, but by an inner necessity growing out of the nature of the movement itself.

As the labor movement illustrates the necessity of organization, so it teaches us the danger which may spring from organization of the wrong kind. Where workmen and employers—fellow-workers in the same industry—have no common organization through which that unity can find expression, suspicion and misunderstanding are inevitable. The natural desire of each group to advance its own interests develops easily into a doctrine of class antagonism. The belief in the essential incompatibility of interests as between labor and capital, and other teachings which foster suspicion and distrust between men could not gain the power they have if they were not systematically inculcated by persons who speak with the prestige which official position gives them.[1] On the other hand, employers' associations, formed for the legitimate purpose of mutual information and helpfulness, may become agents in promoting social suspicion and ill-will, and their deliverances, by their impersonal character, may have weight and influence which no individual utterance could carry. What we need is an organization in which both employers and workers are represented, which can approach the points

[1] Cf. The Constitution of the I. W. W. already cited, p. 38.

in dispute between the parties from the standpoint of the welfare of the industry as a whole.[1] As it is, the inherent difficulties of the situation are aggravated by the machinery designed to deal with them. What should be a help in bringing minds together proves often an agency for keeping them apart.

From this situation there is but one way of escape—better organization. To dispense with organization is the most futile of all remedies for social ills; for organization is of the very essence of life in society. The only way to correct the evils of organization is to devise better methods of organization. The one sure remedy for a bad institution is a good one.

An illustration in point is the present international situation. Why is it that it is so much easier to stir up ill-will between the nations than to bring them together for mutual helpfulness? The answer is obvious—because our political machinery is planned for the first purpose, and not for the second. We have constructed the state on the hypothesis that all other states are its natural enemies, and when we try to bring states together for other purposes than self-protection, the old associations are too powerful to be overcome. We must not only see that the methods we have been following are wrong, we must not only produce a powerful body of sentiment favoring conciliation and peace; we must create the machinery through which this sentiment can function. We must

---

[1] Among the many proposals that are being brought forward for the settlement of industrial disputes, that offered by the Denver Trades and Labor Assembly is especially interesting. The resolution embodying it is as follows:

"Whereas, capital and labor are rapidly drifting toward a condition of industrial warfare which will be disastrous to the general welfare of America, and

"Whereas, we believe that it is the duty of men to reason together rather than to blindly seek selfish advantage, and

"Whereas, labor is willing to rest its case upon the application of the Golden Rule and the teachings of the Carpenter of Nazareth; therefore

"Be it Resolved, That we, the Trades and Labor Assembly of Denver, invite the employers of Denver to appoint a committee of six members to meet with a like number representing the Trades and Labor Assembly and the Building Trades Council, to form a Good Will Council. This body shall select a thirteenth member by mutual agreement to be the presiding officer. We suggest that this 'Good Will Council' meet every two weeks. To this body any industrial dispute or difficulty may be referred."

The Ministerial Alliance of Denver urged the employers to accept the proposal and it is now reported that they have appointed their representatives.

replace the old divisive institutions which have brought civilization to this lamentable pass with new institutions, international in character, whose avowed aim is unity.[1]

This insight is the driving spirit in the movement for Christian unity which is so much in evidence in our day. We realize that our kindly feelings toward our fellow-Christians, to be effective, must express themselves in action. And that means that we must organize. When Rome threatened spiritual liberty, it was necessary to assert the right of the free spirit to break with the past, just as it was politically necessary for our fathers, a century and a half ago, to assert the right to break with the mother country. New occasions teach new duties. Our need to-day is of unity quite as much as of freedom. But unity, in church and state alike, can find expression only through organization.

The present movement for unity takes two forms: that for organic and that for federal unity. The former takes its departure from the nature of the Church, the latter from the need of the world. The movement for organic unity seeks, through a study of the nature and function of the Church as revealed in its foundation and history, to find some way through which the separated bodies of Christians can be brought together in a single visible and corporate body. The movement for federal unity, on the other hand, tries, through a study of the present tasks of the Church, to find a way in which the different denominations which are addressing themselves to these tasks separately may be associated in some co-operative movement which shall pool their resources and give them the authority and spiritual power which they lack when separated. The two are not necessarily inconsistent. Federal union may be a step toward organic union. Organic union when it comes, in church as in state, may prove to be federal.[2]

The chief differences which must be adjusted in any attempt to secure union, whether organic or federal, concern four points: (1) the significance of the institution for religion; (2) the extent of free-

---

[1] More important than any decision which the new Court of International Justice at the Hague may render, is the mere fact that it exists.

[2] On the meaning of the terms Federal and Organic Union and the possible relations between them, cf. W. Adams Brown, "How We May Unite," *Constructive Quarterly,* June, 1921; cf. also "Christian Unity: Its Principles and Possibilities," pp. 8–12.

dom and variety possible within it; (3) the form of organization most to be desired; (4) the means of securing the agreement necessary to bring about the desired results.

2. *Different Views of the Significance of the Church as an Institution*

Fundamental among the differences between Christians is the difference in their view of the significance of the Church as an institution and its relation to the society of free personalities which it serves. The high churchman of every school views that relation as fundamental. It is the institution rather than the persons who compose it which is the channel of divine revelation. The institution, therefore, precedes and makes possible the spiritual society.

Those who take this view do not deny the difference to which we have already referred between the ecclesiastical organization and the spiritual society of which it is the servant and expression; but they regard the former as antecedent to the latter. They believe that it is antecedent in time. Christ founded His Church as an institution in order that He might bring into existence His Church as a spiritual society. They believe that it is antecedent also in importance. Without the institution, the society of persons could not be; for to it Christ has committed that truth and grace which alone enable it to function effectively in His name. Thus the high churchman finds that everything depends upon the right organization. Apostolic succession does not seem, to the high Anglican, simply a matter of ancient order or of ecclesiastical expediency. It is the condition of the existence of the Church; for without it the grace which makes a valid sacrament could not be conferred.

We have said that this view is common to high churchmen [1] of every school. Anglo-Catholics share it with Roman Catholics. It explains an exclusiveness which many Christians of other schools find it hard to understand. The high churchman does not regard the business of securing unity as a matter of bringing equals together. He sees in it the recall of prodigals to their Father's house.

[1] "High churchman" is used here in a restricted sense to denote those who hold a view of the Church which excludes all Christians who do not accept their definition of what the Church is. The term is often used in a broader sense to include all Christians who have a high sense of the value of institutional Christianity.

This spirit of uncompromising devotion to the institution is found among many who would deny it in theory. High church Presbyterians and Lutherans consider the Bible and not the Church as the pillar and ground of the truth, or rather the Gospel which the Bible enshrines. But since that Gospel is embodied in definite creeds and these creeds are made the test of orthodoxy (in practice at least, whatever may be true in theory) the ultimate outcome is the same. In each case loyalty to the truth is identified with loyalty to a certain institution. In each case compromise with other bodies would involve betrayal of a divine trust. In each case, therefore, the representatives of this view meet any proposal of unity which does not involve the complete acceptance of their terms with a *"Non possumus."*

The difficulty with this position is that it gets us nowhere. The claims of other churchmen equally confident of the right of their position are met in the spirit of absolute denial. Its analogue in politics is the German theory of the state. As state stood over against state in the uncompromising affirmation of sovereignty, so church stands over against church. From this *impasse* there are only two possible ways out—the appeal to force and the appeal to reason. The appeal to force we have abandoned with the Inquisition, and with the cessation of wars of religion. Even in the days when it was practised it was futile. At most it could induce outward conformity, not change of heart. So there seems no way out for modern men but the appeal to reason. If the churches are ever to come together it must be in some such way as this.

By the appeal to reason, we do not, of course, mean the belief that arguments as such can ever produce agreement among Christians. Religion concerns more than the mind, and makes its appeal to feeling and will as well as thought. We use reason in the comprehensive sense of the term to include all the activities of the free spirit as it reacts to its environment and builds up the edifice of conviction out of the experiences which have come to it through its contacts with reality. This is the sense in which our Protestant forefathers understood it when they claimed the right of private judgment against Rome and included among the cardinal loyalties which none could deny without betrayal of trust the freedom of conscience for the sake of which they had broken away from the mother church.

The low churchmen, accordingly, are searching for unity through the consensus of Christian experience. If each man seeks God sincerely in his own way, he will find many joining him in his quest; for God, who is truth itself, cannot be inconsistent with Himself, and what one man learns of Him through his personal experience of salvation will be paralleled in the history of every other man who has passed through a similar experience. If freedom be given full scope, it would seem, then, that unity must follow in due time.

Yet the results which have thus far followed from the application of this method of free experiment might well discourage its advocates. High churchmen rest their case against it on the divisions of Protestantism. They tell us that the private judgment to which liberals so confidently appeal has rent Christendom into a hundred warring sects and divided each of them into different schools of opinion. It has no final authoritative court of appeal. It is impotent to give the certainty for which the human heart craves. In a word, it represents the bankruptcy of religion. When one looks at the situation of Protestantism to-day, one feels that there is much to be said for the high churchman's point of view.

It may prove, however, that the trouble is not so much with the method as with the way in which it has been used, and above all with the anticipations which have been entertained concerning it. The old ideal of uniformity dies hard, and the Reformers who broke with Rome in their theory of the way revelation came, preserved the assumption of the older Church as to the marks by which it was to be recognized. That God should speak to different people in different ways, that a man might reject their conception of truth and yet be in the way of salvation, seemed to our fathers difficult if not impossible to believe. The divisions of Protestantism were the inevitable result of the attempt to secure complete agreement on the basis of freedom. Each variation of opinion required a new organization, because it could not find the liberty it required in the old.

From the difficulties of this situation the historical spirit helps to deliver us. It shows us that the causes which gave birth to the Protestant churches were entirely natural and inevitable. Some of them were the expression of different ideals of the religious life, ideals which have persisted to this day and have present significance for us. Some of them, like the great organization which Wesley founded, came into existence because definite tasks needed to be performed. Still others owe their perpetuation to differences of tradition or sentiment, loyalty to some leader, or response to some æsthetic value rooted in the past. These differences have not the momentous and necessarily divisive effect our fathers thought they had; but they are not purely arbitrary or negligible. Some of them have served a useful purpose in the past; others still serve such a purpose to-day.

We may learn a lesson here from the Roman Catholic Church. We think of the Roman Catholic Church as realizing in a high degree its ideal of unity; but it is unity in variety. In Catholicism, too, different types of religious experience are found, and theologians differ as to the correct interpretation of doctrine. Nor are these differences merely private and academic. They have embodied themselves in institutions with a long history and powerful organization. What the different denominations are to Protestantism, the rival orders are to Roman Catholicism. The struggle for power between the Franciscan and the Dominican, and later between the Society of Jesus and the older orders, fills many a page of church history. So generally recognized is the fact of difference that it has found expression in official Roman Catholic theology in the distinction between the religious and the secular life. The saint is held to a higher standard than the ordinary Christian and may be granted exemption from the ordinary means of grace upon which less advanced Christians must rely for their salvation.[1]

In the light of these facts the older ideal of uniformity is being generally abandoned by thoughtful Christians. The unity now sought is a unity which makes room for difference. The surrender

[1] It was not an easy task to bring the different Protestant organizations together in the General War-Time Commission of the Churches. But if we have been correctly informed, it was no less difficult to reconcile the different interests which co-operated in the National Catholic War Council. Cf. Williams, "American Catholics in the War," p. 114. "Despite the contrary opinion held by so many non-Catholics, the fact remains that there are no more convinced and at times stubborn individualists than Catholics. The idea that they comprise a vast, compact organization, which can be set in motion at a touch from authority, the impulsion of the central will operating efficiently and immediately through the bishops and the priests, is true only and solely in purely spiritual matters—in the region of the defined dogmas of the Faith. In all other concerns, and in all questions of methods, Catholics, and in particular the Catholics of the United States, constitute a very large aggregation of separate schools of thought and types of action."

of the convictions which any group of Christians hold sincerely is
not asked, nor the repudiation of a past laden with sacred memories,
rather the inclusion of these treasures in a larger unity. "The
philosophers of religion," once said a great philosopher, "have all
been right in their affirmations. Their error has lain in their
denials." We are coming to see that this may be true of the Christian denominations.

3. *Different Views of the Limits of Legitimate Variation within the Church*

How shall we determine the extent of legitimate difference?
Can it include the existing denominations or must they give way
to other forms of Christian organization? Or shall we retain some
and suppress others, and if so, which? These questions introduce
us into the very heart of the present debate concerning church
unity.

Formidable difficulties meet us in every phase of the Church's
work—in its doctrine, in its organization, in its mode of worship.
Recent proposals for church union have tried to reduce the range of
debate by specifying certain irreducible *minima* which may be taken
as the basis of further discussion. Thus the well-known Lambeth
quadrilateral specified the Apostles' and the Nicene creeds as the
irreducible *minimum* in the field of doctrine; the two sacraments
with the words of institution in the field of worship; and the historic
Episcopate in the field of organization.[1] Unitarians would reject
the second as committing them to the doctrine of the Trinity. The
stricter Baptists would be dissatisfied with the third as not exclud-
ing infant baptism or insisting upon immersion as the only valid
form of this ordinance; while most Protestant Christians, especially

[1] "I. The Holy Scriptures of the Old and New Testaments as 'containing
all things necessary to salvation,' and as being the rule and ultimate standard
of Faith.

"II. The Apostles' Creed, as the Baptismal Symbol; and the Nicene Creed,
as the sufficient statement of the Christian Faith.

"III. The two Sacraments ordained by Christ Himself—Baptism and the
Supper of the Lord—ministered with unfailing use of Christ's words of institution, and of the elements ordained by Him.

"IV. The Historic Episcopate, locally adapted in the methods of its administration to the varying needs of the nations and peoples called of God into
the unity of His Church."

Quoted in Manning, "The Call to Unity," New York, 1920, p. 123.

those of Congregational or independent antecedents, would object to the fourth as unduly limiting the form of the Church's organization and above all as denying the title of church to bodies of Christians not episcopally organized, although they have shown in their history and experience all the marks of the presence of God's Spirit. The Disciples on their part would reject all three conditions as adding man-made requirements to the sole condition of church membership properly to be required of the Christian; namely, the acceptance of the Bible, as interpreted by the individual conscience, as the final and sufficient standard.

A further difference of importance relates to the extent to which the Church as an institution may rightly enter into political and economic questions. Some denominations are conservative on this point, maintaining that the sole duty of the Church is to win individuals to Christ through the witness of the Gospel and that any attempt to realize a Christian society that is not based upon such antecedent conversion is in effect a perversion of the Christian witness. Others favor a wider extension of the Church's mission. Agreeing that it is the Church's duty to witness to the truth, they think that one of the chief reasons why that witness has so little power is the indifference of Christians to the patent facts of social oppression and injustice, for so long as these remain uncorrected they constitute a most powerful argument against the reality of the Christian God.

More important, however, than any differences in the conclusions reached are the different presuppositions from which the disputants approach the debate. One group believes that the Church has a certain definite and fixed constitution which was imposed upon it by Christ at its foundation, and which cannot be altered or modified without the sacrifice of the grace which makes it a supernatural institution. It is not a question of what we think desirable for the Church, but of what Christ has revealed concerning the Church. When that has been determined, the time for question is over. It becomes our duty loyally to follow the direction which our Master has given.

On this common basis we find wide varieties of individual interpretation. Indeed, it is instructive to observe what strange bedfellows philosophy makes of men. Both the high church Episcopalian and the Southern Baptist believe that there is divine authority for but one view of the Church's constitution. Each holds that Christ has definitely prescribed a certain way of observing His ordinances. Each makes unquestioning obedience to the divine command his justification for the refusal of fellowship with those who think otherwise.[1] The result is the lamentable condition of our divided Christendom.

Observing such an outcome, many Christians are convinced that there is something wrong in the process by which this conclusion is reached. They, too, believe that the Church as an institution has a divinely appointed mission to fulfil in the world and that it is not a matter of indifference how it is organized on lines of creed, polity, and worship, but they are convinced that the way to discover the true method of organization is to study the lessons which God's Spirit has been teaching His people in the course of the Church's entire experience. They think of the Church as a living organism consisting of persons spiritually united to Jesus Christ and progressively taught by Him as to His will. In the course of its history under the guidance of God's Spirit this living organism develops the external forms through which its inner life is expressed. These forms are not arbitrary or unimportant. They grow naturally and inevitably out of the past. They assimilate the results of past experience and hand them down to future generations; but they are not rigid or immovable. Nothing that is alive is changeless. It is always creating new organs of expression. The Church, which is the creation of Him who is life indeed, is no exception to this rule.[2]

---

[1] An interesting example of the strict views of the Southern Baptists was their refusal to allow any money given to their chaplains to be spent on a communion service. Cf. War-Time Agencies of the Churches, p. 21, "It was specified that no part of the $250 was to be used for the purchase of a communion set, as the Council believed it necessary to have a local church membership present in order to hold a communion service."

[2] One of the most interesting things about the recent pronouncement of the bishops at Lambeth was the extent to which it recognized the justice of this point of view. Cf. "Christian Unity," pp. 359–360. "On the one hand there are other ancient episcopal Communions in East and West, to whom ours is bound by many ties of common faith and tradition. On the other hand there are the great non-episcopal Communions, standing for rich elements of truth, liberty, and life which might otherwise have been obscured or neglected. With them we are closely linked by many affinities, racial, historical, and spiritual. We cherish the earnest hope that all these Communions, and our own, may be led by the Spirit into the unity of the Faith and of the knowledge of the Son of God."

In discussing the questions on which we differ from our fellow-Christians we must approach them with an open mind, asking first of all what agencies the Spirit of God has used in the past, and how these agencies can be made to serve the need of the new day and generation. Such widely accepted forms of organization and worship as, for example, the historic Episcopate and the Liturgy, have played so important a part in the life of the Church that the members of the non-Episcopal and non-liturgical churches may well ask themselves whether the time has not come to make place for them in their polity and practice. But such acceptance, if it is to promote true unity, must be made willingly to meet a felt need, and cannot be imposed from without as a condition of reunion.

The two ways of approach which we have thus briefly contrasted correspond roughly to the differences between the advocates of organic and those of federal union. The contrast is, to be sure, not an absolute one, but it is sufficiently accurate for our purpose. Most of those who have been most active in the cause of organic union have been so because they have believed that Christ intends the corporate, visible union of His Church and that the way to bring this about is to discover by discussion, conference, and study of the authoritative records of the past what the marks of such an outward and visible Church must be. Those who advocate federal union, on the other hand, believe that such discussion, however useful it may be as providing points of contact, will carry us but a little way, because it leaves out of account the most important of all our data; namely, the experience of the living Church which is working out the true form of its organization in the laboratory of life. To the question what this form is to be, they can give no final answer. Only experience of the future can teach us what the Church of the future is to be like. We must learn by actual experiment which of the existing forms of church organization are so essential that they cannot be spared and which can now properly be dispensed with.

What interests us in all this is the fact that these experiments are actually being tried. The goal of union is being sought by a number of different methods, and each method holds out promise of real accomplishment. We have spoken of two of the best known of these methods, the method of organic union and that of federal union. But there are others which are not less worthy of study because they are more modest, and less widely advertised. There is the method of administrative union, as it is illustrated in such interdenominational agencies as the Home Missions Council, the Foreign Missions Conference, and other similar agencies. There is the method of local co-operation, as it meets us in the federations of churches and in the community church. There is the union of Christian individuals in unofficial, yet powerful, organizations such as the Young Men's and the Young Women's Christian Associations. There are the conferences that bring together official and unofficial bodies in Ecumenical Councils and in Continuation Committees. All these are ways through which the Christian spirit is manifesting itself to-day. Through each experience is being garnered which will be of service in shaping the lines of the Church of the future.

4. *Inferences as to the Future Organization of the Church Derived from a Study of Present Tendencies*

Can we discern the lines along which this movement toward unity is likely to develop? One hesitates to forecast the outcome of a situation so complicated, but if the past is to be any measure of the future, some such development as the following would seem not unlikely: (1) Denominations of the same or closely related families will be grouped or merged, and as a result the denominational machinery and denominational consciousness will be strengthened not only within each nation, but, in the case of the stronger communions, on an international scale; (2) the leading Protestant communions will be united in a nation-wide Federal Council; (3) the existing agencies of interdenominational administrative union will be perfected and grouped into certain main divisions such as (a) home missions, (b) foreign missions, (c) Christian education, etc.; (4) special questions or tasks on which the opinion of the Church is not sufficiently united to make official action possible or expedient will be referred to commissions or associations of individuals for study, experiment, and report; (5) agencies of local co-operation will be multiplied and united on a nation-wide scale; (6) intermediate interdenominational organizations will be developed on state or other convenient geographical lines; (7) periodic conventions will be held representing all the interests concerned to give public expression to the unity of the Christian forces in the nation; (8) similar National Councils will be created in other countries and united in an International Council embracing all sections of the Christian Church willing to join in it.

We shall reserve for later consideration [1] the relation of these different lines of development to the movement for organic union. It is enough to say here that if organic union is ever to be realized on a comprehensive scale, this would seem to be the way in which it must come about. Organic union, to be effective, must be the expression of a preceding spiritual union, and spiritual union between those who accept the Protestant principle of freedom can be achieved only through some such process of life as we have briefly sketched above.

In the fields where progress has actually been made toward the corporate union of churches, that of denominational groups holding the same polity or of groups of closely related denominations within a definite geographical area, practical co-operation has preceded official action. In each case the contacts already established through missionary work have proved the most potent influence in bringing the churches together. The world's need has proved the Church's teacher. In seeking to serve others it has discovered its true self.

We have an instructive analogy in the life of the nation. Where organic union has been achieved on a large scale, as in the case of our own United States, it has been on the basis of a preceding federal union. The long struggle for liberty taught the American colonies their need of one another and they came together in a provisional organization which retained for the co-operating units their full sovereignty and liberty of secession. But experience soon showed that without a strong central government the common interests could not be adequately conserved, and the present Constitution of the United States was the result of this discovery. Even so it took nearly two generations and a bloody war before the older theory of state sovereignty was definitely outgrown and the right of secession at will finally abandoned. It was the experience of working together for common ends that made possible the degree of national unity which the United States now possesses. If unity is ever to come in the Christian Church, it must be in some such way as this.

[1] Cf. Chapter XIII.

There are encouraging signs that this fact is being widely recognized. The pressure of the world's need is forcing Christians together in many ways, and the contacts so brought about are producing corresponding changes in organization. We have studied one notable illustration of this in the General War-Time Commission of the Churches. What was done successfully in war may be done, must be done, in peace. It is significant that the bishops at Lambeth should have associated with their moving appeal for the organic union of Christendom this significant resolution: "The Conference recommends that wherever it has not already been done, councils representing all Christian communions should be formed within such areas as may be deemed most convenient as centres of united effort to promote the physical, moral, and social welfare of the people and the extension of the rule of Christ among all nations and over every region of human life."[1]

In the meantime, the movement for organic union is going on in the lesser and more closely related groups to which reference has already been made, and lessons are being learned and experience gained which will be invaluable for the larger movements which lie ahead.[2]

For it is important to remember that the different manifestations of the spirit of union which we have reviewed are not arbitrary or independent. They are parts of a single movement which is going on before our eyes—a movement as natural and inevitable as any other life process. It meets obstacles as every life process does; obstacles in the realm of theory and even more serious ones in the realm of sentiment and habit. There are irreconcilables on the right hand and on the left; absolutists who insist that it must be all or nothing and individualists who cheerfully meet this challenge with the declaration, "Then it shall be nothing." Behind these, reinforcing them in a hundred subtle and disheartening ways, are the forces of prejudice, ignorance, and inertia, which have been the foes of unity in every country and in every age. Our final question is how these obstacles are to be met and overcome.

---

[1] Conference of Bishops of the Anglican Communion, Holden at Lambeth Palace, July 5 to August 7, 1920; Encyclical Letter from the Bishops with the Resolutions and Reports, Resolution 13, p. 31. Society for Promoting Christian Knowledge, London, 1920.

[2] One of the most instructive illustrations is that of the churches of Canada of which some account is given in Chapter XIII, pp. 259 sq.

5. *Principles which Condition Future Progress*

First of all and most important of all there must be contact, and this contact must, so far as possible, be natural and unforced. Hence every form of private and unofficial conference between Christians is to be encouraged in order that those ties of understanding and confidence may be formed that make official union possible. Undue haste is to be deprecated. He goes far who goes slowly.

This contact, to be effective, must be in both the realms in which the Christian experience moves—service and worship. We must work together and we must pray together. The precondition of any effective union between Christians is the development of a common religious experience; but that we may worship together effectively we must have some common task ·which sends us together to God for light and strength.

Our most pressing need, therefore, is to find some form of common work in which we can engage together. This work, to be significant, must be important enough to require the services of trained men for its successful accomplishment. Hence administrative union, or the union which grows out ·of the practical co-operation of those who are already serving their respective organizations in a representative capacity, is the best place at which to begin more formal relationships.

However long delayed, sooner or later official denominational co-operation there must be; for unless those who are the official leaders of the different bodies feel the responsibility for educating their constituents in their relationship to Christians of other churches, their power to work together will be limited in ways which we shall study more carefully in the chapters that follow.

The test of effective co-operation, in church affairs as everywhere else, is financial. What men pay for they feel they own. To make the churches realize their partnership in a common task, this partnership must appear on the balance-sheet.

To this end there must be effective publicity, a publicity that uses the agencies of the denomination to educate its members in their responsibility to the larger Church of which the denomination is but a part. The key to interest is always knowledge. To arouse enthusiasm we must impart the facts.

Above all there must be absolute frankness in facing the situation as it exists. There is much glib talk of unity which does more harm than good, since it ignores real difficulties and seeks to substitute words for facts. Nothing can be more dangerous than to pretend to have spiritual unity when none exists. We have made great progress in getting together. But the process is not yet complete, and it is only right that we should face the fact. Not in minor points only, but in matters that are vital, Christians are still divided in spirit.

The ancient cleavage between Catholic [1] and Protestant still remains, and there are many in the so-called Protestant churches who consciously accept the Catholic view of Christianity, and many more who unconsciously act upon its premises. This fact we must take into account in our future plans for a reunited Christendom. Either we must make place in the reunited church for both types of religious faith and experience, or confess that for the present at least our union must be incomplete.

Apart from this major cleavage between Christians there are other differences to be considered. At some of these we have already had occasion to glance in earlier portions of this chapter. They are found in the field of doctrine, of worship, and of organization. Some of these differences are inherent and must be dealt with by mutual recognition and tolerance. Others are due to misunderstanding or immaturity and can be removed by education. All are real difficulties to be faced frankly, discussed freely, and dealt with in the Christian spirit of faith and love which is the key to the successful resolution of all our difficulties.

Besides these intellectual difficulties there are serious moral difficulties to be overcome. There is the inertia which seems implicit in institutional life. There is the tendency to regard the institution as an end, and not simply as a means. There are the temptations which accompany office-holding and the power of patronage. When an institution becomes as strong as the Christian Church and exercises as wide an influence, other motives lead men to join its ranks than devotion to its ideal. Not all who take the Christian vows are willing to pay the price which thorough commitment to their principles would involve. These facts, too, we must frankly

[1] The term is used here in the same narrow sense in which the word "high churchman" was used earlier in the chapter.

recognize in our plans for the future. Any programme for the Church which requires the sacrifice of prestige or of official position will inevitably meet opposition.

But these difficulties, far from discouraging us, should be but so many motives leading us to a more complete consecration. What the body is to the individual, the organized Church is to the Christian society. It is the organ through which that society acts upon its human environment and shapes to spiritual uses the conflicting purposes of men and women. Organized government, in Church as in state, is an instrument of education by which men are trained to discipline their private likings in order that they may become able to work together and to reap the rewards of such work in greater usefulness and happiness. In this process, as in the simpler process of physical education, mistakes are made and dangers incurred. But there is no way of escaping this. It is the price of progress.

It may be that to some readers of this book this will seem a disappointing conclusion. It may seem to them to lay too heavy a responsibility on human shoulders. They have been accustomed to think of the Church as a great exception to God's customary way of working for man through men. They are asked to see in it one more example, the most conspicuous, of the way in which He trains His children by responsibility. The writer sympathizes with their disappointment. He, too, wishes there were some short and easy road to the great consummation; but it seems this is not God's way. Wherever we look, in nature or in human life, we see God using finite and imperfect instruments for His divine and beneficent ends. Why should it surprise us to find the same true in the Church? What God wished to do for men He elected to do through men with all their weaknesses and limitations. We may wonder at the risks in such a choice. We cannot but accept with joy the splendid responsibility entrusted to us and carry forward in humility and in hope the work committed to our charge.

PART IV

ORGANIZING FOR WORK

CHAPTER XI

1. *The Fundamental Importance of the Local Church for the Forward Movement in Christianity*

THUS far we have been moving largely in the realm of theory. We have been asking ourselves what the Church of Christ would be like if it could realize its divine ideal, and what are the methods which must be followed to bridge the gap between ideal and present fact. We have seen that as the institution of religion the Church exists to make men acquainted with God, and sharers in His plan for their lives; that this plan has to do not with individuals simply, but with society, and that the churches must therefore concern themselves with those wider questions of race, of class, and of nationality which divide men from one another and prevent the realization of the Christian ideal. We have seen that the first and most effective step toward this realization would be for the churches themselves to come together. It remains to ask what chance there is that this will come to pass. What are the churches actually doing and what are they likely to do to realize the ideal of a Christian social order? [1]

The final test of success or failure for the Church must always remain the local congregation. The local congregation introduces us to individual men and women under the normal conditions of life. Here is laid the foundation for the Church's wider ministry in the preaching of the Gospel, and the formation of the habit of worship. Here children are gathered into the Sunday school for religious training and through the children the Church reaches the home which is the fountain-head of all true religious life. Here, too, is the ultimate source of the financial support of the Church— the recruiting ground to which all national organizations must go for supplies for their more ambitious projects. From the local

[1] For the subjects treated in this and the following chapters, cf. "Christian Unity: Its Principles and Possibilities," New York, 1920.

church, finally, come the young men and women who must provide the ministry of the future. To form an intelligent idea of the prospects of the Church as a whole we must begin by studying the local congregation.

In the local church we meet the difficulties which thwart our effort to realize the ideal in their most acute form. The local church stands on Main Street, and is exposed to all the influences which go to make up the life of the average community. Here the individual displays his powers for harm with least check. Whatever there may be of provincialism or narrowness or self-satisfaction in the community at large is reflected in the local church. Yet it is of such churches that the Church consists, and it is in the strength of the spiritual forces found in them that we must go forward, if we go at all.

It is difficult to gather reliable information as to what goes on in our local churches. Statistics can tell us something of their number; of their relative growth and decline; of the number of members in each and how many are without a pastor; of the services they hold; of what they pay for their own support, and what they give to the Church at large. But these statistics mean little without interpretation, and for this interpretation we lack a standard.[1] All that we can hope to do is to register symptoms and tendencies.

[1] An interesting attempt to establish such a standard was made by the Town and Country Divisions of the Interchurch World Movement. In co-operation with the Home Missions Council, they worked out a "par standard" for the local church covering thirty-one points, all of which are regarded as obtainable by many town and country churches. These include "social and recreational equipment, including a stage; a well-equipped kitchen; an organ or piano; separate Sunday-school room or curtained spaces for classes or departments; stereopticon or motion picture equipment; adequate sanitary toilets; horse-sheds or parking space for automobiles; a pastor resident within the same community as the church, who gives full time to the work of that church, conducts services every Sunday, and receives a salary of at least $1,200 a year and house; an annual budget for all money raised; a yearly canvass of all members; sum for benevolences equal to at least twenty-five per cent. of the current expenses; services to all racial and occupational groups which have not their own Protestant churches; Sunday school the entire year; Sunday-school enrollment equal to church membership; provision for bringing pupils into the church; special instruction for church membership; teacher training or normal class; provision for leadership training; systematic evangelism, aimed to reach the entire community and all classes of the community; co-operation with other churches of the community; organized activities for age and sex groups; co-operation with church boards and

On the face of it the situation seems discouraging. We hear constant complaints of the weakness and ineffectiveness of the local church; of the loss of its former influence on individuals and on the community; of the increasing number of parishes without a minister; of the growing difficulty of securing candidates to take the place of the men now in the field. This, true of all parts of the country to a greater or less extent, is pre-eminently true of the country districts. Here we see the effects of the individualism of our American Christianity in its most disheartening aspect. The overchurching of some communities and the all but total abandonment of others; the rivalry of denominations for promising fields and the corresponding neglect of those which are more needy; the loss of the natural constituency of the churches through the steady flow of population from country to city and the failure to devise any effective method for dealing with the situation thus created: these are some of the more obvious aspects of the present situation which strike the superficial observer.

In Gill and Pinchot's study of the country churches of Ohio [1] we have the most complete study at present available of the condition to which this lack of foresight has reduced the Church.[2] It reveals a state of overchurching which is almost unbelievable, with a corresponding state of weakness and inefficiency in the churches which exist. In the entire state there was in 1918 an average of one church for every two hundred and eighty people. Out of every hundred of these churches sixty had less than one hundred members; fifty-five less than seventy-five, and thirty-seven not more than fifty members. Two-thirds of the churches had no resident pastor, even counting in all the rural town churches, while in the open country only three hundred and sixty, or thirteen per cent of the two thousand eight hundred and seven churches, had resident pastors. The average salary paid in the denomination with the largest

denominational agencies; service to the entire community; twenty-five per cent. of members with a definite place in some part of church activities." Cf. Four Country Churches of Distinction—Studies in Church Efficiency, Educational Department, Board of Home Missions of the Presbyterian Church in the U. S. A.

[1] "Six Thousand Country Churches," New York, 1919, pp. 8–11.

[2] It is to be noted that the State Federation of Ohio has prepared a revised survey of practically every county in Ohio based upon the material gathered by the Interchurch World Movement. This is in course of publication in a series of small pamphlets.

number of country churches was eight hundred and fifty-seven dollars and free use of a parsonage; in the denomination with the next largest number, seven hundred and eighty-seven dollars, or six hundred and eighty dollars, if a parsonage was provided.

What has been going on in Ohio has been going on with variations in other parts of the country. The surveys conducted by the Presbyterian Board of Home Missions through its Department of Country Life found essentially the same conditions in each of the several states in which counties were surveyed.[1] In Missouri only four per cent. of the country churches had resident ministers.[2] In a recent survey of two central counties made by Dr. Alva Taylor, Secretary of the Social Service Commission of the Disciples, not a single resident pastor was found.[3] Yet in these same communities there may be two, three, or even four or five different church buildings standing side by side.[4]

It is difficult to exaggerate the disastrous effect of such a state of things. The loss in money and efficiency is obvious; that in prestige is even greater. How can we expect young people to respect an institution which conducts its affairs in so haphazard and unbusinesslike a way? With what conscience can we seek recruits for a

---

[1] Such surveys have been published for counties in Ohio, California, Oregon, Arkansas, Maryland, and Tennessee.

[2] Cf. Alva W. Taylor, "The Community Church the Only Way Out," *The Community Churchman,* April, 1921.

[3] *Ibid.*

[4] From a number of cases in Missouri furnished by Dr. David R. Piper, editor of the *Community Churchman,* we cite the following:

"Callao, population 526 according to 1910 Census, but reckoned now at 450. Four churches: Methodist Episcopal, Southern Baptist, Presbyterian U. S. A., and Disciples. All the buildings are rotting down except the Disciples. Alexandria, a fishing village of about 500, has three churches: Disciples, Presbyterian U. S., and Baptist, and no resident pastor. Presbyterian building in fair condition. Others dingy. Mirable, population 250, has four churches, including Presbyterian U. S. A., and Methodist. Novelty, population 232, has four churches: Disciples, Methodist Episcopal, Methodist Episcopal South, and Baptist (Southern). There is an open country community in the southwest corner of Grundy County, near the village of Hickory where within a radius of three miles are six church buildings. Two of these are Baptist and one Disciples. The farthest of these churches is less than three and a half miles from Hickory, which has one church: Methodist Episcopal. At the time of the survey last fall, no church had a resident preacher."

Dr. Piper comments: "I do not know whether you consider these as flagrant examples. They are the normal thing in northern Missouri."

ministry which offers no larger or more inspiring opportunity of service?

In cities and larger communities, the situation is, of course, better; but here, too, there are disturbing factors. Most noticeable is perhaps the almost complete absence in most of the Protestant denominations of any recognized parish system. Churches are placed at haphazard where the taste and inclination of the members incline, and moved to a more desirable location when the shifting of population seems to make such a change advantageous. As a result we have the familiar spectacle of overchurching in some quarters and no churches in others. The Church as a whole fails to impress itself upon the community as a whole.

Both of these results are due to the same cause, the unrestricted individualism which has hitherto been the dominant factor in our American Christianity. The methods which were appropriate for dealing with a situation of one kind have shown themselves inadequate to meet different conditions. In an earlier study [1] these conditions were summed up as follows: "What is needed in our cities to-day is a group of strong churches, with ample resources, highly organized, fully manned, well equipped for social and educational as well as for distinctly religious work, intelligently linked in a well-planned parish system, with an efficient central organization fitted to cope with new conditions as they arise, and flexible enough to try needed experiments without the sacrifice of continuity of purpose. What we find is a group of churches planted under the conditions of an earlier day, working in more or less isolation and independence, having no definitely marked parish lines, but ministering to people of widely different localities, held together by a principle of elective affinity, and feeling already the drain upon their financial and moral resources, which is due to the increased cost of living and the consequent transfer of many of their most loyal supporters from the city to its suburbs. What is needed in the country, where conditions are exactly the reverse, is a wise husbanding of resources, in which there shall be one church to a community, and in which all waste of men and of material shall be avoided in order that the widest possible territory may be most effectively covered. What we actually see is a group of struggling churches

[1] W. Adams Brown, "Problems and Possibilities of American Protestantism," *Constructive Quarterly,* June, 1913.

planted, many of them, under conditions wholly different from the present, competing one with another for a support which would be scarcely adequate properly to maintain a single effective church."

This state of things has been made possible by the large powers granted to the local congregation in the matter of tenure of property. In the Protestant churches the title to the church building and other permanent funds of the local congregation is ordinarily vested in a Board of Trustees distinct from the spiritual officers of the church, which board is responsible to the state for the administration of the church's finance. In churches of Congregational or independent polity, this control is absolute. In more highly organized bodies like the Presbyterian, Lutheran, and Episcopal churches, where there are certain creedal requirements obligatory on the ministers of the denomination, the control is limited in various ways which it would take too long to describe. But even in these cases the power of the denominational authorities over the property of a self-supporting church is of the slightest and is seldom, if ever, exercised. Only when weaker congregations seek aid from the missionary agencies of the Church has the parent body any effective means of controlling policy, and here, as we have seen, denominational pride or rivalry often makes it difficult to use this power in any effective or constructive way.

But most formidable obstacles can be overcome if the will to overcome be present, and this will is abundantly evident in the matter which we are discussing. We find a growing consciousness of the responsibility of the Church to its environment, whether that environment be rural or urban. We find also an increasing tendency on the part of the churches to come together. In small places this tendency meets us in the movement for the community church; in towns and cities it appears in the rapid increase in the number and influence of federations of churches.

2. *The Expanding Work of the Local Church—The Country Church as Community Centre—The Institutional Church —The Mother Church with Affiliated Churches*

One of the most encouraging features of the church life of our time is the deeper sense of the Church's responsibility for its immediate environment. This is one of the results of the more vivid social consciousness already mentioned. It meets us both in city and country and is producing significant changes in the activities of the Church and, what is still more important, in its ideals. The sense of responsibility to the neighborhood is not only bringing churches closer together; it is also suggesting to them new things which they can do when united. They are facing the problem of the social application of the Gospel in the place where, in the last analysis, it must be met and solved, the place where men have their homes and do their work and bring up their children.

In the country districts and the smaller rural communities, this enlarged sense of social responsibility is closely connected with the movement for a community church. It shows itself in the greater interest of the minister in the week-day affairs of his parishioners and in the increasing effort to make the church a centre for all healthful social activity in the community. A type of minister is coming into existence who takes the country church as his chosen field because he is convinced that it is the key to the life of the community as a whole and that its many-sided contacts bring him into a more intimate relationship with his people than is possible in larger centres. Such a minister identifies himself with what goes on in the township or in the county. He is a member of the grange, interested in the farmers' problems; often he has a bit of land of his own and knows how to cultivate it; above all, he is the connecting link between the local interests and needs of his community and the larger life without.

In the cities and larger towns the sense of the church's special responsibility for its neighborhood is even more apparent. Of the many forms which it is taking two are typical: (1) the institutional church; (2) the mother church with affiliated churches.

The institutional church is the attempt to extend the activity of the local church till it includes every practicable form of ministry to the bodies and the minds of men. In neighborhoods where there are inadequate facilities for education and for recreation the church puts rooms at the disposal of its neighbors and provides workers to lead the various activities which gather about the centre thus provided. St. George's Episcopal Church, in New York City, was a pioneer in work of this kind.

Almost all the typical social and philanthropic activities of our time can now be found in the programme of an institutional city church: boys' clubs, girls' clubs, and clubs for older men and women, classes in language, citizenship, history and literature, good government clubs, societies for civic and social reform, clinics and day nurseries, dramatic societies and music classes. To read the year book of such a church would be an illuminating experience to those who think of the church as an outworn institution.[1]

Because of this many-sided and beneficent work, the institutional church is often regarded as the best model for the church everywhere. It seems a scandal to invest largely in buildings which are used but one day in the week, especially if these buildings are relieved of taxation. To justify such exemption it is felt that the church should be the centre of every form of helpful activity, through the week as on Sunday, in the city no less than in the country. The settlement is held up to the church as a model, or at least as a necessary supplement, for the settlement is simply doing in a voluntary and more or less haphazard fashion what the church ought to have been doing long ago.

There is certainly much to be said for this view. If a man's Christianity means anything it should be as apparent in his life during the week as in his conduct on Sunday. The church as the social expression of the Christian religion may be expected to illustrate this fact in its organized life. It does not, however, follow that because the institutional church is at present indispensable it will always be equally necessary. As the Gospel gains ground and its authority is increasingly recognized, we should expect that all the institutions in society will reflect the new spirit. It will no longer be necessary for the church to do the work of school and clinic and social club, for the existing agencies of the community will provide every needed facility for health, education, and amusement. When the community has become so completely Christianized that the only thing left for the church to do is to provide a centre of social

---

[1] Of special interest is the recent revival of the New Testament ideal of bodily healing as a part of a religious ministry. We owe to the amazing success of Christian Science a strong impetus to regard health as a synthesis to which spirit as well as mind must contribute. Not a few modern churches have clinics where doctor, trained nurse, and minister work side by side, and in such experiments as the Emmanuel Movement and other similar movements the health-giving effect of religious faith is receiving new demonstration.

worship, it will be a most convincing proof that the church has succeeded in its task.[1]

A second way of applying the social Gospel in the local community is through the mother church with affiliated churches. There are many churches located in centres which are adequately provided with social agencies, and do not need the facilities of the institutional church; but they adjoin other neighborhoods which are not so well supplied. In such circumstances it is often possible for the stronger church to establish an outpost, through which it can share its larger resources with those who are less fortunate and supply the means and the workers to maintain the varied ministry of the institutional church.

It is essential to the success of this experiment that the new church centre should be a real church with its own officers and its direct responsibility, not a mere mission dependent for its policy upon the will of the parent body. The affiliated church should command the services of a first-class minister and be able to take its place with the other churches of the city in the larger co-operative movement to which reference will presently be made. Only in this way can it win the support of the self-respecting people to whom it ministers and successfully meet the criticism so often directed against American Protestantism, that it is the church of a class.

A conspicuous example of a successful affiliation of this kind is the Brick Presbyterian Church in New York City, with its two affiliated churches, Christ Church and the Church of the Covenant. Each of these three centres has its independent organization and activities. Together they provide a ministry which spans the city from river to river.[2]

A different application of the principle of affiliation is furnished by the American Parish on the upper East Side in New York City. Here a group of foreign-speaking churches are associated with an

[1] Where the community in which a Protestant church is carrying on an institutional work is predominantly Catholic or Jewish it is not always easy to hold the balance between the function of the church as a representative of Protestant Christianity and its wider activities as a community centre. Some students of the problem feel the difficulties so acutely as to question whether the two kinds of activity can wisely be carried on under the same auspices. They argue that the same expenditure of funds and leadership would yield larger results both for the community and the church if each enterprise operated from its own centre.

[2] Cf. Year Book of the Brick Presbyterian Church, New York, 1922.

English-speaking church through a Board of Pastors under the chairmanship of the pastor of the latter, all the churches receiving support in money and workers from the other churches in the Presbytery working through the Church Extension Committee.[1]

An advantage of the system of affiliated churches is that it makes possible a multiple pastorate. In so extensive a work, men of different talent and training may find their place. The wisdom and judgment which come with long years of experience are needed to balance the fire and enthusiasm of youth. For the minister of such a parish the dead-line has no terrors, for he has something to give which is needed for the largest success of the whole.

In the extension of this system, and its application in varying degree to the different conditions which obtain in the country, is to be found one way of meeting the difficulty, referred to in an earlier chapter, of the future of the older man in the ministry. When we cease to make the individual congregation our sole method of measurement it will be possible for us to work out combinations in which men of different ages as well as of different temperament and training can find their appropriate place.

This consciousness of common responsibility for community problems is having its reflex influence upon the relation of the churches to one another. The federation movement, of which we shall presently speak, is one example of this influence, but it is paralleled by a similar movement within each denomination. Where a city-wide organization already exists, as in churches of Episcopal and Presbyterian polity, it is being more effectively utilized. Where it was lacking, as in the case of Congregational and Baptist bodies, it has been created. More and more it is recognized that as no congregation can solve its own problems alone, so each is responsible for helping the others to meet the larger demands which are laid upon all alike.

So our study of the enlarging work of the Church leads us inevitably to the other tendency of which we have spoken, the movement for unity. What can be done by the local church alone, even with the best will in the world, is limited. The last illustration we have used—that of the American Parish—is the best proof of this. What is being done by the churches of this parish is made possible

---

[1] Cf. "The Church and the City." An account of Home Missions and Church Extension in New York Presbytery. New York, 1917.

because of the support of the presbytery as a whole. The more earnestly we try to enlarge the work of the local church and to increase its usefulness, the more clearly we perceive that without the co-operation of all the churches our effort is doomed to failure. Apart from the closer denominational relationship just referred to, this co-operation may take two main forms according to the size of the community with which we are concerned—that of the community church and that of the federation of churches.

3. *The Movement for the Community Church—Its Present Status and Possible Lines of Future Development—The Three Forms of the Community Church* [1]

By the community church in the sense in which we shall use the term here, we mean a church which aims to provide religious facilities for all the people who live in a definite locality, so that there will be no need within that geographical area for any other Protestant religious organization.[2] It is evident that the community church as so defined, must be confined to places with a limited population. In cities and larger towns other means must be found to express the unity of Christians.

The term "community church" is sometimes used in a different sense to describe such an experiment as is being carried on by Dr. John Haynes Holmes in New York City, where a number of persons, desiring an even broader basis for church membership than that afforded by their previous association with Unitarianism, have founded a religious society with no creed or platform other than membership in the community and the desire to do good to one's fellowmen.[3] Such a use of the term, however legitimate, is for our present purpose confusing and we shall ignore it here.

We have already sufficiently described the situation which the community church is designed to correct. It is the overchurching which is the natural result of the unrestricted operation of the de-

[1] Cf. John Haynes Holmes, "New Churches for Old," New York, 1922; Henry E. Jackson, "The Community Church," Boston, 1919; "Christian Unity, Its Principles and Possibilities," pp. 96–110.

[2] The reasons which make it necessary for us to restrict our consideration to Protestant agencies have been already explained. For what can be done in the way of co-operation between Protestants and Roman Catholics cf. pp. 271, 272.

[3] The *Statement of Purpose* is as follows:
"This church is an institution of religion dedicated to the service of humanity.

nominational competition we have already described. In the flow of population westward the new-comers brought their churches with them. If the community seemed at the time too small to absorb the liberal supply of ecclesiastical privileges which they provided, they looked to the future to justify their action. They were building not for a few hundreds on the ground, but for the pretentious town that was presently to be. Denominational rivalry reinforced local pride with a result which we know only too well. When early hopes were disappointed, and the steady sweep from country to city began to empty the villages and little towns of the young people on whom future growth depended, the result was inevitable.

It is a hopeful sign that so many people are awake to the danger of the situation, and are making plans to meet it. These plans agree in this, that the remedy for overchurching is unity. If there are not Christians enough in any one place to sustain more than one strong church, then let them come together and make one. The community church is the name we give to a church which is the outcome of such a union. It has three main forms: (1) the union church; (2) the federated church; (3) the denominational church serving the entire community.

By the union church we mean a church which includes all the persons in its neighborhood without regard to their denominational affiliation. In some cases it proposes its own creed; in others it ignores creed altogether. In some its Christian character is emphasized and its members feel in sympathy with the religious history of the past. In others the point of view is radical, and the ties which bind it to the older churches of the loosest.

It is clear that a church of this kind has significant points of contact with the other kind of community church described above. It is like it in its composite character, and, above all, in its lack

"Seeking truth in freedom, it strives to apply it in love for the cultivation of character, the fostering of fellowship in work and worship, and the establishment of a righteous social order which shall bring abundant life to men.

"Knowing not sect, class, nation or race, it welcomes each to the service of all."

Bond of Union Inscribed on the Church Book

"We, the undersigned, accepting the stated Purpose of this church, do join ourselves together that we may help one another, may multiply the power of each through mutual fellowship, and may thereby promote most effectively the cause of truth, righteousness, and love in the world.

"Persons signing the above Bond of Union are accepted as members of the church."

of denominational connection; but it differs from it in being really
and not simply in ideal inclusive. It is, in fact, what in name it
professes to be, a community church.

It is difficult to know how many such churches there are.
Springing up as they do to meet local conditions, and depending for
their success upon the initiative of individuals, they are only beginning to develop the corporate consciousness which will make it
possible for the movement to give an intelligent account of itself.
In Massachusetts there are more than forty such churches which
meet in annual conference under the guidance of the Massachusetts
State Federation of Churches.[1] In other states the movement has
not developed so rapidly, but it is growing and has its representatives in all parts of the United States.[2]

The advantages of the community church of this type are those
of the Congregational system in its more thoroughgoing form. It
puts full responsibility upon the people of the community, derives
its final authority from them, and leaves them free to shape their
institutions of belief and worship in any form to which the leading
of the present Spirit shall seem to point. On the other hand, its
disadvantages are those of Congregationalism in every form. Its
ties with the past being of the loosest, it misses the steadying influence that comes from tradition and enters an age which has definitely broken with individualism without any effective nation-wide
agencies of unity. What the future of the movement is to be and
how large its contribution to the life of the Church as a whole, will
depend largely upon the spirit in which its representatives approach
this final test of all organized life—the test which is furnished by
the necessity of living and working together.

It is too soon to predict what the outcome of the experiment will
be. Two possibilities seem open; one, that the union church will
form the nucleus of a new denomination of a more liberal and inclusive character—a denomination that, in its desire to be catholic,
is ready to overlook even such ancient distinctions as that between

[1] While forty-one such churches were listed by the Massachusetts Federation of Churches, only twenty-two complied with the request for statistical
reports in January, 1921. The last annual conference (the tenth in number)
was held in Hough's Neck in June, 1921.

[2] Dr. Piper, editor of the *Community Churchman,* states that his card
index contains the names of 325 churches of this type. This list, however,
includes both consolidated churches and those which have been independent
since their formation. Of the latter there are known to be 144.

Christian and Jew.[1] The other and the more likely is that, like so many other liberal movements, it will fulfil itself through its reflex influence on the older churches.

There are, to be sure, some advocates of the community church who predict for it a still more ambitious future. Thus Dr. Joseph McAfee[2] looks for a time when the older denominational distinctions will no longer be tolerated, and membership in the community carry with it *ipso facto* membership in the church. But this would be simply to repeat over again in the name of democracy the experiment of the state church against which American Protestantism was a protest. So long as men sincerely differ in their religious convictions, these convictions must somehow find expression in organization, and the church must take account in its plans for its own constitution of the existing differences in the beliefs and practices of religious people. This insight determines the other forms of community church which we have still to consider—the federated church, and the denominational church functioning for the whole community.

The federated church takes its departure from the existing denominational differences and makes place for these within the membership of the united church. It does not ask the Congregationalist to give up his Congregationalism, or the Methodist his Methodism. On the contrary, it recognizes this membership on its rolls and in the apportionment of its benevolences. When a new convert joins the church he is enrolled in the denomination of his profession. When a pastor is called he may belong to any one of the communions represented in the membership and is so entered on its ministerial roll. But he is called to be pastor of the united church and ministers to all its people alike. Of churches of this kind there are known to be between two hundred and three hundred,[3] and when

[1] The example of the Disciples is instructive here. Like the community church, they began as a protest against denominationalism. Their hope was, by a return to primitive Christianity, to find some simple and inclusive form in which all Christians could unite. In fact, however, the logic of events has forced them against their will into their present position of a denomination among denominations.

[2] *New Republic*, January 18, 1919, pp. 331 sq. The same point of view has been more fully set forth by Dr. John Haynes Holmes in his recent book, "New Churches for Old," New York, 1922.

[3] The list in the office of the Home Missions Council contains 300 names; that of Dr. Piper, 236. Conditions in these communities are so constantly changing, however, that it is difficult to obtain reliable statistics.

one considers the difficulties in such an arrangement, on the whole they are functioning with surprising success.[1]

Yet in the long run it is doubtful if this method will permanently solve the difficulty. It is instructive to remember that in the Plan of Union of 1810, Congregationalists and Presbyterians applied the principle of the federated church to their home-missionary programme; but the time came when both churches agreed that the method had outlived its usefulness and each resumed its original independence of action.[2] The stronger a church grows, the more it will desire a special outlet for its energies. The division of funds between different denominational boards will become increasingly unsatisfactory, and the lack of a unified missionary programme even more so. These difficulties can be successfully overcome only when the churches as a whole recognize their common responsibility and provide an interdenominational programme of work in support of which churches of different denominations can unite. Until this is done the federated church must remain a temporary makeshift —useful as pointing the way to something better.[3]

There remains a third form of the community church which, if it can be had, is simpler than either of the preceding. It is the denominational church functioning for the entire community. It is possible for a congregation of any one of the larger Protestant bodies so to recognize its obligations to the community as a whole and so to plan for the discharge of its communal responsibility that Christians of other denominations will feel that they can join it without loss of self-respect, and find their religious needs and as-

[1] Cf. "Christian Unity: Its Principles and Possibilities," pp. 99–101.

[2] *Op. cit.*, p. 287. "By the provisions of this agreement, which applied to home-missionary soil, each member in a mixed church should have the privileges of the polity of his choice. Each church should choose a 'standing committee' which should exercise the ordinary rights of the session, and the delegate of such a standing committee should have full recognition as a ruling elder if sent to a presbytery. Presbyterian and Congregational ministers could be indifferently pastors of Presbyterian, Congregational, or mixed churches, but should be answerable for discipline according to the polity they represented."

[3] The term "federated church" is sometimes used in a different sense to describe (*a*) two churches of different denominations employing the services of a single pastor; (*b*) a church in which a pastor of one denomination serves a church of another; (*c*) churches having as temporary members persons of different denominations as in the case of the American churches in Europe or in the Canal Zone.

pirations satisfactorily met. There are doubtless many hundreds, it may be thousands, of such churches.[1] But the movement meets with two obstacles which cannot be overcome without assistance from without: (1) the possible opposition of the denominational authorities; (2) the difficulty of providing in the same service for the needs of members of the liturgical and of the non-liturgical churches.

One of the great advantages of the denominational community church is that it can count on the help and support of the denominational Board of Missions. In weaker communities this is an asset of no slight importance. But the denominational connection may be a liability as well as an asset, and be used to prevent Christians coming together as well as to help them to do so. There are communities to-day not strong enough adequately to support a single Christian church, into which the money of more than one Christian denomination is being poured. Such waste of resources is little short of criminal, and it is a happy sign that the conscience of Christians is increasingly setting itself against it.

All the more refreshing is it to note instances in which the influence of the central bodies is being thrown in the interest of co-operation and comity. Through such enlightened leadership Maine has long been grappling successfully with the problem of the local church. The same is true of Massachusetts. In the State of Vermont not less than eighty-two churches in thirty-eight localities have gone on a community basis during the past four years. The most recent example of intelligent planning is Montana, where in 1919 the Home Mission authorities of the State combined in an "Every Community Service Endeavor." One of the features of this plan is the development, wherever possible, of the community church of the denominational type.[2] These are but the most striking examples of a movement which is nation-wide and which is full of promise for the future of Christianity.[3]

---

[1] The line which separates such a denominational community church from a denominational church of the conventional type is so vague that it is difficult to obtain reliable statistics. Dr. Piper puts the number above 500. A list furnished me by the Massachusetts Federation of Churches reckons 240 in that state alone.

[2] Cf. "What Montana has Done and is Doing in Christian Co-operation." Home Missions Council, New York, 1921.

[3] A recent editorial in the *Christian Century* (December 29, 1921), while recognizing the good done by this movement, sounds a needed warning against

More difficult to deal with is the other obstacle, that which grows out of sincere difference in religious conviction and experience. While it is true that most Protestant Christians can pass from one denomination to another without the sense of serious loss, there are exceptions to the rule. In churches like the Episcopal and Lutheran, which have cultivated a strict sense of denominational responsibility, many persons feel recreant to their Christian duty unless they can have access to the sacrament in the particular form in which they are accustomed to receive it from a minister of their own communion. The same is true of those Baptists who practise close communion. In this fact is the most serious obstacle to the present movement for the community church.

We have in mind a community of four thousand people in which a single church has been ministering with acceptance to the Protestant Christians within its limits. Members of no less than twenty-one communions, including the Episcopalians, who stand fourth in its membership, unite in its service and contribute to its support. It has a neighborhood house which cares for the social and recreational needs of the whole community. It has a minister who commands the confidence and affection of all who know him. Yet this happy state of things is threatened because a few individuals in the community feel that they cannot do justice to their religious convictions without having a church of their own.

Such facts give significance to the proposed Concordat between the Episcopal and Congregational churches. This is an arrangement by which, without sacrificing his standing as a Congregational minister, a man may receive Episcopal ordination for the purpose of ministering to those Episcopalians in his congregation who desire to receive the sacrament from a priest of their own communion.[1] Unsatisfactory as a permanent solution of the problem of Christian unity, this would relieve the strain in many a local situation, and it is much to be hoped that no obstacle will prevent the experiment from being tried.

---

interpreting the principle of denominational comity too narrowly. It reminds us that in the matter of church relationships there is no such thing as a vested right. The denomination exists to serve the community, not *vice versa;* and in the complicated situation which faces us to-day no solution which proceeds on the basis of mathematical equivalents can be satisfactory.

[1] For the text of the proposed Concordat cf. Manning, "The Call to Unity," New York, 1920, pp. 144–152.

But the denominational church alone, useful as it may be, cannot solve the problems of the community. The difficulties already noted in the case of the federated churches reappear here and the remedy is the same. The denominations themselves must come together and create some central missionary agency through which the common work to which all alike are committed can be carried on. When this central agency has been created, denominational rivalry will be attacked in its citadel. If all are working together through the same agency for the same end, it will not make much difference through which denominational treasury the river of benevolence reaches the common reservoir.

A factor which is destined to play a far larger part in the life of the local church in the future is the growing influence of women. In the church at large it may be possible by the mere force of tradition or inertia to continue present methods for a considerable time. There are men enough to fill the existing positions without calling upon the women. Moreover, the latter find scope for their expanding activities in their own boards, many of which raise large sums of money and employ a large number of missionaries. In the local church this is not the case. Here all the resources available are insufficient to meet the need. The spectacle of two or three incompetent or inefficient men controlling the policy of a church in which all the energy and much of the spiritual force is supplied by women is too anomalous to continue. Sooner or later place will be found for the women on the official boards of the local church. In some denominations, as we have seen,[1] this has already been done, and when it becomes the rule rather than the exception we may expect a new accession of energy and of devotion that will mean much for the Church.

The movement for the community church is still in its infancy. The denominations have recognized its importance by creating departments of rural life, country church, and the like.[2] It has enlisted the active support of the leaders of the agricultural colleges and other influential persons who realize the fundamental place held by the farmer in our national life. It has already found an organ of expression in the *Community Churchman,* a quarterly

[1] *E. g.,* The Methodists, cf. p. 30.
[2] Cf. Chapter XII.

journal published in Excelsior Springs, Missouri, which represents, besides the denominational churches already mentioned, more than five hundred community churches in the technical sense.[1] Through this and similar agencies experience will be shared and standards developed, and with the co-operation of all who are interested we may confidently expect great progress in the near future in grappling with this most serious and perplexing of all the problems of our American Christianity.

4. *The Federation of Churches—Its History and Present Status—*
   Larger Aspects of the Federation Movement [2]

The second form of the movement for local unity is the federation or—as it is becoming more common to call it—the council of churches. This is the most practicable way of securing co-operation in those larger centres where the religious needs of the community can no longer be met by a single church.

It is not necessary here to rehearse the causes which make some form of federation necessary. In our large cities we have all the evils with which denominationalism has plagued the smaller communities and others besides. In some quarters we find too many churches; in others too few. Everywhere we discover needless competition and waste. What is more serious still, we find the churches lacking moral and spiritual influence on the community as a whole. What they might do in the cause of civic and social righteousness if they were united, is undone. What they try to do in the sphere in which they are actually working is twice done or half done. To correct these evils a few earnest and ardent spirits a few years ago initiated the movement which we now know as the federation of churches.

The federation of churches differs from the federal movement in the larger sense in which we have already considered it in that while the latter deals with the denomination as a whole, this is confined to the local congregation. The movement has passed through a period of experiment in which mistakes were made and experience gathered. In the course of this experience it has worked out a set of principles which are now commonly accepted by those

---

[1] *E.g.*, union or federated churches.
[2] Cf. "Christian Unity: Its Principles and Possibilities," pp. 110–122.

who have studied the situation with which they are designed to deal.[1]

There are three possible ways of forming a federation. It may be formed by a group of individuals, ministers or laymen, who associate themselves for the study of community problems and do whatever they can to promote co-operation among the churches. It may be formed by the local congregations, choosing delegates to represent them in a council which shall consider their common interests and report their recommendations to the parent body. Finally, in those cities which are so large that the missionary task of the Church can not be adequately handled by the local churches themselves, it may be formed through the union of the City Missions Societies or Church Extension Societies which the denominations have created to carry on their missionary work or even by the denominations themselves. The first and third are devices designed to meet exceptional situations. The second is the prevailing method in cities of moderate size.

In New York City all three of these methods may be studied. The size of the city is so great, its problems so difficult, its changes so rapid and bewildering that until recently no effort to bring about a comprehensive organization for the greater city had been successful. The geographical and economic difficulties, in themselves all but insuperable, are accentuated by the division of responsibility between dioceses, conferences, classes, and presbyteries. Under these conditions it has been hard to work out a single comprehensive organization for the city as a whole. Manhattan has been working in its field through its Federation and City Missions Council, and Brooklyn and Queens through their own organizations. Only recently has it been possible to create an organization comprehensive enough to take in all parts of the greater city.

The New York Federation of Churches in its older form illustrates the first of the three methods of approach to the city problem. It began as an organization of individual pastors and laymen

---

[1] The story of these experiments is told by Dr. Roy B. Guild, Secretary of the Commission on Councils of Churches of the Federal Council, in the chapter on this subject in the volume on "Christian Unity" already referred to, as well as in various publications by the Commission (*e.g.*, "Practicing Christian Unity," New York, 1919; "Community Programs for Co-operating Churches," New York, 1920). To these we may refer the reader who wishes fuller information as to details.

who believed in federation and were working to bring it about. It did not officially represent the churches as a whole. The Federation has done indispensable work in investigating conditions, disseminating information, and forming public opinion, but its unofficial character has prevented it from becoming a true federation of churches in the sense in which this is true of other organizations which we are presently to describe.[1]

To supplement this lack the New York City Missions Council was established. This is a committee consisting of officially appointed delegates of the responsible ecclesiastical bodies carrying on missionary work in Manhattan and the Bronx. It includes representatives of the Episcopal, Presbyterian, Lutheran, Methodist, Baptist, Disciples, and Dutch Reformed churches and of the City Missions Society. The basis of representation differs in different cases. In the case of the Episcopal Church the diocese is the unit represented; in the Dutch Reformed Church the classis; in other cases the responsible Church Extension or City Missions Society is the appointing body. The powers of the Council are purely advisory and consultative; yet it has done much to establish principles of comity and to create in its constituency a spirit of confidence and co-operation.

Recently the Council has united with a similar organization in Brooklyn to form a comprehensive body taking in the entire field of greater New York. This enlarged Council has undertaken a study of the religious needs of the greater city which it is hoped will prove a useful guide for further planning.[2]

Neither Federation nor Council in its present form is adequate to meet the needs of the greater city, and plans are already under way and indeed far advanced to supply New York City with a really responsible and representative federation. In this case, owing to the size of the city, the unit of representation will not be the individual church, but the denomination. The right to vote for

[1] On the history and work of the New York Federation cf. the files of *Federation*, published by the New York Federation of Churches, esp. VII, No. 4, April, 1914.

[2] A similar organization has existed in Chicago for many years. It includes five denominations—Methodist, Presbyterian, Baptist, Congregational, Disciples—and operates under an agreement which binds the co-operating bodies to submit all plans for locating new churches to the Council for its approval. This Council must not be confused with the Comity Committee of the Chicago Federation of Churches, which includes sixteen denominations.

directors and to determine the general policy of the Federation will be vested in the representatives of the denominations which co-operate. Provision will be made through a class of general members for representatives of the co-operating local churches and others whose participation in the work of the Federation is desirable. A similar federation exists in Chicago, in which sixteen different denominations co-operate on a basis of proportional representation.

Reference to the Church Extension and Home Missions Committees calls attention to another feature of the churches' local administrative machinery, of which brief mention must be made, namely, the denominational committees in the different localities which are charged with the responsibility of caring for the weaker churches and otherwise promoting their missionary and educational work. In cities like New York and Chicago these are powerful bodies raising and expending large sums of money, employing a considerable staff of workers, and commanding skilled leadership. In smaller communities the service rendered is usually by volunteers and the machinery much simpler. These local organizations are the natural points of contact between the local community and the nation-wide work of the Church of which we shall speak in the next chapter, and their efficient co-operation is a necessary condition of carrying through any comprehensive plan.

The conditions which obtain in New York City and Chicago are exceptional. In most cities the natural units to be federated are the local congregations. Such federations exist in forty-five cities,[1] and as we have already seen have accumulated a considerable body of experience and a definite set of ideals.

The following principles have been agreed upon by the representatives of the movement as essential to a successful federation. In the first place, the organization must be official, not voluntary or individual; that is, the units which form the federation must be congregations, or the larger bodies through which they co-operate officially. In the second place, adequate financial support must be secured before a beginning is made. The movement must be co-operative in support as well as personnel, and this support must come not simply from well-disposed individuals, but from the bodies which the federation proposes to unite. Finally, there must

[1] According to the list compiled by the Commission on Councils of Churches, as of December 31, 1921.

be a paid secretary, giving his entire time to the movement, and sharing his experience with other secretaries engaged in similar work. The burdens to be carried are too heavy to be borne by amateurs. For the initiative and guidance of a successful federation, only a professional is adequate.[1]

In the volume on Christian Unity already referred to, Dr. Guild outlines the programme of a typical federation which has served as a basis for more than a dozen others. Among its objects he enumerates the following:

"(a) To make a continuous religious survey, to furnish reliable information and a basis for intelligent action.

"(b) To prevent unnecessary overlapping and competition between the denominations, and to see that all communities are adequately churched.

"(c) To endeavor to arrest the attention of the city with the claims of Christ through a strategic programme of evangelism in all the churches individually, and unitedly where possible, depending almost entirely on local leaders.

"(d) To study the outstanding industrial and social needs of the city, and to apply Christianity in an effort at solution.

"(e) To effect a policy of recreation which will afford to all the people as much as or more than the saloon has given, and to make all the recreations wholesome and uplifting.

"(f) To present a programme of Christian education that will meet the needs of the city.

"(g) To interpret Christian democracy, especially to the alien, non-English speaking groups in the city.

"(h) To give proper publicity to Christianity, to the churches, and the religious interests of the city.

"(i) To make religion effective and attractive in the city, and to apply to the work of the churches the best modern business principles of efficiency and economy."[2]

What is planned in this programme is already being put into effect in a number of American cities. Chicago, Pittsburgh, Indianapolis, Cleveland, Louisville, Baltimore, Detroit are but a few of the more conspicuous examples which could be given. In Indian-

[1] Cf. "Christian Unity: Its Principles and Possibilities," pp. 110–122.
[2] *Op. cit.*, p. 119.

apolis, community evangelism has been carried on with increasing success.[1] Elsewhere religious education has been stressed,[2] or social service.[3] In Atlanta, excellent work has been done in securing publicity for Christian interests, notably through a series of remarkable editorials in the *Atlanta Constitution*. In Dayton, provision is made for a worker in the juvenile courts who represents united Protestantism. Portland has developed a department of international justice and goodwill. The Chicago Federation has given special attention to work in public institutions.

From the cities the movement is already beginning to extend to the counties and states. Massachusetts has had a state federation for years which has rendered most effective service. Similar federations are found in California, Connecticut, Indiana, Ohio, and Pennsylvania.[4] Through such state federations the interests of the community church are being actively pushed and the two streams that we have thus far been studying separately have already joined their waters.

In addition a movement for county federations is beginning, and one or two have already been established with permanent paid secretaries;[5] but their function still needs to be defined and their usefulness proved.

More important than any specific thing the federations have done has been their success in creating a common consciousness and developing a method of procedure. Pastors who have been oppressed by the difficulty of their task have been encouraged by the discovery that they were not working alone. Congregations that were facing problems they did not know how to solve have been helped by an exchange of experience with others who have been more successful. The primitive Christian conception of the

[1] Detroit and Pittsburgh are also doing good work along the line of evangelism.

[2] *E.g.*, at Toledo, Cincinnati, Detroit, Rochester, Chicago, St. Louis, Duluth, Portland, Oregon, Newark, and Erie. Specially significant has been the work done by the Toledo Federation in supervising the work of community weekday Bible schools.

[3] *E.g.*, at Boston, Pittsburgh, and Chicago.

[4] The Ohio State Federation, in co-operation with Ohio State University, maintains a two weeks' summer school for country pastors. The Connecticut State Federation holds a similar session in connection with the State Agricultural College.

[5] *E.g.*, Wayne County, Indiana, and Louvain County, Ohio.

church in the city has through this movement become a reality for multitudes of Christians.

The federation is not simply a clearing-house of information within its own community; it is a means of exchange between community and community. Through periodic conventions experience is interchanged, and contacts established between the local community and the wider movements in the nation at large. Thus the federation movement is increasingly a source of inspiration and education for all who take part in it.

A typical example was the convention held in Cleveland in 1920. An inspiring programme was presented covering not only the local problems of the different cities represented, but the larger aspects of the Church's task at home and abroad. Such questions as the responsibility of the Church for promoting a better social order and a more sensitive international conscience had their place side by side with the older and more permanent topics of evangelism and education.

The educational possibilities of the movement were emphasized at a gathering of federation secretaries held at the Union Theological Seminary in New York in June, 1921. Thirty different communities were represented, a force whose influence on the future development of the Church it would be difficult to over-estimate. In these men, met for a week of quiet study and thought on the greatest of all themes, the two most important movements in the religious life of the present were represented—the movement for Christian unity and the movement for the social application of the Gospel.

But, after all, what can be done through local co-operation even with the best will in the world is limited. In city and country alike there are problems beyond the power of those on the ground. Only specialized study by men set apart for this purpose can adequately aid us here. For such specialized service, we are dependent upon national agencies. What these are and how they function will concern us in the next chapter.

5. *Consequences for the Work of the Minister—Need of a Recon-
sideration of the Function and Responsibilities of the
Protestant Ministry*

Before we turn to this new phase of our subject there is one
aspect of the local situation that requires further consideration,
and that is its bearing upon the life of the minister. We have seen
that changes are taking place in the institution he serves. It is
inevitable that these should have a reflex influence upon his own
responsibility and functions. Such an influence is in fact being
exerted, but in ways more or less unpremeditated and haphazard.
It is worth while to consider with some care what its effects are
likely to be.

We have noted two tendencies in the local church, a tendency
to enlarge the scope of its activity, and a tendency to unite with
other churches. Little churches are coming together to form bigger
ones and the bigger churches are doing more things and more kinds
of things than they did before. Group enterprises are being undertaken and, as a result, new demands are being made upon the
minister. He is asked to do more and he has less time to do it in.

One may differ in one's interpretation of this situation. One
may believe with the advocates of the institutional church that the
tendency to expand the church's activities is likely to continue
indefinitely. Or one may believe with the present writer that the
present condition is a temporary one, due to causes in our social
environment which it is the duty of the church to correct and
remove. In either case, no intelligent observer can fail to recognize
that this expansion of function is taking place to-day. This being
true, the ministry must adjust itself to the change both in theory
and in practice.

The adjustment in practice is going on at the present time in
many interesting ways. But the theoretical adjustment has not yet
kept pace with the changes in practice. The minister of to-day is
doing a great many things that his predecessor was not expected
to do, but men's thought about him still moves in the old groove
worn when Jonathan Edwards preached his Stockbridge sermons
and Whitfield swept the country with the fire of his revival preaching. The contrast between the theory of the ministry and the practical conditions in which individual ministers find themselves work-

ing constitutes one of the greatest practical difficulties in the way of the modern ministry.

We have already considered what some of these difficulties are—the insecurity of tenure, the limitation of outlook, the lack of any adequate relation to the larger interests of the Church as a whole. We have traced these to their roots in the conception of the minister as an isolated individual dealing with other isolated groups which we call local churches. We have seen how this isolation creates the uncertainty and restlessness which we have already noted. The congregation does not wish to call any minister for whom it may be expected permanently to provide. The minister who feels that he is not rightly placed has no self-respecting method of bringing about a change. In the meantime he is asked to do all kinds of things for which his previous training may not have fitted him and the distinctive work for which he is called as a preacher and a pastor suffers.

Such a conception of the minister's responsibility does not correspond with the conception of the Church to which the facts of modern life are forcing us. The barriers between the churches have been breaking down and the Church is coming to be thought of as a great social institution with a many-sided life, employing men of different talents and training who can co-operate with one another in carrying out a common plan. This corporate conception of the Church, long characteristic of such highly organized bodies as the Methodists, the Presbyterians, and the Episcopalians, is showing itself to be the only conception which is able to stand the strain of modern life.

It is clear that such a conception of the Church requires a modification of the earlier conception of the ministry. Either the minister in the conventional sense must add to his duties as preacher, pastor, and leader of worship other functions as social leader, man of business, and the like, or we must develop a differentiated ministry in which, besides the ministers who preach and lead in worship, men—and for that matter women—may be called to serve the Church as its recognized ministers who are not expected to do any of these things.

This change is already taking place in the ministry of the foreign field. In a list of forty-three persons recently commissioned for service by one of our foreign-mission boards, only seven were ordained ministers.[1] The others were teachers, nurses, physicians, men of business, all going out with Christian motives as servants of the Church to do forms of the Church's work.

A parallel expansion of function is going on in the Church at home, but it has not yet resulted in any corresponding differentiation in the function of the ministry. It is true that a beginning has been made. The teaching ministry is beginning to differentiate itself from that of preaching, and the directorate of religious education is becoming a recognized profession. But religious education is only one of many functions which are being carried on in the modern Church. The pastoral work of the Church, too, requires specialized training. Boys' clubs and girls' clubs, civic forums and good government clubs, and all the range of social activities which are included in the work of a modern institutional church are so many opportunities for pastoral contact. Trained leaders are needed who share the ideals of the minister who preaches. For such a ministry, women as well as men may well be set apart, and within it differences of age and talents may find free scope. Music and the arts, too, will take their place in this comprehensive ministry, and the organist and the choir-master be recognized as ministers of religion and judged accordingly.

Such a differentiation of the minister's duties would free the minister who preaches from the strain which is now put upon him by the multitude of his duties. It would make it possible to restore worship to its central place in his interest and give dignity and restfulness to the service of prayer and praise. Above all, it would make place for the older man in the ministry who is now too often crowded out by the younger man, not because he does not do well the thing he is fitted to do, but because he is expected to do other things which are not part of his business and which can be done much better by younger and differently trained men.

To do this would be to restore to modern Protestantism the conception of the ministry which was prevalent in its beginning. In Calvin's plan for the church of Geneva four different kinds of minister were recognized. Besides the pastor was the elder, who had charge of discipline; the deacon who cared for the poor; and the teacher who was responsible for religious education. We need to revive this conception of a differentiated ministry and extend it

[1] *Presbyterian Advance,* December 1, 1921.

to fit the conditions of the modern Church. We must take the new activities which have grown up in the churches in voluntary and unofficial ways, and make a place for them as parts of our more formal and recognized ministry. We must release the rarer spirits who have the gift of preaching from other duties and give them the time and opportunity they need for this most important task.

The foundation for this differentiated ministry is already laid in the present organization of the Church. The Congregational churches, including the Baptists, have their deacons as well as their ministers. The Presbyterians add the elder to the minister and the deacon. The Episcopalians and Methodists have their deaconesses. All denominations have their trustees who, as the local representatives of the congregations, hold property and represent the churches before the courts. There is no reason why other officers should not be added. There is every reason why the existing offices should be more fully utilized, assigned larger responsibility, and, if need be, made salaried positions.

In the larger institutional churches this is already taking place. A staff of paid workers is employed, including men and women. On the bulletin of any large city church to-day you will find printed beside the name of the minister the names of parish visitors and other church workers; but their work has not yet received full theoretical recognition. Their position has not yet been raised to the dignity of an independent and permanent life work.

It is because the Young Men's and the Young Women's Christian Associations provide in their secretaryships such permanent positions that they are attracting so many men and women who, if a similar opportunity were offered them, would be glad to work in the regular churches. The time will surely come when this lack will be rectified and the Church provide not only opportunity, but recognition for the highly trained service of which it is in need.

For this there is need of a change in the organization of the Church. The forces which are bringing about unity in the local community must expand until they take in the Church at large. A good beginning has already been made. In the mission boards of the churches as well as in the Christian Associations the conception of a differentiated ministry functioning in the name of the whole Church is already accepted. What these organizations are doing we shall study in the chapter that follows.

CHAPTER XII

1. *The Need of Specialization in Christian Work—The Survey as a Condition of Effective Specialization*

WE have seen that both in the smaller communities and in the larger cities influences are at work and problems arise which cannot be dealt with adequately without the assistance of specialists. This fact the churches are beginning to recognize, and in various ways they are adapting their methods to meet the new situation.

The agencies through which the churches are addressing themselves to their new responsibilities are the boards of the different denominations, and various voluntary societies, of which the most important are the two Christian Associations. To these may be added the Salvation Army, an organization with methods so distinctive as to require separate consideration.

The boards of the churches are one of the most interesting and instructive developments of American Protestantism, deserving far more study and attention than they have hitherto received. They are not only agencies of missionary service, but instruments of government adapted to the peculiar needs and ideals of Protestantism. Through its Boards of Home and Foreign Missions, a congregational church like the Baptist, jealous of the rights of the local congregation and repudiating with decision the claims of the Episcopate in every form, is furnished with an instrumentality through which all its congregations can act as one, and the secretaries of these boards have an administrative responsibility comparable only to that of an archbishop. It is instructive therefore to note what these representatives of the churches are doing with the powers which have been entrusted to them.

To deal wisely with the problems of modern missions, whether at home or abroad, it is necessary, first of all, to secure accurate knowledge of the situation to be met and, secondly, to provide the proper agencies to meet it. The boards are doing these two things in ways which enlarging experience is constantly making more effective.

The method used by the boards in assembling the facts that they need to know is known technically as a survey. A survey is an intensive study of a particular geographical area, such as a city, county, or state, with a view to discovering the religious conditions and needs of the people living in it, the methods used by the existing churches in ministering to those needs and what still should be done to supplement or correct the Church's ministry at those points where it is now faulty or insufficient. Such a survey may be made either by the resident Christian forces or by representatives of the boards, or, better still, by both combined.

The conditions of an effective survey are that it should be thorough, accurate, economical of time and money, and above all adapted to the purpose which it is designed to serve. It is not too much to say that much so-called survey work is useless or worse than useless, either because it is conducted by persons not sufficiently familiar with the subject to be studied to estimate correctly what they find or because it is not so planned as to seek the facts that are really relevant. What is needed is not so much statistics obtained from house-to-house visitation by persons who have never done such work before, as careful study of significant and representative areas and intelligent interpretation of the vast mass of statistical material already available from other surveys.

A well-planned survey will be designed for one of two purposes: to determine a policy, or to inspire people to execute it. These two purposes, however intimately related, must be clearly distinguished. The difficulty of doing this may be illustrated in the case of the survey undertaken by the Interchurch World Movement. The idea which underlay it was an admirable one—to give a comprehensive picture of the world-wide task before the Church in such a way as to inspire the churches to discharge it adequately, and at the same time to furnish the information which would make that discharge possible. Unfortunately the pressure of time compelled emphasis upon the first aspect of the survey to the injury of the second. To provide campaign material for the drive it was necessary to have the survey material available at a certain time, and this necessitated such haste in the preparation of certain parts of the work as to sacrifice much of its usefulness as information on which to base a trustworthy policy.[1]

The lesson so painfully learned is not likely to be forgotten. Most of the survey work done by our mission boards is careful, accurate, and intelligent. The survey is made by persons who are trained for the work, and after models whose usefulness has been tested by experience. The same is true of the work done by the Young Women's Christian Association.[2] Some of the studies made by this Association have proved useful not only to churches, but to governments. Notable examples are the recent study of women in industry conducted by the Young Women's Christian Association and published by the United States Department of Labor,[3] and the survey of the city of Prague, conducted by the same organization at the request of the Czecho-Slovak Government.[4]

The two examples just cited illustrate two different kinds of survey which it is important to distinguish: first, a study of some particular local situation which presents peculiar problems or difficulties; second, a study of some particular problem which may enter into a number of different local situations but which can only be properly dealt with on the basis of knowledge derived from a comparison of all available instances.

After securing such knowledge, the next step is to agree upon a policy and to provide the agencies to carry it into effect. Dr. Charles L. Thompson, the veteran secretary of the Presbyterian Board of Home Missions, was one of the first to direct the attention of the home mission forces to the new problems before the

[1] It should be said that this criticism applies in different degrees to different parts of the work. Thus the educational survey assembled much information of permanent value which had not hitherto been accessible, and the same was true of the survey of rural conditions. More than a dozen publications owe their existence either directly or indirectly to the investigations which the Interchurch World Movement set on foot. Other contributions may be expected from the Committee on Social and Religious Surveys, a voluntary committee formed to carry on the uncompleted work of the Survey Department of the Interchurch.

[2] The Young Men's Christian Association, while it has conducted a number of investigations for special purposes, has published little material in this field.

[3] The New Position of Women in American Industry: Bulletin of the Women's Bureau, No. 12, United States Department of Labor, Washington, D. C., 1921.

[4] Cf. The Survey, June 11, 1921.

Church and to devise plans which would make it possible to deal with them effectively.[1]

2. *Resulting Changes in Organization—The Department as an Agency of Specialized Service—Other Forms of Specialization at Home and Abroad—The Resulting Need of Unity*

In Dr. Thompson's church, the Presbyterian, the need of specialization was met by the creation of departments to care for particular phases of the home-mission task, such as immigration, country life, social service, and the like. The same practice is common in other denominations. Even those which have not found it advisable to create separate departments have seen the importance of setting apart men for special forms of service and of giving them a training not required by the general body of workers, who are engaged in the more familiar tasks of evangelization and education which will always occupy the greater number.[2]

When the new departments were first established, the line between the newer and older forms of work was strongly emphasized, but as time has passed and experience has accumulated, it has become apparent that the function of the new departments is not to relieve the other workers of responsibility for the kind of work the departments are doing, but rather to gain a body of knowledge and experience which can be shared with the Church at large so that all its work may become more effective.

[1] Cf. Thompson, "The Soul of America," New York, 1919.

[2] The American Baptist Home Mission Society has secretaries for English-Speaking Missions and Indian Work; Social Service and Rural Community Work; City and Foreign-Speaking Missions; Education; Evangelism; as well as an architect secretary.

The Board of Home Missions and Church Extension of the Methodist Episcopal Church has superintendents for the following departments: Church Extension; City Work; Rural Work; Frontier Work; Evangelism; Indian Mission Work; and directors of the following bureaus: Publicity; Foreign-Speaking Work; Colored Work.

The Board of Home Missions of the Reformed Church in the U. S. has a superintendent for immigration.

The Department of Missions and Church Extension of the Domestic and Foreign Missionary Society of the Protestant Episcopal Church in the U. S. A. is the latest national organization to appoint a secretary for work among Foreign-Born Americans.

The Board of Church Extension of the American Moravian Church has a Country Church Commission.

The relation between these two phases of the Church's work may be illustrated in connection with the board with which the author is most familiar, the Board of Home Missions of the Presbyterian Church in the U. S. A. Of the specialized work carried on by this board, the most instructive for our present purpose is that done by its Departments of City and Immigrant Work, of the Church and Country Life, and of Social Service. The first deals with the race question as it meets us in our great cities and industrial centres; the second, as its name implies, with the country church; the third with the questions at issue between capital and labor, and especially with the group of workingmen who are alienated from the Church.

The first business of the Department of City and Immigrant Work has been to gain an understanding of the conditions to be met. This has been done by surveys of selected fields in this country, supplemented by special studies of the home conditions of the nationalities among whom work is being carried on. Through the offer of immigration fellowships it has been possible to send selected men from the seminaries for a year of study in the different countries from which these new citizens come and thus to secure for them that familiarity with the language, the national traditions, and the social customs of various immigrant groups which is an indispensable condition of effective work.

As a result of this experience the department has acquired a body of information which it can use in the training of workers and in advising the communities which ask its help as to how they can best deal with their own peculiar conditions. In co-operation with other workers in the same field it is helping to create a literature which makes a useful addition to our knowledge of the immigrant.[1]

Besides studying conditions and training workers, the department undertakes to prepare a definite plan of work for any community that requires it. Such plans have been made for cities as well as for smaller communities and are being successfully put into

[1] Cf. the series of racial studies prepared under the New Americans Division of the Interchurch World Movement, six of which are being published for the Home Missions Council and the Council of Women for Home Missions by the George H. Doran Company. The studies are as follows: "The Czecho-Slovaks in America"; "The Russians in America"; "The Poles in America"; "The Italians in America"; "The Greeks in America"; "The Magyars in America."

effect in many places. In a church like the Presbyterian, where the local presbytery is responsible for all work done within its boundaries and representatives of the Home Board can gain admission only through the invitation of the presbytery, this requires close and friendly relations between the board and the presbytery which are equally advantageous to both parties.

The final test of success is met in the fourth and last form of the department's work; namely, that of inspiring the home church to co-operate in the plans when made. In a task so great as that of home missions, what can be done directly by any board, even the strongest, is limited. The most that it can hope to do is to set a standard and devise methods which may commend themselves to the judgment and secure the support of the great mass of Christians everywhere. In exceptional cases, to be sure, as a temporary expedient, the department may assume full charge of the work of a definite locality; but this is not the ideal. The ideal arrangement is for the department to find a man and put him at the service of the local community, leaving them to work out their problems together.[1]

What the Department of City and Immigrant Work is doing for the foreigner in our cities the Department of the Church and Country Life is doing for the neglected country churches. Among the influences which have helped to direct popular attention to the serious condition of our country districts, the activity of this department has not been the least. It has been conducting surveys, trying experiments, publishing literature, securing recruits, preaching the need of a resident ministry, and demonstrating by example what can be done by such a ministry if it can be secured. It has been holding summer schools for persons interested in the country church and co-operating with the agricultural colleges in imparting

[1] San Francisco Presbytery is a good illustration of this kind of co-operation. A different form is illustrated in New York City in the relation between the department and the Church Extension Committee of Presbytery. Here three different factors are co-operating in a harmonious way—the local congregations which furnish the field and the people, the Church Extension Committee of the Presbytery which raises the money and provides the buildings, the Department of Immigration which furnishes the superintendence and trains the workers. As a result of this co-operation a continuity is given to the work which could not otherwise be secured, and methods worked out which have been found useful in dealing with similar problems in other cities.

the information necessary to fit a minister to become not simply a preacher of the Gospel, but a leader in all the social and educational influences which centre about the church.

An interesting indication of the success of the department's work is the number of requests which have come to it from presbyteries that it take over a part or all of their work for a term of years as a sort of experiment station. Twenty-six parishes are now under the care of the department, and in several cases (*e.g.*, French Broad Presbytery in North Carolina, Cumberland Mountain Presbytery in Tennessee, and the Southwest Bohemian Presbytery in Texas) the department has assumed responsibility for the entire work of the presbytery. But such experiments must always be regarded as experiments merely, which fulfil their aim in the measure that they set a standard for the work of the Church as a whole.

What the Presbyterian Church has been doing through the departments described above, other churches have been doing through similar agencies. As already stated, the reason for choosing these particular examples for illustration is not that they are more important or more successful than others, but simply that the author happens to have first-hand knowledge of the work which they are doing.

Significant as a sign of the time is the interest of the churches in the industrial problem. This is dealt with in different ways by different churches. Some employ a special agency like a Social Service Committee; others a Department of Social Service attached to the Board of Home Missions. In the Presbyterian Church both methods have been followed, but the first has now been superseded by the second.

The Rev. Charles Stelzle was a pioneer in this work. As a member of a labor union he keenly felt the alienation of labor from the Church and he worked successfully to overcome it. By addressing mass meetings of workingmen on religious subjects, by correspondence and editorials in the labor press, by instituting the office of fraternal delegate,[1] and above all by the opening of the Labor Temple in New York City, he helped to direct the attention

[1] A fraternal delegate is a minister who is invited to sit as corresponding member in a labor union, or a labor man to whom a similar courtesy is extended by a local ministers' association.

of labor to the churches and to make workingmen realize that the churches were not indifferent to questions of social welfare and justice.

The Labor Temple is a Presbyterian church on the corner of Fourteenth Street and Second Avenue, in New York City, which was taken over by the Church Extension Committee when its congregation was about to abandon it, and turned over to the Home Board to be used as an experiment station by Mr. Stelzle in his effort to establish a point of contact between labor and the church.[1] It has been at work for twelve years, and it may be said with confidence that it has succeeded in fulfilling the purpose for which it was established. The methods used are those of the modern institutional church: Sunday services in different languages, clubs and classes through the week, a settlement house with resident workers, public lectures on topics of public interest, and the like. Characteristic features have been the open forum where from week to week current industrial questions are discussed by men of different shades of belief, and the hospitality extended by the authorities of the Temple to labor unions for their private meetings. In times of unemployment the Temple has helped its neighbors to find work. In times of strike it has offered a safe place of meeting to young girls exposed to the temptations of the street. To a gratifying degree it has gained the confidence of the working people, as an exponent of a type of religion which they can understand and appreciate.[2]

What the Labor Temple has done in New York, other centres are doing with success in other cities. There is a growing disposition on the part of the churches to hear both sides of the industrial question and to state the Christian position on the relation of the Church to industry not only in the safe seclusion of the sanctuary, but in open debate where the opponent can bring his objection and receive an answer.

Another way in which the Church's interest in industrial questions has been shown is through the appointment of special committees to investigate strikes and other industrial disputes. The Interchurch investigation of the steel strike is the best known, but

[1] The work is now under the charge of the Presbytery of New York.
[2] Cf. "The Church and the City," pp. 48–64.

by no means the only example of its kind. The action of the Congregational churches in the case of the Lawrence strike [1] and of the Denver churches in the case of the recent car strike in that city are cases in point.[2]

The serious criticism which has been passed upon the Interchurch steel investigation should not blind us to the importance of the issue at stake. If it be true that the labor question is at heart a moral question with which the Church as a moral teacher is necessarily concerned, it follows that the churches must have access to the information which will enable them to speak authoritatively or to know when they ought to remain silent. Such information it is not at present easy to obtain. A number of the denominations have established Social Service Commissions or Departments whose secretaries co-operate through the Social Service Commission of the Federal Council.[3] This commission has recently established a Bureau of Research for the purpose of concerted study of industrial questions from the Christian point of view. A more ambitious proposal has been made by Professor Small of the University of Chicago, who suggests the appointment of a permanent commission of the most eminent men in the Church to investigate controversies between capital and labor from the point of view of the moral issues involved.[4]

The cases which we have thus far cited, of immigration, country life, and social service, are but the most conspicuous examples of administrative specialization. Other illustrations which might be given are Sunday schools, freedmen, church erection, and temperance, all of which have their special agencies, in some cases independent boards, in others departments or committees. It is a fair question whether this division has not been carried too far. Would it not be better if all the work of the denominations were grouped in three or at most four comprehensive agencies—which might then

---

[1] Cf. "The Causes of the Trouble in Lawrence: A Report on the Recent Strike," by the Rev. Charles R. Brown, D.D., 1919, *The Congregationalist,* June 5, 1919.

[2] Cf. "The Denver Tramway Strike of 1920," by Edward T. Devine, Ph.D., Rev. John A. Ryan, D.D., and John A. Lapp, LL.D., published by the Denver Commission of Religious Forces, 1921.

[3] *E.g.,* Baptist, Congregational, Disciples of Christ, Episcopal, Lutheran, Methodist, Presbyterian, Reformed.

[4] Cf. A. W. Small, "The Church and Class Conflicts," *American Journal of Sociology,* March, 1919.

subdivide the work as experience showed to be most wise? [1] This is a question which is likely to be much debated in the next few years. However it is decided, we may be sure that the result reached will not mean the abandonment of specialization, but only the effort to guard against the dangers involved in over-specialization.

What the home boards are doing for the home field, the foreign boards are doing for the work across the sea, the only difference being that in their case a single agency is responsible for a variety of work which in this country is distributed among many different agencies. The resulting problems of organization include all the problems of the home boards and others beside.[2] Here also there is need of specialization in study and execution—a need intensified by the fact that the workers are dealing with a foreign language and an unfamiliar civilization. Here, too, we face the double problem of discovering what ought to be done and of securing the means to do it. Here above all we find the constant demand for men and women competent to do what needs to be done, and with a training that will fit them to do it. With such responsibilities it is not surprising that our foreign boards have sometimes failed to realize their ideal. The wonder is that they have been able to do as much as they have done.

In spite of the disadvantages which go with this wide extension of responsibility, the advantages of united leadership more than counterbalance them. Those who are responsible for our foreign-missionary policy are by the nature of the case forced to consider the field as a whole. All the problems which at home are divided between different agencies—education, building, social service, and the like, as well as evangelism in the narrow sense—

[1] The present practice differs widely in the different communions. In some churches administrative responsibility is concentrated in comparatively few agencies, in others it is widely distributed. Thus the Board of Missions of the Protestant Episcopal Church includes both home and foreign missions, whereas the plan followed in the Presbyterian Church has separated interests as closely related as home missions, freedmen, church erection, and Sunday-school work. Other denominations uniting home and foreign missions under a single board are the Disciples, the Evangelical Association, the Evangelical Synod of North America, the Free Methodist Church of North America, and the Methodist Episcopal Church, South.

[2] *E.g.*, the diplomatic problems which grow out of the fact that the work of the foreign boards is carried on in a number of different countries, each with its own government and laws.

come before them for consideration. The result is a comprehensive grasp of the larger problems of missionary policy. A similar concentration of leadership and policy is necessary at home, to fit us to deal suitably with such perplexing questions as, for example, the supply of the ministry.

So far we have been speaking of the work done by the men's boards. But we must never forget that this is only a part of the specialized work which the Church is doing through its official agencies. The women also have their boards of home and foreign missions. The question arises whether the present division of administrative responsibility between men and women is a wise one and, if so, whether the present line of division is rightly drawn. As a matter of fact, there is no consistent principle followed in the existing division of responsibility. In some cases, as in the Board of Missions of the Methodist Episcopal Church, South, men and women sit together in a single board which has complete charge of the church's missionary work. In others, as in the case of the Woman's Board of Home Missions of the Presbyterian Church in the U. S. A., the women assume responsibility for the administration of a special branch of the work—in this case schools and hospitals. In still others, as in the Woman's Board of Foreign Missions of the same church, the woman's board has been a money-raising organ for the men's board, all the responsibility for administration being concentrated in that agency. It does not seem likely that the latter arrangement will prove permanently satisfactory. With the growing self-consciousness of women they are certain to demand and to receive complete administrative responsibility for their missionary enterprises, and if this is granted it will be increasingly difficult to draw the line between the spheres in which each sex is to function independently. Some unified plan of missionary administration including both men and women seems to be the goal toward which we are moving.[1]

As we study all these interests we are constantly reminded of the central importance of sound methods of education. The boards are not simply agents to carry out the will of the churches; they are in a very real sense teachers of the Church as to what ought to be done. Much of their energy is spent in preparing informational literature and in bringing home to the consciences of their constituency facts regarding the needs of their field by

[1] Cf. p. 253.

means of the spoken voice. This work is so important and difficult that they are unable to do it full justice alone and have created to assist them special agencies like the Board of Missionary Preparation.[1]

We are thus brought to the most fundamental of all the tasks of the Church, upon the successful performance of which all the others depend—the task of Christian education. There are many different agencies operating in this field. These agencies are of three kinds: (1) those which have to do with the Sunday school; (2) those which are concerned with students in educational institutions—schools, colleges, and universities; (3) those which are responsible for recruiting and training the ministry. In addition should be mentioned the promoting agencies which serve all alike.[2] The relations between these bodies and the resulting problems of unity, both within the denomination and without, will later claim our attention.

3. *Agencies for Interdenominational Administrative Unity—The Home Missions Council and the Foreign Missions Conference—Corresponding Agencies in the Field of Christian Education.*

A survey of the organizations through which the churches are trying to meet specific tasks makes it clear that it is impossible for them to work well in isolation. Denominational agencies are already co-operating in various ways and are creating the necessary and appropriate machinery. The term "administrative union" has come to be used to describe such official co-operation.

The missionary agencies of the churches are united in the Home Missions Council and the Foreign Missions Conference of

[1] The Board of Missionary Preparation was founded in 1911 as a result of a recommendation of the Continuation Committee of the World Conference of 1910, to secure the most adequate kind and quality of preparation for those who are training for foreign-missionary service. It is appointed by, and responsible to, the Foreign Missions Conference of North America, the official agency through which the foreign-missionary boards of the United States and Canada co-operate.

On the educational work of the home-missionary agencies, cf. p. 237. The most important part of this is done through the Council of Women for Home Missions, which has prepared a series of textbooks for mission-study classes which are used by all the co-operating denominations. Cf. also p. 228.

[2] Of these the most important are the Boards of Publication which print the literature which the other boards require for the prosecution of their work.

North America, both of which are official bodies, representing and financed by the co-operating boards,[1] maintaining their own offices and paid secretaries, meeting annually for the discharge of business, and functioning in the interim through committees appointed for that purpose. With these should be associated the Council of Women for Home Missions, and the Federation of Woman's Boards of Foreign Missions of North America.

The Foreign Missions Conference of North America includes all the foreign-missionary societies in the United States and Canada. It meets once a year for the discussion of common problems, and in the course of its history has succeeded in bringing about a notable spirit of unity and sympathy between the responsible heads of the Church's missionary enterprise. It has its permanent office and paid secretaries and functions during the intervals of its stated meetings through a committee of twenty-eight persons called the Committee of Reference and Counsel.[2]

It has been the practice of the Conference not to initiate work except at the request of some of its constituent boards, and then only with the approval of the other members. In the course of its history it has done a number of important and significant pieces of work, among which may be mentioned the recent study of rural education in India [3] and the comprehensive investigation of missionary education in Africa and in China.[4] In these studies it has co-operated with the missionary agencies of other countries in establishing standards which will affect the work of missions as a whole.

In addition to its educational work and its function as a clearing-house of information, the Foreign Missions Conference has been able to deal with a number of difficult and perplexing questions which no single missionary board would have been able to

[1] This is true wholly of the Home Missions Council. In the case of the Foreign Missions Conference, the contributions of the boards are supplemented by private gifts.

[2] The permanent office of the Committee of Reference and Counsel of the Foreign Missions Conference of North America is in New York. Mr. Fennell P. Turner and the Rev. Frank W. Bible are its secretaries.

[3] Cf. "Village Education in India: Report of a Commission of Inquiry," New York, 1920.

[4] The results of these investigations are now being published by the Foreign Missions Conference of North America under the titles, "Report of the Africa Educational Commission" and "Report of the China Educational Commission."

cope with alone. It has provided an agency through which the missionary forces could approach the government of the United States as well as the governments of other countries in connection with the many problems which affect the missionary interests in the countries in which the boards are at work.

The organization of the Home Missions Council is similar, except that it does not include all the Canadian Home Mission Societies.[1] Thirty-six home-missionary organizations are represented in its membership. It has its office in New York and maintains a considerable office staff.[2] During the earlier years of its history the Home Missions Council was primarily a consultative body and was concerned with matters of comity between the denominations. But in recent years it has begun to assume a much larger measure of responsibility and is now functioning actively through a number of special committees which deal with such subjects as Alaska, Indian missions, migrant groups, Negro Americans, new Americans, Spanish-speaking peoples, comity and cooperation, etc.[3]

The organization and function of the women's boards are similar to those of the men. The Council of Women for Home Missions includes nineteen constituent, twelve affiliated, and five co-operating agencies and makes a specialty of publishing mission textbooks. The Home Missions Council and the Council of Women for Home Missions have offices side by side. They have joint committees dealing with almost every phase of home-mission work. They publish literature together. They make a joint annual report and use a common letterhead. Financial appropriations are frequently made by one to the other. The annual meetings of the two Councils are held at the same time and place and many of the sessions are joint sessions.

In the foreign-missionary field the relation between the men's

---

[1] At present two Canadian boards are members, the Board of Home Missions and Social Service of the Presbyterian Church in Canada, and the Missionary Society of the Methodist Church in Canada.

[2] Rev. Alfred Williams Anthony, D.D., is secretary, and the Rev. Rodney W. Roundy, associate secretary.

[3] There are no less than eighteen joint committees at present maintained by the Home Missions Council and the Council of Women for Home Missions. These committees not only include members of the constituent bodies, but other co-opted members whose services are desired. In this way the co-operation of representatives of the Christian Associations is secured in the fields where they are at work.

and women's organizations is even closer. In this case the women's societies have equal representation with the men's in the Foreign Missions Conference as well as upon all its committees. The same is true of the Young Women's Christian Association. The Federation of Woman's Boards of Foreign Missions of North America brings together the representatives of the women's foreign-missionary boards for purposes of consultation on matters of common interest,[1] but the representation of the individual boards in the Foreign Missions Conference is independent of their relation to the women's organization.[2]

It has been the policy both of the Home Missions Council and of the Foreign Missions Conference to proceed slowly and not to seek executive responsibility. As the names indicate, they have been primarily bodies for conference and counsel. Including as they do representatives of churches of very different views, they have hesitated to do anything which might alienate any part of their constituency. As is so often the case, the body that goes slowest tends to set the pace for the rest. Under the circumstances, the policy followed has probably been a wise one, and the attempt to assume executive functions would have been premature.

At the same time this caution has not been without its drawbacks. Had the Home Missions Council and the Foreign Missions Conference been in a position to assume more active executive responsibility, the Interchurch World Movement might have taken a different form and its worst dangers and evils have been avoided. In theory, as we have seen, the Interchurch World Movement was a movement for administrative union which is just what these bodies are designed to promote. As it was, instead of beginning with these bodies and using their experience and agencies as the nucleus for expansion, a start was made from a completely new centre, with a corresponding loss of energy and prestige.

In the case of the Foreign Missions Conference, this failure has been less serious than in the case of the Home Missions Council, because in the various continuation committees[3] the Boards of

---

[1] *E.g.,* on such matters as recruiting for missionary service, the support of union women's colleges in the foreign field, etc.

[2] Where the women's boards are separate organizations, they appoint their own delegates. Where men and women are working together in a single organization, the representatives are appointed by the unified denominational agency.

[3] Cf. p. 53.

Foreign Missions had a provisional organization through which they could function in the field.[1] In general it may be said that as between the home and foreign mission interests, the consciousness of unity is more highly developed in the latter than in the former. This is due no doubt in part to the greater pressure of need in the foreign field, but also in no small measure to the fact that the foreign boards, operating at a distance from the home base, are more independent of their constituency than those boards which are dealing at firsthand with the local churches from which the bulk of their support is drawn. A further difficulty in the way of securing unity at home is due to the fact that the agencies uniting in the Home Missions Council are not only more numerous, but represent a much wider distribution of authority and overlapping of activities.[2]

But the difference is, after all, only one of degree. Both in the foreign field and in the home field we need to strengthen and dignify the existing organs of unity. Much will depend for the future of the Christian Church upon whether the gap left vacant by the Interchurch shall be filled by the development of the agencies we already have, or whether a new agency must be created. For it seems clear that some responsible interdenominational body is needed that can not only think but act on behalf of the churches.

Such a central executive body is needed in the home field not only to do the things which the experience of the boards shows to be desirable, but because of its reflex influence upon the local church. We have seen that the community church movement faces difficulties because of the lack of a common outlet for its missionary zeal. Either it must divide its contributions between the denominations, or all its gifts must go to one. If the denominations themselves maintained a single responsible agency through which interdenominational work was being carried on on behalf of all, this difficulty would be removed. There would be an object, equally dear to all, to which all could give, and the union which the community church illustrates at the bottom would be matched at the top.

It is gratifying to know that distinct progress is being made toward realizing this end. In a number of different fields the work

---

[1] A significant step toward such an organization in the home field is the recent organization of the Home Missions Council of Montana.

[2] Cf. "Report of the Home Missions Council," 1921, pp. 254, 255.

of the denominations has already been unified by the Home Missions Council. Conspicuous among these are the work in Alaska, for the Indians, at Ellis Island, and in the field of foreign-language publications.[1] We have elsewhere referred to the admirable work done by the Council in Montana in unifying the home-missionary agencies of that state. The same is true to a less degree in Utah and in Colorado. Much progress has been made toward unifying the work for Mexicans and for Negroes, and a promising beginning has been made in co-ordinating the recruiting activities of the various denominations.

The same influences which are bringing the home and foreign-missionary agencies together are operating in the field of religious education, and in all three of the different spheres to which we have already referred. The Sunday-school workers have had no less than five different interdenominational associations—the International Sunday School Association, the Sunday School Council of Evangelical Denominations, the American Sunday-School Union,[2] the International Sunday School Lesson Committee, and the World's Sunday School Association, of which the second (the Sunday School Council) consists of the official Sunday-school agencies of the denominations. Negotiations have just been completed for a union between the Sunday School Council and the International Sunday School Association, which have combined to form the International Sunday School Council of Religious Education. In the Council of Church Boards of Education the workers in the cause of religious education in colleges have an effective organization.[3] Most recently the theological seminaries of the country have formed a conference,[4] meeting biennially, which furnishes a convenient means for the interchange of opinion among those who are working in this responsible field. Besides these larger and better known agencies there are a number of other associations and committees

[1] The Joint Committee on Foreign Language Publications under the Home Missions Council is planning the joint publication of one strong periodical for each language group and the production of a series of tracts which can be used by any denomination under its own imprint.

[2] The American Sunday-School Union differs from the others in that it is not an educational but a promoting agency. Strictly speaking, therefore, it should be classified either with the Home Missions Council or with the voluntary societies like the Christian Associations that administer as well as teach.

[3] Cf. *Christian Education,* January, 1922, "What the Council of Church Boards of Education is Doing."

[4] Cf. pp. 322, 323.

dealing with some specialized form of religious education, such as the associations of college pastors in state universities and of Biblical instructors in colleges and universities. In all no less than fourteen interdenominational or undenominational agencies are functioning in the field of religious education.[1]

All these are distinctly religious organizations. Besides these are the secular educational institutions of the country, our schools, our colleges, and our universities, with the various societies and associations through which they function. Many of these are governed and taught by Christian men and women who share with us our interest in the moral and spiritual issues at stake. No programme of Christian education can be adequate which fails to utilize their experience and to enlist their active co-operation. If religion be the central and all-important fact that we believe it to be, we shall never fully accomplish our aim until this fact is recognized in the secular teaching which forms the thinking of the most influential leaders of the modern world.

There is thus no lack of agencies at our disposal through which to carry out our campaign of education, if our forces are properly unified and co-ordinated.

An invaluable pioneer work in the way of co-ordination has been done by the Religious Education Association, a voluntary society including not only Protestants, but Roman Catholics and Jews. Through this association the field has been mapped out and some of the outstanding desiderata charted.[2] More recently

---

[1] The International Sunday School Council of Religious Education, the Council of Church Boards of Education, the International Sunday School Lesson Committee, the American Sunday-School Union, the World's Sunday School Association, the Religious Education Association, the Missionary Education Movement, the International Committee of the Young Men's Christian Associations, the National Board of the Young Women's Christian Associations, the Board of Missionary Preparation, the Conference of Theological Seminaries, the Association of Biblical Instructors in American Colleges and Secondary Schools, the Conference of Church Workers in Universities, the United Society of Christian Endeavor, the International Association of Daily Vacation Bible Schools.

[2] During the twenty years of its existence, the Religious Education Association has gathered those who have been interested in this subject for periodical conferences. It has impressed church leaders and teachers with a new and deeper sense of the need and value of religious education. It has enlisted scientific educators in the task of religious education and broadened the popular conception so as to include vital and social processes as well as formal instruction. It has developed a professional group in its field, pointed the way to new and better methods, and secured the co-operation of persons of

the attempt has been made to create a permanent organization of
the various interdenominational agencies that represent organized
Protestantism. At the suggestion of all the bodies concerned tlíe
Federal Council called a conference of the representatives of these
agencies to consider the needs of the field as a whole. This conference met at Garden City on May 12-14, 1921, and appointed a
Continuation Committee to effect a permanent organization. In
the meantime this committee was given authority to provide for
such preliminary committees as seemed called for. At the request
of the Committee on the War and the Religious Outlook, the Continuation Committee has assumed the responsibility for bringing
out the projected volume on "The Teaching Work of the Church,"
to which reference has already been made. In this volume it is
hoped to give a bird's-eye view of the entire field of Christian
education, to point out the problems which need to be solved and
the agencies which are at work on their solution, and to suggest
the most important lines of progress for the immediate future.

4. *Voluntary Agencies for Specialized Service—The History and
Expanding Work of the Christian Associations—Problems
Confronting the Associations To-day*

No study of the co-operative movement would be complete
without some account of the voluntary societies through which
Christians of different denominations are working together in unofficial but none the less effective ways. They deal with many different phases of Christian activity. Among the best known are the
American Bible Society, the American Sunday-School Union, the
Young Men's Christian Association, the Young Women's Christian
Association, the American Tract Society, the Young People's Society of Christian Endeavor, the Anti-Saloon League, the Women's
Christian Temperance Union, and the American Sabbath Association. The Bible Society is officially recognized by most of the
churches. The Temperance and Sabbath Associations have received the endorsement of many of them. Together they consti-

all sects, faiths, and communions. It has published about 15,000 pages of
material, held hundreds of conventions and conferences, conducted surveys,
promoted experiments, established standards, and brought about co-operation.
It conducts a bureau of information, a reference library, a personnel bureau,
and a clearing-house of activities.

tute one of the most characteristic expressions of American Protestantism.[1]

The two Christian Associations will serve as illustrations. Of all the voluntary societies of Protestantism they most nearly parallel the work of the churches. Other organizations deal with some particular phase of Christian service, such as education or missions, but in the Associations the only restriction is that of age and sex.[2] Whatever can be done to help young men or young women, whether along physical, intellectual, social, or religious lines, comes within their scope. Geographically, too, their service has no boundary. Like the churches, they work in the foreign field as well as at home. In the course of their work they meet all the specialized problems we have been considering. It is instructive, therefore, to learn how they are dealing with them and what relation their work bears to that of the agencies already described.

The Young Men's Christian Association began as a highly specialized and thoroughly democratic institution. It was an association of Christian laymen who had banded themselves together to work for young men; or rather, it was a group of associations. The central organization that we now know as the International Committee came into existence later and its relation to the co-operating associations which form its constituency has been progressively defined as a result of enlarging experience.[3]

The history of the Association has been marked by three features: (1) an enlarging programme; (2) increased resources, both financial and personal; (3) a growing tendency to extend its work along lines which parallel the work of the denominational boards.

The programme of the Association includes, as is well known, social and educational as well as religious features. It does for the young men and boys who are its members what the institutional

---

[1] Cf. Willett, "Undenominational Movements in the United States" in "Christian Unity," pp. 258–283.

[2] Originally interested mainly in evangelistic and social work, they have added educational and physical features, a field in which they have anticipated much that the churches are now doing.

[3] On the history of the Y. M. C. A., cf. R. C. Morse, "My Life with Young Men: Fifty Years in the Young Men's Christian Association," New York, 1918; Year Book of the Young Men's Christian Associations of North America, New York, 1920; Summary of the World War Work of the American Y. M. C. A., New York, 1920.

church tries to do for all the people in its neighborhood.[1] In addition the Association has been led by a natural and entirely legitimate process to do other things which do not concern young men and boys simply, but have to do with the welfare of the community for which it works or the group of people whom it serves. Thus the city work of the Association has led it to gather representatives of the churches for conference on civic betterment. Its county work has made it necessary to work for women as well as men. In local communities where the church was recreant to its duty the Association has found itself forced to make up for this lack by ministering to the family. On the foreign field especially the relation between the Association and the churches has been especially close, and while scrupulously observing its charter as an agency of the churches, not as a rival denomination, it has yet been doing things which in other places the missionaries are doing themselves. As a result, the line of demarcation between the sphere of the official and voluntary agencies has become increasingly difficult to discern.

This is especially evident in the field of publication and religious education. Through its press and its Bible class work, the Association has entered a field which is of the highest importance to the churches, and the need of a correlation of programme and a definition of responsibility becomes increasingly apparent.[2]

What is true of the Young Men's Christian Association applies to a less but still to an appreciable degree to the Young Women's Christian Association.[3] Beginning in a restricted sphere, this Association has also been led to extend its activities and to enter fields in which other agencies of the Church were already at work. Like the Young Men's Christian Association, it begins to parallel the work of the Church both at home and abroad. Some definition of its relation to the official women's agencies of the churches as

[1] Of its million members, over twenty per cent. are boys in their teens.

[2] An interesting experiment in co-ordination is being tried under the auspices of the Council of Church Boards of Education through the so-called Geneva plan—a plan through which the official representatives of the churches co-operate with the Association in presenting the appeal of the various forms of church work to the students gathered at the summer conferences of the Association.

[3] Cf. Wilson, "Fifty Years of Association Work"; cf. also the Handbook of the Young Women's Christian Association Movement, 1916; Report of the War Work Council of the Young Women's Christian Associations from 1917–1919.

well as to the Church as a whole seems therefore a desideratum.[1]

The problems thus briefly suggested have been accentuated for both Associations by the war. The war proved that in these organizations the Church possessed auxiliaries of the highest value, but it showed also the need of defining the sphere in which each was to work and the limits of its responsibility. We must find answers to such questions as these: How far are the Associations, as at present organized, prepared to do the work which they are actually doing? How far do they need changes in their theoretical basis and methods of administration? What should be the relation of the Associations to each other? Is the present policy of independence a good one; or has the time come for a merger or, if not, for some supplementary organization including both men and women and operating with the family as its basis? What is the relation of the Associations to the churches? Is the present state of independence still desirable, and if so how can we secure that thorough co-operation of all the Christian forces which the Interchurch World Movement tried to bring about and which is needed now more than ever?

The question how far the Associations as at present organized are fitted to do the work which they have set themselves to do is one which primarily concerns the Associations themselves, and involves matters of detail which it would be manifestly impossible, even if it were proper, to discuss here. But the central question is one of general interest, for it has to do with principles which apply to the denominations as well. That question is this: How far can executive responsibility of the magnitude and importance of that now exercised by the Associations be wisely assumed by a group of independent and self-governing bodies like the local associations which meet in convention only once every two or three years? What authority shall attach to the central body appointed by this convention to act for it during the interval between conventions? In what ways shall this body keep in touch with its constituency

---

[1] In two respects the Young Women's Christian Association is doing important pioneer work of special value for the churches. In its training school for secretaries it is working out methods for the training of women workers which deserve careful study by those who are responsible for the training of such workers in other fields. In the vexed field of industrial relations it is conducting studies and establishing relations that are full of promise for the future.

and to what extent should it feel free to act on its own responsibility in initiating changes in policy which may seem necessary to meet some unforeseen emergency? In view of the important questions of principle to be determined by the Associations, such questions as their future industrial policy or the religious basis of their membership, it is essential that the question of primary responsibility should be clearly defined.

Other questions which press for a solution concern the relation of the Associations to each other. During the war the Young Men's Christian Association employed women workers. Are they still to do so now that peace has come? In many communities the Young Men's Christian Association find women for whom no work is being done by women. Are they to neglect them or shall they broaden the basis of their appeal? So in the war the Young Women's Christian Association opened Hostess Houses in the camps which, while primarily designed for the wives and sisters of the soldiers, helped to keep up the morale of the men as well. Are they to do similar work in peace? Have they a ministry to men as well as to women?

The question becomes acute in smaller communities where the number of the population does not justify specialized work either for men or women. What is to be done here? Some inclusive organization seems called for which, operating on the same principles as the Associations but with the family as its unit, can co-operate with the local church in bringing to the community every form of helpful influence.[1] The question is at least worth raising whether the time has not come for such an inclusive organization. If we decide that it is needed, the further question arises how it shall be constituted. Shall it be formed by the union of the present Associations or, if this seems inexpedient, can some larger body be created in which both Associations and churches shall be represented to map out the field as a whole and delegate to each agency the task which it is best fitted to discharge?

The experience of the Salvation Army is a case in point. The army is an agency in many respects like the Associations, although governed in a more autocratic way. It specializes in ministry to the outcast and the submerged, but makes no distinction of sex.

[1] It is interesting to note that in some counties (*e.g.*, Nassau and Suffolk Counties, Long Island) the two Associations are already co-operating along the lines suggested in the text.

Its unit is the family, and this is true not only of those for whom it works, but of the workers as well. In the army there is complete equality of the sexes. Men and women work side by side; and a woman may command as well as a man. In the Salvation Army we see the Roman Catholic conception of a monastic order joined to the Protestant principle of the family. It is worth considering whether the method thus followed is not capable of wider adaptation; whether in ways more democratic, but no less effective, it may not be possible to utilize the immense spiritual resources of America, its womanhood as well as its manhood, for a constructive, nation-wide work that shall translate the dream of the Interchurch World Movement into a reality.

This leads us to the last of the questions concerning the future of the Associations; namely, that which has to do with their relation to the churches. At present that relation is an anomalous one.[1] It is their wish to be auxiliaries of the churches, not rival denominations. Yet they are entirely independent and self-directing. Unlike the orders in Roman Catholicism which give us our nearest parallel, there is no central authority to which they owe allegiance. Whatever adjustment there may be between them and the official church agencies must be voluntary. Several possibilities suggest themselves. The churches may be given the right to appoint representatives on the governing boards of the Associations as has been proposed by the National Council of the Scottish Y. M. C. A. to the Presbyterian churches of Scotland.[2] Or there may be stated conferences at which policies are agreed upon and spheres of influence defined.[3] Or some larger inclusive body may

---

[1] This fact has been recognized by the Young Men's Christian Association which at its convention in Detroit in 1919 authorized the International Committee to appoint a commission to enter into negotiations with the leading evangelical denominations for a careful study of the relations obtaining between the evangelical churches and the Association. Cf. the Report of the Commission on the Relation of the Young Men's Christian Association to the Churches; also "Christian Unity," pp. 126–132, esp. p. 132.

[2] For the details of this proposal cf. the Statement of Progress made toward a Closer Relationship and Co-operation between the Young Men's Christian Association and the Churches in Scotland, by the Church and Y. M. C. A. Relationship Committee, Edinburgh, 1921.

[3] Opportunities for such conference are now furnished by the presence of representatives of the two Associations as consulting members of the Administrative Committee of the Federal Council, of which a fuller account will be given in the next chapter. A representative of the Y. M. C. A. is an honorary member of the Home Missions Council and several of its secretaries are

be created in which both may be included, in which executive as well as advisory powers can be centred and which would represent the Church as a whole.

Whatever the final adjustment may be, it must be such as to conserve the freedom and initiative of the Associations. In an enterprise as many-sided as that of the Christian Church, it is never possible to move the whole body as fast as it ought to go. There must always be pioneers who go before and map out the course. To these must be accorded the freedom to experiment in new fields. Such pioneers the Associations have been, and they will be truest to themselves if they keep to this conception of their task. Much that they were once doing alone is now being done as well or better by the churches. Where this is true let them be glad and count it the highest proof of their success. There are broad fields still unoccupied in which the kind of service the Associations can render was never more needed than to-day. In entering these fields the Associations will find opportunity for an enlarging ministry. Only let it be clearly understood on both sides what these fields are, and as they move forward may it be not as rivals but as allies of the churches.

An indispensable condition of any satisfactory adjustment is that the churches themselves should come together. With a divided Church it is impossible for bodies as strong as the Associations to deal. Hence we are led inevitably to the third and last branch of our practical inquiry; namely, what the churches in their corporate capacity are doing to realize their union with one another.

members of the sub-committees of that body. The Y. W. C. A. as a consulting body is a member of the Council of Women for Home Missions and representatives of the Y. W. C. A. serve on the committees both of the Home Missions Council and of the Council of Women for Home Missions, as well as on the joint committees of the two bodies. Both the Young Men's Christian Association and the Young Women's Christian Association are constituent members of the Foreign Missions Conference and their representatives are eligible for service on its various committees.

CHAPTER XIII

1. *Obstacles to Christian Unity Presented by the Existing Situation in the Denominations*

By whatever road we have travelled we have been led to the same conclusion, that the chance of the Church's becoming what it ought to be depends upon the churches getting together. We have seen this in connection with our study of the local congregation. We have seen it in connection with the administrative work of the churches as carried on by their official boards. We have seen it finally in connection with the relation between the churches and the Associations. In each case the attempt to secure effective co-operation meets obstacles which can only be overcome by the united action of the denominations as a whole. This is the situation which the movement for unity in its inclusive form is designed to meet.

This movement, as we have seen, encounters an unexpected difficulty. It is the difficulty of the lack of unity within the denominations themselves. Even if they wished to unite, they are not in a position to do so effectively, for they have not yet devised the agencies through which they can put the will to unity into practice.

This weakness in denominational organization appears both in the nature of the governing bodies, and in that of the intermediate divisions through which these bodies function.

There is great variety in the method by which the different churches are governed. In some the affairs of the church are cared for by a General Council or Convention, meeting only once in three or four years; in others the supreme judicatory meets annually. In some it consists of two houses, as of bishops and lay delegates. In others it is a single assembly. In some it commands large powers, and can act on its own initiative. In others these powers are strictly limited by the necessity of reference to the congregations represented. In some this representation is immediate and

249

all churches have a right to send or at least to vote for delegates. In others the representation is mediate, through presbytery, classis, or diocese. But in each case the power to act for the denomination as a whole is confined to the highest body, and during the period between the sessions of this body this power is correspondingly limited.

This difficulty, as we have seen, was keenly felt during the war. In the case of those churches whose supreme body did not meet in 1917, various devices had to be resorted to. Agencies of the Church designed for different purposes were forced to act to meet the emergency. Others were created by voluntary action in the hope that what they did would be ratified later. The same causes which made it desirable for the churches to be able to act promptly during the war are operative in peace, and their inability so to act has similar disastrous consequences.

It may be said indeed that this need of a permanent executive is supplied by the various boards and other agencies whose work we have described. Up to a certain point this is true. But these boards are strictly limited by their charters to specific tasks. They have no power to assume new responsibility. In the division of powers between them many promising opportunities go unutilized. What is needed is some permanent body inclusive of the different interests which can be clothed with the full powers of the denomination, and can act in its name during the interval between conventions or assemblies. The Christian Associations, facing a similar problem, have created such central bodies in the International Committee and the National Board. The churches have no corresponding central executive authority, and this lack is one of the most serious obstacles to effective Christian union.[1]

Apart from the limitations thus put upon the ability of the churches to co-operate effectively, there are various ways in which the lack of such a central executive body limits the efficiency of the denominations themselves. It makes impossible any comprehensive plan for the location or merging of churches. It leaves the

[1] This is true not only at home but on the foreign field. A more serious obstacle to union even than the presence of separate denominations working side by side is the existence of a number of independent local committees within the same denomination without any central executive competent to speak for the mission as a whole. One of the most encouraging steps toward unity on the foreign field has been the progress which has been made toward unifying the different missions within each denomination.

individual minister at the mercy of the local congregation; or at best of the intermediate ecclesiastical body of which the congregation is a constituent part. It leaves the church theoretically one, but without any agency through which to realize its unity in practice. It is as though Congress tried to run the government without any executive and then decided to meet only once in two or three years, and never for more than a week or ten days.

In more highly organized churches like the Presbyterian and Episcopal, these difficulties are partially overcome by the existence of intermediate units like the presbytery or the diocese. In theory it is the duty of the presbytery as it is of the bishop to care for the churches within a definite geographical area; but apart from the fact that the power thus theoretically given is often unused or used ineffectively, the plan makes no provision for securing unity of action between the executives of the intermediate units. One bishop may pursue a policy in his diocese which is diametrically opposed to that of his neighbor in the next. The existence of a strong, well-organized presbytery or classis is no guarantee at all that its neighbor's presbyterial duty of supervision will not be altogether neglected. In the Methodist Church alone, through its system of rotation in office, an administrative policy is possible on a truly national scale, and even here the power of the church to initiate radical change is limited by the infrequency of the meetings of the General Conference.

Serious as is the weakness of the present system on its administrative side, its failure as an educational agency is even more serious. In the Protestant Church, no central executive authority can impose its will from without. The Church as a whole can do only what its constituent members determine shall be done, and for this there must be a common public opinion formed by intelligent discussion in the light of all the facts in the case.

At no other point is the weakness of our present denominational system more apparent. There exist no adequate organs for the formation of public opinion on the questions which concern the denomination as a whole, nor is it likely that this need will be supplied until a central body is established charged with responsibility for the affairs of the entire denomination and obliged, therefore, to consult its constituency as to what the denomination shall do.

The larger denominations are beginning to realize the disadvantages of the present state of affairs, and various attempts are being made to secure the needed unity. Among them may be mentioned the denominational forward movements to which we have already referred, such as the Presbyterian New Era, the Methodist Centenary, the Baptist New World Movement, and the like.[1] These movements, like the Interchurch World Movement, have limited powers and are concerned more with raising money for the churches than with spending it. Still they have proved useful in developing the sense of denominational responsibility and unity, and may well serve to prepare the way for something better.

A characteristic feature of these denominational forward movements has been the attention given to education in denominational responsibility. A campaign has been carried on in the different churches, not in the interest of any particular board or agency, but of the work of the Church as a whole. Literature has been created and thought has been stimulated; and while mistakes have been made which larger experience might have avoided, there can be little doubt that the net result has been good.

A second method of securing the needed unification is through the creation of a central Executive Committee to represent and act for the denomination between conventions. Thus the Episcopal Church has its presiding Bishop and Council; the Presbyterian Church its Executive Commission; the Lutherans their Executive Board; the Baptists their Board of Promotion, and so forth.[2] These are useful additions to the machinery of the Church. But they are weak in two respects. They do not include all the men most important for determining the Church's policy; they lack the requisite power to act effectively in matters of consequence.

[1] Cf. p. 120.

[2] The ad interim committees of the various larger denominations are as follows: The Presiding Bishop and Council of the Protestant Episcopal Church; the Executive Board of the United Lutheran Church in America; the General Board of Promotion of the Northern Baptist Convention; the Council of the Boards of Benevolence of the Methodist Episcopal Church; the Executive Commission of the Presbyterian Church in the U. S. A. The Congregationalists have no single co-ordinating committee that acts for the denomination as a whole. There is, however, a Commission on Missions of the National Council which is provided for constitutionally and elected by the Council to co-ordinate all its missionary work. Other matters that affect general denominational interests are dealt with by the Executive Committee of the National Council.

Both these limitations are due to the distrust of a strong central authority which has been so characteristic of American life. The churches, like the cities and states after which their government was modelled, have preferred to suffer the tyranny of irresponsible bosses whose acts they could disown, rather than to entrust power to responsible agents whom they could control. In the Presbyterian Church this fear of centralized authority has been carried so far as to disqualify any one who is a member of any of the boards of the church from serving upon the executive commission which is to determine the policy which the boards are to execute.

There can be little doubt that the pressure of need will lead to a change in this policy. Indeed, signs are not wanting to show that such a change is already taking place. In the Presbyterian Church a Committee of the General Assembly is at work upon plans which, if carried out, would greatly strengthen the central authority.[1] Both in the Episcopal and Lutheran Churches the existing committees are proving themselves effective unifying agencies. Even in the Congregational and Baptist Churches the centralizing tendency is evident, and during the interval between conventions, the permanent officers are assuming larger executive powers.

A further difficulty in the way of effective union is found in the nature of the intermediate divisions through which the churches function. In all the larger denominations it has been necessary to establish intermediate agencies between the central national body and the local bodies it represents; and the same is true of the Christian Associations. These units differ in different churches. In the Episcopal Church this unit is the diocese. In the Presbyterian it is the presbytery and the synod; in the Dutch Reformed the classis; in the Methodist Church the district, and so on.

[1] Since these lines were written the Committee's report has been adopted by the General Assembly. This report consolidates the sixteen boards and agencies of the church into four new boards, namely, the Board of Foreign Missions, the Board of National Missions, the Board of Christian Education and the Board of Ministerial Relief and Sustentation. The Boards of Foreign Missions and National Missions will be composed both of men and women in the proportion of twenty-five to fifteen. The Assembly further referred to the presbyteries for their consideration the Committee's recommendation that a council of twenty-seven members should be created with a permanent paid executive, on which representatives of the new boards should serve with other members appointed by the church at large.

These different bodies have different powers, and if their personnel be reactionary or unsympathetic can effectively block a policy which has the approval of the central body. This provision, like the parallel arrangement between the state and the nation, has its advantages in that it increases the opportunity of experiment, and so the interchange of experience, but it makes it difficult to carry out a consistent national policy.

A more serious difficulty is found in the fact that the intermediate bodies do not correspond with one another. Each church has mapped out its local divisions without reference to the others, with the result that even when unity is achieved at the top or at the bottom, it is impossible to secure it in the middle, or, if not impossible, so difficult that the cost is practically prohibitive. Thus in New York City to unite the churches in support of a city-wide programme it is necessary to secure the consent of two Presbyterian bodies, fourteen Lutheran, five Methodist, and two Episcopal, not to mention bodies like the Baptist whose organization covers the city as a whole. A similar difficulty is met in dealing with larger areas like the state. Even the Associations have done nothing to remove this difficulty. The Young Men's Christian Association is organized by states, the Young Women's Christian Association by fields which cross state lines.

For this maladjustment the obvious remedy would seem to be the adoption of a uniform standard of division—say the state or some convenient group of states, with such smaller sub-divisions as experience might suggest—and the regrouping of the existing ecclesiastical divisions so as to make them conform as nearly as possible to this arrangement. Such an adjustment would take time and patience, but it would bring its reward in increased effectiveness, and there is no reason why, through the formation of state federations or other central committees, it should not in time be effected.

A possible agent through which to bring about this readjustment is the state federation of churches where one exists. Such federations, as we have seen, are found in a number of states and are doing increasingly useful work. In Montana the Home Missions Council has taken the initiative. The entire state has been parcelled out between the different denominations and a united state-wide work is being carried on in the name of the Church as a whole. The experience gained in such a common enterprise is bound to have a reflex influence on those who take part in it, and where clumsy or ill-adapted denominational machinery stands in the way of efficient service, there is good reason to hope that it will be discarded.

2. *The Movement for the Reunion of Denominational Families— Its Difficulties, Practical and Theoretical*

The difficulty of bringing about union is enhanced by the fact that we are not dealing simply with half a dozen large and compact organizations, but with a large number of smaller bodies. The last Census reports some two hundred denominations in the United States, and while a number of these are so small as for our purpose to be practically negligible, there remain of bodies over 50,000 no less than forty-six.

Serious as the situation is, however, there are compensating features. Of the existing denominations, many, as we have seen, owe their organization to local or passing conditions, and only a few represent real differences of fundamental conviction. It is possible to group the leading denominations of the United States into seven or eight families which between them include by far the larger number of Protestant Christians, and the problem of Christian unity, therefore, would seem to require first the union of the separated members of these families with one another.

This movement is, in fact, going on with varying degrees of success. The Lutherans, until recently the most divided of all the denominational groups, have given the most encouraging example of reunion. Three of their larger bodies [1] have come together to form the United Lutheran Church, and seventeen bodies co-operate in the work of the National Lutheran Council.[2] Reunion is being

---

[1] The General Synod of the Evangelical Lutheran Church in the United States of America, the General Council of the Evangelical Lutheran Church in North America, and the United Synod of the Evangelical Lutheran Church in the South.

[2] The United Lutheran Church in America, the Joint Synod of Ohio, the Evangelical Lutheran Synod of Iowa and Other States, the Lutheran Synod of Buffalo, the Immanuel Synod, the Jehovah Conference, the Augustana Synod, the Norwegian Lutheran Church of America, the Lutheran Free Church, the Evangelical Lutheran Church of America (Eielsen's Synod), the Church of the Lutheran Brethren, the United Danish Evangelical Lutheran

actively discussed by the churches of the Presbyterian and Reformed families. Three of the Presbyterian bodies have already
come together [1] and negotiations are now on foot between five
of the remaining.[2] Among the Methodists and Baptists progress is slower. The race question, as we have seen, presents difficulties which have not yet been overcome. Yet the sentiment for
unity is present, and among the Methodists at least a way is likely
to be found in the not too distant future.[3]

Scarcely less serious than the obstacles to reunion which grow
out of the past history of the denominations are those which are
due to the division of sentiment among the present members. By
this we do not refer simply to the divergent views as to the importance of uniting with other churches, but to differences of
opinion as to the degree of freedom which the Church should allow
its own members. In such a body as the Protestant Episcopal
Church, for example, a wide difference of theological belief exists.
All shades of opinion from Catholicism without the Pope to the
most radical Protestantism are represented. This breadth and
inclusiveness is a source of pride to some of its most distinguished
bishops.[4] Other leading churchmen regard the presence of Protestant beliefs within the Church as a serious disadvantage, which, if
they could, they would remove. Far from thinking of the Church
as a half-way house between Roman Catholicism and Protestantism,
they maintain that it belongs wholly on the Catholic side. To

Church of America, the Danish Evangelical Lutheran Church in America, the
Icelandic Lutheran Church in North America, the Suomi Synod, the Finnish
Evangelical National Lutheran Church in America, the Finnish Apostolic
Lutheran Church of America.

[1] The Presbyterian Church in the U. S. A., the Cumberland Presbyterian
Church, the Welch Calvinistic Methodist Church.

[2] The Presbyterian Church in the U. S. A., the Presbyterian Church in the
U. S., the United Presbyterian Church, the Reformed Church in the U. S.
(Dutch) and the Reformed Church in America (German).

Since the above was written, the negotiations between the Northern and
Southern Presbyterians have been broken off for the time being. Discouraging as this failure is, its importance should not be exaggerated. The factors
which are working for the reunion of denominational families are deep-seated
and persistent. Their operation may for the time being be delayed, but it
cannot be arrested, as the progress of the negotiations in the Canadian church
abundantly proves.

[3] For information as to the present state of the unity movement among the
denominations cf. "Christian Unity," pp. 45–95.

[4] E.g., Bishop Manning, "The Call to Unity," pp. 88–91.

their thinking it is one of the three historic divisions of the one true Church from which the bodies which they call sects have schismatically separated themselves. It is obvious that when influential leaders differ so fundamentally it is not easy to secure effective action on behalf of unity.

What is true of the Episcopal Church is true with variations in each of the larger bodies. The form varies; the issue remains the same. Each church has its high and its low churchmen, its liberals and its conservatives. Each is itself an epitome of the larger Church and faces similar problems. The situation in each case reacts upon the larger problems of unity. The conservatives fear any movement which would seem to justify the liberals in their position. The liberals hesitate to assent to action which might increase the power of the conservatives.

Illustrations of this divisive tendency could be given in the case of denominations where every practical consideration would point to unity. Among the reasons for the hesitation of the Southern Presbyterian Church to accept the proposals for union made by the Northern church is the fear that its own orthodoxy may be weakened by the infusion of a more liberal type of theology. In the case of the Baptists, the division between North and South, originally caused by the race question and still perpetuated by it, is reinforced by the uncompromising insistence of the Southern Baptists upon close communion, and their more conservative view of the Bible.

Even Congregationalism is no exception to this rule. If it be asked why Unitarian Christians, originally members of the Congregational family, still constitute a denominational group of their own, the answer lies in the field of doctrine. To unite with the Unitarians, the Congregationalists must sacrifice their present close relations with other churches which hold strictly to the Trinitarian faith. Even if they were willing to do this, the cause of unity would not be advanced. To seek union on terms which would result in a new division is a poor way to promote the cause of unity. Let us first unite those who are already closest together. Then we can see what can be done for those who are farther away.[1]

[1] One great advantage possessed by the movement for unity in the local field is that it makes possible discrimination not feasible on a nation-wide scale. In certain of the local federations of New England Unitarian churches are to-day co-operating with churches of other bodies in various forms of

3. *Organic and Federal Unity—Reasons why We Must Begin with the Latter—The Federal Council, an Agency of Nation-wide Christian Co-operation*

It is against this background that we must approach the movement for Christian unity in its larger aspects. That movement, as we have seen, has two phases—the movement for organic unity and the movement for federal unity. The first seeks to substitute for the present denominations some more inclusive organization; the second takes the present denominations for granted and attempts through them to work out the most effective and practicable forms of co-operation.

The movement for organic union in turn has two phases, of which one seeks the reunion of Christendom as a whole, the other is content to unite the different churches within a definite geographical area like the nation. The outstanding example of the first is the proposed World Conference on Faith and Order. Examples of the second are the movements for unity in Canada, Australia, and New Zealand, and the recent proposal for the organic union of the American churches made by the Philadelphia Conference of 1920.

Important as these movements are, all but the last lie outside the scope of the present discussion. Of the first it is sufficient to say that the refusal of the Pope to be represented in the conference proves what careful students of the subject have long suspected—that any movement for union which tries to include Rome is for the present foredoomed to failure. It is necessary, therefore, either to abandon the hope of union altogether, or to confine the movement to such bodies as are sufficiently close in sympathies and ideals to make present contact fruitful. Such movements, on the other hand, as are going on in Canada and Australia would seem to show that among Protestant bodies, at least, if enough time and pains be taken, organic union on a national scale is not impossible.

With the refusal of the Pope to take part in the Conference on Faith and Order, the position of the Greek Orthodox Church be-

---

practical Christian activity. Through the contacts thus made, possible misunderstanding is being removed and progress made toward that mutual spiritual appreciation and sympathy which is the prerequisite of any effective outward unity on a large scale.

comes one of exceptional interest. There are many indications that in this quarter the approach of the Protestant churches will be met in a very different spirit. The bonds of spiritual sympathy forged in the fires of the Great War and its resulting sufferings have been further strengthened by the visits of representative Greek prelates.[1] In Russia especially, the future of the Greek Church will be a subject of special interest to American Protestants. It is the one stable institution which has survived the cataclysm of Bolshevism, and there is much to be said for the view that the true way to advance the spiritual interests of Russia is not to compete with the work this church is doing, but to strengthen it in every possible way.

Yet to allow our desire for closer relations with the Greek Church to divert us from the more obvious duty of securing an effective union of American Protestantism would be short-sighted in the extreme. To sacrifice possible union here in the hope of securing unity elsewhere would be to retard rather than to advance the cause we have at heart. The stronger and more united the American Protestant Church, the more persuasive will be its appeal to our brethren of other churches.

Especially interesting and significant for our American unity movement is the experience of our sister churches in Canada, New Zealand, and Australia, which have already made substantial progress toward organic union. In Canada a vigorous movement for the union of the Presbyterian, the Methodist, and the Congregational churches has been in progress since 1902. In 1909 and 1910 the basis of union for the United Church of Canada was approved by a large majority of all the churches, and while the size of the minority which in the Presbyterian Church was not yet ready for union made it seem wise not to press the matter at the time, it now seems that the patient effort of twenty years will soon be crowned with success and the United Church of Canada be translated from an ideal into reality.[2]

A similar movement is on foot between the Presbyterians, Congregationalists, and Methodists of Australia and New Zealand, and

[1] *E.g.,* Most Rev. Meletios Metaxakis, Œcumenical Patriarch of Constantinople, and Bishop Nicholai of Ochrida.

[2] William E. Gilroy, "Church Union in Canada," *Christian Century,* September 8, 15, 1921; The Right Rev. the Bishop of Ontario, "The Church of England in Canada and Reunion," *Hibbert Journal,* July, 1920; "Christian Unity: Its Principles and Possibilities," pp. 352, 353.

is apparently meeting with similar success. There seems good reason, therefore, to hope that here, too, a strong national church will be formed by the coming together of these three bodies.[1]

If these movements encourage us to believe that organic union is possible between Protestant bodies within definite geographical areas, they warn us that this will require much time and patience. This seems to be the lesson taught by the failure of the Philadelphia plan above referred to.[2] This plan was the outcome of a Conference on Organic Union held in Philadelphia in 1918 at the invitation of the General Assembly of the Presbyterian Church in the U. S. A., which was attended by representatives of nineteen communions. It provides that when six denominations shall have certified their assent, a council may be convened to function for what shall be known as the United Church of Christ in America. The plan contemplates a federal council with enlarged powers which, besides general duties of an advisory and judicial character, shall have power "to direct such consolidation of the missionary activities as well as of particular churches in over-churched areas as is consistent with the law of the land and of the particular denominations affected."[3] After two years of discussion by the committee appointed to prepare it, this plan has now been submitted to the constituent bodies, but if present indications are to be trusted, there seems to be slight chance of its acceptance. Even the Presbyterian Church, which was responsible for the initiation of the conference, has thus far failed to secure the assent of the requisite number of presbyteries to the proposed plan.

One reason for the failure of the plan has already been mentioned—the limited time which has been given to its preparation. Such a union, if it is to succeed, must be preceded by a long period of education and be the expression of a spiritual sympathy gained through years of practical co-operation. A second reason is the fact that what is proposed is simply a federal council with enlarged powers. This being the case, it has seemed to many that it would be more sensible to strengthen the Federal Council that we now have than to create a new one with different duties and authority.[4]

[1] Cf. "Christian Unity: Its Principles and Possibilities," p. 353.
[2] *Op. cit.*, pp. 156, 355–358.
[3] *Op cit.*, p. 358.
[4] It is only fair to say that those who advocate the Philadelphia plan do not apprehend any serious difficulty on this score. They point out that the two bodies have different functions and authority, and that it would be

Under existing conditions, therefore, the natural point of departure for the movement for unity in this country would seem to be the present Federal Council. We must therefore inquire what qualifications it has to become the central unifying agency of which we are in search.

The Federal Council is an organization which came into existence in 1908 through the action of twenty-nine co-operating churches, to which in the course of the following year four more were added. It consists of a body of delegates officially appointed by their constituent bodies for the purposes set forth in the constitution as follows:

"I. To express the fellowship and catholic unity of the Christian Church.

"II. To bring the Christian bodies of America into united service for Christ and the world.

"III. To encourage devotional fellowship and mutual counsel concerning the spiritual life and religious activities of the churches.

"IV. To secure a larger combined influence for the churches of Christ in all matters affecting the moral and social condition of the people, so as to promote the application of the law of Christ in every relation of human life.

"V. To assist in the organization of local branches of the Federal Council to promote its aims in their communities."

These delegates meet in council every four years, or more often if they shall so decide. In the interim the authority of the Council is exercised through an Executive Committee of one hundred members meeting annually, which in turn is represented by an Administrative Committee which meets monthly. This committee includes, besides the official representatives of the denominations, certain individuals elected by the Executive Committee and certain corresponding members representing other organizations.

The work of the Council is carried on by permanent committees known as commissions, as well as by temporary committees. The most important of the former are the Commissions on Councils of Churches, on Evangelism and Life Service, on the Church and Social Service, on International Justice and Goodwill, on the Church and Race Relations, and on Army and Navy Chaplains. Other

entirely possible for those churches who accept the Philadelphia plan to continue in the existing Federal Council their relation with their sister churches who are not ready to move forward so fast.

commissions are concerned with Relations with Religious Bodies in Europe, with Temperance, and with Christian Education. The personnel of these commissions is made up of persons interested in the matters with which they deal, and so far as possible representative of the constituent denominational bodies. The more important have paid secretaries who, together with the general secretaries, form the Secretarial Council.

The financial support of the Council has hitherto been drawn from three sources: the contributions of the denominations; gifts from friends interested in the cause of Christian unity; special funds raised by the various commissions. During the period of experiment through which the Council has been passing, it has been forced largely to rely upon individual support. This has been recognized as a weakness, and at its recent meeting in Boston the Council decided to appeal to the denominations to assume the full support of the work.

During the years of its existence the growth of the Council has been rapid and steady. It has assumed new duties as occasion demanded, and is to-day recognized as an indispensable organ of the churches. It would seem therefore the natural nucleus for the co-operative movement of the future.

So far as its theoretical basis is concerned, the constitution of the Council leaves little to be desired. Including to-day thirty-one co-operating churches,[1] organized on a thoroughly representative basis for purposes which our entire study has shown us to be of fundamental importance, it is an organization which expresses in official form the highest measure of co-operation which the churches

[1] The Northern Baptist Convention; the Free Baptist General Conference; the National Baptist Convention (African); the American Christian Convention; the Christian Reformed Church in North America; the Churches of God in North America; the Congregational Churches; the Disciples of Christ; the Evangelical Association; the Evangelical Synod of North America; the Friends; the Methodist Episcopal Church; the Methodist Episcopal Church, South; the Primitive Methodist Church; the Colored Methodist Episcopal Church in America; the Methodist Protestant Church; the African Methodist Episcopal Church; the African Methodist Episcopal Zion Church; the Moravian Church; the Presbyterian Church in the U. S. A.; the Presbyterian Church in the U. S.; the Reformed Presbyterian Church; the Protestant Episcopal Church (through its Commissions on Christian Unity and Social Service); the Reformed Church in America; the Reformed Church in the U. S.; the Reformed Episcopal Church; the Seventh Day Baptist Churches; the United Brethren in Christ; the United Evangelical Church; the United Presbyterian Church; the United Lutheran Church (consultative body).

of America have yet attained. Objections to it on the ground of theory are based either on misapprehension of the facts, or fear that any form of federal union may prove so satisfactory to those who take part in it as to make them indifferent to any larger movement.

On the score of achievement, too, the record of the Council is enviable.[1] With scanty resources and little official support it has performed many services of great value to the Church. Through its committees and commissions it has done good work in important fields, notably in the fields of social service, evangelism, local federations, and international relations. It has served as a means of communication not only between the churches of this country but of Great Britain and Europe as well. It has been the means of raising large sums for the weaker churches of France and Belgium and through its Commission on Oriental Relations [2] done much to promote better feeling between this country and Japan. To meet the war emergency it created the General War-Time Commission of the Churches, with its daughter, the Committee on the War and the Religious Outlook.[3] Judged by its accomplishments, hitherto, the Federal Council would seem to deserve the confidence of the churches.

It is doubtful if so representative a gathering of American Christians had ever assembled in this country, or so inspiring a programme been outlined as at the quadrennial meeting of the Federal Council in Boston in December, 1920.[4] The spirit of the meeting was expressed in the closing message to the churches from which we make the following extract:

[1] For a full account of the Federal Council the reader should consult the substantial volume entitled "The Churches Allied for Common Tasks," which contains its last report to the constituent bodies. In four different ways the Council is serving the churches: (1) as a means of information on matters of common interest, as through the publication of its Year Book and monthly bulletins; (2) as a co-ordinating agency in the fields where the churches are already actively at work, *e.g.*, evangelism, religious education, social service, etc.; (3) as a pioneer in new work for which the churches have as yet no adequate official agencies, *e.g.*, race relations, international relationships; (4) as an organ of communication with other bodies, national and international, *e.g.*, the Washington office, the Commission on Relations with Religious Bodies in Europe, etc.

[2] Now merged with the Commission on International Justice and Goodwill.

[3] Cf. Chapter VI, pp. 111–113.

[4] Cf. "The Churches Allied for Common Tasks," edited by Samuel McCrea Cavert, New York, 1921.

"To all who love and would follow our Lord Jesus Christ:

"In the midst of world-wide unrest and uncertainty, we, the members of the Fourth Quadrennial Meeting of the Federal Council of the Churches of Christ in America, face the future with confidence and hope. Wherever we look, in our own country or in foreign lands, we find tasks which challenge and opportunities which inspire. The time calls the churches to resolute and united advance.

"There is a message of faith and hope and brotherhood which must be brought to a despondent and disheartened world.

"There are starving peoples to be fed. In China, in the Near East, in the countries lately devastated by war, men, women, and little children are crying to us for help.

"In our own country there are wrongs to be righted and injustices to be removed in order that there may be a more abundant life for all.

"Millions are struggling for better economic and industrial conditions which will enable them to realize their full personality as sons of the Most High God. These desires we must help them to fulfil.

"There are problems involved in the relation of the races in our country and in other lands which can only be met by the methods of co-operation and conference which befit the children of a common Father.

"There is a reconciling word to be spoken to the peoples with whom we have lately been at war and with whom we hope soon to be associated in the constructive tasks of peace.

"Perplexing questions are at issue between our own country and our neighbors in Mexico and in Japan that need for their solution the spirit of mutual understanding and sympathy which Christianity inspires.

"There are aspirations after international justice and goodwill which must be realized in an association of the nations for mutual helpfulness and world service.

"There is a world-wide ministry to be rendered to men of every nation and every race—a unity of the spirit to be achieved which shall make possible all the lesser unities that we seek.

"To these tasks we would consecrate ourselves anew, to this ministry we would invite men of goodwill everywhere.

"What is this work to which our Master summons us? It is to help men everywhere to realize the kind of life that befits free personalities who accept the standards of Jesus Christ. We must show men not by word only, but by deed, what Christian discipleship means for men living in such a world and facing such conditions as confront us to-day—what it means for the family, what it means for industry, what it means for the relation of race to race and of nation to nation.

"But that our witness may be effective, our conduct must match our profession. A self-centred church cannot rebuke the selfishness of business. A self-complacent church is helpless before the arrogance of race. A church which is itself the scene of competition and strife is impotent in face of the rivalries of the nations. When men see Christians forgetting their differences in common service, then and not till then will they believe in Christ's power to break down the barriers between classes and between races.

"We welcome, therefore, the voice that comes to us across the sea from our fellow-Christians in Lambeth, joining with us in calling the churches to more complete unity. We reciprocate the spirit of their most Christian utterance. We believe with them that we are already one in Christ and are persuaded that the way to manifest the spiritual unity which we now possess, and to make possible its increase in ever enlarging measure, is for all those who love our Lord and Saviour Jesus Christ to join in discharging the common duties whose obligation all alike recognize.

"In this hour fraught with the possibilities of healing or of disaster, one thing only can save the nations and that is a will to united service, born of faith in the triumph of the good. To this faith we summon all men in the name of Him who died that we might live and who is able by His spirit to bring out of the failure and disappointment of the present a far more abundant and satisfying life. In this faith we would rededicate ourselves to the service of the living God, whose Kingdom is righteousness and peace and joy."

The detailed programme of the Council was embodied in the report of the Committee on Methods of Co-operation. This report begins by endorsing the report of a previous committee presented at Cleveland, in which the legitimate business and duty of the Federal Council were described as follows:

"To provide points of contact between the denominations through their recognized representatives, in order to facilitate understanding and sympathy between them;

"To study the programme of co-operative tasks, suggesting measures and methods by which such tasks can be done effectively; and undertake whatever work properly falls within its sphere;

"To speak with care and a due sense of responsibility for the churches on those matters on which there is a general agreement;

"To serve as a clearing-house of information about those things that are being done by its constituent bodies and other organizations affiliated or co-operating with it;

"To be an organ of publicity through which that which is of interest to all may be effectively conveyed to each and to the public;

"To function in other forms of co-operative work for which there may be no adequate provision."

After paying a tribute to the work now being done by the existing commissions of the Council in various important fields and emphasizing the need of still further strengthening and developing this work, notably in the fields of evangelism and Christian education, the report then goes on to speak of "other concrete needs not now provided for in the Council's agencies which in our judgment call for some provision, either directly by the Federal Council or indirectly through it by related co-operative agencies. These include: (1) the friendly and mutually assisting integration of the denominational promotional or forward movements; (2) the provision of some board or committee of forethought and outlook which will study and plan for us all, with no administrative authority, but to suggest approaching needs and the requisite preparations to meet them; (3) some adequate arrangement for supplying information and interpretation regarding the work and activity of the churches; (4) an adequate, continuous, and wisely directed endeavor of all our forces in behalf of a more general acceptance of true principles of stewardship both of money and of life; (5) some facilities for the general relationship of all the Christian organizations and activities of women which would provide them with a common meeting-ground and clearing-house and make the facts of their work and relationships accessible to the churches; (6) some central study of the problem of lay activities in the churches and some helpful interrelation of the denominational efforts to deal with this problem; (7) the promotion of 'works of serving love,' of those deeds of mercy and benevolence in which Christians unite and which powerfully express their common faith."

Here surely is work which needs to be done, if not by the Federal Council, then by some other body similarly constituted.

On the other hand, the Federal Council suffers from certain weaknesses which, if not corrected, will be fatal to its success. It has not as yet had back of it the active support of the constituent bodies in the sense in which the War-Time Commission came to have that support in the war tasks of the churches. They do not yet feel it theirs in the same sense in which they feel this to be true of their own denominational boards and agencies. Above all, it has not yet secured the whole-hearted support of two great bodies whose co-operation was essential to the success of the War-Time Commission, the Protestant Episcopal Church and the United Lutheran Church.

These weaknesses were clearly recognized at the Boston meeting and steps were taken to correct them. Certain changes in the constitution of the Council's committees were approved which would make them more fully representative. Most important of all, the denominations which have hitherto confined their support to the payment of the expenses of their delegates to the quadrennial meetings were asked to assume full financial support of the Council by a pro-rata apportionment of its budget, and encouraging progress has already been made along this line.

A recent statement from the treasurer of the Federal Council reports that of the $250,000 needed for next year's budget, $155,000 have been approved either conditionally or unconditionally by the co-operating churches. In some cases the appropriation has been made from denominational funds already existing; in others in the form of recommendations to the churches. As compared with the situation which existed prior to the Boston meeting, in which the total of the denominational contributions to the Council amounted to no more than $16,000, this represents a substantial gain.

In the case of the communions not now formally members of the Federal Council, progress has also been made. The Episcopal Church, already represented through two of its Commissions, is in unofficial ways co-operating with the Council along many lines. It is greatly to be hoped that in the spirit of the Lambeth recommendation as to the formation of councils in convenient geographical areas [1] the next General Convention will approve the suggestion already made by many of its members that the church assume full membership in the Council. In the case of the Lutheran Church there are certain difficulties to be overcome which grow out of the historic position of that church toward all forms of co-operation which are not doctrinally safeguarded. But here, too, there is a growing spirit of co-operation. Full conferences have been held between a committee of the Administrative Committee and a committee of the United Lutheran Church, as a result of which the latter has recommended that the church assume a consultative relationship to the Council and in addition share in the work of certain of its commissions,—a recommendation which has since been acted upon favorably. It is greatly to be hoped that this may be only a first step toward full membership.

A further adjustment is needed between the Federal Council

[1] Cf. p. 188.

and the central administrative agencies like the Home Missions Council, the Foreign Missions Conference, and the corresponding councils in the field of Christian education, whose important work we have studied in our last chapter, as well as between the Federal Council and the Christian Associations and other nation-wide voluntary societies. The representatives of these bodies sit in the Administrative Committee of the Council as consultative members, and the relation on both sides is most cordial. As administrative agencies, however, the different bodies are entirely independent. It is a fair question whether the time will not soon come—if indeed it has not already come—when some closer relationship may prove desirable, some relationship which, while preserving the full autonomy of each body within the sphere assigned to it, will make it clear to the world that the Church of Jesus Christ in its Protestant branch is in the truest sense one.[1]

We have an analogy in the late war. For years the Allies fought under divided leadership with all its disadvantages in loss of time and efficiency. Only the most urgent need induced them to give

[1] It is interesting to note that the Roman Catholic Church, as a result of its war experience, has established such a central agency. Cf. *Catholic World*, January, 1922, p. 482. "It was natural that this lesson should find co-ordinated, immediate expression for the time of peace, and when the war ended, almost of itself, the National Catholic War Council became the National Catholic Welfare Council. As with its predecessor, unification and co-operation are its watchwords. In this continuation, by the Hierarchy, of an American Catholic organization, we have the best proof that the effort which originated during the days of the war will extend with power into the future. We cannot dwell here upon the splendid programme which the Welfare Council has set for itself, but we can, at least, call attention to its general object; for the object of this latter union is akin to that of the former—to give national expression to the thought of American Catholics upon spiritual and moral matters that affect the welfare of the country. Unification is necessary that such thought may have concrete and weighty value as the expression of all Catholics; co-operation is necessary that it may be clearly seen that this Catholic thought is also truly American." On the relation between the church and the Knights of Columbus, cf. *Catholic World*, January, 1922, p. 476. "In regard to this matter, a statement of Bishop Muldoon, Chairman of the Administrative Committee of the National Catholic War Council, deserves to be cited: 'Some people have said the Church has stepped in and tried to rob the Knights of Columbus of their glory. The Church, instead of absorbing them, has embraced them and held them up to the world as her adopted children. The Catholic Church by adopting the Knights of Columbus as her agent, has broadened the service of the Knights of Columbus. She stands behind them with all her power, and gives them the blessing of the Beloved One.'"

Foch the supreme authority he required and to furnish him with a reserve which should represent neither France, nor England, nor Italy, nor the United States, but the Allies as a whole. During the period of transition, the danger of division was minimized by the creation of the liaison officer. This was a man who was set apart by one army to serve as a constant means of communication with the forces with which it was co-operating. Through him each knew what the other was doing and the danger of divided counsels was averted.

Pending the fuller union to which we look forward, we need such liaison officers in the Christian church, and the Federal Council would seem to be an agency through which they could render most effective service. What would it not mean for the future of the Church of Christ if in each of the more important denominations there should be an officer as able and representative as the men who are now secretaries of denominational boards, whose sole function it was to represent the Church in interdenominational relations and report to his constituency the ways in which they could most effectively co-operate in common tasks. Such an officer would ordinarily be a member of the central council or commission of his own church and so in touch with all its work. But he would be free from other executive duties and so be able to give all the time that is necessary to consider the important work that affects all alike. The existence of such a body of men, serving with the full approval of the constituent bodies, would do more than any other single thing to promote the union of American Protestantism and bring a united Church within the range of practical politics.

4. *The Larger Aspects of the Unity Movement—The Relation of the Protestant Churches to Other Bodies, Religious and Non-religious—Possible Ways of Securing International Co-operation between the Churches*

There is a word still to be said of the relation of the Protestant churches to the other national bodies, both in this country and across the sea, with which their work brings them into natural contact. These include the various philanthropic and charitable societies that operate on a nation-wide scale, religious bodies like the Roman Catholics and the Jews, with which any direct co-operation in religious matters is for the time being impossible and yet who share with the Protestant churches certain spiritual and moral ideals and purposes, and finally, the churches in other countries whose co-operation is essential in the formation of an international Christian opinion.

In the past there has been little direct contact between the organized philanthropies of the country and the churches. Individual Christians have been active workers in every good cause. In the local field the relation between the church and the different educational and charitable organizations has been helpful and often intimate. In connection with a few great causes such as temperance and the suppression of commercialized vice the churches have definitely supported organizations like the Anti-Saloon League and the Sabbath Association, which have worked for reform legislation by the usual methods employed by political organizations. But in general the churches have left the field of organized charity and of moral and social reform to the many private societies which make it their specialty. In the annual congresses of philanthropic workers, the representatives of the churches are not often found.

Yet it is a question whether in the future so wide a separation is desirable. It is easy to understand how the separation has come about. We have seen that as the institution of religion the Church has a sphere of its own which it must guard with care. The fact remains that with the growth of the social interest to which we have already alluded, the churches find themselves more and more concerned with the questions with which the organized philanthropies of the country are dealing. Granting that there are many things which these societies can properly do which the churches cannot do, it is still a fact that the churches command the moral influence without which reforms cannot be effectively carried through. It would seem desirable, therefore, that there should be an understanding between the representatives of the churches and the leaders of the different reform and philanthropic movements as to what the churches can properly be asked to do to promote the causes in which both alike are interested and where this responsibility ceases.

In the past the churches have had no agency through which such contact could naturally be brought about. To-day such an agency exists in the Federal Council. Through its Commission on Social Service the Council is in constant communication with the leaders of the different social and charitable organizations of the country, and in its bi-weekly bulletin provides a convenient source of information for those church people who desire to know what is being done in these circles to promote the moral and spiritual issues they have at heart.

In the case of the non-Protestant religious bodies the situation is somewhat different, for here a new and distinctive factor enters in. Beside the general desire for social betterment our fellow-citizens of other religious faiths share with us our interest in the spiritual interpretation of the universe. Can we meet them on this ground as well as on the more neutral territory of moral and social reform?

Once in a while we find Roman Catholics and Protestants participating in a religious service, as in the great religious meeting held in the Madison Square Garden at the opening of the war. But such opportunities come seldom, and for the most part we must be content to find our contacts in such matters of common concern as temperance, the battle against commercialized vice or the cause of industrial justice. An interesting example of such co-operation was the report of the Denver Commission of Religious Forces on the recent car strike in that city, a report in which representatives of the Federal Council's Commission on Social Service and the National Catholic Welfare Council co-operated with the local authorities in studying the situation and making recommendations.

In connection with the observance of November 13, 1921, as Labor Sunday by the Boston Federation of Churches, Cardinal O'Connell, after conference with representatives of the Federation, issued a pastoral letter to the Roman Catholics of Boston, urging them to make a similar use of the day.

A further example of co-operation was the recent appeal for a Federal investigation of the situation in the bituminous coal fields issued jointly by the Commission on the Church and Social Service of the Federal Council and the National Welfare Council of the Roman Catholic Church.

An even more interesting example of co-operation in the field of distinctively religious interest took place in Detroit when Roman Catholics and Protestants together approached the mayor with the request that all business be suspended on Good Friday between one and three o'clock. This action was possible because Detroit has a strong federation of churches which could speak for Protestantism as a whole. If there is ever to be effective co-operation between Roman Catholics and Protestants at any point, it will be because the Protestant forces themselves are independently and strongly organized.

With the Jews we have the common interest of the Old Testament and a spiritual interpretation of the universe. But the natural opposition of the Jews to proselytizing, as they regard any attempt to win their members to Christianity, makes co-operation in the field of religion difficult. Yet when one considers the situation in a city like New York, where thousands and tens of thousands of young men and women of Jewish antecedents are growing up without any contact with the synagogue,[1] it would seem as if it ought to be possible to find some form of spiritual ministry to these young people in which Christians and Jews alike could co-operate.

An interesting example of co-operation between Protestants, Catholics, and Jews occurred during the war in connection with the so-called Committee of Six. This was a small committee including Protestants, Roman Catholics, and Jews who, at Secretary Baker's request, acted as advisers to the War Department on matters of interest to the groups concerned.[2] Among other things they inspected the chaplains' school at Louisville at the government's expense, and made certain recommendations which were approved by the department. In addition Roman Catholics and Jews have co-operated with Protestants in the Religious Education Association, and they are working together cordially in the World Alliance for International Friendship through the Churches.

The third group of relationships to be considered is that of our American Protestant churches to their sister churches in other countries. If we are ever to deal effectively with the international problems before the Church, Christians of different countries must work together, and for this some form of international organization will be necessary. Either a national council or committee may be formed in each country to co-operate with similar committees in

[1] Cf. Robert W. Anthony, "A Study of the Jews in Greater New York," published by the Board of Home Missions of the Presbyterian Church in the U. S. A.

[2] The chairman of the committee was Father John Burke, Chairman of the Committee on Special War Activities of the National Catholic War Council, and the other members were Dr. Robert E. Speer, Chairman of the General War-Time Commission of the Churches, Colonel Harry Cutler, Chairman of the Jewish Welfare Board, Dr. John R. Mott, Bishop James De Wolf Perry, Jr., and the writer. While holding responsible positions in their several organizations, these gentlemen served on the Committee of Six in their individual, not in their official, capacity.

other countries; or the point of contact may be found in denominational gatherings of international character, such as the Lambeth Conference, the Alliance of Reformed Churches throughout the World Holding the Presbyterian System, the World Conference of Methodists, and the like. Both methods have their advantages and may profitably be used; but of the two, the former is the more promising. Both from the point of view of geographical convenience and from that of the factors to be united, the nation is the natural unit. One of the chief reasons for the impotence of the Church to-day in international affairs is that we have as yet no effective national churches which can combine in an international organization of a truly ecumenical character.[1]

In the meantime American Christians will follow with interest the movements which are taking place in the different countries of Europe to strengthen and unify their respective churches. In addition to its bearing upon the reunion of Christendom, the recent Lambeth Conference was significant because it showed us the Church of England in the act of defining its own conception of its duty as a national church. No less significant is the corresponding movement going on among the non-conformist churches which has resulted in the creation of the Free Church Council of England and Wales, the first really representative organ which the free churches of England have possessed; nor should we forget the promising movement for union between the Established and the United Free Churches of Scotland.

What is going on in Great Britain is taking place in different forms in other countries. We have already spoken of the movement for a national church in India and in China. In France and Switzerland Federal Councils have already been formed and similar action is contemplated in other countries. With the passing of the State Church in Germany the way is open for the formation of a free

---

[1] An interesting argument against the view here expressed is made by Paul Hutchinson, in his suggestive little book, "The Next Step," New York, 1922. In this book he argues for a world-wide Methodist Church as against independent national churches. But his argument overlooks the fact that nationalism is not the only divisive force to be contended against. Denominationalism itself may be such a force. It is true that to create national churches without uniting them in a larger international church would not realize our ideal of Christian unity. It is no less true that to extend the existing rivalry of denominations within different countries to the world as a whole would be equally to fail of the mark.

German church.[1]   In Czecho-Slovakia a remarkable religious revival is carrying hundreds of thousands into the old national
church.   In the Scandinavian churches Archbishop Söderblom is
organizing Christian sentiment in favor of an international organization, which shall mobilize the spiritual forces of the churches
against war.

It is too soon to predict what form such an international organization will take.   We are still in the preliminary stage of discussion
and experimentation.   From at least three different centres this
discussion is proceeding.   One centre is the proposed Conference on
Faith and Order.   Concerned as this is with the problem of organic
union and planning to include all Christian bodies but the church
of Rome, it necessarily moves slowly and is content to leave to
others the discussion of plans for practical co-operation on a smaller
scale.   Within the latter field two bodies are at work, the World
Alliance for International Friendship through the Churches and
the Federal Council's Commission on International Justice and
Goodwill.   The former is an association of individual Christians
which aims by free discussion to educate public opinion in favor
of world peace.   It includes Roman Catholics and Jews.   The other
is composed of official representatives of the larger Protestant
bodies and desires to co-operate with similar organizations in other
countries in establishing a responsible Federal Council of Christians
which shall carry with it the moral support of the co-operating
churches.

Especially important in its promise for the future is the international student movement.   The World Student Federation was
one of the few Christian bodies which maintained its international
relationships unbroken through the war and it is already taking
active steps to unite the Christian students of the world in support
of a campaign for world brotherhood and peace.

However useful and necessary such informal contacts may be,
they will not fulfil their purpose unless they result in some permanent international organization which has back of it the united
support of the Christian forces of the different countries.   What is
true of the unity movement within each country is true of its larger
international aspects.   The sentiment for union developed through
informal conference must be made effective for use through the

---

[1] Cf. Kaftan, "Zur Frage der Kirche," *Die Eiche,* Munich, October, 1921.

concerted action of the official representatives of the churches. Only when a Federal Council, thoroughly representative of the Protestant forces of America, finds similar responsible organizations in other countries through which it can work with its fellow Christians for world brotherhood and peace, will the Church be in a position to exert an effective influence in international affairs. Only through the experience gained by contacts of this kind can we learn what further steps are feasible in the direction of the organic union of the churches.[1]

It is against this background that we have to picture the opportunity and responsibility of the American church. Nothing could do more to encourage those who are working for Christian union elsewhere than to see in a country like America, where individual liberty plays so large a rôle and where there is no national establishment of religion, the churches effectively organized for common service. For this reason it is to be hoped that no desire to knit more closely the bonds of international denominational fellowship, however legitimate and important this desire may be, or to express Christian sympathy and fellowship with congenial sister churches of other lands, will divert the leaders of our American churches from their major and most critically important task—that of providing an agency through which the sentiment for unity in the American churches may find expression in a united Protestant Church.

[1] For this reason importance attaches to the proposed Conference on Life and Work which it is hoped to bring together in the course of the next two or three years. This is a conference which, unlike the Conference on Faith and Order, aims to deal with present and practical issues. Leaving the divisive questions of faith and order in the background, it is proposed to ask what the churches as at present organized can do to make the principles of Jesus Christ a factor in forming an international public opinion so powerful that it cannot be ignored. Committees are being formed in the different countries to further this conference. The head of the English committee is the Archbishop of Canterbury; of the Swedish committee, Archbishop Söderblom; of the American committee, Dr. Arthur J. Brown. Preliminary conferences are being arranged to prepare for it, and in other ways a campaign of education is being carried on so that when the conference meets it will have back of it the united Christian sentiment of each of the countries represented. Cf. "Christian Unity," p. 368.

PART V

TRAINING FOR TO-MORROW

CHAPTER XIV

THE CHURCH AS A SCHOOL OF RELIGION

1. *The Revival of Interest in Religious Education—Its Connection with the General Educational Movement—Aspects of the Church's Educational Task*

As we have studied the situation which faces the church in America we have everywhere been made aware of impending changes, of new movements in thought and in practice. We have seen much that is inspiring and that gives us ground for hope. Yet we are more than ever conscious of the distance which separates attainment from ideal. No one of all these movements has yielded a result commensurate with its promise. Individuals have been earnest and active. Groups have succeeded to a high degree in expressing the spirit of true Christianity. But the rank and file of church members have for the most part returned to the narrow realm of interests from which the war called them. To make satisfactory progress with our practical tasks we must capture the imagination of these backward Christians. This is the work of Christian education.

In many different quarters, attention is being directed to the educational field and experiments are being tried which affect all phases of religious education.[1] Much time and thought is being given to improving methods of religious instruction through the use of graded lessons, more modern and better lesson helps, and the provision of effective teacher-training classes. Efforts are being made to supplement the inadequacy of Sunday schools by pro-

[1] For a full account of what is being done in this field compare the forthcoming report of the Committee on the War and the Religious Outlook on "The Teaching Work of the Church." Much useful information may also be found by consulting the files of *Christian Education,* the official organ of the Council of Church Boards of Education, and of *Religious Education,* the organ of the Religious Education Association. Cf. also W. D. MacKenzie, "The Church and Religious Education," Committee on the War and the Religious Outlook, New York, 1919.

viding week-day religious instruction either by means of some form of co-operation with the public schools like the Gary plan, or by vacation Bible schools, or other voluntary supplements of the present educational facilities. Some reformers would go farther still and substitute for the present Sunday school a church school which combines week-day with Sunday instruction as parts of a comprehensive plan, including all that is now being done in the church which has educational significance.[1] Plans are under way for a unified system of religious education in the local community, through the co-operation of the local churches with voluntary bodies such as the Young Men's and the Young Women's Christian Associations. Special attention is given to the facilities for advanced religious instruction provided by our colleges and theological seminaries, as well as to the need of an adequate specialized training for lay workers, both men and women. The perplexing problems presented to the teacher of religion by the period of adolescence are receiving intensive study.

This many-sided activity is the natural result of our new realization of the power of education as a social force. The example of Germany has shown us what can happen to a whole nation because of what is taught in its schools. Americans are apt to believe that education has some uplifting and purifying power apart from its content, and that if we establish enough schools the results will necessarily be good. We are learning our mistake. Knowledge is simply another name for opportunity. It is so much added power, good if rightly used, but in the hands of selfish and designing men an added danger. Educate a rascal and you make him more of a menace than when he was ignorant. We must not only teach; we must teach what is true in order to inspire to what is right.

This insight conditions the newer ideals in education. We have learned that we must not only impart information; we must also train character. So the older catechetical method is being superseded by the newer experimental method. The modern teacher respects the potentialities of his pupil. He is always looking for the larger and more mature self which is presently to emerge. He believes that this self may be trusted to form its own judgments

---

[1] The church school so defined must be distinguished from the parochial school. In the parochial school the Church as such makes itself responsible for the entire education of its children and young people, completely paralleling the work done in the public or private schools.

and assume its own responsibilities, and he regards it as his duty to hasten the time when this can safely be done.

We are coming also to understand that education is a social process. No human being can be educated alone. In the life of the mind as in every other phase of our human activity we are members one of another. We not only experiment; we experiment together. When we study, we exchange ideas and experiences and form our convictions as groups as well as individuals.[1]

These new insights are paralleled in the field of religious education. Bushnell's conception of religious education as nurture of the growing personality has been reinterpreted by modern scholars who have drawn new material for educational theory from the study of the psychology of the religious experience.[2] We now understand that the Christian teacher is not simply responsible for telling his pupils what they ought to believe about Christianity. He must try with all possible tact and patience to present the Christian view of life in a way that will command their voluntary assent. This is a different and a far harder matter.

The influence of these ideals of education appears in the organization and curriculum of the Sunday school. They affect the methods of recruiting and training teachers, the planning and construction of the school building, the underlying conception of the relation of the school to the church as a whole. Instead of putting every one through a single uniform curriculum, advocates of the newer methods adapt their teaching to the age of the child. For children of four to five they have kindergarten classes, and afterward group the ages in grades that correspond to the groupings of secular education. They not only tell stories; they set the children thinking about what the stories mean. They not only teach the Bible; they try to make their pupils relate what they learn in Sunday school to what they are doing at home or at school or at their play. They think of the world as a laboratory in which the teaching of the school is to be tested, and try to form in their pupils habits of independent thought in the field of religion.

It is, of course, true that in comparison with the total number of Sunday schools, the schools in which modern methods are being

---

[1] Cf. the interesting essay by Vera Lachmann, "As Youth Would Have It," in *The Survey*, February 4, 1922.

[2] Cf. especially Coe, "A Social Theory of Religious Education," New York, 1917.

followed are still comparatively few. Even in these they are carried out to a very unequal degree. Nevertheless, if we compare the educational methods of to-day with those of a generation or even of a decade ago, we find real progress. The character of the lesson helps and of the training courses for teachers is steadily improving and the principle of a graded instead of a uniform system of instruction finds increasing acceptance.

These improved methods appear not only in the work done by individual specialists, but in the activities of the official church agencies, both denominational and interdenominational. The unity movement which we have studied in other branches of the Church's work has affected the Sunday school,[1] and the contact of different points of view has tended, on the whole, to a broader and more intelligent approach. The old rivalry of competing agencies has been steadily reduced and in most well-organized denominations there is a single agency which is responsible for preparing and unifying the material to be taught.

But the Sunday school is only a part of the field to be cultivated. We do not stop learning when we leave school. If we wish to have a really intelligent church membership we must remember the needs of older people. The outlook is not so bright in this direction. One of our chief difficulties is due to the contrast between the ideal of religion which inspires the teaching in our best Sunday schools and the prevailing conditions which the pupils meet when they enter the Church.[2] Our Protestant ideal of a faith grounded in knowledge requires us to conceive of the Church's educational task as a whole.

That task has several aspects, distinct yet intimately related. In the first place, it is the Church's duty to win individuals to Christ's service by the intelligent presentation of His cause. In the second place, the members of the Church must be trained to understand the religion they profess and to practise what they have learned. In the third place, Christianity must be interpreted to the wider public in order to create an intelligent opinion in matters bearing on the Christian ideal. Finally, constructive thinkers must

---

[1] Cf. p. 240.

[2] Any one who has talked with thoughtful parents will realize how great this difficulty is and what a handicap to their efforts to win their children to the Church is the persistence in the local congregation of methods and standards, both intellectual and moral, that fall below those to which the child has become accustomed at home and at school.

be found and trained, not only that the Church may have teachers and preachers, but in order that the process of self-criticism which is essential to the healthful development of every growing institution may be carried on.

2. *Winning Recruits—The Teacher as Evangelist—The Social Gospel as Material for a New Educational Evangelism*

Evangelism and education were once contrasted as two independent and separate Christian activities and men used to debate which was the more important. This contrast has its roots in a false theory of education. Ideas are not something which exist for themselves apart from their appeal to the will; they are the raw material of character—the stuff out of which decisions are made.

The consciousness of the intimate association between theory and practice underlies all modern education. We try to find the point of contact between interest and personality. We encourage our pupils to ask what things mean, and what they are worth. What the evangelist does when he stands on the platform and makes his appeal for decision the teacher is now doing. He invites his pupil to put truth to the test of action.

This is eminently true of the religious teacher. He is trying to make the fact of God real to his pupils, and the test of his success is their response to the presentation of the ideal. His invitation to them is that of Philip to Nathanael: "Come and see." He invites his students to become familiar with the Bible not primarily because it tells us what God did long ago, but because it enables us to understand what God is doing now. He urges the practice of prayer not simply as a duty but as a privilege, as something that helps us to become bigger and better personalities, to find and express our truest selves.

The present emphasis upon religious education is therefore not to be understood as a depreciation of the evangelistic spirit. Rather is it a plea for another and a better kind of evangelism. The trouble with much of the older evangelism was that it was not evangelistic enough. It appealed to a part of man and left another part out. It tried to grip the will without winning the assent of the mind. When Paul urged his converts to bring every thought into captivity to the obedience of Christ,[1] he gave an admirable

[1] II Cor. x, 5.

definition of religious education. It is capturing men's thought for Christ.

Judged by this test, the earlier evangelism had serious limitations. Many older evangelists failed to recognize the changes in men's point of view which had been brought about by modern science with its emphasis upon law and its recognition of development. They phrased their message in terms which for many of our college-trained young men and women had lost their meaning. Thus moving in a world of thought which was unfamiliar to their hearers they diverted attention from the immediate duty of the will by raising difficulties for the mind.

These difficulties have been in a measure removed by the new theology.[1] The new theology accepts the results of modern science at their face value, but it shows that they do not alter the essential issue which religion raises—that of a man's personal attitude toward God. We know to-day that God's way of revealing Himself has been more gradual and many-sided than it was once thought to be. He comes to us in a different environment from that in which He met our fathers and speaks to us in different ways. The new theology interprets the old phrases of Bible and creed in the light of this new environment and illustrates them by analogies taken from present life. Thus it recalls the hearer to the main matter with which the evangelist is concerned, the immediate issue for the will.

But, after all, as we have seen, this helps us with a limited number of people only, people who have learned to think for themselves and who realize the difference between the intellectual world of our fathers and the new world of science in which we are living to-day. The great majority have no clear-cut philosophy of life. If the evangelist fails to grip them it is for a different reason. His failure is due to the fact that he does not relate his preaching definitely enough to the conditions in which they are living. Uncompromising in his dealing with individual vices like drink and impurity, he has not been equally searching in his probing of those deeper social evils that grow out of the relation of men to one another in industry and in politics. His call to repentance has not reached the grasping employer or the selfish labor leader or the cynical politician or the man who foments suspicion and hate among the nations. We must emphasize these phases of man's duty to reach the will of the mod-

[1] Cf. W. Adams Brown, "Modern Theology and the Preaching of the Gospel," New York, 1914.

ern man. Education helps us to understand and to deal with them discriminately.

We shall completely misunderstand the group of interests which we commonly sum up under the name of the Social Gospel if we think of them as in any sense a substitute for the old Gospel of individual conversion. They are not a substitute, but an exposition. They help us to realize what it means to a modern man to be converted. They do for him what John the Baptist did for the converts who had been stirred by his preaching and came to him with the searching inquiry, "What shall we do?" They give a clear-cut test by which the sincerity of a man's repentance can be tested.

Our modern Christianity needs such a test. It is still true in some parts of the mission field that when a man confesses Christ it costs him something. He may risk his home, his property, the esteem of his friends, or even life itself; but in our conventional churches no such test exists. It costs nothing to join the Church. When Edwards preached hellfire men trembled. It was so with Finney and with Moody. When Billy Sunday preaches, many laugh and troop to shake his hand in the spirit of delegates visiting the White House. We need to put the iron back into religion. We need some test to determine beyond the shadow of a doubt whether a man professing Christianity means business or not.

Such a test is provided by the Social Gospel. This brings religion into daily life and meets a man in the place where he lives six days in the week. He is asked to prove his faith by the way he acts toward other men, and by the way he uses his property. Such decisions are of a piece with the personal choices for which the older evangelists made their plea. They bring religion into the realm of reality; they associate confession with conduct.

Education, then, is not a substitute for evangelism, but the means by which evangelism may be rendered effective. Education furnishes the language which the evangelist must speak, and what is more important still, the ideas. Education creates the sympathetic relationship between the preacher and those to whom he speaks, which is the indispensable condition of a receptive hearing.[1]

[1] This gives significance to such a volume as "The Church and Industrial Reconstruction." It is not simply material for religious education; it is a *vade mecum* for the evangelist. It helps him to visualize the situation in which the men to whom he preaches are living. It adds to his catalogue of

We need educational evangelists, men who will interpret the Gospel to modern men in the situation in which they now find themselves. We cannot wait for men to come to us; we must go after them, and that means that we must develop a specialized evangelism adapted to the needs of the modern age. Just as the old rescue missions established themselves where degradation was deepest and addressed men and women in language they could understand, just as the Salvation Army developed its particular organization for the special work it set out to do, so we must devise agencies which can win men to the Social Gospel.

For this we must call upon men of the same class as those whom we would win. Employers must win employers, and labor leaders must win labor leaders; editors must influence editors, and lawyers must influence lawyers; university professors must gain the allegiance of university professors, and public men that of public men. Wherever there are problems to be worked out in the application of Christianity to present conditions, we must have men who know these conditions and who can speak with the authority which knowledge gives. As the work of the Church expands, our responsibility increases for seeing that the opportunities it offers are made known. Every profession must have evangelists bringing their technical training and knowledge to bear upon the specialized tasks for which they are best fitted.

This does not mean that the call to Christian service is to be resolved into a humanitarian appeal. It is meant that our plea to men to surrender their lives to God should grow out of definite human needs and carry with it a correspondingly definite objective. A man who gives himself to God's service should know exactly what he is doing and why. What the Student Volunteer Movement did for the past generation, we need to do to-day for the Church at home. As the foreign-missionary appeal has broadened until it is heard not only by ministers, but by teachers, doctors, nurses, settlement workers, and practical men of affairs, so it must be in the home field. Such an enlargement of our programme will give a new reality and definiteness to the call to Christian service. Men and women whom we could not otherwise have

---

sins. He is to preach to men not simply as drunkards and wastrels, but as men who have been squandering the most precious of all the Father's gifts— their chance to do their part in making the world a better place for all God's children to live in.

reached will be convinced that Christianity is in fact what it professes to be, a religion for every day.

Above all we must avoid the Pharisaic note. It is not for us to decide for others. The most that we can do is to present the opportunity as we see it, and let it speak for itself. Each must respond as he will and work out the consequences in his own way.

3. *The Church's Responsibility for Educating Its Own Members—*
Special Importance of This in Protestantism—What
Christians Need to Know about Christianity

But winning men is only the first step. They must be trained after they are won. Unless the body of church members know what they believe and are able to give a reason for the faith that is in them, it is hopeless to expect them to influence public opinion in matters of religion.

The development of a body of intelligent lay Christians has always been the ideal of Protestantism; for Protestantism, as we have understood it, stands for democracy in religion. It is based upon a double faith, faith in the capacity of the individual to know God for himself and faith in the possibility of social action on the part of those who share similar religious convictions. Such common convictions may be imposed by Catholicism from without. In Protestantism they can only be created by a process of education.

There is no such consensus of conviction in the Protestant churches to-day. What is more serious, no adequate steps are being taken to secure it. There has been no systematic instruction for the average church member in the history of the Christian religion, or in the beliefs and ethical ideals of the different Christian denominations, or in the present organization and activities of the Christian Church. Even the necessary literature is lacking through which such information could be obtained.

This state of things is no doubt mainly due to the fact that in our Protestant churches the work of religious education has been largely entrusted to the Sunday school. But the great majority of our Sunday schools reach only the children and these only for a single hour in the week. Young men and young women of college age are not present there in any large numbers, although they are the very people who most need the kind of teaching we have in mind. Other methods must be devised to reach them. The older men and women, too, are facing complicated problems—economic, social, and political. They need to know what the Church can teach them about ways of applying the principles of the Christian religion to such problems. The pulpit must resume its teaching office, too long neglected in Protestantism; and through books and the public press an extensive educational work be undertaken. Above all, the home must be restored to its original function as an agency of religious education.

In saying this we would be the last to depreciate the importance of the Sunday school or to minimize the great service which it has rendered to the cause of Christian education. Of all the educational tasks of the Church, none is comparable in importance to the training of the young. It is right that the agency which is charged with this duty should be given the central place in the Church's educational system. Necessary as it may be to preach the Gospel to adults and try to win them to Christ by conversion, the great evangelistic opportunity of the Church lies with the children and young people who are growing up under Christian influence. All that we would insist on here is that the child to be taught is the potential man or woman and that the whole process of Christian education must be shaped with this in view.

We may learn a lesson here from the Roman Catholics. For years they have been giving special attention to the religious education of laymen. In many a Roman Catholic church you will find a little rack at the front door in which is placed a plentiful supply of pamphlets setting forth in clear and simple language the teaching of the church upon such matters as the sacraments, confession, indulgences, and the like.[1] Anyone who reads these pamphlets will learn what the Roman Church teaches on the subjects which are regarded as most important in religion. The Protestant layman will find no similar means of information in the average Protestant church, and the lack of definite textbook instruction is seldom supplemented by any clear-cut teaching from the pulpit. Doctrinal preaching has fallen out of fashion and expository preaching of the old-fashioned kind which took a book of the Bible for its subject and led the hearer step by step through its argument is a forgotten art. Whereas Protestantism began by aiding the layman to understand the doctrines and precepts of the Christian religion, while

[1] Thousands of these racks have been sold by the Paulist Press of New York City.

the Roman Church deliberately fostered his ignorance, to-day all this is reversed. It is the Roman Church which provides instruction in religion for its laymen. The Protestant Church too often leaves its members to pick up for themselves such knowledge as they can.

This failure is the more serious because there is no other agency which feels the responsibility for filling the gap. In most European countries, the colleges and universities include religion among the subjects on which they give instruction, but in this country only the private and denominational institutions do so. As a result of the divorce of church and state, the responsibility for religious education has been assumed by the Church and all teaching of religion is banished from the public schools.[1] The same negative attitude is taken in the normal schools and state universities, and while many denominational colleges provide required courses in the Bible and in the evidences of Christianity, the older Christian universities make such instruction entirely voluntary. Thus it comes to pass that a generation of young men and women is growing up in the country whose only means of learning about Christianity is the Sunday school.

Yet this is a very inadequate provision for so great a need. Even in the best of our schools the time given to the study of the lesson is seldom more than half an hour, and the instruction is given by volunteer teachers. There are multitudes of children whose attendance even on this brief course is for a part of the year, and a great number are not in Sunday school at all.[2]

A further difficulty is the impossibility of providing for a comprehensive course of study in the available time. Few of the sub-

[1] Sometimes the fear of introducing religious teaching into the schools is carried so far that even the reading of the Bible without comment is prohibited. Elsewhere reading is permitted and in some cases a simple commentary is added. The subject of the extent to which it is possible for the public school to make place for moral and religious instruction without being involved in denominational differences is too large to be entered upon here.

[2] Exact statistics on this subject are not available. The statement quoted by Dr. John Haynes Holmes on the authority of the Interchurch ("New Churches for Old," p. 14) that "three children out of every four in the country never receive any religious instruction of any kind" is not supported by the best authorities. The figures, to which Dr. Holmes refers, were reached by including all children in the country, including infants between the ages of one and five. It is obvious that any such basis of calculation is wholly misleading. Still, when every allowance has been made, the situation is serious enough.

jects with which an intelligent Christian ought to be familiar can be included in the curriculum of even the best regulated Sunday schools. Portions only of the Bible are taught in many of our Sunday schools, and these in detached bits not correlated with the rest of the book. Of historic and literary interpretation there is far too little, and for the later history of the Church, even in its most outstanding features, there is seldom time.[1] Under these conditions, the wonder is not that so many Christians should be ignorant of the history and tenets of their own church, but that in spite of this ignorance it should be possible for the Church to maintain a vigorous and useful life.

For consider what a Christian ought to know if he is to be a really intelligent church member. He should know something about the history of his religion, the past which lies back of it, and the relation which it bears to other existing religions; he should be familiar with the beliefs which it presupposes, the living convictions as to God and His plan for man which inspire Christian activity; he should certainly understand the present organization and activities of his church, the institutions through which it functions, the programme it is trying to realize in the world. Just as we should consider an American unfit for citizenship who knew nothing of the past history of his country, was ignorant of its present constitution and laws, and was out of sympathy with the spirit of its institutions, so we should judge a Christian uneducated who is content to remain in ignorance of the most elementary facts about his religion and his church.

The teacher's opportunity begins here. He must plan a comprehensive course of study which takes in the most important subjects on which the intelligent Christian needs to be informed.[2] This course must tell the story of the Christian religion. The pupils must learn how Christianity began, what stages it has passed

---

[1] It should be stated that the history of the Church is being included in some of the recent graded lesson series, such as the Christian Nurture series, Scribner's, and the International.

[2] It is encouraging to know that the attempt is being made to provide such a comprehensive course of study by such publishers as Scribner's Sons and the University of Chicago Press. The new denominational courses like the Christian Nurture Series and the new Beacon Series are also making serious efforts in the same direction. The same is true of the International Graded series, published by the Congregationalists, Methodists, and Southern Methodists, and used by others.

through, and under what forms it exists in the world to-day. They must study the Bible, of course, but they must not stop with the Bible. They must be familiar with the history that came out of the Bible and with the effects which faith in Christ has since produced in the lives of men. They must know the Church as a present factor in human society; not their own particular branch of the Church only, but the other churches which together make up the one great Church. This is a study which cannot be finished in Sunday school. It is something at which we must be working all our lives. It requires the co-operation of all the different agencies at our disposal—the minister in his pulpit, the missionary societies and the Christian Associations with their literature, the press which keeps pace with the present progress of the Kingdom of God. The point is that the Sunday-school curriculum should be planned with this later study in view and that provision should be made through other agencies of the churches to carry further what the Sunday school begins.

At two points in particular there is need of more thorough instruction. In the first place, we need instruction in the beliefs which Christianity presupposes. Our age is characterized by an extraordinary dislike of doctrinal teaching, which is in part a natural and justifiable reaction against an earlier attempt to enforce uniformity of belief by external authority. This dislike has had unforeseen and lamentable results. In our reaction against the creeds of the past a generation has been brought up to believe that creeds can be dispensed with altogether, or, if this prove impossible, that each individual can improvise his own creed without regard to what his predecessors have believed.

To break so completely with our own past would be to lose one of the most precious of all the gifts of the Christian religion—the fellowship into which it introduces us with those who have explored the mysteries of life before us. Christianity, we must never allow ourselves to forget, does not offer us simply the satisfaction of our own individual needs. It brings us insights which have been progressively verified through the centuries. Christian faith is a common faith, just as the Christian task is a common task. Theology, as the study which interprets the historic beliefs of the Christian religion, must be a part of Christian teaching. We must know what convictions the Christian faith implies, to what courses of action it commits us, and upon what grounds it is based. These subjects should be of interest to every intelligent person, and they can be presented so as to command that interest.

Whoever has faced in an intimate and personal way the mystery of life will be thankful to any one who can help him to an assurance that at the heart of things there is a Spirit who answers to his spirit, a God, personal, moral, Christlike, to whom he can look up in prayer and from whom he may receive strength in his struggle for the good. He will welcome convincing evidence that the Christian recognition of Christ as Saviour, Master, and Friend is valid; that Jesus' ideal of a new social order in which helpfulness is the rule and service the test of greatness is a practicable ideal.

This evidence is in the last analysis the history of the Christian religion itself. The proof that there is a good God like Jesus Christ is the fact that men are living in the faith that the good God exists and are finding satisfaction in so living. The proof that Christianity is a practicable religion is the fact that it is actually being practised and that when it is practised the expected results follow.[1]

An intelligent church member should therefore be acquainted with the agencies through which the Church's activities are now being carried on in the world. Christianity has been the mother of institutions, and these institutions are functioning to-day, offering the modern Christian opportunities for service which he could not have alone. Among these the most important is the Church itself in all the many-sided activities which we have been passing in review.

It is, of course, true that the Church is not the only agency through which the Christian ideal is being realized in society. Each of the different institutions which man has devised to express and further his social relations has its part to play in the creation of the new social order—the family, the school, the courts, the complex machinery of industry, commerce and finance, literature and the arts, the state. Without their co-operation the Christian ideal for society could not be realized. Protestantism has recognized the sacredness of all life and permits men to regard every calling as a form of ministry. But the fact remains that there is no other human institution except the Church which has for its sole function the promotion of man's higher spiritual life. If we wish to gain an

[1] For a brief statement of the evidence for this belief cf. W. Adams Brown, "Is Christianity Practicable?", New York, 1916.

adequate conception of the forces which are working for social betterment, it is essential that we should understand the Church.

Our Protestant teaching has hitherto conspicuously failed to bring about such an understanding. In our reaction against Roman Catholicism we have conceived a deep-rooted suspicion of institutional religion. This has extended even to those institutions in which the Gospel has found social expression in Protestantism. Certain branches of the Church, notably the Church of England and the Protestant Episcopal Church in America, have retained a strong churchly feeling which affects the character of their religious teaching; but this is not true of the great majority of Protestants. Religion has meant to them primarily a relationship between the individual soul and God. The significance of Christian institutions, even their own, has not been adequately apprehended.

Thus it has come about that in planning courses of religious study Protestant teachers have not paid sufficient attention to what God has been doing through the Church since the year 100 A.D. The old word of Chillingworth about the Bible may or may not be true of Protestant religion, but it has certainly been true of Protestant education. The Bible and the Bible alone has been the textbook of Protestants. A generation has grown up almost completely ignorant of the history of the Church since post-Biblical times and of the forms in which Christianity finds organized expression in the world to-day. For this lack we are suffering to-day in many ways— most of all in that we have developed among Protestant Christians so little intelligent consciousness of the Church as a whole. As a result we lack a public opinion strong enough to support those who are trying to unify the churches. To create this opinion we must teach our people the history of the Christian Church and help them to understand the origin and present significance of the main forms of contemporary Christianity.

A good point of departure is the history of missions, for missions furnish at once one of the most interesting and one of the most instructive manifestations of contemporary Christianity. In foreign missions we see the Christian Church making earnest with the ideal of world-wide evangelism, facing the divisive influences of race, of class, and of nationality, and overcoming them in original and suggestive ways. Here, too, we learn how much this effort is hampered by our denominational differences; in what practical ways the need of Christian unity makes itself felt.

In home missions we find the same difficulties facing us in personal and embarrassing ways. The study of the literature of modern home missions will dispel the complacency of many a conventional Christian and make him realize, if he has not already done so, that the most difficult mission fields in the world are not China or India or Japan, but American cities like New York and Chicago, where all the races of the world meet and where the problems of industrial strife, race rivalry, and national ambition confront us in their most extreme and perplexing forms. It is encouraging to know that through the agencies we have already described so much is already being done to inform modern American Christians of the present state of the missionary problem both at home and abroad. Through the agencies of missionary education the subject of the modern Church is finding its way into the Sunday-school curriculum and a large and constantly increasing literature is coming into existence which is indispensable to the understanding of present-day Christianity.

No less important than the study of the history of the Church is an understanding of the Church's existing organization and methods. It has been suggested that the ignorance of the average Christian on these points is a good sign, for it shows how loosely denominational ties sit upon him. Yet the fact remains that whether we realize it or not, the denominational differences of the various Protestant churches are serious obstacles to unity, and that these differences will never be overcome until the individual Christian takes the trouble to understand them.

One difficulty in the way of interesting the average Christian in the study of Christian institutions is the denominational spirit. This spirit treats the part as if it were the whole. The Presbyterian is taught something about the laws and creeds of Presbyterianism, the Episcopalian of Episcopacy, etc., but such an isolated study is neither sufficiently informing nor inspiring. Differences can only be understood through comparison. If one could study his own church not as an isolated phenomenon, but as an example of a type of organization which has recurred from age to age and from country to country, he would begin to understand its true significance. It is especially important that we should study sympathetically the types that are not congenial to us. Thus the liberal should understand the conservative and the conservative the liberal. The Episcopalian should comprehend the genius of the non-liturgical churches, and the Christian who does not use the liturgy should realize what the sacrament means to the high-church Episcopalian. Only through such sympathetic study of contrasted types can we create intelligent public sentiment and prepare the way for the larger unity to which we look forward.

It is vital that we should teach our people the meaning of worship. Worship is the very heart of the Christian religion. In worship we practise the presence of God and realize not only that He is, but that He is with us. Unless we can learn to worship together, all our other approaches to Christian unity stop short of the mark. Yet there is no part of our Christian practice in which there is a greater lack of common understanding. The two main types of approach, the liturgical and the non-liturgical, each have their difficulties and limitations, yet each seems the expression of some deep-seated human need for which provision must be made in the Church of the future. How important it is, then, that Christians should be trained to understand and appreciate both forms of worship, and above all that those who lead in worship should feel their responsibility for cultivating that mingled reverence and intelligence which is the proper attitude in which to approach the object of Christian devotion.[1]

Above all we must familiarize our people with the movement for Christian unity. We have seen how vigorous and deep-rooted it is; in how many different forms it manifests itself. Yet comparatively few Christians have ever made it the subject of serious study. Few could even name the existing agencies for promoting unity, much less tell what each is doing and why. Without such intelligent understanding on the part of the laymen of our churches, the support that is necessary to the success of the unity movement will not be forthcoming. Not until they study the situation for themselves and realize how progress is hindered by imperfect methods of organization will an interest be aroused which will make the necessary changes possible.

4. The Church's Responsibility for Forming Public Opinion in Matters Bearing upon the Christian Ideal

The training of its own members in the principles of their religion does not exhaust the Church's educational responsibility.

[1] Cf. W. Adams Brown, "Worship," Association Press, New York, 1917.

Besides the special groups who are gathered in congregations and the individuals who can be won by an evangelistic appeal, there are individuals and groups outside any ecclesiastical organization who help to form that potent force we call public opinion. There are earnest people who for one reason or another have been alienated from the Church and yet are working unselfishly for worthy causes through other agencies. There are larger masses of thoughtless and unimaginative people ready to respond to any passing impulse who, because they have no deep and settled conviction, become the easy prey of propaganda carried on by selfish and narrow interests. To each of these groups the Church has a duty. The children in our Sunday schools, the young men and women in our congregations must study and work and play in the atmosphere which public opinion creates, and will be helped or hindered in their efforts after the Christian life according to the standards of the society in which they move. Christians who are members of contemporary social agencies, industrial, commercial, and political, must share with those who are not Christians the responsibility for common action in national and international affairs. It is essential, therefore, that the Church should do everything possible to elevate public standards so that the conduct of church members as citizens and workers may not contradict their profession as religious believers. Above all it is essential that the Church should appeal to the widest possible public because in this public are found the men and women who might be won to the Christian cause, but who now hold aloof either because of indifference or of misunderstanding.

In the foreign field the primary work of the Christian teacher is with those who have grown up in non-Christian surroundings and who approach the deeper questions of life without sharing the Christian presuppositions. In preparation for such work much time must be given to discovering points of contact and in finding words and, what is even more important, ideas which will convey the Christian message.[1]

A similar situation meets us at home. The world of organized religion is still an unknown country to multitudes of people. It is

[1] An eminent Chinese missionary, the late Dr. Jones of Shantung, spent most of his life in making a dictionary of Chinese philosophical terms because he was persuaded that without the aid of the exact phraseology which such a dictionary would give, it would be impossible for the Christian teacher to convey the Christian beliefs about God and Jesus Christ to educated Chinese in such a way that they would be really understood.

not simply that they are not church members or that they have difficulties with this or that doctrine; they have lost touch with Christianity altogether. They do not take it into their account as a factor with which as intelligent and conscientious persons they have to reckon.

Some who are alienated from Christianity owe their present condition to ignorance. They have been brought up in homes where the Christian religion was ignored and the Church treated as negligible. They have found satisfaction for their higher impulses in the pursuit of science or in the service of some one of the many causes in which the spirit of altruism expresses itself to-day. Others know the Church only too well and have reacted against what they regard as its narrowness and superstition. Both alike need what Christianity at its best can give. It is our business to find out where these people are, to gain a point of contact with them, and to create the language through which the Gospel message may be conveyed to their minds.

So far as this problem concerns those who are already in educational institutions, we shall come back to it in a later chapter.[1] Both in connection with the public schools and the state universities, we have already faced the fact of a secularized education and the problem it presents. Even among those who have been educated in Christian colleges there are many whose acquaintance with the Bible and with Christian truth is so superficial as to be practically negligible, and the problem how to reach them and interest them in the Christian religion is one whose importance it is difficult to exaggerate.

We are thinking here, however, primarily of the persons who are not readily accessible through the ordinary educational channels— business men associated in their chambers of commerce and manufacturers' associations; workers in the various philanthropic and reform associations which are concerned with the betterment of human society; members of labor unions and of the various organizations representing more radical opinion, like the Socialists and the members of the I. W. W. Lawyers and doctors should not be neglected, nor the journalists who play so large a part in moulding public opinion. These are all factors to be considered by those who believe that the Church has a Gospel for the whole of society and

[1] Cf. Chapter XV.

commands forces which it is a duty to mobilize for the welfare of the race.

Apart from the general interest of the Church in establishing contact with every group to which human beings look for moral and intellectual stimulus, there is an added reason why a teaching Church should take account of what is being done in these circles. They, too, are becoming educational agencies. Partly unconsciously, partly of set purpose, they are forming the beliefs of men for the purpose of shaping their activities. Sometimes this is done in a superficial or even dangerous way as propaganda in defence of preconceived opinions, but in many cases a higher motive is operative and a more serious purpose is manifest. Both in labor [1] and in business [2] circles serious study is being undertaken on such subjects as the conditions of human welfare, the relation of capital and labor, the nature and limits of the responsibility of the state, and an attitude of mind is being developed which opens the way to the consideration of the great themes of religion.

To this new spirit, wherever it may be found, the Church must appeal. We must show men what the churches are actually doing in the field of social service and public morals. We must frankly confess wherein the churches have failed and are failing. Above all, we must define our ideal and invite the co-operation of all men of goodwill in its realization.

For this we shall need to create a new literature of interpretation. It is characteristic of a living religion like Christianity that it must always be inventing a new language in which to say over again the old truths. Even for Christians the old books will not do. We are continually finding the need of new ones. How much more for those who do not understand our Christian language and need to begin from the beginning?

When we speak of literature we are not thinking primarily of books. These have their place and we need them.[3] We are thinking

[1] Cf. the Report of the Proceedings of the First National Conference on Workers' Education in the United States Held at the New York School for Social Research, New York City, April 2–3, 1921. Workers' Education Bureau of America, New York, 1921.

[2] Cf. the recent report of the New Jersey Chamber of Commerce on the relation between capital and labor, *New York Times,* February 5, 1922.

[3] Of our need of more and better Christian literature we have already spoken. In our output of reading matter there are surprising and lamentable gaps. Individual scholars are making their contributions in the field where their primary interest lies, but there is no one who is responsible for survey-

of the literature of the people, the daily press and the periodicals. We need to use this tool far more than we have yet done for purposes of Christian education.

One agency whose possibilities have not as yet been adequately developed is the denominational religious press. As at present conducted this reaches for the most part only readers of its own communion and with notable exceptions has thus far been too largely concerned with local and denominational interests to make possible a comprehensive treatment of the larger elements of church life. Opportunity for a more thoroughgoing discussion is furnished by such interdenominational journals as the *Constructive Quarterly* and the *International Review of Missions*, as well as by such weeklies as the *Christian Work*, the *Christian Century*, and others which appeal to a public outside the denomination. But there are many phases of the co-operative movement which still lack adequate interpretation. Is it too much to ask that the religious editors of the country should together face their responsibility for Christian education? They stand at the strategic point where denominational and interdenominational interests meet. They have access to a public which can be reached in no other way. Has not the time come when they should use this contact to interpret the different phases of the co-operative movement to their constituency more fully than has yet been done?[1]

The religious press at best reaches a limited public. For forming public opinion the secular press is the natural point of approach. The columns of the daily papers are open to all religious matters which have news value. Let the Church do or say something of general public interest, and the columns of every daily in the country will be open to it. When an Edinburgh Conference is held, or a campaign for national prohibition is initiated, there is no difficulty in securing all the space that is needed. The case of the Interchurch Steel Report and the recent campaign of the churches for limitation of armaments is evidence of this.[2]

ing the field as a whole and determining where the gaps are which need to be filled. The beginnings of such co-operation have, to be sure, been brought about in the field of missionary literature, but it needs to be carried much farther and applied in all other departments of the Church's work.

[1] An effort to secure such co-operation has been made by the Federal Council through the creation of the Editorial Council of the Religious Press.

[2] In the *Christian Monitor* the Christian Scientists have given us an example of what can be done to make the daily press an organ of religious educa-

Most promising, because more carefully read, is the periodical press. The leading weeklies and monthlies are open to a sympathetic treatment of religion and nothing would do more to bring the interests we have at heart to the attention of thoughtful people than the preparation of a series of articles which should interpret in the language of to-day the spirit of the Church at its best.

One more field for Christian education may be mentioned, and that is our legislatures and the politicians who control them. There are difficult and delicate questions to be considered. The well-established principle of the free state and the free church must not be imperilled. But if political action threatens the ideals to which the Church is committed, the Church must find some way to protest. The power of the Church has been shown in the field of private morals in connection with the battle against drink and commercialized vice. A similar demonstration may be required in the field of public morals where evils cut still deeper and do even more harm.

It is not, however, in the advocacy of particular political measures that the most effective contribution of the Church to political education is to be made. Rather is it in the cultivation of that spirit of faith and goodwill which is the condition of any large measure of social progress. As Christians we are committed to the ideal of a world-wide society in which men of different races and nations may find it possible to live in co-operation and sympathy. There are multitudes of people who.believe in this ideal and would be glad to work for it. But they have been told so often that it is imprac-

tion, and their experiment is well worth studying by all who recognize the increasing power of the press in forming the thought life of the American people.

A promising field which has been far too little cultivated is the county press. A suggestive experiment is being carried on by the New Jersey Herald, which conducts a department called "The Listener's Bench," in which a well-known minister brings a weekly religious message to those who for one reason or another are out of touch with the Church. The purpose of the new department was announced as follows: "Frankly, this is to be the religious department of the Herald. In its other columns expression is given to the political, social, and commercial life of our town and county. And it is fitting, yes, necessary, if this or any newspaper is to meet all the needs of the individual human being, that provision shall be made for those deep, universal, abiding interests that we call religious. And so from week to week the editor and his collaborators will present in this particular space a few brief paragraphs in the hope that they may bring something of understanding, consolation, courage to men and women who, in spite of all burdens and obstacles, want to travel bravely and to arrive." The department has now been carried on for some months and the response from people of all sorts has been most encouraging.

ticable and find in influential quarters so many who repudiate it that they are beginning to lose their faith and to turn regretfully but deliberately to more attainable aims. They need the assistance of organized religion—a renewal of faith through the reaffirmation of the Christian ideal, a reinforcement of will through fellowship with men who are convinced that Christ's way is practicable and who live in this faith. This help the Church should give.

CHAPTER XV

1. The Problem of Educational Leadership in Protestantism—
Fields in which Religious Leadership is Needed—The
Church's Responsibility for Finding and Training
Constructive Thinkers in the Field of Religion

In the preceding chapter we have recognized the central importance of education for the progress of the Church. We have seen
that it is the duty of the churches not simply to instruct their members, present and prospective, in the nature of the Christian religion, but to interpret the Christian ideal to individuals and social
groups out of touch with organized Christianity. We have noted
the need of a new educational evangelism and pointed out some of
the work which this new evangelism might undertake. But where
are the workers to come from and how are they to be trained?

It is clear that they cannot come from the ministry alone. The
undertaking is far too large for this. Nor can they be supplied by
those who are specializing in religious education. The whole work
of the Christian Church is an educational work, and its teachers
must be drawn from every walk in life. Fathers and mothers,
employers and workers, teachers in the technical sense and the
pupils they teach—all are the Church's educational material, the
reserves from which it must draw its recruits.

This enlarged conception of Christian service, forced upon us by
the pressure of the times, is a return to the original ideal of Protestantism, which affirms the universal priesthood of believers. Not
all Christians are called to the ministry in the technical sense, but
all alike share the primary Christian duties of evangelism and education. Protestantism expects every convert to be a missionary,
and that means that every convert must be a teacher. The two
things go together. The appeal to accept Christ and enlist in His
service implies a knowledge of what Christ is and what He requires.
The witness must be an interpreter.

302

What is true of Christians in general is pre-eminently true of those who have gifts of leadership. We need men of such gifts not simply to do definite work, but to show us what more needs to be done and how. The teacher's function, as we now see it, is not merely to impart what he knows, but to encourage his pupils to join him in the search for what still remains to be known. Research shares with instruction the time of the modern teacher, and our great universities are employing men and women who give their time to this and to nothing else.

It should be the same in religion. We are dealing with a growing and expanding religious life. God's work in the world is not finished. New light is breaking forth from the world of nature and from the world of human life. The Bible means more to us than to our fathers and will mean still more to our children. The Church is not a fixed but a developing institution. It is passing through significant changes and is creating untried forms. We have too few leaders to interpret the significance of this process of change. What is even more serious, we do little to develop and utilize the leaders we have.

With the single exception of the provision of an earnest and competent ministry, incomparably the most important of the educational tasks of the Church is to give its own children and young people an intelligent understanding of the Christian religion. It is the most important in bulk, for it affects by far the largest number of teachers; it is the most important in consequences, for it is the foundation on which all subsequent work of a specialized character must be built. The number of persons engaged in Sunday-school teaching in this country at the present time runs into the hundreds of thousands, and of these all but a negligible fraction are amateurs. Obviously, then, one of the Church's most important duties is to find teachers of the proper character and ability and train them to do their work effectively. We cannot any longer take it for granted that every one is competent to be a good Sunday-school teacher. If it takes time and training to fit oneself to teach geography or mathematics, it is certainly not less necessary to make careful preparation for teaching the incomparably more important and difficult subject of religion. We must find persons who are willing to give the necessary time to preparation and we must provide teachers competent to train them.

The Church's aid is also needed by that larger company whose work in religious education begins even earlier,—the parents in our homes. Without the co-operation of the home the work of the best teacher is handicapped; and yet in how many cases that co-operation is lacking. Many parents do not recognize the extent of their responsibility for guiding their children's thoughts about religion, but did they recognize this duty they would lack the training to do so. We have communicants' classes for children and young people. Is it not quite as important and quite as feasible to have classes for the parents of these children? Why should not a parents' class be a feature in every well-organized church school?[1] There are difficulties of time and place, no doubt; yet surely the love of parents for children and their sense of obligation toward the growing life should make it possible to overcome these difficulties.

Of the need of lay leadership in the effort to apply the principles of Christianity to our contemporary political and industrial life we have spoken elsewhere. It is important, however, that we should remind ourselves how much preparation is required for such leadership. The question naturally arises whether in view of the magnitude of the demands made upon the churches in this most difficult field it will be possible to secure adequate service from volunteers. In religious education the impossibility of depending upon volunteer help is generally recognized. Men and women are fitting themselves to teach religion in our colleges and preparatory schools and to take charge of the educational activities of individual congregations as Sunday-school superintendents and directors of religious education. Should not the same be true in the field of applied Christianity? Why should not the churches set apart men and women to give their lives to the study of the industrial question, or the race question, or the international question from the Christian point of view? Something has already been done in our social service commissions and similar agencies, both denominational and interdenominational, but when we consider the greatness of the opportunity we cannot but feel that we are only at the beginning of what may become a development of great significance.

[1] There is such a parents' class in the Union School of Religion, the practice school conducted by the Department of Religious Education of the Union Theological Seminary in New York City.

The most obvious and best recognized field of Christian leadership is, of course, the Church itself. We have seen what a great enterprise the Christian Church has become, what vast resources it commands, what a varied work it carries on at home and abroad. Considered simply as a business enterprise the missionary work of the American Protestant churches is immense. When to the raising and expending of many millions of dollars annually we add the cost of administering the home churches, the responsibility of our church leaders is apparent.

But the business side of the churches' work is the least part of their responsibility. They shape policies which affect the spiritual life of millions of men. They conduct a great educational enterprise containing in its classes twenty million persons. They are the ambassadors of an international brotherhood which has no boundaries of race or nation. Above all, they maintain an institution of worship which lifts men's hearts to the God of all the earth and reveals their spiritual kinship with one another. The men who control the policies of such an institution have a responsibility second to none, and the problem of their selection and training is of pressing importance.

This problem meets us in its most acute form in connection with the local congregation. All the different interests of the Church at large impinge at last upon the group of men and women who find the centre of their spiritual life in the local church. What the great Church is doing is known to them only through their own particular section of the Church, and the man who is responsible for bringing such knowledge to them is the local minister. He is at once preacher, pastor, leader of worship, administrator, missionary, social-service worker, and teacher. Or, if he be not all of these himself, he is responsible for seeing that each of these interests is properly cared for by persons duly chosen and trained for the purpose. The tone of the Church at large will not conspicuously rise above the tone of the individual minister. The recruiting of a competent ministry and the provision of proper facilities for its training becomes therefore a paramount interest for the Church as a whole.

What is true of the local minister is true *a fortiori* of the greater Church to which his congregation belongs. Its multiform activities require the services of a numerous staff. The boards of home and foreign missions need competent executives; so also do the educational agencies of the denominations. Apart from the administrative work done by volunteers which, in many cases, is very heavy, the regular business of each denomination occupies the full time of a greater or lesser number of persons, while besides the administrative work of the different denominations there is the wide field of interdenominational activity as it is carried on by the Federal Council, the Home Missions Council, the Foreign Missions Conference, the Council of Church Boards of Education, the International Sunday School Council of Religious Education, and the different state or local federations. Most of these require the undivided service of able men and women.

Thus far the Church has made meagre provision for the preparation of those who are to hold these responsible positions. They have been drawn mostly from the active pastorate. Latterly, however, the number of persons who have chosen the administrative service of the Church as a life work has increased, and the need of specialized training for them has been accentuated. Such training is necessary not simply to fit them for the technical work they have to do (that can be learned by practice as it is learned in other businesses and professions) but to give them the breadth of outlook and background of knowledge which will enable them to act wisely in the important matters which are constantly coming up for decision.

This brings us to the last of the Church's educational responsibilities, that of developing constructive thinkers in the field of religion. Such constructive thinkers are needed to guide the Church in its planning for the future, and this all along the line. We need them to instruct and inspire the younger generation who have been taught in the university to prove all things and need to be assured that a man can be a good Christian and yet keep an honest mind. They are required to assist the older men and women in the wise use of the resources which they control and to win to the Church the individuals and the groups now alienated through misunderstanding or ignorance. Above all they are necessary to furnish our executives with the technical knowledge through which alone a missionary programme for the Church as a whole can be wisely developed.

Where are these thinkers to be found? Clearly wherever men

and women exist with capacities which fit them for this unique service.

There are four sources of supply to which we would naturally turn for constructive thought in the realm of religion: our theological seminaries; our colleges and universities; our ministry; the leaders of our missionary and ecclesiastical organizations. In each case we find that the energies which should be given to work of this kind are largely diverted to what seem to be more pressing tasks. Our theological teachers recognize their responsibility for research in the field of religion, but hitherto their main energies have been devoted to the history and criticism of the past. They have not as yet to any considerable extent made the living Church the subject of their critical inquiry. Our college and university professors are active in research along many different lines, but thus far they have failed to give adequate attention to the claims of religion as a subject of scientific investigation. Our ministers in America (unlike their colleagues in Scotland where the scholarly tradition is bred in the bone) find themselves almost immediately immersed in a multitude of details from which it is all but impossible to extricate themselves. The same pressure of detail hampers those who ought, of all men, to be most free to devote themselves to constructive religious thinking—our missionary and ecclesiastical leaders.

Evidently one of the most important parts of the Church's educational work is to direct the attention of those in responsible official positions to the need of finding men and women who have the capacity for constructive thought and of setting them free for this indispensable service. Without such thoughtful leadership, effective action on a large scale is impossible. In the university, teaching and research go hand in hand; it should be the same in the Church.

In the light of these general considerations we must consider the Church's responsibility for the training of its leaders. This is not a responsibility which can be assumed by the theological seminary alone or by the institutions which fit men and women for specialized forms of church work. It rests also upon our colleges and universities. Above all, it is the responsibility of the living and working Church which, in its present activities, is the greatest of all educational institutions, the laboratory in which all the theories of the schools must be tested.

2. *Agencies Available for the Higher Religious Education of Laymen—The Responsibility of Our Colleges and Universities for the Teaching of Religion.*[1]

Among the agencies to which we must look for help in our effort to secure adequate religious leadership our colleges and universities hold a foremost place. Our ability to do what needs to be done will depend largely upon the attitude of the men who are responsible for shaping the policies of these institutions. It is important, therefore, for us to understand just what this attitude is and what chance there is of securing their effective and intelligent co-operation.

What, then, have we a right to ask of our colleges and universities in the way of religious education? *For one thing we have a right to ask that they give to every student who comes under their influence some intelligent conception of the place of religion in human life, the part which it has played in history and the institutions through which it functions to-day. We have a right to ask further that they give their students such an acquaintance with the contents of the Bible as will make them at home in its great passages and furnish those who care to carry the study farther the foundation of knowledge which will fit them to become teachers of the Bible to others. We have a right to ask that at some appropriate place in the course each student find a sympathetic treatment of the intellectual difficulties in the way of faith and the attitude of the great thinkers of the past who have found a reasonable faith possible. Finally, we have a right to ask that they awaken in a certain proportion of the abler students such an interest in the larger aspects of religion as will fit them for leadership in the Church in one or other of the lines we have just indicated.*

In some of our colleges and universities these conditions are to a large degree realized. In others little or nothing is done to secure them. In far too few has the problem been seriously faced and the full responsibility of the institution accepted. To understand the situation in its varying aspects a brief historical retrospect is necessary.

[1] Cf. Foster, "Religion in American Universities," *Christian Education,* June, 1921; "Schools of Religion at State Universities," *Christian Education,* April, 1922; Thompson, "Christian Education in Colleges and Universities," *Christian Work,* February 18, 1922.

In the earlier educational history of this country the teaching of religion played a prominent part. The original impulse to the establishment of the older colleges was the desire to furnish facilities for the education of a competent ministry. Theology was taught as a college subject and all students were expected to study it, not only those who looked forward to the ministry as a profession. Later the seminary was separated from the college and became a professional school either entirely independent of the college, with a governing board of its own, or in affiliation with the institution of which it had originally been an integral part.

This change was due in part to the natural tendency toward specialization which was felt in all the professions; in part to the increase in the number of college graduates who looked forward to business as their life work. It was accompanied by a change in men's attitude toward formal creeds and by the growth of a more liberal, not to say lax, view of religion. With the weakening of the older conception of the Church's authority, the instruction in our colleges and universities tended more and more to confine itself to science and the humanities, leaving formal instruction in religion to be provided by the churches through voluntary agencies or in institutions definitely under church control. A system of secularized higher education continued the secular education of the public schools. The establishment of the state universities was an important step in this process, but it was only one element in a larger movement. In the older private institutions of the East, founded by Christian people for definitely religious purposes and still Christian in character and spirit, changes were taking place which restricted the time given to formal instruction in religion. An increasingly large number of students graduated who possessed but the slightest acquaintance with theology and the history of the Church. The more strictly denominational colleges, on the other hand, continued to require the study of religion by all students, and emphasized the responsibility of the college to win each student, as far as possible, to the Christian faith.[1]

In analyzing the present attitude of our colleges and universities

---

[1] The report of the Standardization Committee on Biblical Departments for 1921 lists 307 colleges and universities giving instruction on religious subjects (including the Bible). They are divided into four grades according to the quality of the instruction given, of which A includes 88 institutions, B 51, C 102, and D 66.

toward religion we have to distinguish three different kinds of institutions: the state universities, powerful institutions with great prestige, large financial resources, and many thousands of students, from which until recently all formal teaching of religion has been banished; the strictly denominational institutions, usually much smaller and less well endowed, though not necessarily less efficient within the field of their choice, in many of which at least a certain amount of religious instruction is required of all students;[1] and the privately supported colleges and universities in the older parts of the country. These are still Christian in sympathy and include religion among their subjects of instruction, but they do not ordinarily require it as part of the conditions necessary for graduation.[2]

As the state universities gained in strength and prestige, not a few Christian people came to look upon them as godless institutions from which no help could be expected for training young people for an active religious life. Appeals on behalf of denominational colleges were often based upon the irreligious character of the state universities. The attempt was made to develop a system of higher education under church control which should parallel their activities and make adequate provision for the education of the children of the Church. It soon became clear, however, that such a duplication of educational facilities was impracticable, and in many parts of the country the policy of co-operation replaced the earlier attitude of opposition and rivalry.[3] It was recognized that the students in our state universities often came from Christian homes, and what was needed was to supplement the opportunities provided by the university by adequate facilities for religious instruction, very much as the Sunday school supplements the work of the public schools.

[1] It is to be noted, however, that even in the strictly denominational colleges the number in which the study of religion is required is diminishing. The tendency is to rely upon the quality of the instruction offered to attract students.

[2] Of the 450,000 students in our colleges and universities, about half are in tax-supported institutions; of the remaining 225,000 somewhat less than half are in the private colleges and universities, leaving somewhat more than a quarter of the whole number in strictly denominational institutions. Exact figures are not at present available.

[3] In the South, the attitude of the churches to the state institutions is still largely one of suspicion. The recent attempt in the Legislature of Kentucky to secure the prohibition of the teaching of evolution in tax-supported institutions is only one of a number of indications of this attitude.

This was attempted in various ways. Voluntary Bible classes were provided under the auspices of the Young Men's Christian Association and the Young Women's Christian Association. The equipment of the local churches was strengthened. College pastors were called to look after the students of the several denominations; buildings were erected where the students of a particular denomination could be cared for under helpful influences. Most recently the experiment has been tried of providing courses in the Bible and other religious subjects of such high character that the university has been willing to give those who take them academic credit.[1]

The proposal to establish interdenominational schools of religion in connection with state universities suggests a development of great promise. A beginning has been made at the University of Missouri, where the Disciples Bible College has added a Presbyterian teacher to its staff and is planning to add representatives of other denominations. The University of Texas has an Association of Biblical Instructors in which different denominations are represented. The Iowa State University is at work upon plans for an affiliated school of religion to be co-ordinated with courses of a religious nature at the university; and similar plans are under consideration at other universities.

Of special interest as an example of co-operative work is the recently organized Council of College Pastors at Cornell. Six different denominations are represented in this Council which has a single treasury. Each pastor is responsible for a definite part of

[1] The Methodists and the Disciples have been specially active in this, the former through the Wesley Foundation, the latter through Bible Chairs, and in some instances Bible Schools maintained at university centres. Illinois, Wisconsin, Missouri, Indiana, and Kansas may be mentioned as examples of universities where such co-operation exists. Dr. Cope, Secretary of the Religious Education Association, has compiled a list of thirteen state universities at which extra-mural credit is given for courses in religion and the Bible; namely, California, Colorado, Illinois, Indiana, Iowa, Kansas, Michigan, Missouri, Ohio, Pennsylvania, Nebraska, Texas, and Wisconsin. On the subject of credit for religious subjects taken at other institutions cf. *Christian Education*, April, 1921, pp. 9 sq.

Some state universities themselves offer courses in religious subjects. The University of Michigan is an interesting example. One of the curriculum courses in Biblical literature of this university had this year an enrolment of 195 undergraduates. Courses in New Testament Greek and the Philosophy of Religion are offered by Iowa State University, which will form a part of the combined offering of the proposed school of religion.

the work; the Baptist takes charge of friendly relations, the Episcopalian is responsible for the cultivation of the devotional life, the Congregational for extension work, the Lutheran for the missionary interest, the Methodist for vocational guidance, and the Presbyterian for voluntary Bible study. At Ohio State University a number of denominations have united in the support of a single student pastor to represent united Protestantism, and the same is true of the Michigan Agricultural College.

The original impulse to this activity came from the various denominational boards which were interested primarily in looking after the students of their own denominations. Since the establishing in 1911 of the Council of Church Boards of Education, however, it has been possible to deal with the situation in a more thorough way. Under the auspices of this representative body a systematic study of Christian education in our colleges and universities has been undertaken and unified policies have been developed.[1] A monthly journal serves as a clearing-house of opinion and furnishes an indispensable source of information.[2]

In addition to studying the state universities, the Council of Church Boards has devoted attention to the denominational colleges. There are no less than four hundred and twenty of these, and they constitute an exceedingly important factor in our educational life. Distributed all over the country, many of them in smaller communities where the cost of living is less than in great cities and which are easily accessible to the neighboring towns and country districts, they care for many thousands of students and form the largest single recruiting ground for the Christian ministry. In recent years much has been done to improve their quality and strengthen their resources, and they are to-day one of the most interesting fields for the study of what is possible in the way of higher instruction in religion.

A different and in some respects more difficult problem is presented by the colleges and universities in the eastern and middle states. These institutions are definitely Christian in character and

[1] Among the special pieces of research done by the Council may be mentioned a study of the Congregational colleges undertaken at the request of the Board of Education of that church. At present the Council is engaged in a study of the present status of theological education in the United States. It is much to be desired that the resources at the disposal of the Council should be increased in order that it may be able to do more work of this kind.

[2] *Christian Education*, 1916 sq.

make provision in various ways for the teaching of religion. They have daily chapel and university preaching on Sunday, at which in some cases attendance is compulsory. They offer courses on religious subjects both for undergraduate and for graduate students. Some universities maintain theological faculties with a professional standing equal to that of their faculties of law and of medicine. A few make provision for a college pastor. In others the main reliance for the maintenance of the religious life of the students is placed upon the voluntary services of the Young Men's and Young Women's Christian Associations and the work of the neighboring churches. For the good work now being done we may be grateful. Yet it is timely to inquire whether taking them as a whole our eastern colleges and universities have yet faced in a comprehensive way their responsibility for meeting all the different claims which may legitimately be made upon them.

There are three groups of students whose needs must be considered separately: first of all, the rank and file of students who are not themselves actively interested in religion but who should be given an intelligent conception of the place of religion in human life, of the function of the Church in modern society, and of the contents of the great classic of English literature, the Bible; secondly, those students who are now or may become actively interested in religion and upon whom the Church is to draw for lay volunteer leadership; finally, the still smaller group who are to make the service of the Church their life work in the regular ministry or in some one of the various specialized forms of service. No university can properly be said to have done its duty as an educational institution that has not made definite and adequate provision for the needs of each of these three groups.

There are two ways in which the university can make provision for the first of these needs. One is through special courses in the Bible, comparative religion and the philosophy of religion, given either as parts of the regular curriculum or as electives. The other is by making place for a treatment of religion in the general courses which deal with history, philosophy, psychology, sociology, and the like.

With the present pressure upon the curriculum and the delicate questions that grow out of denominational and theological differences, it is not probable that the amount of time given by the average undergraduate to special courses on religious subjects will materially increase. An occasional new course may be added, and the quality of the existing courses may be improved, but these courses will never of themselves accomplish all that is needed, if for no other reason than that they are taken by a limited number of students. To give the rank and file of students the desired familiarity with the facts about religion and the proper sense of their importance it will be necessary to interest those members of the faculty who teach other subjects. Much more is being done along this line than is commonly recognized. The history of the Church and the philosophy of religion are dealt with in general courses in history and philosophy. Great figures in the world of religion are discussed in the courses on literature. But such discussions are usually due to the interest of the individual teacher and form no part of a comprehensive plan. If there could be in each institution some one person whose function it was to correlate what is now being done in the different classrooms and to suggest further points which could be wisely emphasized, a stronger impression would be produced than is possible under our present happy-go-lucky system.[1]

Much would depend on the personality of the teacher. The only sure way to make students realize the importance of religion as a subject of study is to let them see that teachers whom they respect regard it as important. Required instruction in religion given by men who do not appreciate the significance of religion is often worse than useless. But when the student hears his professor of history or of politics or of psychology calling attention to the part played by religion in human life, or explaining the function of the Church as a social institution, the effect is all the more impressive because the reference is unexpected.[2]

[1] It is of interest to know that in the introductory course on the Problems of Civilization required of all freshmen at Columbia, the subjects of religion and the Church receive due recognition as factors indispensable to the understanding of the world in which we live. For a further account of what is being done along this line the reader is referred to the author's address delivered before the Yale Convocation entitled, "The Responsibility of the University for the Teaching of Religion," *Yale Divinity Quarterly*, June, 1920.

[2] This would seem to be a field which might be cultivated with profit in the state universities. Many of the teachers of these universities are Christian men who would gladly co-operate in any plan to give the subject of religion the attention it deserves in those courses to which such a study would be germane.

Here is an opportunity for the educational evangelism of which we were speaking. Much has been done to win college students to Christianity. Little has been done to enlist the co-operation of the members of the faculties. Yet in proportion to their numbers the faculty members probably exercise a greater influence than any other body of men in the country. Our universities and colleges give the tone to our national life. From them come nine-tenths of the leaders in every walk of life. To them therefore the Church must look for leadership.

Beside the students whose interest in religion is of a general character, there are two other groups to which the university has a special obligation: the thoughtful students who are to be the volunteer lay workers in our churches, and those who are going to make the service of the Church their life work. The needs of the first group can be met by special courses similar to those designed for the whole body of the students, but more thorough. Men expecting to enter the ministry should be treated like the students of other professional schools for whom the university provides courses designed to lay the foundation for their later and more technical studies.

In this connection a word should be said of the opportunity offered by the summer school for developing an interest in religious research. Such schools are held every summer by our great universities (*e.g.*, Columbia, Chicago, and Harvard), and are attended by thousands of students. Among the subjects taught in these schools religion is included. At Columbia and the University of Chicago the courses given are somewhat technical in character and are designed primarily for theological students or for those intending to specialize in some form of religious education. At Harvard the courses are briefer and meant to meet the needs of ministers who cannot afford to give the time required for courses which count for a degree. It would be interesting to know whether there is a public which would be attracted by plans of a different character. A summer school of religion modelled after the Williams College School of Politics would be an interesting experiment and might set a standard for similar work in other places. In such a school special attention could be given to the responsibility of the Church for dealing with social and political problems, and teachers of national repute could present the results of the best Christian thinking to men and women who were themselves at work in these fields.[1]

In addition to all that the university does to provide instruction for special groups of students, it must endeavor to create a general atmosphere of interest in the theoretical aspects of religion. The questions before the Church cannot be dealt with in a narrow or partisan spirit. They require consideration by thoughtful men of different departments under such conditions as exist in the graduate schools of our great universities. For this reason we welcome the action taken by some of our leading universities [2] in providing for the inclusion of religion among the subjects for which the degree of Ph.D. is given. This is an encouraging indication of a growing recognition by the university of a responsibility for training thinkers as well as workers in the field of religion.

How can a sympathetic attitude toward the study of religion on the part of our college and university teachers be further cultivated and developed? There is just one certain way, and that is to make the Church such a significant factor in modern life that it will be impossible to ignore it. When our teachers see the churches doing the things that seem to them important within the fields which they are studying, they will begin to take note of this fact in their classrooms. Whatever we can do, therefore, to make the Church stronger and more effective will help to win a larger place for the teaching of religion in the curricula of our institutions of higher education.

These considerations have a direct bearing upon recruiting for the ministry. Much may be done to win men for the cause by individual appeal and by group conferences, but the one argument that cannot be resisted is the presence in the ministry to-day of men who are doing work which is evidently worth while. Such men create their own successors, and without the reinforcement of such examples every other argument must fail. This introduces us

[1] A word should be said of the summer conferences for students held at Geneva, Silver Bay, Blue Ridge, and other centres, under the auspices of the Y. M. C. A. and the Y. W. C. A. These gatherings have done much to interest students in the study of religion and give them an intelligent appreciation of the missionary work of the Church.

[2] *E.g.*, Yale and the University of Chicago. Until recently Harvard also gave the degree of Ph.D. in religion, but this has now been superseded by the degree of Th.D., administered by the theological faculty.

naturally to the next subject to be considered, the present state of ministerial education.

3. *Recent Developments in Ministerial Education—Training for Other Forms of Specialized Service—The Church's Responsibility for Training Its Workers in the Field* [1]

Important as it is to increase the number of laymen trained to think independently about religion, we shall not accomplish what we desire unless we can effect corresponding changes in the character and training of the ministry; for the Church is at heart, as we have seen, an institution of worship, and the man who leads in worship gives tone to the life of the whole.

This fact the churches of America have fully appreciated. They have made generous provision for the training of their ministers, at first in connection with the existing colleges, then in denominational seminaries provided for the purpose. These seminaries, now about one hundred and fifty-three [2] in number, command large resources in property and men and together constitute a factor of importance in moulding the religious life of America. It is instructive to inquire what influences are at work in them and what ideals control their policy.

Like the denominations which have created them, the seminaries of the country differ widely. In a conservative body like the Lutheran, where doctrinal orthodoxy is strongly insisted on, the seminaries are under strict denominational control and the character of the teaching conforms closely to the official standards of the church. In loosely organized bodies like the Congregationalists and Baptists, greater freedom obtains, and the character of the

[1] Cf. W. Adams Brown, "Theological Education," printed in *Monroe's Cyclopedia of Education,* New York, 1914, Vol. V, pp. 582–606.

[2] These figures, supplied by Dr. Kelly of the Council of Church Boards of Education, include only the Protestant seminaries. Of these 22 are exclusively for Negroes. In addition there are 32 Roman Catholic seminaries, 2 Hebrew seminaries, and 9 theological departments in colleges and universities. A careful list compiled by the librarian of the Union Theological Seminary puts the number of Protestant seminaries (both white and colored) at 167. The denominational distribution is as follows: Baptist, 29; Congregational, 12; Lutheran, 22; Methodist, 27; Presbyterian, 27; Protestant Episcopal, 13; other bodies, 29; undenominational, 8. The discrepancy in these figures is doubtless to be accounted for by the use of different principles of classification.

instruction given is determined by the judgment of the faculty and the prevailing opinion of that section of the church in which the graduates of the seminary are expected to work. In the Presbyterian, Episcopal, and Methodist churches the method of control varies. The theoretical right of the church to determine the character of the teaching is generally recognized, but in practice the entire management of the school is committed to the trustees or governing boards of the several institutions.

From the seminaries under denominational control must be distinguished those theological schools which are entirely independent. These are of two kinds: the theological faculties of our great universities like Harvard and Yale, which are university faculties in the strict sense and are governed by the corporation of the university, and independent schools like Union Theological Seminary in New York City, which may have university affiliation but which are governed by their own self-perpetuating boards of trustees. The tendency to secure freedom from ecclesiastical control which we have already noted in our study of colleges and universities reappears in the seminaries. Even where the connection with the denomination still remains, the number of seminaries which for all practical intents and purposes may be regarded as independent is increasing.

In general the seminaries of the United States have faithfully reflected the qualities which have characterized the religious life of America. They have regarded it as their prime responsibility to train men for the ministry of their own denomination and have given relatively little attention to the affairs of other churches. If the tenets of other bodies have been taken into account, it has been to point out their errors and to contrast them with the purer and more adequate statements of the teacher's own denomination. The theology taught has been for the most part highly individualistic and has presupposed a view of the world in which nature and the supernatural are sharply contrasted. The curriculum has been simple and has varied little in the different schools. It included a knowledge of the languages of the Bible, exegesis, church history, systematic theology and practical theology, which included homiletics and pastoral theology.

This conception of ministerial education is gradually changing as a result of a number of influences, some of which we have noted. Among these the most important are the general acceptance of the scientific method, the growing interest in questions of applied Christianity, and the weakening of the barriers between the denominations.

Of the first of these we have spoken elsewhere. The influence of the modern scientific movement upon education in general has been reflected in our seminaries and has affected both subject matter and method of teaching. Critical and historical questions occupy a larger space than before and the rival theories of specialists fill much of the time previously given to mastering the contents of the Bible. The attitude taken toward the new science varies in the seminaries as in the denominations they represent, and the effects have been on the whole similar. In the more conservative seminaries the critical study of the Bible is still looked upon with suspicion, and the conclusions of the more radical critics are uncompromisingly opposed. An increasing number both of teachers and of students, however, approach all religious questions with an open mind and find no difficulty in reconciling a whole-hearted Christian faith with the acceptance of the point of view which controls men's thinking in other spheres of human interest.

A greater interest in applied Christianity is shown in many ways. More attention is given to the practical problems of the modern Church. Christian ethics, once taught as a part of systematic theology, becomes a separate study in which the difficult question of applying Christianity to our contemporary economic and political life is discussed. Christian missions at home and abroad is made the subject of special instruction. The practical work done by the students in the different churches and philanthropic institutions is supervised and the conception of the city as a laboratory for the study of religion in action is emphasized.

The emphasis upon the practical application of the Gospel brings many students to the seminaries which are located in the larger centres of population where they can enjoy the advantages of the existing educational and philanthropic institutions. In New York there are three theological seminaries. In Chicago and its neighborhood, there are eight; in Boston, six. Some of these have close affiliations with Columbia, the University of Chicago, or Harvard. All recognize the advantage of the practical contacts afforded by the life of a great city. Institutions like the Union Settlement, South End House, and the Chicago Commons give the students an exceptionally favorable opportunity to study human problems. They go out equipped with more practical experience than could otherwise have been acquired. There is, of course, a danger in the pressure of conflicting interests. Schools like the Protestant Episcopal Seminary at Alexandria, Virginia, where quiet hours with the great thinkers of the past are still possible, will always maintain their place. For the present, however, the tendency of students to congregate in the great cities seems likely to continue. As long as this is true it is natural that students of theology should be there too.

Among the important influences which are further affecting present methods of theological education is the spirit of Christian unity. Denominational barriers are more and more breaking down. Men may pass freely from the seminaries of one denomination to another. At Princeton, the leading representative of Presbyterian orthodoxy, twenty-three denominations are represented in the student body. At Union Theological Seminary in New York there are thirty-one. In most of the larger seminaries this state of things can be duplicated. What is more significant, we find seminaries in which the same catholicity appears in the constitution of the faculty. At Union six different communions are represented in the faculty; at Harvard, five; at Yale, four; at the University of Chicago, six.

The broadening of the constituency of the seminary is reflected in its teaching, which becomes less rigidly denominational, more catholic and inclusive. The consciousness of the larger Church is beginning to invade even the most conservative of the seminaries, and this fact is rich in promise for the future of the American Church.

It is interesting to note that the line between conservative and liberal, could one be drawn, would not correspond with denominational divisions. Each large denomination has its more liberal and its more conservative schools, with the various shadings within each. In each case the sympathy that grows out of similar temperament and outlook cuts across denominational lines. The writer belongs to a theological society composed of teachers from a dozen of the leading theological schools of the different denominations— Presbyterian, Episcopal, Methodist, Baptist, Congregational. The subjects discussed are of the most fundamental and divisive character and the differences in opinion of the participants are often great. Yet in method of approach, in unity of aim, in deep spiritual sympathy with one another, in the consciousness of belonging to a single unbroken fellowship the members of the society are at one. In this they are typical of a far larger number of teachers in all branches of the Church.

Under these influences we see the curriculum broadening and becoming more flexible. New subjects are included, such as the history of religion, the psychology of religion, and sociology. Many modern seminaries have a department of religious education where instruction is given both in the theoretical and the practical aspects of the subject. Electives multiply until they run up into the hundreds. The student with a practical interest finds it possible to specialize, while higher degrees encourage the more thoughtful student to prolong his studies for one, two, or three more years.

In two particulars this tendency to specialize is noteworthy. One is the attempt to adapt the studies carried on in the seminary to the work for which the student is preparing himself after graduation. The differentiation of tasks of which our preliminary analysis has reminded us requires corresponding differences in training. This the seminaries are beginning to provide. In addition to the subjects which must be included in every minister's education, special preparation is needed by the minister of a country parish, by the man whose work is in the congested districts of our great cities, by the specialist in religious education, by the missionary who goes to the foreign field. These needs are met by special courses leading in some cases to vocational diplomas.

The second form of specialization is in connection with scholarship and research. From the first the seminaries have recognized their obligation to contribute to the scientific study of religion, and the long and constantly increasing number of monographs in the various fields of religious knowledge have for the most part seminary professors for their authors. In the past these volumes have been written on the familiar subjects of the older curriculum, the criticism and interpretation of the Bible, church history, theology, and the like. More recently the practical problems before the Church have been studied and teachers of Christian ethics and its allied subject, Christian institutions, are contributing their share to the theological output. The psychology of religion and the theoretical aspects of religious education, as well as the history of religions, are receiving increasing attention.

It is, of course, true that the extent of these changes differs in different institutions. Some seminaries have felt the new influences little, some consciously repel them. None are entirely unaffected by them.

A subject which concerns all seminaries alike is the number of men who are entering the ministry without a thorough preparation. Statistics are not available to show how many ministers in the Protestant churches are without either college or seminary training, but we know that they are very many and that the number appears to be increasing.[1] What is more serious, we find that a campaign is being carried on against the seminaries which insist upon a high standard for their graduates. They are attacked as out of touch with the churches and congregations are urged to take men who have a more direct and vital Gospel. This campaign is closely connected with the revival of premillenarianism. A fertile field for this propaganda has been the Bible Institutes, which, originally designed for the training of lay workers, are now sending many of their graduates into the ministry.[2] Many of the teachers in these schools are committed to a literal interpretation of the Scripture which insists upon the visible, personal second coming of Christ. They suspect Christians who do not hold this view, however conservative in other respects their theology may be. Those who accept the modern critical view of the Bible are regarded as enemies of the faith and an active propaganda is carried on against them.

One salutary effect of this campaign has been to unite the friends of a thorough training for the ministry. The recent formation of the Conference of Theological Seminaries of the United States and Canada was an encouraging evidence of such union. This conference, begun four years ago at Harvard at the invitation of President Lowell, brought together representatives of more than fifty seminaries. It was repeated two years ago at Princeton where thirty-five institutions were represented. It has now become a biennial affair. Teachers of different denominations, widely separated in theological and ecclesiastical position, meet for friendly discussion of their common problems. Provision has been made for a Continuation Committee which is to meet in the interim, and

---

[1] Some of those who have studied the situation estimate that taking the country as a whole less than half the present ministry have had both a college and a seminary course, and a very large number of ministers have had neither.

[2] This is notably true of the Institutes at Los Angeles and Chicago.

other committees are conducting investigations which will be to the mutual advantage of all concerned.[1]

The existence of this Conference, with its committees, opens the way for a serious consideration of some of the larger questions of ecclesiastical policy, of which one of the most important is what can be done to provide a ministry for those churches which cannot afford the highly trained graduates of the seminaries which require a college degree for entrance. At present the Bible Institutes are definitely trying to meet this need. It is for the educational authorities of the churches to decide whether they will provide briefer, although still thorough, courses of instruction for men without college training.

There are two possible ways in which this could be done. Some of our existing seminaries could be equipped with facilities to do the work on a large scale;[2] or new institutions could be established with their own governing boards and faculties. The latter would only be possible on an adequate scale if a part of the funds now directed to the higher education of the ministry were diverted to this purpose and the gap filled by the consolidation of existing institutions. If our seminaries are to justify the large sums spent upon them, something of the sort should in any case be done. A study of the whole field is needed in order to ascertain where the major needs lie and what changes or additions are desirable.

Such a study should also include a survey of the facilities available for fitting men and women for other forms of specialized religious service.[3] Many of those who are fitting themselves to teach religion now receive their training in our seminaries.[4] Secretaries of the Young Men's and Young Women's Christian Associations are prepared for their work in special institutions created

[1] *E.g.*, on the subject of pre-seminary studies; on the opportunities for theological study for American students in the universities of Great Britain and the Continent, and on similar facilities offered to foreign students in the institutions of this country, etc.

[2] Bangor and Hamilton are examples of seminaries which have definitely adopted the policy of training men for the ministry who are not college graduates.

[3] In the April number of *Christian Education* for 1921, O. D. Foster gives a list of sixty-four such institutions with statistics of the number of students attending them. This study makes apparent the almost complete lack of standardization in this field.

[4] Hartford maintains a separate School of Pedagogy, giving the degrees of Doctor of Philosophy, Master of Pedagogy, and Bachelor of Pedagogy.

for the purpose.[1]   But there is a wide field in which little or nothing is being done except by voluntary agencies like the Bible Institutes.   Certain denominations provide training schools for lay
workers where elementary instruction is given for a year or two
years.   The Episcopalians and Methodists have their deaconess'
schools, but the work is of an elementary character and leads to
no recognized degree.   A promising experiment is the Social-
Religious Workers' course for college graduates carried on jointly
by the Methodists and Presbyterians in connection with Teachers
College.[2]   A similar school is being conducted by the Methodists
at Evanston.   These are beginnings, all but negligible in comparison with the greatness of the opportunity.   A comprehensive survey of the whole situation would lead to a closer co-ordination of
our existing facilities, and might raise the question whether in
addition to the existing schools for vocational training there is not
room for some central institution, either independent or attached
to an existing seminary or university, which could do for religious
education what Teachers College does for secular education.   Such
a central institution might set a standard which would elevate the
tone of religious teaching the country over.

Scarcely less important than to guard the entrance into the
ministry and to provide adequate training for lay workers, is it
to see that those who have entered these callings without sufficient
education shall have an opportunity to supplement their deficiencies
after they are in.   It is to the credit of the Methodist Church that
in theory at least it has grappled with this problem and made continued study a requirement for the body of its working ministry.
Its annual conferences bring together untrained or half-trained
ministers, examine them on a course of reading prescribed for the
year, and give them a course of lectures by older and more experienced teachers on themes of central importance, both theoretical
and practical.   It is true that the character of the work done in

[1] *E.g.,* The National Training School of the Young Women's Christian
Association, New York; The Young Men's Christian Association College at
Springfield, Massachusetts; the Chicago and Lake Geneva Young Men's
Christian Association College.

[2] Those who take this course live in the different churches and settlements
which they serve and devote half their time to neighborhood or parish work,
sharing their experience with one another and using the city as a laboratory
from which to draw the material which is interpreted to them in the class-
room.

these conferences differs greatly and is often superficial and unsatisfactory. Nevertheless the principle has been established and all that is needed is to improve what has been begun.

What is done for the Methodist ministry by means of conferences is being done by some of our home-missionary boards for their own workers. From time to time they bring together a selected number of workers for a discussion of common problems. Such conferences not only provide needed information and instruction for the individual, but also create an *esprit de corps* which is invaluable. Plans for more extended study are being considered by some of the boards, but have not yet been developed far enough for notice here.

The furlough gives our foreign missionaries a convenient opportunity for more prolonged study, and every year an increasing number come to our seminaries and universities for serious graduate work. It is much to be regretted that the financial pressure upon the returned missionary and the demand for his services as a speaker prevent many who desire to do so from taking advantage of this opportunity.

The intellectual refreshment which the mission boards provide for their workers through their group conferences ought to be available for all the ministry. Something can be done by the seminaries through summer schools and conferences. Such conferences have been held at Harvard, Union, Auburn, Chicago, and elsewhere with gratifying success.[1] Yale holds an annual convocation lasting a week, which is attended by many ministers, and the same is true of Bangor. In several denominations annual congresses have been held which have proved a fruitful source of instruction and stimulus, all the more because they have brought together for friendly conference men of very different theological and ecclesiastical positions. But such occasional and unrelated meetings reach only a comparatively small number and leave untouched those who most need stimulus and guidance. To deal with the situation on an adequate scale it will be necessary for the educational authorities of the several denominations to co-operate with the colleges and seminaries in some nation-wide plan of extension work, making

[1] A special word should be said of the work that has been done at Hampton Institute through the summer conference for Negro ministers. Howard University is also carrying on extension work in the same field.

possible for the Church as a whole what the Methodist Church now offers its ministers.

One educational agency of great promise has been almost entirely overlooked, and that is the stated meetings of the ecclesiastical bodies themselves. Beside the national conventions and councils which reach only a few and where the volume of work makes any large educational programme impossible, there are intermediate bodies like the presbytery, the diocese, the classis, the district convention, which include all the clergy within a specified area. The meetings of these bodies are often taken up with details of a more or less unprofitable character and leading ministers are often conspicuous by their absence. If these units would constitute themselves study groups for the consideration of the vital problems and would appoint committees to gather material during the year which could be presented for discussion when the body meets, they might in time do much to change the intellectual outlook of the ministry.[1]

The conception of the Church as an educational institution brings before us with renewed force our need of leadership. Important as it is for us to see that our ministers are encouraged to study, it is no less important that they should be furnished with the best possible helps to effective study; but for this there must be extensive co-operation. Not enough is being done to bring together our constructive thinkers; not enough to direct the young men, who are beginning their studies, to the fields which most need to be cultivated; still less to interpret to those who are actively at work the lines along which the best contemporary thought is moving. There are many minds at work, but we have as yet no common mind. This introduces so important a subject that we must reserve it for another chapter.

[1] In the Presbyterian Church an interesting experiment is being tried. In some of the Western synods, notably Oregon and California, a week is given up to the meeting of synod and the religious condition of the state is made the subject of concerted study. Those who have attended meetings of synod under the new plan report the change in the spirit of the meetings as remarkable and the effect upon those who attend as far-reaching.

CHAPTER XVI

THINKING TOGETHER

1. The Christian Way of Dealing with Difference—The Church as a Training School in Co-operative Thinking

THE preceding pages have made us familiar with what has thus far been done to bring about co-operation in the American churches. It is an encouraging story. In spite of much limitation and failure, there has been a steady progress in understanding and sympathy. Barriers have been broken down. Contacts have been established, in the local community, in our educational and missionary agencies, in the Church at large. What is needed now is to carry the process farther, to relate the groups that are still independent, to co-ordinate the agencies that now parallel or compete with one another, to provide adequate leadership for the Church as a whole.

This is not simply a matter of setting up new machinery. It may be necessary to do this—we shall give reasons for thinking that it is—but of itself it will not accomplish what we want. What is needed is a new mental attitude. We must not only be willing to work with our fellow-Christians; we must be willing to *think* with them, which is a different and a more difficult matter.

We may learn a lesson from the students of physical science. They have carried co-operation in research farther than any other group have done, and to this fact their extraordinary successes are largely due. No other field of study has been so well organized, and nowhere else have the results of research to date produced more revolutionary effects upon practice.

But organization could not have produced such results without the *spirit* of co-operation. In all the great branches of research men are working side by side, sharing one another's insights, testing one another's conclusions, rejoicing in one another's successes, making each new discovery common property that it may form the point of departure for the next forward step, by whomever it may be made. Science is only another name for thinking together.

327

Why can we not do the same thing in the Church? In his recent book, "The Mind in the Making," [1] Professor James Harvey Robinson suggests an answer. He contrasts the divisions and prejudices which characterize our thinking about the human problems which bear most directly upon our daily welfare with the unity and precision with which students of the physical universe approach their problems. Why is it, he asks, that while in a comparatively short time our attitude toward nature has been revolutionized and we command powers of which our fathers never dreamed, we have made such slight progress in dealing with the infinitely more important problems of government and education? He concludes that the trouble is with our way of thinking. To our study of the physical universe we bring a perfectly open mind. In our attitude toward our fellow-men, on the other hand, tradition still holds sway. We assume that what is old must be good. It not only hurts us to change our minds; it seems to us immoral. What the scientist regards as the greatest virtue, the patriot and the preacher condemn as the unforgivable sin. Professor Robinson insists that this attitude must be changed if we are to make progress toward a better society. We must rid ourselves of our prejudices in favor of the old and be ready, if necessary, to break completely with the beliefs of the past. [2]

There is enough truth in the contrast to provide food for self-examination. Yet of itself it does not tell the whole story.

The divergence of which Professor Robinson reminds us is not simply due to a difference in the mental attitude of those who are studying; it grows in part out of the nature of the subject to be studied. The physical sciences deal with objects which can be touched and measured, and the problems which they propose for

---

[1] New York, 1921.

[2] Cf. especially p. 25. "In order that these discoveries (of physical science) should be made and ingeniously applied to the conveniences of life, it was necessary to discard practically all the consecrated notions of the world and its workings which had been held by the best and wisest and purest of mankind down to three hundred years ago—indeed, until much more recently. Intelligence, in a creature of routine like man and in a universe so ill understood as ours, must often break valiantly with the past in order to get ahead. It would be pleasant to assume that all we had to do was to build on well-designed foundations, firmly laid by the wisdom of the ages. But those who have studied the history of natural science would agree that Bacon, Galileo, and Descartes found no such foundation, but had to begin their construction from the ground up."

solution lend themselves to laboratory experiment. In social matters, on the other hand, we are dealing with human beings who have wills of their own and who must consent to what is proposed to them. If the chemist or physicist makes a mistake in his calculations and finds it necessary to correct his hypothesis, no great harm is done. In spite of this, prejudice is not unknown, and the spirit of co-operation has to make its way against obstacles. In our study of man's social relationships these obstacles are immeasurably greater. This is a field in which personal interests are affected. A miscalculation may bring sorrow and misery to multitudes. It is not strange that men's minds should move more slowly here and that prejudice should be harder to overcome.

We may illustrate this in connection with our social and industrial problems. Much of the resistance to progress in our day is due to personal selfishness, the resolute determination to hold what one has at any cost. But much of it is due to honest doubt as to whether the changes proposed will really be for the better. With this doubt, reinforcing and dignifying it, goes the sense of responsibility for the human values which may be imperilled if any mistake be made, values cherished not for ourselves alone, but for other lives as well. This fear of change has its evil consequences against which we must always be on our guard, but it has often proved a useful balance-wheel. It has held society steady when some untried theory has been proposed as a new Gospel of salvation, and it has forced the advocates of change to justify their claim by winning the consent of those who must pay the price of the experiment.

In religion we face the ultimate realities and define our relation to the supreme values. We can afford, least of all, to make mistakes here. Here, therefore, we find ourselves most hesitant to venture into unknown fields. In religion the problem of difference becomes most acute, and the obstacles in the way of unity seem most difficult to overcome. To the natural preference of each for his own way, to the ever present obstacles of inertia and prejudice are added nobler motives, the sense of fellowship with martyrs and saints in the past, the consciousness of responsibility for handing down to the future the truth and grace entrusted to us by God.

But if religion accentuates our difficulties it helps us to deal with them. Religion lives by faith, and faith furnishes the atmosphere in which differences may be most helpfully approached. The triumphs of science have been possible because those who have studied science have believed that success was attainable. No number of past failures has been able to shake the student's faith that the next experiment might succeed. The spirit in which our human problems have been approached has too often been the very opposite. We have been content with half measures and compromises because it was too hard to believe that anything better was possible. We have made the past the measure of the future and met each proposal for a forward step in church or state with the sweeping assertion that it is impossible to change human nature. Because man has sinned and blundered in the past therefore he must always continue to blunder and sin. Because he has lacked faith in the past, therefore he must always continue faithless. That which blocks progress at every point is fear born of unbelief. No diagnosis of our present social ills is complete which does not recognize man's distrust of his fellow-man. Why will not capital do the obvious thing for labor? Because capital does not trust labor. Why does labor pursue its short-sighted and selfish policy? Because labor fears that if it do otherwise capital will take some advantage. Why does not France disarm? Because France fears what Germany will do, and so with all the other nations. From this *impasse* we can escape only by the way of faith. If we are to go forward it can only be as we are willing to help one another to live the better life. For this we must trust one another and wish one another well. Religion makes possible this mutual sympathy and goodwill. It shows us the unrealized capacities of our fellows and interests us in their progress and welfare.

Of all men, therefore, religious people ought to be most willing to open their minds to new light and to approach life's tasks and problems together. The habit of thinking together, to be sure, will not of itself put an end to difference. Indeed it may well accentuate it. But it will give difference a new significance. It will put it in the right place. Men are often divided by unreal differences. They hold aloof from those with whom they are really in sympathy and try to work with those who, at heart, care little for what they value most. Contact will dispel these misunderstandings. It will bring those together who belong together. It will join conflict on real issues.

Not only will the right attitude help to limit the number of our differences to those which have real significance; it will show us how to deal with those which remain. Perceiving the causes which have produced our differences we shall be able to treat them more intelligently. We shall understand even where we cannot approve. We shall sympathize even where we cannot agree. Where a plain moral issue of right and wrong is presented, we shall meet it with the courage that is born of a knowledge of the facts.

Thinking together, we must never forget, does not necessarily mean thinking alike. One of the most valuable lessons a man can learn is how to differ without loss of respect. For the Church this lesson is of fundamental importance; for it is the indispensable condition of any real progress toward a united Church. The first step toward Christian unity must be taken within, and this involves the facing of differences in the fraternal spirit. Whatever may be the outcome I will at least try to make my brother's point of view my own. I will see with his eyes and think with his mind and feel with his heart and I will dare to believe that what I am willing to do for him he will be willing to do for me. Where this attitude prevails unity may not at once be possible, but diversity will be robbed of danger.

This applies to the theological differences which separate Christians. They are not unimportant or negligible. We deceive ourselves if we pretend they are. They have deep roots in human nature and testify to realities which cannot be ignored. Whether God reveals Himself gradually and through natural means, as the new theology maintains, or instantly by miraculous means, as is believed by advocates of the older view, is not a scholastic question. Practical issues of large significance hang on the decision. But of one thing we may be sure, that if we are to make progress in the right direction it will be by trying with all our might to understand what can be said for the position we do not hold. It may be that neither of us has grasped the full truth. It may be that some new synthesis can be found that will make place for the truth of both. In the meantime let us rejoice in that which we hold in common—our mutual faith in the good God whom Christ reveals.

Our differences as to the nature of the Church, too, are far from negligible and we should be foolish to minimize them. It is not easy to over-estimate the contrast between the independent who distrusts all organization and finds his ultimate social unit in the free spirit which responds individually to the Spirit of God, and the high churchman to whom the institution as such is God's organ of revelation and the sacrament is the very heart of religion. But these differences, also, can be approached in an attitude of faith and goodwill. We must pay to the man from whom we differ the respect that we ask for ourselves. We must believe that God may speak to him as truly as He speaks to us, even if in language strange to our ears. We must learn to understand what worship means to him and to feel toward it as he feels. We may find to our surprise that he has discovered something precious that we have overlooked. This much is certain; if we are to share with him the insights we have received from God, it can only be through some point of contact won in this way.

The opportunity for such contact the Church should provide. It should be a school for co-operative thinking in which mind meets mind in a common quest of truth.

2. What It Means to Think Together—Fields in Which Co-operative Thinking Is Needed in the Church

What, then, are the conditions of successful co-operative thinking? They are many, but two are indispensable—time and contact. Under the conditions of our American life they seem almost impossible to secure.

Fruitful thought requires concentration. The mind must be free from the pressure of conflicting interests, and to attain this a busy man requires more than ordinary resolution. We must realize that to make room for thinking is so important that it is worth a sacrifice. A distinguished Frenchman was asked to give his impression of our American universities. "You Americans," he said, "respect scholarship; but you do not respect the conditions of scholarship." We like the results of thought, but we are too busy doing things to pay the price of thought.

This preoccupation with doing strikes an observer from the older world as one of the characteristic features of American life. Speed seems to us the thing supremely important. We are always hurrying, and if anyone can tell us how we can go faster still, we are eager to follow him. Quantity rather than quality of output is the aim of our manufactories. Too often it seems our ideal in the Church.

We have said that we are too busy to think. This is not quite true. We are not too busy to think about methods—at least within certain limits. If anyone can invent a labor-saving machine we are eager to hear about it, and will scrap any amount of old machinery to install it. But the question whether the thing we are doing is really worth while; whether the product we manufacture serves a useful end; whether it would not be better in the long run if we directed our energy to some altogether different occupation: for such questions as these, we have little time. Indeed, there are many of us who seem scarcely to suspect that these questions exist.

This lack of proper forethought explains the incredible waste of American life. We see it in the relation of capital and labor. Labor turnover is one of the biggest items in the modern employer's balance-sheet. Industrial unrest with its resulting unemployment and stagnation of industry is responsible for·vast sums every year. Yet only recently have employers begun to realize that there are human factors to be taken into account which need to be studied with as much care and attention as the scientists study the laws of motion. Fewer still have time for the bigger questions which concern the industry as a whole—time to ask themselves what is the use of their business to society, what its relation to other industries as part of the complex social machine that serves the nation and mankind.

More tragic than the waste of economic resources is the waste of those priceless treasures—faith and goodwill. There are infinite stores of these in human nature. They reappear in every new generation of children. The disposition to think well of life and to hope for·the best—how hard it dies in these prospective citizens and Christians. How quickly it responds to friendly treatment. How easy it would be to translate it into social service, if our existing institutions were not built upon a different philosophy and did not ruthlessly contradict the idealism which the child is taught in school.

A well-known I. W. W. agitator thus explained the method of his propaganda. He would gather a number of men in some logging camp in Washington or Oregon and talk of the common things they saw about them every day. "You meet a lame dog," he would say, "and are sorry for him. You see a man abusing a valuable horse and it makes you angry. Yet you pass a suffering woman or a crying child and it never occurs to you to do anything to help. You take such things for granted as part of the order of things.

How do you account for this? How has it come about that the pity which we instinctively feel for suffering animals is so often absent where human suffering is concerned? It is because of our unnatural social·order. We .have been trained to be indifferent to our fellow-men and this training has inhibited our natural impulses of kindliness and friendliness." This method of approach, he declared, had never failed to win him the sympathy of his auditors.

There is a clue here which is worth following by others. There are stores of faith and goodwill in the average man which are available for our use; but we are too busy running the machine in the way it has always been run to ask ourselves whether there is not a better way. Only recently have people begun to wake up to the folly of this procedure and to ask themselves seriously whether there is not some way of testing modern methods in business and politics by Christian standards.

One of the most interesting signs of the times is the awakening of modern business men to the losses they have sustained because they have made no proper provision for systematic study. Many of them are reorganizing their personnel so as to leave some of the staff free for travel and research. They are turning to the colleges for help where expert advice is needed. They are doing this not simply in technical matters of finance and invention, but in connection with that more subtle and difficult factor in industry, the men and women who work. Recently a large employer commissioned two college professors to give a year of study to the methods of labor adjustment used in certain large plants in which he was interested. This is typical of the new spirit in industry; the spirit that seeks to realize problems as a whole, and is ready to take the time which is necessary.

How much more essential is such study in an enterprise as complex as the Christian Church! For here we are dealing with man not simply as a factor in industry but in all the complicated relationships that make up his life in society. We are trying to form standards for judging our conduct and the methods proposed to improve it. This is not work for any single individual, or number of isolated individuals. It must be done by all of us working together.

With time must go contact. We must not only take time to think ourselves; we must take time to know what other people are thinking. We have been recently reminded of the significance of the group for the formation of opinion.[1] Discussion carried on with an open mind reveals unsuspected possibilities. A result reached through conference is different and usually much better than a result reached through the same amount of effort on the part of individual members of a group working separately. Such progress as we have already made in practical co-operation has been made possible by group thinking. But we should have more of it, and for this we need to multiply our opportunities of contact.

Such group thinking, to be sure, will not render individual initiative any less necessary, but it will furnish the impulse which sets the gifted individual thinking. "Imagination," it has been said, "is not a group quality," but the contact of mind with mind which the group makes possible starts processes of thought which may ripen in lonely hours when the other members of the group are far away.

One sometimes wonders what test Jesus would use to-day if He were to enter our modern world with His words, "Follow me." In speaking to our young men what would He substitute for "Go, sell all that thou hast?" We do not know. But one thing we are sure He would say: "Be willing to talk to your neighbor. Remember that he is a fellow-man with personal interests at stake in the issue between you. Recognize those interests in your attitude toward him. Before you decide against him hear what he has to say." What incalculable harm would have been saved the world if this principle had been acted upon. How many wars, industrial as well as international, might have been avoided, if considerations of prestige had not prevented the principals from meeting face to face while there was yet time.

Our business men are recognizing that a change is needed. Some are beginning to abandon the autocratic methods which have hitherto prevailed in their industries and to provide for group discussion between management and workmen. They are taking their employees into their confidence and trying to create a group morale which will give those who work a sense of partnership in the enterprise. A large concern engaged in international banking recently at great expense brought to New York all its foreign representatives for a week's conference on the business for the purpose of removing possible misunderstanding and securing unity of spirit in the con-

[1] Cf. Follett, "The New State: Group Organization the Solution of Popular Government," New York, 1920.

duct of the business as a whole. The same motive underlies the movement for the democratic control of industry, whether in its more conservative form of shop councils or the more radical plans which involve profit sharing or some other method of the employees' participation in management.

A similar movement is apparent in international affairs. We are coming to see that there are only two ways of settling differences between nations, war or conference, and the best brains of all the different peoples are now engaged in finding some way in which the second method may become a part of our accepted international procedure.

In the Church, too, we need to multiply our opportunities of group contact. We need such contact between the leaders to secure agreement in policy. We need contact all along the line to make sure that the results reached by the leaders are understood and approved by those whom they represent.

It may be said that in our higher institutions of learning the Church is already provided with all the needed facilities for co-operative thinking. Our universities and theological seminaries ought to be the places where group thinking about social and religious questions is carried on most effectively, to which, therefore, we should look for guidance in the solution of difficult church problems. They are in fact doing much to help us, for which we are thankful. But even our universities have not wholly resisted the American tendency to measure results by quantity rather than quality. They have yielded to the prevailing cult of the specialist, dividing department from department, and making each supreme in its own sphere. In the physical sciences, to be sure, a large share of co-operation has been realized, but the social and political sciences are still for the most part unorganized. We know much about many things, but to inquire what these many things mean and how they are related seems to be no one's business. Philosophy, in the old sense of the quest of wisdom, has been dethroned by science and the correlation of knowledge is left to be dealt with by amateurs.[1]

Even if the thinking of our universities and seminaries were better organized, it would still remain true that it is not properly interpreted. We have not yet devised the way in which the results of the best thinking in the humanities can be made practically avail-

[1] Cf. W. Adams Brown, "The Future of Philosophy as a University Study," *The Journal of Philosophy*, Vol. XVIII, December 8, 1921.

able like the results of research in chemistry and physics. The ordinary man grows up in ignorance of many of the things he most needs to know, and there is no one to whom he can turn to supply his lack. He knows a little about many things, and a great deal about some one thing. But he has no comprehensive view of life as a whole, and there seems no one who can give it to him. The specialist cannot give it to him because he is a specialist. The elementary teacher cannot give it to him because he does not know enough. There would seem to be need of a new profession, that of intellectual correlator, or liaison officer in the realm of the mind— the man who assembles the results of the specialist's work on the subjects of living human interest in such form that they can serve as the basis for general education.[1]

In religion most of all we need some one to bridge the gap between the specialist, whose interest lies on the border-land of our knowledge, and the uninformed teacher, to whom most of us must look for instruction. We need to increase the number of those who can teach teachers, who can popularize the results of research.

Such correlation of knowledge is needed not simply for information and general culture; it is needed still more for effective action. In a particular business it may be possible to overlook this necessity for a time, because the interests involved are special. But those who are concerned with personal relationships, as is the case with workers in state or church, cannot shut their eyes to the larger whole of which they are a part. Unless each of the smaller units is rightly related to all the others, they cannot succeed. They have a vital interest, therefore, in bringing about such mutual understanding between the different persons who must co-operate that the net outcome of their effort will be for the common good.

This need of entering into others' thought may be illustrated in each of the different fields which we have been studying. It may be

[1] Cf. H. G. Wells, "History for Everybody," *Yale Review*, July, 1921, p. 676: "The modern community has yet to develop a type of teacher with the freedom and leisure to make a thorough and continuous study of contemporary historical and other scientific knowledge in order to use these accumulations to the best effect in general education." Such a task Mr. Wells has attempted in his "Outline of History," and whether he has succeeded or not, no one can deny that he has tried to do a thing which needs to be done. On the difficulty of gaining accurate knowledge on contemporary affairs and the resulting danger to society, cf. Walter Lippmann, "Public Opinion," New York, 1922.

illustrated in the local community. The difficulty with so many congregations that are living at a poor dying rate is that their members have never been able to form the habit of thinking of anything but themselves. They do what they are doing because it is the thing they have always been in the habit of doing. It does not seem strange to them that there should be a Presbyterian, a Methodist, and a Baptist Church standing side by side in a community which has only people enough to support one vigorous church, because so far as they can remember there always have been three churches there. It is not that their wills are perverse but that their minds are limited. They need to rub up against their neighbors. They require to be converted to the community spirit. When once they have formed the habit of thinking together, nine-tenths of their difficulties will disappear and they will be surprised to find how much better off everybody is under a co-operative than under a competitive system.

What is true of the local congregation is true of the Church as a whole. Its members need to learn what their fellow-Christians are thinking. In important phases of the Church's life this lesson is rapidly being learned. It is being learned in the field of missions. In the work that Methodists or Presbyterians are doing for India or China, they are conscious of a corporate responsibility which lifts them above their provincialism and makes them in a true sense citizens of the world. The same is true in increasing degree of the men and women at work in the home field; but their influence reaches only a part of the church membership. In all our denominations there are multitudes who are still living without the larger vision. They need to be shaken out of their self-sufficiency and made to realize the larger whole of which they are a part. The corporate consciousness which so largely dominates our missionary activity must become part and parcel of the life of the Church as a whole.

Most of all, understanding is needed among leaders. They are dealing with great interests and they need all the help they can get. This help can come only through co-operation as they pool their resources of insight and knowledge and make provision for a collective attack upon the problems that remain.

But for this organization is necessary. What, if anything, can be done here?

3. *Wanted: an Organ for Collective Thinking for the Church as a Whole*

In a recent number of the *New Republic,* Walter Lippmann reviews a book by a Frenchman named Pierrefeu on the French high command. He points out that the significance of the book lies in the fact that it shows the extraordinary part theory played in the conduct of the war. "One conclusion," he writes, "is fairly plain. It took nearly three years for the French General Staff to understand the character of the war it was fighting. . . . We are almost justified in saying that the long deadlock in the West was in the last analysis a time in which both commands were vainly trying to *conceive* the war. The soldiers held while the generals thought; the soldiers wasted themselves in fruitless attack while the staffs painfully searched for the right method of attack." [1]

It is a picture of what is going on in the Church. The soldiers of Jesus Christ, the privates in their several parishes scattered all over the land, are wasting themselves in fruitless attacks because their leaders have not yet found the right *method* of attack. One reason why they have not found it is because they are not looking for it together. The Church needs a unified leadership such as is furnished to the army by the general staff.

What is the general staff? It is a committee for continuous collective thinking. The staff is a group of men taken from the line or, in other words, the men actively at work in the various departments of the army—infantry, artillery, cavalry, and engineers—to think for the whole. They are to the army what the brain is to the individual, the centre from which the whole nervous system radiates, the co-ordinating machinery. Their business is to see things in relation and perspective, to test what is being done, not only by the technical standards which prevail in this or that particular branch of the service, but by its usefulness for all. They look forward and back, studying the history of past wars, forecasting the possibility of future wars, planning what can be done with the resources available to increase the strength of the army either for offence or defense. They draw their recruits from men of practical experience, taking them from all arms of the service alike. They send them

---

[1] Cf. *New Republic,* January 19, 1921.

back from time to time to refresh themselves with new experience. Individuals may change. The group remains, thinking for the whole, studying the things that need to be studied, sharing with the men who must execute the wider knowledge that is necessary to make action in any particular field a success.

Without such a staff the army could not function as a whole. Its success depends in the last analysis not upon the number of men it contains nor the amount of munitions at its disposal, nor even the resources in men and money which it can command, but on its ability to use these at the time and place where they are needed. No preconceived idea of what each arm of the service is fitted to do, or the proper method of using cavalry or artillery as they have been used in the past, must divert the commander from his main objective, which is to defeat the enemy. Marshal Foch, in his book on the "Principles of War,"[1] has expressed this truth in the formula of the economy of forces—the formula which shows how each part, by timely combination with the others, may be made to multiply its own effectiveness many fold.

What is true of the battles of war, technically so-called, is equally true of the spiritual struggle which is going on all the time. That side will win which is able to concentrate its forces most completely at the point where the contest is most severe. In his suggestive book, "Democracy after the War,"[2] Professor Hobson points out how the vast spiritual energies which are going into the struggle for a better world are neutralized and thwarted by the fact that these energies are divided. Each group is working at its pet interest as if it were the whole, and because there is no unified leadership positions of fundamental strategic importance are lost for lack of the help which others might easily have given. If we would work together effectively we must first learn to think together.

An impressive plea for such united leadership in the Church has been made by Earl Haig.[3]

"I have seen in my own sphere of activity the working of a General Staff. I understand how, without interfering with the discretion of those on the spot in matters that concern them and them

[1] New York, 1918, pp. 48 sq.
[2] London, 1918. Cf. esp. pp. 145–161.
[3] Cf. extracts from his address to Scottish churches given in Professor Curtis' suggestive article in the *Hibbert Journal* on "A League of Churches," January, 1921.

only, it is yet able to give singleness of purpose to diversified operations in many theatres, . . . yet more particularly, how it is able to instil life, energy, resolution, and drive into the actions of all, inspiring all with the feeling that they are working to a common end, that their efforts are interdependent, their failure involving more than their own ruin, and their success guaranteeing the victory of others. I want to see established a General Staff for the Christian churches of the Empire, some body at least analogous in the ecclesiastical sphere to the position held by the Imperial General Staff in the military organization of the Empire. There need be no interference in the internal economy of the churches, whether on their spiritual or their temporal side. What it seems to me is needed at once is a strong representative body, not too large for energetic action, which can direct the general policy of the churches, infuse them with new energy, and strengthen their resolution in the great crusade of brotherhood, on the long road on which the war has set our feet. This central body must proceed to the further development of an organization suited to the needs of the Empire. We are entering, we hope, upon an era of peace, bought by vast sacrifices. The object of every one of us is to make that peace secure and permanent. To my mind, the one means by which that end can be achieved is to develop—not merely in Scotland and England, but throughout the whole of the British Empire and the whole world—the spirit of brotherhood born of war. For that great work we need the active help of a strong, vigorous, national Church —a Church which has risen superior to the forces of disruption, and is itself a living embodiment of the principles of fellowship and unity." [1]

But the example of the army can be followed only in part by the Church. The staff is not only an organization for collective thinking; it is also the official adviser of the responsible executive head of the army. Such concentration of power is not possible in the Protestant Church. Rome can command the kind of leadership found in the army because it has embodied in its constitution the principle of external authority. Our Protestant ideal is different. The only leadership possible for us is group leadership. We must assemble our leaders from different branches of the Church, and they must rely for their influence on the full assent of those to whom their counsel comes.

But *this is all the more reason why we need to assemble them.*

[1] The proposal of Earl Haig for a central council to direct the thinking of the Church in its international relations is paralleled by the plea of Professor Small elsewhere referred to for a central body to advise the Church in industrial and economic matters. Cf. p. 232.

There are groups thinking to-day in many different places, but their thought is partial and unrelated. We need to unify these groups and to relate them one to another so that those who are now working independently may work together and the Church as a whole may make its impact felt upon the world as a whole.

It may be objected that we have too much organization as it is. Committee succeeds committee in interminable succession. It is so in the denomination; it is so in the interdenominational field. Most of all it is true in the field of religious education. Of interdenominational organizations alone we have no less than fourteen which have to do with religious education. It would seem as though our trouble were too much organization rather than too little.

Whether we have too many organizations the present writer is not prepared to say, but it seems clear that those which we now have are not functioning as effectively as they might. We are not getting in results a product commensurate with our output. The men who are running the different parts of the machine are too busy doing so to take time to find out how the whole can be run better. If this be true the remedy is plain. We must find men who are willing to give the time and we must put them in the place where they can work together effectively.

There are two ways to set about the creation of such a central correlating agency. It may be brought about through the voluntary action of individuals or it may be made an integral part of some one of the existing interdenominational agencies.

We have already spoken of the Conference of Theological Seminaries as an organization which brings together many of the men who are actively carrying on research in the various problems concerning the Church's life and work, and pointed out the need of taking steps to correlate their work so that it may bear more directly upon the needs and tasks of present-day Christianity. This is but one of many groups which are doing similar work and present a similar opportunity. Most of the different educational agencies of which we have spoken are doing research work, some of it of a high order. Our boards of home and foreign missions are doing it, as well as the interdenominational agencies through which they function. The same is true of the Christian Associations. From the men and women engaged in these various enterprises a voluntary organization might be formed to study the tasks of the Church as a whole and to give their conclusions wide publicity.

Such a method of procedure would have much to commend it. It would have the advantage of securing the utmost freedom and impartiality on the part of those who took part in it; but it would have the disadvantage of all voluntary organizations. It would have no official standing in quarters where its influence was most needed. It would be difficult to secure for it the services of many of those whose contribution was most desirable. If inadequately financed, it would be hampered in its work. If privately financed on an adequate scale, like the great foundations in the field of education and medicine, it would lack the close touch with the organizations to be influenced, which would be the case if it drew its resources as well as its personnel from them.

For every reason, therefore, it would seem desirable to attach the committee to some existing organization. Such a point of contact might be found either in the Federal Council [1] or in the proposed Council of Christian Education.[2] The determination of this question is less important than the definition of the function of the committee and its right relation to the existing agencies of collective thinking in the Church.

Essential to the success of such a committee would be the provision that it should have no executive responsibility. It should be purely a body for study and advice. Apart from the fact that the churches would be unwilling to surrender to any such central body the powers which they have hitherto exercised, it would introduce a disturbing element into the committee's work. Its members would become so much interested in the things that needed to be done immediately that their attention would be diverted from the wider outlook. They would no longer be a strictly impartial body whose duty it was to report on the facts as they found them, but the executives of a policy which other parties in the Church would feel they must oppose.

Yet though the work of the committee should be purely advisory, it should none the less be concerned with matters of present and vital interest. It should study the questions proposed to it as they meet us in the existing world situation and bear upon the tasks of

[1] The Social Service Commission is not the only commission of the Federal Council which is conducting research. Each of the commissions is studying its own field in its own way, but the work they are doing has not yet been effectively correlated. Moreover, each can spare but a part of its time from other duties.

[2] Cf. p. 242.

the present Church. The conclusions reached should be verified by all available experience and put in the form of suggestions which could be further tested in practice.[1]

The definition of its task would determine the personnel of the committee. It should include not only official representatives of the churches, but men and women who are now doing constructive thinking about religion in every sphere of life; professors should be on it, and men of business, labor leaders and scientists, as well as ministers and church officials—whoever has knowledge of the matters that the leaders of the Church need to know or judgment which will help them in making right decisions. Not all these persons need to serve continuously, though they should be available for service when needed. But there should be a permanent executive committee to give continuity to their work, and map out the special tasks to which they are to be assigned.

This central committee should be in touch with similar committees operating on a smaller scale and dealing with more detached problems than can be handled by the central committee. Each denomination should have such a committee, as well as the Associations, the local and state federations, and the national interdenominational agencies. They should be available for whatever service may be required of them, within the local community as in the Church at large. Does a serious labor dispute break out in a certain industry? There should be a competent and representative committee of the Church to see whether any moral principles are involved, in which the public opinion of the community ought to be educated. Is there a race riot, as at Tulsa? There should be a similar group to determine how far the churches are responsible for the existence of the causes which led to it, and what they can do to remove them.

In planning the work of such a group of committees care should be taken to distinguish two different kinds of work: that of determining principles, and that of applying them in detail. The former

---

[1] A suggestive precedent is furnished by the Committee on the War and the Religious Outlook from whose studies we have drawn so liberally in the preparation of this volume. This committee was official in the sense that it was created by the joint action of the Federal Council and the General War-Time Commission of the Churches, but it was left entirely free to act on its own initiative in its choice of subjects and methods of work. What was more important, it had no executive responsibility of any kind. It was chosen for one purpose and for one alone, to do collective thinking.

should be the task of the central committee; the latter may well be left to those on the ground who are more familiar with the facts to be passed on.[1]

The need of such a central committee becomes specially apparent when we consider those larger questions of race and nationality which affect all branches of the Church alike. On world problems the whole Church must learn to think together, for the problems which confront any one part of the Church confront the other parts as well, and only unity all along the line can bring success. The case of disarmament is such a problem. War, as we have seen repeatedly in the course of this study, is the result of causes that are often remote from the immediate issue and sentiments which must be dealt with at the source. It is clear that in a question of this magnitude and complexity no one branch of the Church alone can do what needs to be done. All the churches must work together and together create the common sentiment about war which in the end will make it impossible.

In this spirit of world-wide service we in America ought to approach the tasks and problems of our own home church. Nothing could do more to promote the cause of world brotherhood than to see the churches of a country like America effectively organized for national service. And nowhere could this organization better begin than with the creation of such a central committee as we have briefly sketched. It would help to form the public opinion which would shape the policy of all the constituent churches. It would suggest improvements in the existing organization of the churches, and make it easier to bring them about. It would reinforce the efforts of those who are recruiting for Christian service, by helping to define more clearly the object for which life service is asked. Above all, by bringing to clearer expression the central loyalties and convictions which all Christians hold in common, it would help to fuse the many minds within the Church into a common mind.

[1] An example of the more detailed study needed is the survey of St. Louis recently completed by the Committee on Social and Religious Surveys. A similar study is greatly needed for New York City. This is a field in which every kind of difficulty is to be met with and success is possible only through the most intelligent and complete co-operation. Yet it is a field in which there is as yet not only no adequate co-operation of Christians, but no complete marshalling of the facts we need to know in order to make such co-operation possible.

CONCLUSION

THE CHURCH AND THE DEMOCRACY OF THE FUTURE

CHAPTER XVII

THE CONTRIBUTION OF THE CHURCH TO THE DEMOCRACY OF THE FUTURE [1]

1. *The Spiritual Significance of Organization as a Challenge to Christian Citizenship and Churchmanship—Need of an International Organization to Unify Democracy*

WE have reached the end of our study. It remains to sum up our conclusions. We began by raising two questions: first, what modern democratic society has a right to expect of the Church; secondly, what reason we have for believing that this just expectation will be realized. We are ready now to give our answer: *Democracy has a right to expect of the Church a unifying spiritual influence, springing from a common faith, and issuing in common action.* Our reason for believing that this just expectation can be realized is the increasing number of persons who accept this ideal of the Church's function, and the demonstration which they have given of the possibility of united action when the will to union exists. But whether this reasonable hope will be fully realized will depend upon what we who belong to the Church of to-day do to overcome our divisive sentiments and habits and to carry to completion the work which our predecessors have begun.

We end with an opportunity, not a certainty. Fulfilment will not come of itself. There is a condition attached, simple in principle but infinitely complex in its application. These pages have been devoted to showing what that condition is. *It is the whole-hearted co-operation of all those who have felt the world's need of a united church in making the Church what we know it ought to be.*

It is difficult to over-estimate the strength of this appeal. Every chapter of this book has brought its cumulative evidence of the magnitude and gravity of the crisis we face. We are standing between two worlds—the world of selfish competition whose reliance is only on force, and the world of mutual helpfulness and co-opera-

[1] A few sentences in this chapter have been taken from an address of the author entitled "The Contribution of the Church to the Democracy of the Future," *Religious Education*, October, 1918.

tion which appeals to reason and goodwill. We have seen the outcome of the first method when practised on a world scale and we dimly foresee possibilities ahead more appalling still. The second method, successful within limited groups, has still to be tried on a world scale. There are many who fear that, if tried, it cannot succeed. There are a few who for their own reasons do not wish to have it tried.

The issue is all the more serious because it is a moral issue. It is a conflict of philosophies—rather, shall we say, a conflict of religions. Two theories of world organization are contending for the mastery: the soldier's theory and the teacher's theory—the theory that would unify by conquest, working from without, and the theory that would unify by consent, working from within. Between them there can be no compromise; in the end one or the other must conquer.

We have enlisted on the side of democracy. We believe that the bond which is permanently to unite the peoples must be an inner bond. Against the forces which autocracy commands, there is only one power which can prevail, and that is the power of an ideal.

The difficulty with the democratic method of securing unity lies in the presence of ideals that conflict. When we appeal to men on the basis of their present aspirations we find these aspirations working for division rather than for unity. We see this in the intensified group consciousness which expresses itself in the desire of different bodies of men to break away from the larger units of which they form a part and to live their own lives in independence. Where we have to do with homogeneous groups within the same territory we may hope for a unity which is consistent with freedom; but when men of different race or class are living side by side the problem is more difficult. Here unity is possible only through the discovery of some ideal more inclusive than either race or class, something which makes appeal to a larger faith and calls forth a deeper loyalty.

Such an ideal is citizenship. The nation may include persons of different racial stock and conflicting economic interests who are yet one in loyalty to its institutions and obedience to its laws. Take Switzerland, for example. Switzerland contains elements, on the face of them, most unfavorable to unity. Yet its national life has persisted unbroken for centuries. It includes races as antagonistic as the French and the Germans. It has no natural economic unity, no obvious geographical boundary. It has not even unity of language. Yet it has stood the test of the last war successfully, though appealed to by the most powerful motives from either side.[1]

Our own country is another illustration. All the different countries of Europe have poured their streams into the broad sea that is America. The ancestors of the men who fought shoulder to shoulder at Gettysburg in defence of the Union had fought one another in the lands from which they came. Yet here they found something which made them spiritually one. The same is true of the men who yesterday were fighting with us in France, men with names that we find it hard to spell, much more to pronounce. Poles and Russians, Czecho-Slovaks and Austrians, enemies at home, and still separated by language, tradition, and even by religion, have become fellow-citizens in the United States.

It is clear that if we are to realize our hope of world organization, we must discover some inner principle of unity that will do for mankind at large what patriotism does for individual peoples. It must be intimate and concrete, operating through sentiments and habits as well as through reason; for reason plays a very modest part among the factors which actually influence man. It must be familiar and ancient, growing out of the past, which does not need to be explained; something that we can take for granted, as the nation takes for granted the loyalty of its citizens when danger threatens the national independence or integrity. Without such an inner bond all forms of outward organization will be futile. If we are to have an organized world we must have a world soul.

There are groups in all the different countries who perceive this. Notably is it true of the radical groups, whether they hold the Socialist creed or the more individualistic philosophy of the Industrial Workers of the World. In each case they see that if the new world order for which they are striving is ever to be realized, there must be a community of sentiment as well as of interest among the members who compose it. They are trying to create such a unity where it does not exist, and to give it an organ of expression where it is already present.

But they are handicapped by the narrowness of their horizon.

---

[1] Cf. Bryce, "Modern Democracies," London, 1921, Vol. I, pp. 367 sq.

Their appeal is a class appeal. In their new world order there is a place for the working classes of all countries, but those who uphold the capitalistic system are enemies who must be subdued or expelled. Russia has given us an illustration of the extremes to which this philosophy may go. We have seen the Bolsheviki turning the guns which were used in the war against Germany upon their own countrymen in order to establish the Soviet Republic and demanding unconditional submission to the will of one class—the proletariat—as the first step toward realizing the true social ideal.

The radical movement is further handicapped by its lack of historical perspective. It is not only a class movement; it is a modern movement. Like all revolutions, it is ready to break with the past in order to create a better future; but it has no adequate substitute to offer for that which it surrenders. It has no great tradition reaching back across the centuries uniting it to men of other times and of other faiths; no common symbol which it shares with those who feel themselves the heirs of all the ages.

Here, then, is the opportunity of the Christian Church. Christianity, like Socialism, is an international movement, but it embraces men of all classes as well as of all races. There is no spot on earth where Christianity has not made itself a home; no special stratum from which it has not drawn adherents. In time as well as in space it is ecumenical. It reaches back through the centuries and finds something good in each; but its face is turned toward the future. Its word to the individual is: "You must be born again;" to society: "The Kingdom of God is at hand." Thus uniting reverence for the past with limitless anticipation for the future, the Christian religion possesses qualities which fit it to become the unifying element for the democracy of the future.

But these splendid possibilities must be utilized, and for this organization is necessary. Priceless as is our inheritance it will not become truly ours until we make it ours by use. To this use the living Church must point the way. We must take the old words which long association has clothed with a remote and artificial sanctity and make them a part of the vital thought of to-day; we must devise the new forms of social organization through which the ideals they express may be translated from hope into accomplishment; we must add to the lesser loyalties which divide the citizens of the different nations, the inclusive citizenship of the Kingdom of God.

2. *The Contribution of the American Church to the Larger*
Democratic Experiment

At the beginning of our study we warned our readers that our
inquiry would concern itself with many questions of organization
and polity which seemed remote from present spiritual interest,
but we have signally failed in our purpose if it has not become clear
in the course of our discussion how large a part these matters play
in the development of that vital religion for the sake of which
alone the Church exists. Constitutions and committees are only
machinery; and, like all machinery, they need to be tested by use.
But like the wires that convey our electricity they are indispensable for the transmission of power. If contact be not made
between the dynamo and the lamp to which it supplies light or the
engine which it is to drive, the power which nature has stored up
for our service will waste itself without result or become a minister
of death instead of life. So the spiritual potentialities which God
has provided for our uplift and our happiness will never reach us
unless a contact is made and man is brought into touch with his
fellow-men whom God's Spirit has touched. God is the power-
house from which all goodness and all healing spring. It is for the
Church to make the contacts that will set His Spirit free to do His
beneficent work.

It is against this background that we must set the study to
which the foregoing pages have been devoted. We have been studying the American Church not for its own sake simply, but to understand its contribution to the larger democratic experiment. For as
the Providence of God—using methods we could not foresee and
can not control—has brought the American people to the place
where what they do and what they refrain from doing affects not
their own destiny only, but all the peoples of mankind, so He has
given the American churches an opportunity which they hold in
trust not for themselves alone, but for the Church universal.

This opportunity is compounded of different elements. It is due
in part to the strategic position held at present by the American
people. Whatever may be in store in the more distant future, it is
generally conceded that in the years immediately before us the
course taken by the United States in world affairs will be of momentous consequence for the future of civilization. With our vast
territory and all but exhaustless natural resources, with our tradi-

tion of independence and inventiveness, with the absence of external danger and of the suspicion and fear which accompany such danger, with our young men still largely spared to us although others have lost their millions, we represent a reservoir of energy of incalculable power for good or incomparable possibility for harm. It will depend largely upon what the American churches do in the next generation whether the rôle America plays in the world brings blessing or bane.

This opportunity is due also to the Church's inheritance of the democratic spirit. In the weakness as well as in the strength of this spirit, the American Church has shared to the full. But when all allowance has been made for democracy's failures, it is still true that in democracy the world's hope lies.[1] If the ideals we cherish are to be realized at all, they can be realized only through the co-operation of free men. But the Church is of all American institutions the freest. Its laws are of its own making; its standards self-imposed. As it has developed its institutions little by little to meet the changing needs of the past, so it can modify them as experience may show to be necessary to meet the new needs of the future. In the Church, therefore, we have the opportunity to try the democratic experiment under the most favorable auspices.

This opportunity is due, further, to the intimate relation which exists between the American churches and their sister churches of other lands. No form of living Christianity anywhere but has its representative here. No experiment tried here, therefore, but will have its reflex influence upon those who are our spiritual kin. What we do to bring the churches of America together will encourage those who are working for Christian unity everywhere. What we achieve in Christianizing our social and industrial relationships will increase the faith of all those the world over who are trying to prove that Christianity is a practicable religion.

For all these reasons we need enlightened and united leadership. Upon all who are responsible for the shaping of the Church's policy during the next few years, particularly upon those in official position, rests the most solemn of duties: to see to it that each thing they do and each decision they make in the particular part of the Church they serve, promotes and does not hinder this larger consummation. Above all it is their duty to foster the spirit of sympa-

[1] Even Dean Inge admits that with all democracy's faults he sees no more promising alternative. Cf. "The Future," *Atlantic Monthly*, March, 1922.

thetic understanding and brotherly goodwill without which effective co-operation on a world-wide scale is impossible.

One more factor in the case needs to be added, and that is the urgency of the situation itself. We are not referring here to any of the outward difficulties and dangers which we have passed in review, but to something more intimate and vital still. We refer to the deep need of God which has been born out of the darkness and despair of the time. All over the world there are men and women who are spiritually orphaned, longing for some clear revelation of goodness at the heart of things. To-day as in every past age men need to be assured that there is a good God who cares, and that when Jesus said, "He that hath seen me hath seen the Father," he spoke the truth. This reassuring message only a reunited Church can give, for to be given effectively it must be expressed not in words but through deeds.

In the light of this world-wide opportunity the Church makes its appeal to the young men and women of our country. This is the real call to the Christian ministry—not simply to the ministry of preaching, but to the wider ministry which includes every individual, the ministry of which Jesus offered the great example when He gave Himself on the Cross for the life of the world.

INDEX

Adams, Henry, 144.
Ad interim committees in denominations, 252.
Administrative Committee of the Federal Council, 103, 247, 261, 267.
Administrative Committee of the National Catholic War Council, 268.
Administrative union, 186; what is meant by, 235; agencies for interdenominational, 235-242; see also Union.
Administrative workers, need of more effective training for, 306.
Adventists, 66, 87.
Africa, 9, 49, 236.
African Methodist Episcopal Church, 262.
African Methodist Episcopal Zion Church, 262.
Africans, 51.
Agencies of local coöperation, 186.
Alaska, 237, 240.
Alexandria, 198, 320.
Alliance of Reformed Churches throughout the World Holding the Presbyterian System, 83, 273.
Allies, 268, 269.
Amalgamated Garment Workers, 38.
America, 49, 54; as a Christian nation, 80.
American Baptist Home Mission Society, departments of, 227.
American Bible Society, 103, 242.
American Christian Convention, 262.
American Christianity and international problems, 46-60; democratic character of, 64; provincialism of, 73; denominationalism of, 73; hopeful factors in, 87-91.
American Church, 46, 126; differing estimates of, 5-7; an experiment in democracy, 63-65; importance of, for the understanding of the American people, 64; provincialism of, 72; individualism of, 74; present responsibility of, 275; possible contribution to world-wide union, 275;

function of, 345; contribution of, to the democratic experiment, 353-355; opportunity of, 353; strategic position held by, 353; its inheritance of the democratic spirit, 354; freedom of, 354; relation of, to other churches, 354; see also Church.
American churches, number and resources of, 65-72; denominational distribution of, 65, 66; in Europe, 209.
American Expeditionary Force, 47, 106.
American Federation of Labor, 38.
American International Church, 36.
American labor movement, 40; see also Labor.
American parish, 203, 204.
American Protestant churches, 171; relation to their sister churches in other countries, 272-275; different forms of possible coöperation, 272-273.
American Protestantism, denominational distribution of, 69-70; outstanding characteristics of, 72-76; see also Protestantism.
American Sabbath Association, 242.
American Sunday-School Union, 41, 240, 241, 242.
American Tract Society, 242.
American women, religious experience of, 27; critical attitude toward the church, 27; see also Women.
Andover, 41.
Anglican, 178.
Anglicanism, 64
Anglo-Catholics, 178.
Annual Conferences of Methodist Church, 324.
Annuity funds, 129.
Anthony, Alfred Williams, 237.
Anthony, Robert W., 272.
Anti-Saloon League, 242, 270.
Apostles' Creed, 182.
Apostolic succession, 178.
Applied Christianity, 319.

357

menace to peace, 50; significance for American Christianity, 70; Christian view of, 168, 170.
Radical, radicals, 160; propaganda, 39; Protestantism, 256; movement, limitations of, because of its restriction to class, 351; because of its lack of historical perspective, 352.
Rauschenbusch, Walter, 90.
Recruiting for the ministry, 305, 316.
Recruits, 283.
Red Cross, 55, 96.
Reformation, 139, 142.
Religion, 5; unifying influence of, 5; of the average American, 9, 15-33, 34, 36; of American young men, 15-23; of older men, 23; of American women, 27-31; of American children, 31-33; decay of in the home, 31; teaching of, in schools, 79; in the new intellectual environment, 137-152; as a permanent human interest, 147; different types of, 148; rational element in, 179; what is meant by appeal to reason in, 179.
Religious corporations, law governing, 80.
Religious education, 20, 147, 218, 222, 235, 279, 321, 342; revival of interest in, 279-280; imperfect methods in, 282; Protestant ideal of, 282; as evangelism, 283; of laymen, neglect of in Protestantism, 288; attention given by Roman Catholics to, 288; content of an adequate, 290, 291; of laymen, agencies available for, 308-316; history of in America, 309; need of a comprehensive survey of facilities for lay workers, 324.
Religious Education Association, 311; important work done by, 241, 242; coöperation of Roman Catholics and Jews with Protestants in, 272.
Religious experience, Protestant type of, 148; Catholic type of, 148.
Religious liberty, 139.
Religious literature, 287.
Religious press, importance of, 299.
Reformed, 65, 66, 70.
Reformed Church in America, 256, 262; Progress Campaign of the, 120.
Reformed Church in the U. S., 256, 262; Forward Movement of the, 120.
Reformed Episcopal Church, 262.
Reformed Presbyterian Church, 262.

Reformers, 139, 141, 180, 232.
Reform legislation, 270.
Relations with Religious Bodies in Europe, Federal Council Commission on, 262.
Repentance, 284, 285.
Representation, immediate in Congregational churches, 249, 250; mediate, 250.
Required instruction in religion, 314.
Rescue Missions, 286.
Research, 303, 321, 327, 342; need of, in religion, 316.
Reunion in the Presbyterian and Reformed family, 256.
Revelation, 332.
Revival movement, 74.
Richards, Timothy, 88.
Ritschl, Albrecht, 159, 160.
Robinson, James Harvey, 327.
Rochester, 218.
Roman Catholic, Roman Catholics, 20, 65-66, 102, 106, 110, 178, 205, 274, 288; number of in America, 66; basis of estimation for church membership, 67; element, relative strength of compared with Protestants, 67; view of church unity, 173; reasons against, 173-174; orders, 181; relation to Protestants, 271, 272.
Roman Catholic Church, 72, 76, 150, 173, 289; in America, need of a sympathetic treatment of, 68; its social outlook, 75; unity in, 181, 268; differences in, 181, 268; National Catholic War Council, 181, 268; National Catholic Welfare Council, 268, 271.
Roman Catholicism, 137, 293; see also Catholicism.
Rome, 8, 142, 159, 174, 177, 179, 180, 258, 294, 341.
Rotation of office, 251.
Roundy, Rodney W., 237.
Rowntree, Seebohm, 165.
Rural Community Work, 227.
Russia, 35, 40, 49, 56, 352.
Russians, 36, 228, 351.
Ryan, John A., 154, 232.

Sabbath Association, 270.
Sacrament, Sacraments, 21, 146, 182, 288, 332.
Sacramentarian Christianity, 83.
Sacramentarianism, 81.
Saint, 181.
Salaries of ministers, 65, 129, 196.